Lisa Cooper is Associate Professor of Near Eastern Art & Archaeology at the University of British Columbia. She is the author of *Early Urbanism on the Syrian Euphrates*.

'Although Gertrude Bell has been a favourite subject for biographers, their focus on her travels, romances and political role has often overshadowed the significance of her archaeological work. Lisa Cooper's lively, authoritative and very welcome account reveals Bell as a scholar rather than a dilettante. As the author makes very evident, it was Bell's interest and involvement in the archaeology of the Middle East that shaped her approach not merely to the understanding of its vanished civilizations, but also to the peoples and societies that she encountered in her travels. This work situates Bell within a network of pioneering individuals that were transforming archaeology into a serious, scholarly discipline but this is far from a dry, academic survey of archaeological activity. Rather it brings us closer to understanding Gertrude Bell's appreciation of Iraq's past, a vision that would inform her later activities in shaping the region's future.'

Paul Collins, Jaleh Hearn Curator for Ancient Near East,
Ashmolean Museum

Lisa Cooper

In Search of
Kings and
Conquerors

Gertrude Bell and the Archaeology of
the Middle East

I.B. TAURIS
LONDON · NEW YORK

Published in 2016 by
I.B.Tauris & Co. Ltd
London • New York
www.ibtauris.com

ISBN: 978 1 84885 498 7
eISBN: 978 0 85772 896 8

A full CIP record for this book is available from the British Library
A full CIP record is available from the Library of Congress

Library of Congress Catalog Card Number: available

Typeset in Stone Serif by OKS Prepress Services, Chennai, India
Printed and bound by CPI Group (UK) Ltd, Croydon, CR0 4YY

For Richard and Julianne:
'Light of mine eyes and harvest of my heart'

CONTENTS

LIST OF ILLUSTRATIONS

PREFACE AND ACKNOWLEDGEMENTS

Gertrude Bell has held my fascination for many years. I became acquainted with her about three decades ago when, as an undergraduate student of Near Eastern archaeology, I bought a copy of her biography by H.W.F. Winstone and marvelled over her travels and political activities. A few years later, as a graduate student, I worked on an archaeological project in southern Iraq that was supported by the British Institute for the Study of Iraq (then the British School of Archaeology in Iraq). The fact that this institution had been established in memory of Gertrude Bell, Iraq's first Director of Antiquities, piqued my interest in her again, as did the prospect of taking a day trip to the west of the Euphrates River to see the ruined castle of Ukhaidir, which Bell had documented in 1909 and 1911. Regrettably, the excursion did not take place, but the allure of that desert castle had taken root in my imagination, and I longed to know more about it and what exactly Bell had achieved there.

The war in Iraq and the looting of the Iraq National Museum in April 2003 brought my focus back to Gertrude Bell, this time in a more substantive way. I gave several public lectures, both at my own institution of the University of British Columbia (UBC), in Vancouver, and at the Canadian Society for Mesopotamian Studies, in Toronto, on the life and archaeological activities of Gertrude Bell and her important connection to the Iraq Museum, as its founder in 1923. As I began to probe further into her archaeological work, however, I became aware that while Bell's biographers routinely referred to her as an archaeologist, they failed to report in any detail just what sort of activities she had undertaken, particularly in the years before World War I, and what kind of achievement in archaeology, if any, they amounted to. These omissions in Bell's otherwise well-documented life prompted my own research into this topic. The work was further encouraged in 2008 by funding from a Hampton Research Grant from UBC, and a Research Grant from the British Institute for the Study of Iraq. I am tremendously grateful for this generous support, which enabled me to carry out the bulk of my research over several years.

I undertook a trip to Syria in April 2009 to retrace the journey that Bell had made down the eastern bank of the Euphrates River almost 100 years before, and to visit and photograph the same archaeological sites and monuments that she had documented. I wish to thank Stephen Batiuk for accompanying me on that short but memorable trip. I shall not forget the kindness and hospitality shown to us in the hotels, taxis, buses and restaurants of Aleppo and Raqqa, the two bases of our excursions, and it pains me to think about the dire present predicament of the people of these two remarkable cities.

In the autumn of 2010, I travelled to the UK to visit the Gertrude Bell Archives in the Special Collections of the Robinson Library of Newcastle University. Thanks go to the librarians of the Special Collections, who were most helpful in expediting my access to Bell's papers, as well as to Mark Jackson of the School of History, Classics and Archaeology at Newcastle University, then keeper of Bell's photographic archive, who provided digital copies of some of Bell's photographs and cheerfully answered numerous questions about her travels and archaeological activities. A short train ride up to Edinburgh University also brought me into contact with James Crow, the former keeper of Gertrude Bell's photographic archive, and I am grateful also to him for taking the time to share his knowledge about Bell, especially regarding her archaeological photography. Lastly, a visit to the Royal Geographical Society in London, where several of Bell's field notebooks are housed, was facilitated by Joy Wheeler of the RGS, who provided me with access to Bell's field notebooks and subsequently arranged for the reproduction of images from select pages.

In later stages of production, I wish to thank Vicky Manolopoulou of the School of History, Classics and Archaeology at Newcastle University for providing me with numerous additional images from the Gertrude Bell Archive and granting me the necessary permissions. Ian Johnson, Head of Special Collections and Archives at the Robinson Library at Newcastle University, also helped me to secure permissions to reproduce excerpts from Bell's diaries and letters and miscellaneous works. In all, the Gertrude Bell Archive at Newcastle University is to be congratulated for making its online access to Gertrude Bell's diaries, letters and photographs so accessible and user-friendly, without which this distant researcher from Canada would not have been able to accomplish anything at all.

Other individuals who have assisted in some way with my research by directing me to useful sources or photographs include Joan Porter MacIver, Thomas Leisten, Jens Kröger, Josef Moradi, Ed Keall and Julia Gonnella. I am grateful to Antionette Harri of the Fondation Max van Berchem, Hannah Westall, Archivist at Girton College Cambridge, Kiersten Neumann of the Oriental Institute Museum, Irmgard Wagner of the Deutsches Archäologische

Institut, Friedrich Polleroß of the Institut für Kunstgeschichte der Universität Wien, and Joachim Marzahn and Helga Vogel of the Deutsche Orient Gesellschaft, for their assistance in procuring images for this book and permitting their use. Henry and Emmanuelle Ritson provided transcriptions and translations of two of Max van Berchem's letters (in French) to Bell. I am tremendously grateful for the lively and productive conversations I had with Marcus Milwright and Maya Yazigi on the topics of Islamic history, art and architecture. I also enjoyed talking to Leilah Nadir and getting her unique insights into Bell.

At UBC, student research assistants greatly helped me in my work over the years, namely Carrie Arbuckle, Christine Johnston, Alexandra Harvey and Chelsea Gardner. They combed through Gertrude Bell's diaries and letters for all references to her archaeological activities, researched past and contemporary individuals who figured in her writings, and organized and researched relevant archaeological photographs. I must also thank Alexandra Harvey and Lisa Tweten for their assistance in producing digital adaptations of Bell's plans of the Great Mosque of Samarra and the palaces at Ukhaidir and Qasr-i-Shirin. Transcriptions and translations of letters (in German) to Bell from Ernst Herzfeld and Walter Andrae were capably provided by Lydia Jones and Stephanie Revell of the Germanic Studies Program in the Department of Central, Eastern and Northern European Studies, at UBC.

Encouragement, guidance and research assistance were provided to me by my colleagues in the Department of Classical, Near Eastern and Religious Studies. I am truly fortunate to have co-workers who possess not only wide learning but genuine interest in their colleagues' research. James Russell was a fountain of knowledge about Bell's archaeological activities in Anatolia and was among the first to impress upon me the quality and importance of her archaeological observations, plans and photographs. Hector Williams, Toph Marshall and Susanna Braund alerted me to several sources pertaining to Gertrude Bell and her contemporaries. Roger Wilson provided helpful information about Roman tower tombs, while Leanne Bablitz and Charmaine Gorrie clarified details about Roman governors, brickwork, and the campaigns of Trajan and Septimius Severus.

During the writing stage, I owe a debt of gratitude to my husband, Richard, for reading many sections of the manuscript and making an effort to pare down my unwieldy and wordy prose. Lynn Welton acted as a valuable sounding board for some of my ideas and made useful suggestions to my manuscript in the eleventh hour. I was also exceedingly fortunate to have the highly capable editing skills of Dania Sheldon, who seemed to be able to get through each of my chapter drafts without losing her patience or good cheer. I am tremendously grateful for her effort in improving my work, particularly in the final stages of its production.

Richard and our daughter, Julianne, put up with the countless hours I required to work on this book, and I regret that I did not get to spend as much time with them as I wanted, especially on weekends. Through it all, however, they did much to preserve my sanity and good spirits, and provided me with constant, happy companionship and affection. My research on Gertrude Bell began the year that Julianne was born, and these two female persons – one growing up before my eyes and the other coming to life from her many writings and images – have, in a rather odd combination, greatly enriched my life over the past seven years, filling that time with wonder, fascination and delight.

INTRODUCTION

Arriving at Cairo's Grand Continental Hotel in late November 1915, Gertrude Bell hurried down to dinner, anxious to hear the latest news of the East from her dining companions – among them David Hogarth and T.E. Lawrence – and weigh in with her own thoughts on the personalities and politics of the Ottoman Empire's Arab provinces.[1]

It had been a difficult and sad year for Bell. The outbreak of war a year previously had put an end to her rollicking travels and stimulating archaeological projects. A man she had dearly loved had been killed in the Dardanelles. Her war work to this point had involved the heartrending job of tracing the missing and the dead lost in the battlefields of France. But now her life was charged with a new purpose and promise, and she brought a revived spirit and fresh energy to the mission with which she had been tasked.

The war would change the direction of Bell's life and radically transform her relationship with the Middle East, where she found herself once again. She knew this part of the world very well. She had been to Egypt on multiple occasions, and she had travelled up and down the coastal regions of the Levant and through Anatolia. Recently, she had made an intrepid journey into Arabia. Her explorations had included the lands watered by the Tigris and Euphrates Rivers, and she knew the deserts and mountains of Persia. The accounts of her travels had produced lively travelogues that, when published, were eagerly received by a public fascinated with this adventurous, resilient woman. Perhaps even more significant, however, was the aim that drove many of Bell's trips to the Middle East. Her intense interest in the antiquity of these lands, and her desire to find, map, describe and understand the rich histories, peoples and settlements that had once existed, were often the motivations that inspired her long journeys into remote places.

Now in 1915, however, Bell's engagement with the past had been pushed aside by present realities. In Cairo once again, her purpose was of a different character. No longer was she in the East to explore and identify ancient sites, plan monuments and trace the routes taken by long-ago kings and their armies; her task was to provide descriptions of the modern groups she had seen in the course of her travels. As part of a newly created office of British military intelligence that would soon be known as the Arab Bureau, she had been charged with listing the present location of Arab tribes and their sheikhs, estimating their numbers and judging their loyalties to the British and the Turks.[2] This was to be Bell's part in the British war effort to defeat Germany and its ally, the Ottoman Empire.

One hundred years later, musing over that pivotal year in Bell's life as she officially entered the arena of modern politics in the midst of a world war, I cannot help but reflect on my own relationship with the Middle East, and how my engagement with it up to this point has been, like Bell's, primarily from the perspective of exploring its lands in pursuit of the rich past. Although three decades of archaeological fieldwork and research have been fascinating and productive, my engagement with the ancient Middle East has never been far removed from the current conditions of the countries in which I have worked. Calamitous developments – notably the wars in Iraq and now the violence and destruction that rage across Syria – have affected my own research, and more importantly, the lives of people I have known. Ancient settlements and artefacts that I have seen and explored have been severely damaged or destroyed, and many of the people who shared with me in uncovering Iraq's and Syria's ancient heritages have undergone unbelievable hardship and suffering.

My experience with the current misfortunes of the Middle East is naturally different than the circumstances faced by Bell as she embarked on her official war work in Cairo in 1915, but it shares across the century the inseparable relationship between one's search for the past and the inevitable confrontation with the often dramatic and tragic realities of the present. Moreover, the past and present are entangled, the present often being closely linked to the actions of the past, arising from it or replicating what has played out many times before. Bell was aware of this, and even as she optimistically played her role in the post-war effort to introduce a new order in the Middle East to replace the shattered Ottoman Empire, she knew of the many previous imperial powers that had taken control of these lands before her, stretching back millennia to the dawn of history. Their glories had been brief, however, and they had fallen time and time again, trampled into the dust by the feet of later kings and conquerors. Today, almost a century after the bold schemes ushered in by the European powers with which Bell was associated, there still has been no long-lived or peaceful resolution in the Middle East. We are forced to recognize once again the folly of imperial ambitions and ineffectual meddling which have plagued the peoples and nations that have forever been dismantled and refashioned anew.

While one can be critical of the role Gertrude Bell played in the politics of the Middle East, there is no question that this period of her life was fascinating and eventful. Indeed, the majority of written accounts about her place a huge emphasis on this latter phase of her life, especially her part in the creation of the state of Iraq shortly after the end of World War I.[3] The selection of the country's first king and the drawing up of its modern political borders – in which Shi'ites, Sunnis, Kurds and Christians were all placed under a united flag – can be traced to the British colonial government in which Bell, as the administration's sole female political officer, played an active and influential role.

But Bell's biographers have not hesitated to report on other aspects of her remarkable life as well, among them mountain-climbing expeditions and intrepid travels into remote regions of the Middle East where few Europeans had previously ventured. Bell rubbed shoulders with colourful, prominent personalities, including Winston Churchill, Lord Cromer, Edward Grey, Mark Sykes, Ibn Saud and T.E. Lawrence. Even her love life, while ultimately tragic, was the stuff of high romance. Her engagement at a young age to a dashing but penniless lord amid the deserts of Persia was forbidden by her parents, and in any event, the suitor died of pneumonia within a year. Later in life, Bell had a clandestine affair with a highly respected, married military officer and diplomat whose death on the battlefield at Gallipoli cut short what had been an all-consuming passion. These sad affairs and Bell's death, the cause of which appears to have been an overdose of sleeping pills on a stifling summer day in Baghdad in her 58th year, elicits a melancholy fascination for this remarkable woman who seemed to have everything and yet nothing.

What of archaeology, the subject that triggered her full engagement with the Middle East in the first place? To be sure, all accounts of Bell's life have listed archaeology among her many accomplishments, but most have never pursued this topic very far, usually failing to describe in any detail the specific kind of archaeological work in which she was engaged, or the impact that her research made in the fields of Byzantine, Islamic and ancient Near Eastern studies. Attention is often paid to the travels that Bell undertook to visit archaeological sites and the written and photographic records she kept of these archaeological journeys. However, little has been done to assess the quality of this work and its significance both in her time and up to the present. Lacking, in particular, are any serious accounts of Bell's 1909 and 1911 visits to, and study of, the magnificent Islamic-period castle of Ukhaidir. Not insignificantly, Bell's work at Ukhaidir resulted in several scholarly publications, including her magisterial 1914 monograph *Palace and Mosque at Ukhaidir*.[4] Nevertheless, Bell's biographers give short shrift to the site, and if her visit is mentioned at all, they simply prefer to describe her energetic measuring and photographing of the castle, and her clothing: a 'white cotton shirt, petticoat and long patch-pocketed skirt, black stockings and laced-up shoes, a dark *kafeeyah* wrapped around her sun helmet'.[5] Ukhaidir is sometimes also mentioned in the context of Bell's disappointment at finding that German archaeologists had also been to the site, and that their report was to appear in print before hers.[6] This emphasis on the Germans' achievement at Bell's expense has had the regrettable effect of overshadowing her work. The erroneous impression one gets from this superficial treatment of Bell's research of Ukhaidir (as with the treatment of her other archaeological endeavours) is that she surveyed the ruins and took some good photographs, but her work was that of an interested dilettante.

In one of the few accounts of Bell's life that outlines her archaeological work more substantively, Julia Asher-Greve perceptively notes that even in Bell's own time, her contributions to archaeology tended to be downplayed by her contemporary male colleagues. Their recurring references to 'Bell's family wealth and connections, couture clothes, eccentricities, or alleged intelligence activities' served to cast doubt upon her scholarly capacities, 'emphasizing her gender and thus her outside status'.[7] It is particularly surprising to read the comments of the archaeologist Walter Andrae, the German director of the excavations at Assur. Bell held him in such deep esteem for his archaeological activities in Mesopotamia and for his collegiality and friendship that she dedicated her 1914 Ukhaidir book to him.[8] But in his autobiography, rather than commenting extensively on Bell's archaeological career, Andrae noted that her ability to speak several foreign languages, including German, was the result of her family's wealth and status, which provided her with good connections to European diplomatic circles and facilitated her wide travels.[9] In addition, Andrae wrote that back in 1911, when she had visited him at Assur, he had already suspected she was 'on a diplomatic mission in Mesopotamia'.[10] This appears to be a tactful way of saying that he guessed she was a British spy. That Bell was engaged in official intelligence activities before the outbreak of World War I is at best debatable, but Andrae's comments serve to further obscure Bell's primary reason for journeying to Mesopotamia in those years: her genuine and intense interest in the antiquities of the region, and her wish to make a name for herself in archaeological circles.

Finally, it may not have helped that Bell herself, when writing in her diaries or in her letters to her parents, tended to make light of her archaeological endeavours. She was self-effacing, often undervaluing her scholarly worth. This tendency, coupled with her youthful enthusiasm for her work, often gave the impression that she wasn't to be taken too seriously. For example, in a letter to her parents during her investigations in Anatolia in 1905, she wrote, 'I have had the most delightful day today playing at being an archaeologist.'[11] In 1909, upon her discovery and recording of Samarra in Mesopotamia, she wrote, 'Sometimes [...] I think I'm something of an archaeologist myself – but of course that's going too far!'[12] After the completion of her investigation at Ukhaidir, she wrote with almost school-girlish glee, 'It's the greatest piece of luck that has ever happened to me. I shall publish it in a big monograph all to itself and it will make a flutter in the dovecotes.'[13] Bell's rather romantic writing style may also have contributed to a general tendency to discount her as a genuine researcher. In a letter to her father during a visit to Babylon, she wrote, 'I heard the Mesopotamian nightingale and remembered that these were the same sights and sounds that Nebuchadnezzar had known and even Hammurabi. Were they, I wonder, comforted and sustained by the eternal beauty of the earth and the simple country life of field and river that springs and dies and leaves no marks and never alters?'[14] While these passages read as the lyrical musings of an individual deeply enamoured with the past and her own evocative surroundings, they have the tendency, like the other excerpts quoted, to cast Bell as a lightweight rather than as a serious and committed scholar. It is unfortunate that Bell's biographers have most often tended to cite such passages, since they play up Bell's romantic inclinations and presumed naiveté while ignoring the substance of her observations and conclusions.

In undertaking the research for this work, I aim to compensate for other accounts' superficial coverage of Bell's archaeological activities and accomplishments by bringing them to the fore. I will demonstrate not only that Bell was passionate about the study of archaeology, and set herself to learn a great deal about it (especially the archaeology of Anatolia and Mesopotamia), but that in a short time, she became thoroughly proficient at it, producing a number of learned and valuable archaeological reports. Bell was particularly consumed with the pursuit of archaeology between 1905 and 1914, and she carried out her most significant investigations in the Near East during this period.

At this point, it is perhaps important to discuss what exactly is meant by 'archaeology' as Bell practised it, especially since her work rarely entailed digging into the ground to recover ancient remains. Nor was she part of a larger, officially sanctioned archaeological project or team, with the exception, perhaps, of her collaboration with William Ramsay at Binbirkilise in Anatolia. She did not have the sponsorship of a university or archaeological institute; rather, all of her investigations were supported by her own funds and initiative. Her particular research focus and interests concentrated on ancient architectural forms and their presence through time and across space, and her approach, which entailed a comparative formal analysis, did not require stratigraphic observations through excavation. Nevertheless, there was a fieldwork aspect to Bell's research: she visited all of the sites in which she was interested, and made concerted efforts to comprehend them on the ground through detailed plans and photographs. Moreover, her subsequent research – which entailed looking for comparable sites and structures and endeavouring to situate them according to their periodization, cultural milieu and influences – followed the same type of methodology employed by other archaeologists of her time. If her fieldwork didn't actually include excavation, it was because most of the artistic and architectural forms in which she was interested were still standing above ground and could be documented without the need for more than a minimum of earth clearance around foundations to clarify structural dimensions and forms. Bell's efforts to record other artefacts, such as pottery, terracotta objects, metal fragments, bones and palaeobotanical remains, were either non-existent or, at best, ephemeral or occasional, but it has to be remembered that these were still the early days of archaeological practice. Few of her contemporaries recognized for their archaeological pursuits were carrying out the kinds of systematic and comprehensive approaches to archaeological recovery that became common practice later in the twentieth century.[15] In light of these considerations and the nature of Bell's not inconsequential efforts to examine ancient material remains in the field, I am comfortable with calling her pursuit of the past 'archaeological' in its scope.

In tracking Bell's archaeological efforts, one cannot help but be impressed by the sheer quantity of data with which she dealt, and the breadth and depth of her observations and conclusions. Although her intensive archaeological investigations only lasted about a decade, her scholarly output – which addressed an incredibly wide range of cultures, peoples and historical periods of the ancient Near East and beyond – was prodigious. Faced with this abundant dataset and yet still wishing to highlight her archaeological accomplishments in a meaningful way, I have chosen to focus on a smaller aspect of Bell's work, in particular her investigations of the Sasanian and early Islamic periods in Mesopotamia, represented principally by archaeological sites visited and documented during the course of her 1909 and 1911 travels. Bell's other probes into the past, such as her extensive investigations of the ecclesiastical architecture of Late Antiquity, known mainly from her study of early Christian churches in Binbirkilise and Tur-Abdin in Anatolia, are not extensively covered in this book. Scholars of Late Antiquity have already done an admirable job of presenting Bell's study of Anatolian churches and assessing the merits of her work in that regard, so covering the same subjects would largely replicate these accounts.[16] On the other hand, few have attempted to summarize and assess Bell's work on Islamic and pre-Islamic art and architecture in Mesopotamia, making this subject more worthy of scrutiny here. Her expeditions in Mesopotamia are also significant in that they connect meaningfully with her later activities in the same region during and after World War I, both in her capacity as a political officer and as Iraq's honorary Director of Antiquities.

I aim not only to describe Bell's archaeological work – her visits to ancient sites, the physical acts of planning and photographing ancient art and architecture, and her conclusions – but also to situate her endeavours within the field of archaeological studies, assessing the degree to which her work was favourably received by her contemporaries and subsequent generations. It is difficult not to be impressed by the learned quality of Bell's scholarship, particularly her capacity for finding comparable architectural forms through time and space and tracing their origins back to original Near Eastern sources. While this type of methodological approach is regarded today as flawed – it neglected other strands of artefactual evidence, paid little heed to stratigraphy, and excluded almost entirely issues such as social organization, economy, environment, agency and gender when attempting to understand how people lived and interacted within a particular ancient site or structure – Bell's work was still quite ambitious in its breadth. Although not always correct, she showed a comparable or greater degree of insight to that of her scholarly contemporaries, as will be demonstrated. At the same time, Bell was engaged in archaeological studies precisely when archaeology was developing into a serious, scholarly discipline through the efforts of a number of extraordinary individuals who were pioneering a systematic, careful and controlled form of archaeological inquiry in the Near East. These individuals would shortly eclipse Bell in their own brilliant efforts. She met several of them, including the Germans Walter Andrae and Robert Koldewey, known for their excavations at the sites of Assur and Babylon. Even within Bell's own field of the archaeology of the early Islamic period, there were rising stars like Ernst Herzfeld, whose brilliant insights into the source and inspiration of Islamic art and architectural forms were matching or exceeding her own interpretations of these topics. Bell was well aware of the abilities of these learned individuals, and even before she had left the field altogether, she had in some instances chosen to abandon further research on subjects, knowing that her own efforts would fail to match those of the other scholars.[17]

Bell abruptly abandoned her archaeological work upon the outbreak of World War I, thus severing her ties to the scholarly community. Thereafter she engaged herself in the war effort and actions relating to the political affairs of Iraq, this constituting an altogether different direction and focus than her archaeological exploits. It is true that her role as honorary Director of Antiquities in Iraq in the 1920s re-engaged her in work related to archaeology, but with this new work, Bell acted more in an administrative capacity related to excavations and antiquities rather than as a researcher in her own right. People would henceforth remember Bell as someone involved in political activities, and who in some way was connected to archaeology, but they largely forgot her scholarly output in that field, as prodigious as it had once been.

Bell's turn into politics represented a complete change in the direction of her work, but the experiences she had acquired while travelling in the Near East and engaging in the study of its past did not count for nothing. On the contrary, Bell's familiarity with the archaeology of the Near East, especially with the archaeology and history of Mesopotamia, gave her a special and unique understanding of this part of the world that in many ways influenced her ideas about how the region should be governed and her own place within that scheme. This background, coupled with her romantic sensibilities, as I will relate in the final chapter of this book, worked within Bell to create a very specific, inspired vision for Iraq's present and hopeful future. The success enjoyed by that state upon its creation and the installation of its first king, Faisal, were in part fuelled by the vision of Bell, ever desirous to usher the country into a new and glorious chapter of its rich history. At the same time, the very knowledge of the past that inspired her also made her mindful of the transitory nature of empire. This awareness tempered her optimism, forcing her to recognize the futility of nation-making and the vanity of her own part in this enterprise. Gertrude Bell, for all of her energetic schemes and dreams, could not, in the end, emerge from the shadow of humanity's unendingly tumultuous history.

CHAPTER 1

EARLY LIFE AND FIRST STEPS IN ARCHAEOLOGY

Gertrude Bell's interests in history and archaeology were very much propelled by her fortunate upbringing. She came from a life of privilege, this allowing her to pursue a higher education and exposing her to the wider world through travel. Further encouragement from a number of key scholars, and Bell's own love of ancient ruins and the remote, desert landscapes in which they were often located, gradually led to her sole focus on the archaeology of the ancient Near East. As her knowledge of this field grew, so did her confidence, and she began to pursue the field as a serious scholar. This activity would absorb much of her attention for several years and lead her further and further into the unknown, unexplored parts of the Near East and its fascinating past.

Born in 1868 in northern England, Gertrude Margaret Lowthian Bell was the daughter of Hugh Bell and the granddaughter of the famous Isaac Lowthian Bell. Lowthian Bell, as he liked to be called, was one of England's leading industrialists during the Victorian era.[1] At a young age he had joined his father's ironworks in Newcastle, shortly afterwards pioneering the use of blast furnaces and rolling mills for iron production and operating a chemical factory used to manufacture aluminium.[2] By 1844, Lowthian and his brothers had established a company known as Bell Brothers, and by the 1870s, this firm had become one of the leading ironworks in the English north-east.[3] The company also had colliery properties, steel mills, quarries and mines, and built a railway to convey raw materials, enabling Lowthian to control his own supplies of coal, ironstone and limestone.[4] Not only was Gertrude's grandfather a successful businessman, but he was well educated and a gifted scientist. He had studied physics, chemistry and metallurgy in Germany, Denmark, France and Britain before the age of 24, and had gone on to win many medals over the course of his life for his scientific work, especially in the fields of engineering and industry.[5] He was, for example, recognized as a world authority on blast-furnace technology.[6] As a man with a deep interest in his community, Lowthian Bell also entered into politics. He was elected twice as the mayor of Newcastle, served as high sheriff of the county of Durham, and held a Liberal seat in Parliament for five years. This great man, with his exceptional mind, natural curiosity and limitless vitality, had a tremendous influence on his offspring, and it is to him that we may attribute some of the same qualities seen in his granddaughter.[7] Of course, Gertrude also had the advantage of inheriting much of Lowthian Bell's fortune, and this wealth would contribute significantly to her pursuit of a higher education, her extensive travels around the world and her archaeological endeavours.

In her youth, Gertrude Bell had demonstrated a passion for literature and the arts as well as world affairs and history, and so it was decided that she would be sent up to Oxford University in 1886 to continue her studies. Although Oxford was for men only, a women's college (Lady Margaret Hall) had recently opened, and it allowed a small number of women, including Bell, to attend the university's lectures and sit for its examinations. Despite being one of only a handful of women in lecture halls filled with hundreds of men, Bell flourished in the academic environment. By the end of her second year, in 1888, she had succeeded in receiving a 'first' in Modern History, the first woman at Oxford to achieve that honour.[8]

Travel featured heavily in Bell's young adult life, particularly in the years following university. Her academic pursuits and her interest in history filled her with a desire to journey to the places that she had studied and whose pasts had come alive for her in books and the lecture halls of Oxford. Many early trips, often with family members, featured European destinations such as Germany (1886, 1896), France (1889, 1894), Romania (1888), Italy (1894, 1896) and Switzerland (1894, 1895, 1896). She even travelled as far as Constantinople on one occasion (1889).[9] It was also in Europe that Bell became enamoured with mountains, the Swiss and Austrian Alps holding a particular fascination for her. Lured by the snow-capped peaks and her sense of daring and adventure, she actually established herself as a capable mountaineer. Between 1897 and 1904, Bell climbed no fewer than ten mountain peaks or ranges, each of them more challenging than the previous. These mountains included Mont Blanc (in France), the highest summit in the Alps. This was followed by the Schreckhorn, one of the more rugged and difficult of the 13,000-foot peaks in the Alps, and the seven peaks of the Engelhörner range, none of them having been climbed before. To her tremendous pleasure, one of these peaks was christened after her, and it remains Gertrudespitze – Gertrude's Peak. She also climbed the Matterhorn (1904), but her most death-defying climb was the Finsteraarhorn (1902). Rising to 14,022 feet, it is notorious for bad weather and frequent avalanches. She and her male climbing companions actually got within the final few hundred feet of the peak when terrible weather – a blizzard, a violent electrical storm and

Fig. 1.1 Gertrude Bell, taken around 1895, when she was about 26 years old. By this time, Bell had already travelled widely and had published her first book, based on her impressions of Persia, visited in 1892.

blinding mist – forced them to turn back. By the end of their ordeal, they had spent 53 hours on the rope, and Bell suffered frostbite in her hands and feet. Although this ascent was a failure, it earned her tremendous respect within the climbing community.[10]

While the Alps satisfied some of Bell's physical needs, her emotional and mental capacities continued to be stimulated by travel, and she began looking farther afield, to exotic places that provided fresh landscapes upon which to marvel and peoples and cultures whose poetry, art and literature dazzled her in ways that were not satisfied by the confining, commonplace character of her native northern England. Her wanderlust is perhaps best expressed in her embarking on two world tours, in 1897–8 and 1902–3. The latter trip included a long stop in India, where she witnessed the imperial Durbar celebrating Edward VII's accession to the throne as Emperor of India. Further stops included Singapore, China, Korea and Japan before she returned to England via Canada and the United States.[11]

Above all other places in the world, however, Bell seems to have felt the allure of the lands of the Near East, ignited by one of her earlier lengthy trips to Persia in 1892. Staying in Tehran with her aunt Mary and her uncle Frank Lascelles, the latter having been appointed British envoy to the Persian Shah,[12] she found herself enchanted with the country around her, its breathtaking contrasts of mountains, deserts and gardens, fountains, silvery water streams and luxuriant roses. She also found its people hospitable and Persian art, music and poetry captivating. The sensations aroused within Bell in this exotic land were perhaps all the more keenly felt because she had fallen in love with a junior diplomat in the staff of the British Embassy in Tehran, Henry Cadogan. Their shared passion for poetry and literature, and the excitement of walking or riding together beyond Tehran to rapturously take in Persia's impressive landscapes, only served to heighten and draw out Bell's romantic nature. Sadly, Bell's parents rejected Cagodan's request to marry Bell – they considered him too poor and flawed in character to be an appropriate match. Compounding Bell's bitter disappointment and grief, Cadogan died of pneumonia a year later, dashing any remaining hopes that he might have earned a promotion and thereby increased his eligibility in her parents' eyes.[13]

Despite this grievous setback in Bell's personal life, her love for Persia and the 'East' did not fade, and it may be that she hoped to hold on, as best she could, to the memory of Cadogan by immersing herself in all things associated with Persia and her sojourn there. Upon her return to England, she wrote of her Persian experiences with a 'glowing eagerness'[14] in her first book, *Safar Nameh: Persian Pictures* (London, 1894), and energetically studied the Persian language; after only a few short years, she completed a commendable English translation of the *Poems from the Divan of Hafiz* (London, 1897), which celebrates the verses of that great and highly revered fourteenth-century Persian poet.[15]

If Bell's trip to Persia provided the first spark for her interest in the Near East, her subsequent journeys to the Levant around the turn of the century and in the years that followed consolidated a passion for the 'East' that would continue for the rest of her life. Each trip took her further off the beaten track, developing her self-reliance and resolve, testing her physical endurance and piquing her curiosity for new landscapes, peoples and built-spaces from the past and present. Bell's first major Near Eastern trip, which began in late 1899 and extended to June 1900, included a long stay with family friends in Jerusalem, where she threw herself into the study of Arabic, a language in which she would eventually become fluent.[16] Highlights of this trip included a side visit to Petra (in present-day Jordan; 29–31 March 1900), a venture up through the Hauran and the Jebel Druze to Damascus (25 April–14 May 1900), and a momentous solo journey to Palmyra in the Syrian desert before returning to Beirut on the Mediterranean coast (15 May–9 June 1900).[17]

Other Near Eastern trips followed (in 1902 to Haifa and Mount Carmel), and then a particularly ambitious journey in 1905 (January–May). Aimed at 'wild travel',[18] this trip through Palestine and Syria saw Bell exploring beyond the well-trod paths of tourists, into remoter places, where the well-watered, cultivated fields of the coastal plain gave way to mountains and then the steppe and desert lands of the interior. She retraced some of the earlier steps she had taken in 1900, this time pausing longer in the desert regions around Amman and Damascus, exploring the Jebel Druze at greater length and then moving up through the central part of Syria, taking in the towns and ancient ruined settlements of the Orontes Valley and the rocky hills of the Limestone Massif. She travelled almost entirely independently of other Europeans, escorted only by a small entourage of native guards, guides and a cook.[19] Overcoming obstructive Ottoman authorities through her quick wit and abilities in Turkish and Arabic, Bell managed to visit, document and photograph a wealth of peoples and places over the space of four months. The exhilaration she felt in this journey is reflected in her travel account *The Desert and the Sown*, written upon her return to England, which enjoyed favourable reviews upon its publication in 1907. 'Charming'[20] and 'enchanting'[21] were some of the adjectives used to describe this book, in which nearly every page is filled with colourful descriptions of the people and places she encountered over the course of the journey. Readers were particularly enamoured with her ability to provide 'snapshots' of conversations with the people she met, and in so doing present a vivid and often humorous picture of the speakers and their activities, opinions and customs.[22] Her accounts described her dealings with people of all occupations and ethnicities, from Turkish officials to shopkeepers, soldiers, shepherds, priests, desert sheikhs, 'those who sit around our campfires and those who ride with us across deserts and mountains, for their words are like straws on the flood of Asiatic politics, showing which way the streams are running'.[23]

As one might expect in the writings of an early twentieth-century traveller from Britain, *The Desert and the Sown* contains an Orientalist undertone in Bell's description of the peoples of the Near East and her interactions with them. Confident in her intellectual and moral superiority as an Englishwoman, she sometimes characterized Arabs as existing in a perpetually primitive state, petty, impractical, prone to conflict, and unable to progress towards a state of civilization like the West.[24] A passage in Bell's account, describing an 'Oriental' as being 'like a very old child',[25] underscores her patronizing tone. Nevertheless, she also had the capacity to both admire and respect the people she encountered, accepting differences between West and East and, at her best, recognizing the relative nature of value systems, morals and human organization across cultures.[26] That she was a woman and thus in some ways marginalized within her own English society may have made her sensitive to attitudes of inequality and difference,[27] but it may simply be that as a highly observant individual, her keen recognition and appreciation of human behaviour in its myriad forms often prevailed over other attitudes she might have had about empire, race and gender.

Bell's 1905 Near Eastern journey had another important aspect: it drew into sharp focus her interest in the antiquity of the regions she passed through. She enjoyed contemplating the cultures and peoples who had been here before her and had left their mark through art, architecture and inscriptions. Archaeology and ancient history are very significant motifs in *The Desert and the Sown*, taking up almost as much space as her accounts of modern people and places. Her enthusiasm for history is clearly shown in the wealth of ancient sites on her itinerary, including, for example, the Roman site of Baalbek and the impressive Crusader castle of Krak de Chevaliers.[28] While many of these sites frequently featured in other tourist itineraries, Bell took the time to explore lesser known sites as well, pausing over their ruins and recalling age, date and cultural significance. Travelling up through central western Syria, for example, she described the high mound of Tell Nebi Mend, the site of the ancient city of Qadesh, and the famous battle fought there between the Hittites and Egyptians, this event also known from hieroglyphs and reliefs in Egypt.[29] Beyond Hama, she passed by the ruined Islamic castle of Shayzar (which she called Kala'at Seijar) (Fig. 1.2), describing its impressive situation atop a steep bluff overlooking the Orontes Valley.[30] She observed numerous tell sites further along the way (at Sheikh Hadid)[31] before arriving at the extensive Greco-Roman site at Qal'at Mudiq (ancient Apamea), also giving this site ample attention.[32] Still further to the north, Bell expressed great excitement at encountering the Princeton archaeological expedition at the Dead City of Tarutin, and she spent the day following them, observing members of the team planning the ruins and deciphering inscriptions. Through their efforts, as Bell relates, 'the whole 5th century town rose from its ashes and stood before us – churches, houses, forts, rock-hewn tombs with the names and dates of the death of the occupants carved over the door'.[33] Clearly,

Fig. 1.2 Bell's 1905 photograph of the Arab castle of Shayzar (tenth to thirteenth centuries CE), overlooking the Orontes River (Syria), with a pre-modern bridge over the river in the foreground.

with these site visits and her accompanying descriptions and photographs – the latter often featuring close-up shots of artistic decoration and construction details in the architecture – Bell was beginning to show an archaeological curiosity and knowledge that went beyond the simple attentions of an enthusiastic tourist.

Bell's 1905 journey wasn't her first to take in archaeological sites and monuments. She had demonstrated a keen interest in the past on earlier occasions, as attested in letters to family members in which she often evocatively described ancient sites and historical details. Bell's active imagination and romantic nature were frequently at work, envisioning people and events from the past in the places through which she travelled. The landscapes acted as a time portal, too, transporting her back to an age when charismatic or tyrannical kings had ruled, and to lands through which conquering armies had passed. During her stay in Persia back in 1892, she had recalled a stony, desolate valley ringed by mountains, within which stood a Persian temple of death – a 'tower of silence' – upon which corpses would once have been laid out to be defleshed by vultures. This ancient structure evoked a grim bygone tradition and the many people who had once witnessed it in their 'weary journey' towards death.[34] On one memorable trip to Athens with her father in 1899, Bell had the pleasure of meeting the eminent German archaeologist Wilhelm Dörpfeld, and the archaeologist David Hogarth, brother of her Oxford friend Janet. In her letters, Bell burst with enthusiasm over being able to speak with these gentlemen and then holding 6,000-year-old pottery from Melos, exclaiming that her mind reeled at the experiences.[35] Later in the same year, while walking through the ruins of Ephesus in Anatolia, Bell imagined St Paul with the shining, gorgeous Greek city in front of him, walking up the colonnaded street and the marble steps to the theatre at the end, just as she had walked.[36] She undertook still other archaeologically focussed trips in western Anatolia in 1902: Bell watched with interest as a Byzantine tumulus was excavated at Colophon;[37] she made a six-day trip to visit the ancient ruins at Pergamum, Sardis and Magnesia;[38] and she observed German excavators digging at Menemen, near Smyrna (Izmir).[39]

One can sense within her writing that especially in the lands of Palestine and Syria, which she first visited in 1900, she felt a real rapture for ancient places and the striking desert setting in which they were often found. When Bell and her travelling party visited the desert Nabatean city of Petra (29 March 1900), she could not but be stunned by the natural setting, which provided such a magnificent context for the ancient rock-cut tombs (Fig. 1.3), built into the pink sandstone of the desert cliffs and approached through a narrow defile in the rock:

> We went on in ecstasies until suddenly between the narrow opening of the rocks, we saw the most beautiful sight I have ever seen. Imagine a temple cut out of the solid rock, the charming facade supported on great Corinthian columns standing clear, soaring upwards to the very top of the cliff in the most exquisite proportions and carved with groups of figures almost as fresh as the chisel left them – all this in the rose red rock, with the sun just touching it and making it look almost transparent. [...] We walked about all the afternoon and photographed and were lost in wonder. It is like a fairy tale city, all pink and wonderful, as if it had dropped out of the White King's dream and would vanish when he woke![40]

Bell's first sight of Palmyra (Fig. 1.4) in the Syrian desert in May 1900 made no less of an impression upon her, the barren surroundings providing the context for the ancient site:

> I wonder if the wide world presents a more singular landscape. It is a mass of columns, ranged into long avenues, grouped into temples, lying broken on the sand or pointing one long solitary finger to Heaven. Beyond them is the immense Temple of Baal; the modern town is built inside it and its rows of columns rise out of a mass of mud roofs. And beyond, all is the desert, sand and white stretches of salt and sand again,

Fig. 1.3 Bell's photograph of the rock-cut tomb of Sextius Florentinus (Roman governor of the province of Arabia, 130 CE) at Petra (Jordan) in March 1900.

with the dust clouds whirling over it and the Euphrates 5 days away. It looks like the white skeleton of a town, standing knee deep in the blown sand.[41]

And yet alongside her taste for lyrical musings over ancient sites, Bell was also acutely interested in the detailed features seen amid the ruins, and willing to take

Fig. 1.4   Colonnade inside the precinct of the Temple of Bel, Palmyra (Syria). Modern mudbrick houses, which in 1900 stood right in the midst of the sacred enclosure, were all subsequently removed.

the time to record them in her notebooks. Her writings are filled with such descriptive details, even at Palmyra in 1900:

> There is one splendid tower almost perfect, the Kasr el 'Arus the Arabs call it – the Bride's Castle. It consists of a great chamber 20 ft high, pilasters running up from floor to ceiling and between them rows and rows of loculi, like so many shelves. When I say the floor I might add that the floor is gone and has left a great pit in the shape of a deep basement, arched over formerly, and also full of loculi. Of the roof of the great chamber about 2/3 remains, elaborately carved, stuccoed and painted, and the colours are still quite fresh. At either end of it was a panel containing 4 portrait heads, I daresay there was one in the middle too, but it had fallen in. Over the door was carved the head of a bearded man, the chief of the family perhaps, and at the opposite end the usual Palmyrene stele, 5 busts in a row on an enormous block of stone with a border round which is always the same, a thing like the body of a chess king at either end and a roll at the top ornamented with wavy lines and low cut wreaths of flowers. We climbed up

a broken stair into the next chamber which was much plainer, no carvings
in it. There was still another above which we couldn't get into because the
broken floor prevented our reaching the stair. I believe each loculus was
closed by a portrait bust of the owner but these have long since been broken
or sold.[42]

Such detailed passages of archaeological features continue in all of Bell's
writings. Moreover, one also observes, particularly from 1905 onwards, the
addition of more speculative, scholarly notions, the product of her having
learned more about the cultures and artistic traditions of the sites she visited.
When describing the site of Baalbek, for example, Bell suggested that it was a
'combination of Greek and Asiatic genius that produced it and covered its
doorposts, its architraves and its capitals with ornamental devices'.[43] Bell's
mind was once again speculating on particular architectural traditions when
she passed through the ruined Late Antique villages and churches in the hilly
region to the northeast of Qal'at Siman in northern Syria. Not aware that the
Princeton archaeological team had previously inspected this region,[44] she took
it upon herself to carefully inspect the area and offer some explanation for the
particular appearance of its architecture, which was 'not executed by local
workmen but by the builders and stone-cutters of Antioch'.[45] Such writings
reflect the growing confidence with which Bell explored archaeological sites,
including those outside the usual tourist itineraries, and her efforts to
determine their date and cultural influences.

The improved, scholarly character of Bell's archaeological visits and her
writings by 1905 coincided with her association with Salomon Reinach (1859–
1932), an influential European scholar-savant who had entered her life around
1904. Belonging to a German Jewish family and having studied at the
University of Paris and the French School in Athens, Reinach was by the turn of
the twentieth century a leading expert in Classical languages, the study of
mythology and religion, and art history and archaeology.[46] His archaeological
activities included research in Greece, Asia Minor and French North Africa, the
products of which were scores of works analysing Greek and Roman antiquities
in these areas. He also wrote prolifically on ancient Gaul.[47] As a whole, his
publication record was prodigious for its quantity and scope, featuring books
and journals that included topics as varied as Greek and Latin epigraphy,
Classical and Late Antique art and architecture, the religion of Asia Minor and
the Levant, and European medieval and Renaissance art.[18]

When Bell met Reinach in 1904,[49] he was the director of the archaeological
museum at Saint-Germain-en-Laye, near Paris, a post he would keep until his
death in 1932 (he started in 1902). He was also lecturing on Renaissance painting
as an art history professor at the École du Louvre and editing the prestigious
journal *Revue archéologique*. It seems that Bell had learned about this renowned

European scholar through her friend Eugénie Strong, a Classical archaeologist by training,[50] and she had probably travelled to Paris to see him at Strong's recommendation. Strong herself had made Reinach's acquaintance a decade or so earlier, and attributed her appreciation of the art and archaeology of the western Roman provinces to Reinach's expertise on Celtic and Gallo-Roman archaeology.[51]

As related in her letters and diaries, Bell's visits to see Reinach were exciting and productive. She described intensive days under his guidance, poring over books of engravings, inscriptions and photographs of ancient sculpture and architecture that he brought to her from the shelves of his comprehensive library. She also visited museums with him around Paris, including his own in St Germain, and she was able to see and sometimes handle antiquities – for example, ancient ivories and illuminated manuscripts.[52] Reinach endeavoured to introduce Bell to other notable scholars whose interests in the Near East matched her own, among them Melchior de Vogüé (1829–1916), a French archaeologist distinguished for his investigations and scholarly reports on ancient Cyprus, Syria and Palestine in the 1860s,[53] and René Dussaud (1868–1958), a renowned French Orientalist, archaeologist and expert on ancient religions, who had travelled extensively in Syria and published widely acclaimed accounts of Syrian history, peoples and ancient sites.[54] Overall, Bell liked Reinach tremendously and was impressed with his dedication to his studies and his vast capacity for work.[55] For his part, Reinach found Bell 'quite charming' and extended to her warm hospitality whenever she visited him.[56] He was also generous with his time and wide learning.

Reinach must have been impressed with Bell's scholarly abilities, too, for he asked her to write a review article for *Revue archéologique.*[57] Although anxious about producing an article for such a prestigious academic publication, Bell excitedly accepted this assignment, which entailed reviewing a lengthy work on the artistic and architectural program of the desert palace of Mshatta, a ruined castle in the Jordanian desert south of Amman. The author was the famous Austrian scholar Joseph Strzygowski.[58] The topic was appropriate for Bell: she was already acquainted with Strzygowski's scholarship and could capably read German. Moreover, she had passed by Mshatta during her travels through Jordan in 1900 and was familiar with the controversy over its date and the identity of its builder. As it transpired, Bell's short review article, which appeared in Reinach's journal in 1905,[59] was to be the first of several that he commissioned, the others being Bell's reports on the ruined churches she visited in the course of her 1905 journey through Cilicia and Lycaonia in Anatolia, and a review of a German report on the site of Binbirkilise.[60] These reports gave Bell exposure to the wider world of archaeological scholarship for the first time, and they did not go unnoticed. Strzygowski himself produced a favourable review of Bell's accounts of the Anatolian churches, writing:

I do not know Gertrude L.B. personally, I do not know if she is young or old, therefore my judgement is totally impartial: what she accomplished should set an example for men [. . .] she has presented Christian art of Asia Minor in a way that hopefully the whole world will soon go there to see with their own eyes that Asia Minor is a very fruitful 'Neuland' for art history.[61]

Altogether, the positive encouragement, intensive instruction and introduction to European scholarship that Salomon Reinach provided for Bell contributed significantly to her development as an archaeologist. Her new-found knowledge and confidence boosted her desire to study the ancient world, and her travels to the Near East found additional fulfilment through the scholarly manner in which she now analysed the archaeological sites she visited.

As reported, the final leg of Bell's 1905 Near Eastern journey, in April and May, entailed a visit to the regions of Cilicia and Lacaonia in Anatolia (present-day southern Turkey), where she proceeded to make the careful and comprehensive report of Byzantine churches that would appear as a series of installments in *Revue archéologique*.[62] By far the most fascinating churches were located at Binbirkilise, a remarkable cluster of ruins on the slopes of the volcanic mountain Karadağ, to the south-east of the city of Konya on the central Anatolian plateau. Because of their remoteness, these churches and the numerous structures around them had not been disturbed by later construction, and despite their ruinous state, Bell could often discern some of their original plans and functions. She spent time measuring and photographing the ruins and copying some of the few inscriptions found among them. Fortuitously while in Konya, Bell had a chance encounter with the Classical archaeologist and leading 'authority on the topography, antiquities and history of Asia Minor', William Ramsay, to whom she enthusiastically reported the archaeological wealth of Binbirkilise.[63] They agreed that the site deserved further scrutiny, and so they decided to collaborate on an archaeological expedition to further explore its remains.

Largely financed by Bell's personal funds, the archaeological project to Binbirkilise proceeded in May and June 1907 (Fig. 1.5). The expedition's aim was to acquire a comprehensive record of the site's remains, particularly the churches, and while it did not entail full-scale excavations, a small team of local Kurds and Turks were employed to clear the earth and rubble around the bases of the buildings' walls in order to expose their full dimensions and forms.[64] Bell subsequently travelled to neighbouring areas of Anatolia after the investigations at Binbirkilise, finding and reporting on contemporary examples of ecclesiastical architecture that helped situate the site in its proper architectural and chronological context (she explored further the region of the Karadağ, and then the Hasan Dağ and Karadja Dağ ranges in July 1907). The result of Bell's and Ramsay's intensive research was a co-authored monograph entitled *The Thousand and One Churches* (a translation of the site's Turkish name, Binbirkilise). Published

Fig. 1.5   Gertrude Bell and her servant, Fattuh, standing in front of her tent at Ramsay and Bell's camp at Binbirkilise (south central Turkey), in 1907.

in 1909, the work well reflects the respective expertise of its authors, Ramsay tackling the dating and development of the buildings on the basis of extant historical records and his study of the inscriptions found at the site, while Bell's contribution consisted of a detailed description of each church, accompanied by carefully measured plans and photographs.[65] She also devised a chronology of buildings on the basis of changes observed in their architecture, masonry and decorations.[66] Together, the authors produced an architectural classification of churches that tracked their development between the fifth and eleventh centuries, and they linked the buildings' abandonments, shifts in settlement location, rebuildings or renovations to historical developments such as the Arab Muslim invasions and the later arrival of the Seljuk Turks.[67]

Bell's investigations at Binbirkilise marked her first intensive foray into archaeological work in the Near East, and in this effort we can begin to discern the particular direction of her archaeological interests and her favoured methodology, these largely persisting in all of her subsequent investigations. Without question, a strong influence by 1907 was Josef Strzygowski (about whom more will be said in the following chapter), and we see his signature approach in much of Bell's work in *The Thousand and One Churches*. Her work on the development and character of Binbirkilise's churches, marked by careful attention to their architectural forms and ornamentation, and her attempts to establish cultural contacts and influences on the basis of these observable physical characteristics, closely followed Strzygowski's own comparative formal analysis. Bell's study of the vaults, arches, domes and architectural mouldings of the Anatolian churches, and her consequent determination of the date and cultural character of the buildings in which they appeared, especially exhibited this type of approach. Moreover, her growing expertise in this methodology and her familiarity with such features – their distinctive forms, dimensions, masonry and technology – guided subsequent investigations. Her later treatment of the vaults and domes of the palace and mosque at Ukhaidir (to be considered further in Chapter 3), for example, constituted a critical aspect of her study of this complex, assisting greatly with its dating and identification.

While Bell followed Strzygowski's overall approach to ancient art and architecture, his overly simplistic notions about the primacy of the East to explain the origins of all architectural forms did not match her more nuanced observations of local creative ingenuity and innovation in the architecture of Asia Minor, as Mark Jackson has adroitly observed of Bell's study of the churches of Binbirkilise.[68] But she expressed her diverging views only passively in *The Thousand and One Churches*, possibly in deference to Strzygowski, whom she still highly respected in this early stage of her archaeological career.[69] Nevertheless, they hint at her potential for independent thought as well as her growing ability to recognize the entangled, multifaceted manner of cultural exchanges and their manifestations in art and architecture. These outlooks would find ample expression in Bell's later, more mature scholarly works.

One other significant element of Bell's work at Binbirkilise that deserves mention is her photography. The truly enduring strength of *The Thousand and One Churches* is the richness of Bell's clear, crisp black-and-white photographs.[70] Over 200 of these throughout the work document the site and neighbouring regions' distinctive churches and associated structures. While they hold no particular artistic or aesthetic merit (attained through careful composition, lighting and balance, as seen in the output of other early archaeological photographers such as John Henry Haynes),[71] they cannot be faulted for the clarity they offer of particular architectural features such as carved ornamentation, mouldings, capitals and columns. Bell's photographs occasionally also emphasize the built and natural environments around the churches, providing a wider context for the settlement and landscape in which they existed (Fig. 1.6). The value of Bell's photographs of Binbirkilise is all the more apparent when one realizes that many of the site's structures no longer exist, having either severely crumbled or disappeared altogether (Fig. 1.7). The rapid deterioration of the ruins had already been noted by earlier explorers of the site, including Bell herself, and indeed, part of her motivation to acquire a good photographic record had been her observation of the churches' decline.[72] Altogether, Bell's talent for archaeological photography, practised at Binbirkilise, is a distinctive, much

Fig. 1.6 Bell's photograph of several ruined Byzantine churches at Binbirkilise (south central Turkey), with the hills of the Karadağ range visible behind. Panoramic images such as these, which Bell started taking in 1907, capture nicely the natural landscapes in which ancient sites were situated.

valued feature of her archaeological approach, and it continued into her subsequent investigations, often to great effect.

By the time Bell's Anatolian campaign concluded in 1907, archaeology had become, at least for the time being, the principal calling in her life. Her mountain-climbing exploits, as successful and exciting as they had been, had ceased, and her far-ranging travels that had taken her across the globe now

Fig. 1.7 The ruined interior of Church No. 1 at Binbirkilise (fifth century CE), looking towards its apse.

became focused largely on the Near East. Bell's numerous journeys through the Levant and Anatolia had by this time given her exhilarating first-hand experiences with archaeological remains, and her studies and encouragement by Salomon Reinach had further fuelled her archaeological pursuits and given them a scholarly legitimacy. Finally, her intensive fieldwork and research at Binbirkilise had developed her archaeological skills and knowledge to the point where she could now justifiably count herself among a small group of learned scholars from around the world who were experts on the study of Late Antiquity in the Near East.

But this wasn't enough for Bell. If anything, her achievements whetted her appetite for more ambitious enterprises, and fields of study in which she was thus far only a novice. Moreover, they drew her further and further eastwards, into Mesopotamia, where only a small few Europeans had journeyed before her, and an even smaller number had cared to document its ancient remains. This land, once the 'cradle of civilization', now beckoned to her, and she longed to see its sweeping rivers, wide, dusty plains, and abundance of ruined places, reaching back to the very dawn of history.

CHAPTER 2

EUPHRATES JOURNEY

In a darkened, vaulted corridor of a noisy bazaar in Aleppo, Bell's servant Fattuh purchased string from a shopkeeper. The hank of twine was intended for the long journey upon which they were about to embark, and amid encouragement from passers-by and Bell herself, who were gathered around the stall, Fattuh endeavoured to get the best price for it. The scene nicely evokes the anticipation and excitement felt at the onset of travel and exploration in the Near East. Moreover, the setting in the old covered marketplace – from which Bell could see the sun casting its light upon the even more ancient Citadel at Aleppo – gave a sensation of timelessness, where the past blended seamlessly into the present. One could imagine the act of haggling over string being played out time and time again over hundreds of years in the antique bazaar.

This is the scene Bell gives her readers in the opening pages of her travel book *Amurath to Amurath*, the account of her long, exploratory expedition down the Euphrates River into the lands of Mesopotamia in the early months of 1909.[1] The theme so evocatively introduced in these opening pages, of past and present being melded together, carries on through Bell's entire travelogue, moving the reader between her encounters with the contemporary peoples, towns and landscapes of the Near East, and their rich and eventful histories. Aleppo, a city that 'readily leads one back into the past' with its old bazaars, walls and mosques, was a perfect place to begin the narrative of this unique journey, in which the author describes and celebrates both the historical and the here and now.[2]

Bell's extensive journeys in the Near East, especially those through Palestine, Syria and Anatolia in 1905 and her more recent expedition to Anatolia in 1907, had made her a seasoned traveller. She had become well accustomed to life on the road, and indeed revelled in it, riding every day, eating food prepared by Fattuh over an open fire and sleeping in a simple tent. Her fluency in Arabic and Turkish facilitated interactions with the local inhabitants, Ottoman officials and her entourage of guides, guards and muleteers. Her skill and experience had made her travels relatively untroubled and efficient, and for the most part she passed through places both familiar and remote with an elation and excitement for the road that attested to her voyager's spirit. By 1909, she had become fully aware of and attuned to the past, and it resonated strongly for her wherever she ventured in the Near East. History and archaeology held such a fascination for her that they now took centre stage. The cities and towns she would visit, the route she had planned, all were designed to enable her to connect with ancient places, to record their monuments and to chronicle the stories of the legendary rulers who had once conquered their strongholds and inhabited their lofty halls.

The route of Bell's 1909 Near Eastern journey, which followed the eastern bank of the Euphrates River in northern Syria down into southern Mesopotamia (southern Iraq) before turning northwards and following the Tigris River up into Anatolia (Fig. 2.1), was clearly selected with her archaeological interests in mind, and these were nicely combined with her taste for travelling through remote locales that other Western travellers had seldom frequented. Even by the early part of the twentieth century, many parts of her proposed route had rarely been

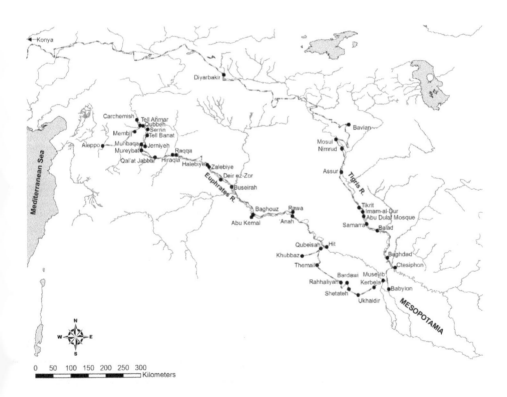

Fig. 2.1 Map of Bell's 1909 Near Eastern journey, showing her route along the eastern bank of the Euphrates River, excursion to Ukhaidir, and journey through Mesopotamia and Anatolia.

visited by Europeans, and its geography, inhabitants and settlements had been only cursorily recorded. The fact that she would be passing through regions where ancient remains were known to be rich and plentiful but still poorly documented further enhanced the pioneering, exploratory nature of her trip.

Bell's planned study of the archaeological remains she would visit during this expedition, however, would be challenging. Not only were there materials dated to Late Classical Antiquity, a period with which she had considerable expertise through her previous work in Anatolia, but there also were remains from both earlier and later eras. The Euphrates River valley and the regions of Mesopotamia on her itinerary were rich in pre-Classical cultures, some hailing back to prehistoric periods over 5,000 years ago. At the same time, she would be venturing through regions that had supported the rich Islamic cultures that came after Late Antiquity, and with them she would have the opportunity to trace art and architectural forms through to their later manifestations, assessing the degree to which they adopted, rejected or transformed earlier Classical forms. In all, the journey would expose Bell to an incredibly rich and varied feast of archaeological remains that attested to the lives and cultures of humans over thousands of years, and she would need steady determination and diligence to keep a careful written and photographic record of all that she came upon. Moreover, at the journey's end back in England, her scholarly abilities would be further tested by the additional research she would need to carry out to make sense of the dates and significance of these remains.

Influences

Bell's itinerary was not devised solely from her own aims and ambitions. She consulted with respected friends and colleagues who were familiar with the regions through which she would pass, receiving from them advice, encouragement and inspiration. Two individuals in particular should be mentioned for their impact on her 1909 trip. They provided her with the most detailed guidance on the specific regions through which she should travel and gave her important background information about the cultures she was likely to encounter. These individuals also had an impact on Bell's methodological approach to the archaeological remains she found, and the emphases she gave to particular materials and their interpretation.

David Hogarth

Among her fellow British acquaintances, no one held a more prominent place in Bell's archaeological life than David George Hogarth (1862–1927) (Fig. 2.2), an accomplished archaeologist, geographer and distinguished author whose expertise included not only the lands of the Classical world, but the regions and peoples of the Near East and Egypt. Since Bell had come to know and respect

Hogarth's work a great deal by 1909, a short overview of his life and accomplishments is warranted here, especially for identifying aspects of his activities and scholarship that had the greatest impact on her own work at this time.

After graduating from Oxford in 1885, Hogarth travelled first to Greece and then to Anatolia, where he joined William Mitchell Ramsay, the celebrated Oxford scholar of Classical Antiquity and Early Christianity (with whom Bell herself would eventually become well acquainted).[3] These journeys honed Hogarth's Classical training, particularly his epigraphic skills, which in his case involved the location, measurement, mapping and copying of countless ancient inscriptions in the hills and valleys of Anatolia's rugged landscapes.[4] Hogarth's first excavation experience was gained on the island of Cyprus, and thereafter he dug in Egypt, Greece and Crete, working alongside other notable archaeologists such as Flinders Petrie, Édouard Naville and Arthur Evans.[5] His archaeological work eventually took him back to Anatolia, where he dug at the site of Ephesus (1904–5), and finally to northern Syria, where he directed the British Museum excavations at Carchemish on the Euphrates River, beginning in 1911.[6] In England, Hogarth was no less busy, becoming Keeper of the Ashmolean Museum, at Oxford, in 1908. He would retain that prestigious appointment until his death in 1927.[7]

Hogarth's numerous scholarly publications included reports of his archaeological excavations, as well as colourful accounts of his travels through places such as Cyprus, Egypt and Anatolia. His other written works included perceptive observations of the modern inhabitants of the lands through which he passed – their cultures, languages, religions and political leanings.[8] Hogarth also observed the geography of the regions through which he travelled, taking careful note of their landscapes and climates, and speculating on how such features would have affected the cultures of the people who lived in them, both past and present.[9]

Hogarth had a particular fondness for exploratory travel, this being in part connected to his long-time fascination with Alexander the Great and 'the spacious world' of the East over which this extraordinary man had moved.[10] Of Alexander's conquests, Hogarth wrote that they 'fired my imagination and stirred a lust for discovery'.[11] His 'explorer's itch' led him to several places in Anatolia and Syria seldom frequented by European visitors, and it promoted his interest in the Arabian peninsula, which had remained a largely unsurveyed and little understood region of the Near East. While it is surprising that Hogarth never actually travelled to Arabia until 1916 – and by this time he was only on official wartime business – he nonetheless acquired considerable knowledge of its geography, history and peoples through various publications.[12] His 1904 work, *The Penetration of Arabia: A Record of the Development of Western Knowledge Concerning the Arabian Peninsula*, chronicled that region's history and geography and made a detailed report of the European travellers who had ventured there up

Fig. 2.2 David Hogarth – traveller, archaeologist, author and political operative – in the centre of the photograph, with T.E. Lawrence (left) and Alan G.C. Dawnay (right). Hogarth was a source of inspiration and encouragement for Bell at the time of her early trips to the Near East. Their association continued into the years of World War I and afterward, when they served as political agents of Britain in the Near East.

to the nineteenth century. The travels of the exceptionally intrepid Charles Montagu Doughty (1843–1926), a distinguished Arabian traveller, were capaciously chronicled in the book, and Hogarth would return to this subject towards the end of his life, when he penned Doughty's biography.[13] While recent travel and the current conditions of Arabia were Hogarth's main subjects in *The Penetration of Arabia*, he did not neglect topics pertaining to antiquity, as evidenced by his report on Roman or pre-Roman inscriptions at Teima, ancient roadways to Petra, Gerra and Sheba, and Ptolemy's map of the peninsula.[14]

Gertrude Bell could be counted among the many readers of *The Penetration of Arabia* whose imaginations were fired up by the prospect of exploring this vast desert land of the Near East, as she was by the other regions through which Hogarth had travelled. But Bell's familiarity with Hogarth extended beyond his writings, as has already been reported. We know that she had met him through his younger sister, Janet, a friend from her Oxford days in the late 1880s. Her letters indicate that she encountered Hogarth on several occasions in the course of her travels through Europe, including in Athens in 1898, by which time he was Director of the British School at Athens and involved in the excavations of the site of Phylakopi on the island of Melos.[15] Thrilled as Bell was by the opportunity to see and handle some of the pottery that had been excavated at that site, we may perhaps credit Hogarth for having sown some of the seeds of her incipient interest in archaeology.[16]

In the years that followed, Bell's own travels in the Near East, especially her journey up through the Hauran of northern Jordan and southern Syria, which she undertook in 1905, did not go unnoticed by Hogarth. He acknowledged her efforts in a lecture on Near Eastern exploration, delivered to the Royal Geographical Society in London in November 1908.[17] That a personal association also continued to exist between the two is indicated by Hogarth's request, prior to her 1909 journey to the Near East, to proceed to the site of Tell Ahmar on the left bank of the Euphrates River in Syria, in order to take additional paper squeezes of the Hittite inscriptions, since his own squeezes of those stones had not been successful.[18] Upon the conclusion of her Mesopotamian journey, we know from Bell's letters that she visited Hogarth in Oxford, reporting on her visit to Ahmar and giving him paper squeezes and photographs. Some of these materials subsequently appeared in Hogarth's published article on Carchemish and surrounding archaeological sites, and Bell must be given credit for their clarity and informative character.[19]

Bell clearly shared Hogarth's love of exploration, as already shown by her earlier travels in the Near East that veered from the paths well-trodden by previous Europeans. One can also detect within Bell, like Hogarth, a similar fascination for Arabia, given its unexplored quality. The central Nejd region of Arabia seems to have particularly captivated Bell, this containing the *Ruba el-Khali*, the 'Empty Quarter', which no European had traversed.[20] Coupled with that was her ongoing curiosity for the House of Rashid, an Arab family of the northern Nejd, which was centred on the city of Hayil. Reports about the goings-on of the prince Ibn Rashid had been made to Bell as early as 1900 during her travels in Syria,[21] and she harboured a fascination for this elusive character that would ultimately be realized by her daring trip to his capital at Hayil in 1914. Hogarth would report the details of this perilous journey in his obituary for Bell in 1926, remarking that she was only the second European woman, after Lady Anne Blunt, to see the Nejd.[22]

For her 1909 journey, Bell selected a Near Eastern itinerary that was considerably less hazardous than the desert wastes of the Nejd she would tackle five years later but still entailed the kind of exploration of which Hogarth would have wholly approved. He himself had noted, in print, sections of the Euphrates River Valley that required closer inspection, and we can guess that parts of her 1909 itinerary were intended to take into account those regions. As remarked above, Bell's visit to the site of Tell Ahmar, downstream from Carchemish, was certainly made at Hogarth's specific request. Her overland route from Aleppo to the Euphrates River, and her further travels down the left bank of the river from Tell Ahmar, as far as 'Anah, appear to have been partly in response to Hogarth's observation – together with Bernhard Moritz's advice (see Chapter 3) – that these areas had seldom been travelled since Chesney's expedition 70 years earlier but were much changed, now dotted with agricultural villages where once had been but a few wandering Arabs,[23] and that many new places needed to be added to the map.[24]

Besides in her choice of travel itinerary, Hogarth's influence over Bell may be discerned in her travel writing. In *Amurath to Amurath*, she provides ample information about the modern conditions of the regions she passed through, including the names of existing villages and towns, along with tribal groups and their pasturing lands, political opinions and sheikhs' names, echoing Hogarth's own tendency to describe current conditions in his travelogues.[25] Historical geography also held a tremendous allure for Bell. Her work attests to the diligence with which she located the ruins of ancient settlement sites, and to her subsequent efforts to discern their ancient names, suggest ancient caravan routes and military tracks, and locate river crossings. Such investigations often involved recourse to pre-modern geographers and historians who provided place-names and reports of the regions through which she had travelled. References to these are liberally scattered throughout Bell's published accounts. Readers of *Amurath to Amurath*, for example, often find themselves assailed with information mined from Classical authors such as Ammianus Marcellinus,[26] Xenophon,[27] Strabo,[28] Lucian[29] and Ptolemy,[30] and ancient works such as the Peutinger Table,[31] the Antonine Itinerary[32] and the Parthian Stations of Isadore of Charax.[33] Nor was Bell ignorant of the Arab historians and geographers Ibn Khordadhbeh,[34] Istakhri,[35] Ibn Jubayr,[36] Yaqut[37] and Abu'l Fida,[38] these also assisting in her identification of pre-modern settlements, the location of older tracks and crossings, and other places and monuments of historical significance. While some of the locations of ancient sites suggested by Bell on the basis of these historical geographical studies have since proven incorrect,[39] her method of inquiry essentially emulated Hogarth's own geographical investigations and his similar recourse to ancient authors.[40]

A final indication of Hogarth's influence is Bell's stepped-up interest in not only the ancient remains from the Greco-Roman periods but also those from the even earlier Bronze and Iron Ages. Bell did not hesitate to speculate on the date and function of several pre-Classical monuments and tell-sites, and she was eager to report these in careful detail. This echoed Hogarth's own interests, which although solidly based in the Classical world nonetheless had veered, through his travels and investigations in central Anatolia and northern Syria, to earlier periods of antiquity. He had become particularly fascinated by the Hittites. We see in Bell an increasing curiosity and interest in pre-Classical civilization as she progressed through her 1909 journey into Mesopotamia, this culminating in her detailed and enthusiastic reports on two of the region's most celebrated ancient cities, Babylon and Assur.

Significantly, Hogarth's association with Gertrude Bell did not end with their shared scholarly interest in the Near East, both past and present. Like Bell, Hogarth played an important role in Arab affairs during World War I. Because of his vast knowledge of the geography and people of the Near East, in 1915 Hogarth was appointed to head up the so-called Arab Bureau of the British Naval Intelligence Division in Cairo, gathering for its top policymakers vital information about the movements and loyalties of the Arab groups of Arabia, Palestine, Syria and Mesopotamia, and their potential alliance to Britain.[41] Hogarth was responsible for recruiting one of his archaeological protégés from the Carchemish excavations, T.E. Lawrence, to make contact with the Arab leadership in the Hejaz, this eventually leading to Lawrence's key role in the Arab Revolt.[42] It was also in his capacity as director of the Arab Bureau that Hogarth invited Bell to join the Bureau in 1915, a move that essentially launched her legendary career in British–Arab affairs and the politics of Iraq.[43] T.E. Lawrence would later commend Hogarth for his great knowledge and careful wisdom,[44] and it is doubtful that Gertrude Bell would have been any less fulsome in her praise, given the force of his impact upon her travels, archaeological pursuits and political activities.

Josef Strzygowski

Discussion of Bell's archaeological interests and activities cannot rightly proceed without the acknowledgement of another source of inspiration and knowledge about the Near East: the German scholar Josef Strzygowski, whom I introduced in Chapter 1 (Fig. 2.3). Strzygowski was especially influential with respect to Bell's work on the art and architecture of the Byzantine and early Islamic periods, and she strongly emulated his scholarly method in her written works.

Born in 1862 in humble circumstances – the son of a cloth manufacturer in Austrian Silesia – Strzygowski was the object of many prejudices in academia, and he was considered something of an outsider in the elite academic circles of late nineteenth-century Germany; such factors may have shaped his combative and iconoclastic personality.[45] He opposed traditional views about art and endeavoured to dethrone the older generation of narrow-minded German academics, whom he believed gave undeserved priority and pre-eminence to Classical antiquity – especially Classical languages – at the expense of other worthy fields of study of the ancient world. In 1909, the year Bell set out on her first journey to Mesopotamia, Strzygowski had just taken up a prestigious professorship in art history at the University of Vienna, remaining there until his retirement in 1934 (he died in 1941).[46]

Strzygowski's special interests and expertise lay with ancient cultures and countries that fell outside the cultural sphere of Rome. Over the course of his career, he studied and published numerous articles, reviews and monographs on the art and architecture of Armenia, and on Byzantine, Slavic, Serbian, Germanic, Coptic and, importantly, Near Eastern antiquities.[47] His focus was primarily the Hellenistic, Byzantine and Early Islamic periods of the Near East, and he acquired an unprecedented knowledge of the material culture of these eras. As his research developed, he became more and more disillusioned with the traditional notion that the Classical world, especially Rome, was the origin of all great Western art, a belief that still persisted among his contemporaries. On the contrary, he argued, the Orient – by which he meant the Near East – was the source of a great number of important developments that had spread to the West and ultimately affected the development of European medieval art and architecture.[48]

Strzygowski's analytical method gave priority to the style and form of art and architecture. Once these formal characteristics had been carefully described, they were then compared with other sites displaying morphologically similar features. Similarities indicated a path of cultural diffusion, whereby the formal characteristics of a particular art style or architectural feature were seen as spreading out from one point of origin through time and across space. This comparative formal analysis was often carried out at the expense of textual sources and inscriptions that could provide a historical context.[49] Nevertheless, Strzygowski argued that only with artefacts could one enter into otherwise inaccessible realms of prehistoric or illiterate cultures for which there are no inscriptions, or the everyday worlds of common people. Thus, he claimed that while 'writing had largely been a pursuit of elites, artistic movements (and the artefacts they generated) reflected much more closely the actual life of the *Volk*'.[50]

Strzygowski's continuing attacks on colleagues, not to mention his odious personality – he was well known for his belligerence and arrogance – made him

Fig. 2.3 Josef Strzygowski, the Polish-Austrian art historian who championed the ancient Near East over Rome as a source of many important artistic traditions that ultimately spread to the West and impacted European medieval art. Bell was strongly influenced by Strzygowski's theories about the primacy of the Near East, and she adopted his formal analytical approach to the study of art and architecture.

unpopular among some of his academic peers.[51] Moreover, his style of inquiry was frequently called into question by more cautious scholars. As one reported, his method was to 'make erratic combinations without the requisite critical sorting of the individual facts', and, this critic opined, such an approach departed 'too radically from the path of prudent method and source criticism'.[52] Despite these shortcomings, however, Strzygowski could not be criticised for the breadth of his interests, his innovative approaches, his unique familiarity with out-of-the-way material, and the fact that a great many of his morphological observations were striking and brilliantly conceived.[53]

None of these accomplishments are what Strzygowski is remembered for today. Instead, he is remembered for his racist leanings. Although he was the Orient's greatest champion over Rome, with the Orient he situated Semitic races and their negative influences:

> Strzygowski claimed that changes in late antique art, and the rise of Christian art were not a Roman development but rather the pervasive and malicious influence of the East, risen again from its slumbers after centuries of Greek dominance to destroy the Hellenic tradition.[54]

His racist themes developed over time, and eventually, he became sympathetic to the Nazi regime that gained power in Germany in the 1930s. It is because of his association with this infamous period of history that Strzygowski's name is seldom uttered today. As one modern scholar writes, 'Discussions of his genuine scholarly significance have always been burdened by excuses or embarrassment, or his work is discredited altogether.'[55] But as J. Elsner cogently writes:

> Stripped of its proto-Nazi politics, the influence of this approach has been fundamental to the establishment of the history of Islamic art, to the study of image production on the eastern peripheries of the Roman empire, with a view to resisting Romano-centrism, and most ironically, to the study of Jewish art, in which Strzygowski can be hailed as a pioneer.[56]

One should keep these things in mind when considering Strzygowski's contributions in the pre-Nazi era of German art-historical scholarship, and the significance of his influence over people like Gertrude Bell.

By 1909, Bell had come to know a great deal about Strzygowski and his specialization in the art history of the Near East. Even as far back as 1896 she had been familiar with his scholarship, reading his books on the train between London and her family home at Rounton in North Yorkshire.[57] Bell's interest in and familiarity with Strzygowski's scholarship had also prompted her to write in 1905 a favourable review of his comprehensive 1904 report on the artistic and architectural program of the desert palace of Mshatta.[58] As mentioned in

Chapter 1, Bell's review was published in *Revue archéologique* at the behest of her good friend and mentor Salomon Reinach.[59] This review, and her own visit to that site, would have drawn her into the world of the Mshatta debate that had been raging for some time, as the site's date and ethnicity were frustratingly difficult to determine.[60] It probably also made her familiar, for the first time, with the scholarship of a young German by the name of Ernst Herzfeld, who was formulating his own brilliant conclusions about Mshatta, and with whom Bell would later enter into a spirited correspondence.[61]

Bell would have known of Strzygowski's other works, including his polemical *Orient oder Rom* (Leipzig, 1901), which argued that the Orient must be given sufficient credit for its creative power, and that it was the source of a great number of artistic developments that spread to the West and influenced European medieval art.[62] Bell also carefully read Strzygowski's next book, *Kleinasien, ein Neuland der Kunstgeschichte* (Leipzig, 1903), which proceeded in a similar vein. It argued that 'Greek and Roman culture had relatively little impact on Asia', and specifically Anatolia, 'where local traditions had persevered'.[63] In this vein, he distinguished between coastal settlements in Anatolia, which through their exposure to Hellenistic culture presented Greco-Roman art and architectural features, and those in the interior, which exhibited wholly 'Oriental' elements. In the interior of Anatolia, for example, one could find 'churches with two towers in the façade, recalling Hittite and Jewish prototypes; doors and windows piercing the lateral walls, as in Syria; compound piers instead of columns; arches instead of architraves; vaults in place of coffered wooden ceilings'.[64]

When Bell first visited the site of Binbirkilise, in Anatolia, she was carrying a copy of Strzygowski's *Kleinasien* in her saddle bag, and it was this work that originally inspired her interest in the early Christian monuments in 1905.[65] She and William Ramsay frequently consulted it when they drew up their plans and conclusions concerning the dates and evolution of late antique ecclesiastical architecture at this site in 1907. In the end, their published work, *The Thousand and One Churches*, which appeared in 1909 (London), was dedicated to Strzygowski. Moreover, Bell's contribution to this work clearly shows Strzygowski's influence, not only in her advocacy of the importance of Near Eastern artistic traditions, but also in how her building typologies and architectural categorizations were formulated, and the emphasis she placed on morphological developments in architectural form and decoration as factors determining developments through time and space.[66]

Bell's study of the ancient sites and antiquities she encountered during her 1909 journey continued to bear the imprint of her mentor Strzygowski, particularly in the use of his comparative, formal analysis of art and architecture. She also accepted the creative, persistent power of the East and continued to seek native Near Eastern elements in the ancient remains she inspected. That Strzygowski was often in her mind when she visited various sites in the Near East is indicated by statements expressed in her letters, such as 'Strzygowski will be off his head with joy over this find: I must write to him now' (regarding her discovery of the castle of Ukhaidir),[67] and 'Strzygowski will be wild with joy over them' (the early fragments of wall stucco patterns she had encountered at Samarra).[68] That she had a personal relationship with him is also indicated in her letters, some of which refer to visits with him in Graz or Vienna.[69] Ultimately, Bell's most ambitious work, her report on the palace and mosque of Ukhaidir, strongly bears the imprint of Strzygowski's art-historical methodology, as I will further discuss in upcoming chapters. Altogether, Strzygowski's formidable presence in Bell's life left a deep mark in her Near Eastern scholarship.

Preparations for the 1909 Trip

By the time she was ready to embark from Aleppo, the official starting point of her journey, Bell was outfitted with all of the provisions and equipment necessary for a proper exploratory expedition into distant parts. She purchased her pack animals in Aleppo, as well as much of her food and fodder, knowing that she could not depend on finding adequate provisions along the remoter parts of the road she was taking.[70] She had an ample supply of clothing for all seasons and temperatures, as well as other personal effects. Canvas tents would serve as private sleeping quarters for her and her men when other accommodations in towns were not available. The tents figure often in Bell's photographs, frequently pitched right amidst the ruins of ancient sites, on the outskirts of inhabited settlements or directly in the open countryside and desert.[71]

Photography

One of the most laudable aspects of Bell's Near Eastern travels was the photographic record she kept of her journey. Having already carried a camera on her 1905 journey through the Levant, then in 1907 when she photographed prodigiously with Ramsay at Binbirkilise in Anatolia, Bell swore by the value of images for properly documenting ancient sites and monuments. In her archaeological research, they were as valuable as her written descriptions and plans for comprehensively recording buildings and monuments, and they assisted in jogging her memory when she got home and engaged in typological, comparative research.[72] For readers of her travels and archaeological reports, Bell's photographs greatly aided their ability to comprehend the places she described and to appreciate more fully their beauty or architectural significance. For us today, Bell's photographs provide an incredibly rich record of a past that in many cases no longer exists, or which has deteriorated considerably since her time.

The survival of Bell's nitrate negatives, which are housed at Newcastle University, indicate that she was carrying portable cameras equipped with film rolls, far better technology than the older and cumbersome cameras that required weighty glass plates.[73] The majority of her photographs in 1909 were taken with a conventional single-format camera, but by this time Bell was also carrying a camera for panoramic images, realizing the value of taking wider shots of sites and landscapes. At the same time, she occasionally attempted to capture wider-angle views through a series of overlapping shots. These panoramic views, as J. Crow has emphasized, are particular effective for conveying the vast emptiness of the Mesopotamian deserts in contrast to the solidary grandeur of monuments standing in their midst, such as the Arch of Ctesiphon or the desert palace of Ukhaidir.[74] As Crow also noted, these views are even more compelling when they include the shadow of the photographer herself, rarely seen on film otherwise.[75]

Field Equipment

Bell did not carry sophisticated mapping or surveying equipment in 1909. For planning archaeological remains, she relied solely on a compass to provide her with cardinal points, then used a simple hand tape measure and foot ruler to measure out the dimensions of walls and other features, which were entered into her field notebooks, these of varying sizes. Some features, especially if they were particularly ruined or of less immediate interest to her, were roughly sketched and then measured by foot paces, which were recorded in her field notebooks.[76] She did not carry a theodolite for taking bearings and planning a proper map until her 1913–14 trip in Arabia.[77] She did, however, carry an aneroid barometer, which helped her to gauge rough elevations above sea level and get an approximate sense of changes in the topography of the terrain through which she was travelling.[78]

Maps

Bell was equipped with the best maps available at the time. As with her earlier travels through the Near East, she relied on maps that had been prepared by the well-known and highly respected German cartographer Heinrich Kiepert (1819– 99).[79] Kiepert's life work had entailed producing detailed maps of many parts of the Old World, and given his interest and background in ancient history, many of these maps sought to identify the locations of ancient cities and towns known to have existed in various regions.[80] Such maps were of tremendous interest and value to many European travellers, whose journeys, like Bell's, were deeply informed by the landscapes of antiquity and by the multitude of cities, military outposts, borders, roadways and ancient campaign routes that populated those regions.

By 1909, Kiepert's cartographic work had been given over to his son, Richard Kiepert (1846–1915), who continued to fill blank spaces on his father's maps. Thus, Kiepert's *Provinces Asiatiques de l'Empire Ottoman (sans l'Arabie)* (Berlin, 1884) was augmented by additional place-names, many of these supplied by more recent

European travellers and scholars who had journeyed through these lands or whose research of Classical or Arab historians and geographers provided educated guesses as to where some ancient places should be located. Such historically rich Kiepert maps were included in the book of the German archaeologist Max Freiherr von Oppenheim, *Von Mittelmeer zum Persischen Golf* (2 volumes, Berlin, 1899–1900), an account of his Near Eastern journey undertaken in 1892–3. On them, one can see, for example, the locations of places that had been reported by Colonel F.R. Chesney during his 1835–7 steamer voyage down the Euphrates into Mesopotamia, and those of his travelling companion W.F. Ainsworth, these having also figured in the original H. Kiepert maps.[81] But in addition are places that had been recognized by more recent European travellers, such as Robert Koldewey, Eduard Sachau, Melchior de Vogüé and Bernhard Moritz.[82]

Bell's own Kiepert maps would have been akin to those produced for Oppenheim. We also know from her diary entries that she had the benefit of looking them over with Oppenheim himself, together with Moritz, when she was in Cairo in January 1909.[83] Upon these occasions, both Oppenheim and Moritz advised her on which routes to take in Syria, Mesopotamia and Anatolia. Further, Oppenheim seems to have provided additional notes for Bell about the left bank of the Euphrates River around the village of Serrin, for he had been there in 1899 on his way to the archaeological site of Tell Halaf further to the north-east, near Ras al 'Ayn.[84] Altogether, the quality of the maps Bell carried on her 1909 trip, along with the sage advice of colleagues who had actually travelled in the regions she was going to visit, prepared her well for the impending expedition.

Euphrates Journey

The Beginning – Aleppo

Bell's trip began in earnest in early 1909, after she had travelled by boat to Egypt and Beirut and by train to Aleppo. The last was, as she remarked, the gateway to Asia.[85] Here, she bought her horses and provisions and hired her baggage handlers for the long trek that would take her down the Euphrates River, into Mesopotamia.

Ever interested in the modern affairs of a place and its residents, Bell wasted no time in meeting the inhabitants of Aleppo – ranging from wealthy businessmen to shopkeepers, soldiers and labourers – and discussing with them current political and economic developments. Foremost in their minds were the reforms to the Ottoman government that had recently taken place, the product of the Young Turks rebellion in 1908, and Bell sought to record their reactions.[86] But her excitement was also kindled by the city's long history, traces of which could be found at every turn. Ross Burns has said that in Aleppo exists 'a sort of time continuum, in which flashes of the past, rather than dissipating with time, accumulate in the present'.[87] Aleppo is believed to be one of the world's oldest continuously inhabited cities, and Bell, as a consummate traveller and history enthusiast, set out to learn as much as she could of its eventful past.

Back in 1909, Aleppo still possessed most of its pre-modern character and charm, and Bell was excited to visit and photograph its many old mosques and khans as well as the great Citadel in its midst. She appears to have been particularly interested in finding traces of Aleppo's earliest history. This included, for example, her report – at the small, sixteenth-century Mamluk mosque of Qaiqan, near the Antioch Gate – of a thirteenth-century BCE block, inscribed in Hittite hieroglyphics, which had been set upside down into the mosque's walls.[88] She spotted more Hittite sculptures in the fortifications of the Aleppo Citadel itself and purchased some Hittite and Assyrian cylinder seals from an antiquities dealer.[89] With respect to later antiquity, Bell visited the twelfth-century Madrasa Halawiye, which incorporated some of the column-capitals of a sixth-century Byzantine cathedral into its domed prayer hall.[90] In her visit to the Al-Shuaibiyah mosque, Bell was particularly taken with its twelfth-century Kufic inscription and carved decoration of interlacing foliage, deeming it one of the 'loveliest monuments of the art of Islam in the whole town of Aleppo'.[91]

Bell was not breaking any new ground with her observations of these antique remains in Aleppo. Most of these sites and monuments were already well known and studied. What is valuable, however, are her photographs, which capture key architectural features of the city, some of which no longer exist or have experienced profound changes over the past 100 years. One may note, for example, that the minaret of the charming fourteenth-century al-Tawashi mosque is no longer standing, although the beautifully carved collonettes on its outer façade (Fig. 2.4) and *muqarnas* decoration in the main entrance, which she nicely captured in photos, were still intact in 2009 when the present author visited the mosque.[92] Sadly, the tall, square-stone, eleventh-century Seljuk minaret of the Great Mosque in Aleppo, proudly rising above the mosque and photographed by Bell (Fig. 2.5),[93] was brought down in 2013 amid an exchange of heavy-weapons fire in the Syrian civil war.

Bell also photographed the beautiful Khan al-Wazir. This seventeenth-century caravanserai was laid out in the typical format, with an open courtyard on the ground floor, surrounded by a two-storey elevation. The rooms on the ground floor served as a storage place for merchants' goods, while its upper storey served as sleeping quarters for guests and the resident merchants, with balconies overlooking the courtyard below.[94] Particularly notable is the khan's monumental doorway, its interior face characterized by two inset windows surrounded by delicately carved ornamentation and two-tone stone masonry (Fig. 2.6).[95] By the time Bell visited the Khan al-Wazir in 1909, it had been transformed into a factory for dyed cloth, although its essential plan was intact.[96] Its elaborate exterior façade, which also features delicate carved decorations around the windows, was obstructed in large part by the narrow streets and the closely built structures surrounding it.[97] Since the 1950s, however, this exterior arrangement has been completely transformed by the construction of a modern road and parking lot, providing an unhindered view of the khan.[98] The khan interior was turned into shops featuring antiquities, carpets and local artisans' work. At the time of writing, it was known that parts of this structure had been reduced to rubble in 2012 in the Syrian civil war, but the full extent of the damage to this exquisite example of Old Aleppo's once-vibrant commercial life remained undetermined.

For Bell, Aleppo was a stimulating and fortuitous beginning to her long journey. With her servant Fattuh's help, her preparations had all gone well, and now with her 12 horses, a donkey, and seven men, she set out from Aleppo through the rolling, open country to the Euphrates River.[99] Already she could see that the landscape was dotted with tells, the grassy mounds that marked the place of ancient settlements.[100] As she set out on her eastward path, she recalled the great historical figures who had ventured this way before her:

> With Xenophon, with Julian, with all the armies captained by a dream of empire that dashed and broke against the Ancient East, the thoughts go marching down to the river which was the most famous of all frontier lines.[101]

First Destination on the Euphrates – Tell Ahmar

Bell and her entourage arrived on the Euphrates River after passing through the town of Membij on 17 February 1909. Thrilled to be seeing this 'noble stream' for the first time, flowing between white cliffs, she observed that its rolling water was 'charged with the history of the ancient world'.[102] Finding the ferryboat by the river's edge, Bell wasted no time transporting herself and her baggage animals to the other side, arriving at the village of Tell Ahmar, situated at the foot of the high-mounded ancient site from which the village got its name.[103] This was the start of Bell's journey down the eastern bank of the Euphrates River, and her archaeological reporting became more detailed; Bell was aware that few who had travelled down this side of the river had made any systematic attempt to record its ancient remains.[104]

Tell Ahmar was an important archaeological stop for Bell. Her friend David Hogarth had been here only the year before, and while inspecting the site, he had come across several carved stone fragments, some covered with as-yet undeciphered Hittite hieroglyphic inscriptions. Anxious to copy these inscriptions, Hogarth had made paper squeezes of the stones, but owing to the humidity of the season, these had not turned out well, and many were illegible.[105] Hogarth had therefore asked Bell to retake the squeezes.[106]

While walking over the site, Bell spotted the carved and inscribed stones in question in a little depression beyond the ancient north-western gate into the city, these all belonging to a single stele originally set up at that locale in antiquity.[107] On one side, the stele had the carved image of a bull and at least one person. With the assistance of the local villagers, Bell dug the engraved stones out of the ground, then took a squeeze of each (Fig. 2.7).[108] This entailed pressing wet, mouldable paper into the inscribed surface of the stone and hammering the back of the paper with a bristled squeeze brush. Once the paper was dry, it was removed from the face of the stone. It now had on it a mirror image of the inscription in raised relief. These squeezes were later taken back to England to Hogarth,[109] who was able to piece together the entire inscription and publish it in an English archaeological journal, along with other findings from Tell Ahmar, Carchemish and neighbouring sites.[110] The article appropriately acknowledged Bell's contribution to this inscription.[111] Significantly, the report also used some of Bell's photographs of other Tell Ahmar carved reliefs (Fig. 2.8), not to mention photographs she had taken of stone reliefs from the site of Arslan Tepe, near Malatya, later in 1909,[112] which provided good *comparanda* to the sculptures of Ahmar and Carchemish.[113] Altogether, Hogarth's published report owed much to Bell, not only for her efforts at copying inscriptions, but also for her photographs, which provided important documentation of the art of the still-elusive Neo-Hittite–Aramaean kingdoms of Northern Mesopotamia.

Later excavations and research at the site of Tell Ahmar, some continuing up to the present day, have generated considerable information about the site, allowing the material investigated by Bell to be put into its proper historical context. French excavations under the direction of the scholar F. Thureau-Dangin in 1929–31, and the more recent work of Australian and Belgian missions under the direction of Guy Bunnens from 1988 onwards, have revealed that this site had been the place of ancient Til-Barsib, part of the Aramaean tribal kingdom of Bit Adini, established sometime in the early first millennium BCE.[114] The Aramaean rulers of this settlement, which was also known by its Hittite name Masuwari, expanded and strengthened the city, and it enjoyed considerable prosperity until being conquered by the Neo-Assyrian king Shalmaneser III in 856 BCE.[115] The site was renamed Kar-Shalmaneser and was transformed into an imperial control centre, complete with a lavish Assyrian palace on its fortified summit. Other Neo-Assyrian period remains have also been found in the lower town, namely the large houses of wealthy elites, some of these featuring elaborate black-and-white pebble mosaic courtyard floors.[116] In addition to the Iron Age remains, excavations have also brought to light materials from a much earlier habitation of Tell Ahmar. Some of this dates back to the mid-third millennium BCE and consists of a richly furnished, monumental, stone-chambered, elite tomb, dubbed the 'Hypogeum', and a temple.[117]

The stone stele fragments that Bell had copied for Hogarth were again seen at the site in 1928 by F. Thureau-Dangin, then transported and reassembled back in the museum in Aleppo (now the Aleppo National Museum).[118] They depict a Hittite storm-god wearing a horned helmet, standing on the back of a bull and

Fig. 2.4 Bell's photo of an intricately carved engaged collonnette and capital on the façade of the fourteenth-century al-Tawashi mosque, Aleppo.

brandishing an axe in one hand and a trident in the other. The Hittite hieroglyphic inscription that Bell so faithfully copied was eventually studied and translated, and we know now that it was written to celebrate the restoration of the throne of Masuwari to the son of the king Ariyahinas after a short period of

Fig. 2.5 Bell's photo of the Great Mosque in Aleppo. Originally built during the Umayyad period in the early eighth century, it was subsequently repaired and refurbished many times, including during the Seljuk period in the eleventh century, when the exquisitely adorned stone minaret was added. Sadly, the minaret was brought down amid an exchange of heavy weapons fire in 2013.

inter-dynastic struggles.[119] Although it provides a chronicle of the city's Aramaean rulers, the stele's inscription was written in Luwian, the language of the Hittites, and its carved motif of the storm-god belongs to the so-called Neo-Hittite tradition of sculpture that was employed at places like the neighbouring city of Carchemish.[120] The explanation is that since Aramaeans at this time had no tradition of their own in terms of monumental art and architecture, the rulers of Til-Barsib chose to adopt the effective medium of propaganda of their powerful neighbour, Carchemish, as a means of underlining their authority.[121]

In 1999, a similar stele was spotted near the village of Qubbeh, just a short distance downstream from Tell Ahmar.[122] Fortunately, the stone, which was found in two pieces, was recovered just before the completion of the Tishreen Dam on the Euphrates and the ensuing rise of the waters, which completely submerged

Fig. 2.6 Bell's photo of the inner façade of the doorway of the Khan al-Wazir, a seventeenth-century caravanserai in Aleppo. The two-tone stone masonry and delicately carved decorations around the upper windows above the entrance greatly enriched the appearance of the inner courtyard.

the area upon which the stele was found.[123] Today, this stele stands alongside the Hogarth–Bell stele in the Aleppo National Museum. With a similar image of the storm-god standing on the back of a bull, its accompanying inscription celebrates the military victories of Hamiyatas, the son of the usurping king of Masuwari, and is slightly earlier than the stele from Ahmar itself that Bell copied.[124] But its composition, style of iconography and use of the Luwian language is very similar to that of the Hogarth–Bell stele as well as others found at Ahmar, and it demonstrates the popularity of the Neo-Hittite commemorative style in the Ahmar region during this period.[125]

Bell did not see this particular stele in 1909, but she did pass through Qubbeh and made observations of other ancient remains, including two other carved stone fragments, one inscribed with Hittite hieroglyphics (Fig. 2.9) and the other with a relief. Further along, she found the head and legs of a basalt lion.[126] T.E. Lawrence

Fig. 2.7   One of the stone fragments of a large stele from Tell Ahmar, from which Bell obtained a squeeze impression of its Hittite hieroglyphic inscription. Also adorned with the relief image of the Neo-Hittite storm god, the stele celebrates the restoration of the throne of Masuwari (ancient Tell Ahmar) to the son of a local Aramaean king in the early part of the first millennium BCE.

also spotted a relief carving in the village of Qubbeh, possibly the same one seen by Bell.[127] Recently, yet another relief fragment was found near the village. Given this amassed evidence, it seems likely that Qubbeh was the place of an ancient settlement contemporary to Tell Ahmar.[128]

Carchemish

While still camped at Tell Ahmar and before embarking on her journey down the Euphrates, Bell resolved to make the short trip up to the site of Carchemish, fully aware of its importance as a 'great capital'.[129] Her visit required a ferry ride back across the swiftly flowing Euphrates to its western bank and then northward overland on horseback.[130] Approaching the massive, mounded site, its north-eastern citadel rising upon the 'majestic sweep of the river', Bell declared no

Fig. 2.8 A carved stone orthostat with the image of a winged, eagle-headed genius, from the village at Tell Ahmar, dated to the early first millennium BCE, located and photographed by Bell.

other site on the Euphrates to be as imposing as Carchemish, except for Babylon itself.[131]

Carchemish had a rich and long history. Occupied from the fourth to the first millennia BCE, it had attained considerable importance during the Hittite empire period, especially around 1352 BCE, when the king Suppiluliuma I captured the city and installed his son to act as Hittite viceroy of Syria.[132] This royal dynasty lasted for several generations, maintaining the site's commercial and political importance within this region of northern Syria and surviving even after the end of the Hittite empire, around 1200 BCE.[133] Carchemish regained some of its prominence during the so-called Neo-Hittite period, beginning in the tenth century BCE and continuing until around 717 BCE, when the city was ruled over by two successive dynasties belonging to the houses of Suhi and Astiruwa.[134] This period was punctuated, however, by Assyrian conquest and imperial expansion, and during this time the Carchemish kings often opposed or had to pay tribute to Neo-Assyrian kings.[135] The last Neo-Hittite king of Carchemish was deposed during the reign of the Neo-Assyrian king Sargon II in 717 BCE, and thereafter the city and its territory were directly administered by an Assyrian governor. The site was ultimately abandoned shortly after 605 BCE, the year in which the Babylonian crown prince Nebuchadnezzar inflicted a crushing defeat on Assyria's Egyptian allies, led by the pharaoh Necho II.[136] Carchemish was partly reoccupied much later, during the Hellenistic period, under the name Europos.[137]

By the time Bell visited Carchemish in 1909, the site had been explored and excavated by Europeans, including Patrick Henderson, who between 1878 and 1881 had exposed a large stairway bordered with carved stone reliefs on the south-western side of the citadel mound. Six of these carved stones had been sent back to London, but the rest of the reliefs remained in situ and partially exposed to the elements; Bell spotted and photographed these as she walked over the site.[138] In the spring of 1908, David Hogarth had visited Carchemish along with several other sites of archaeological interest in the region, including Tell Ahmar. Only shortly after Bell's visit, Hogarth, sufficiently impressed with the potential of Carchemish to yield further significant remains, including the highly desired Hittite hieroglyphic inscriptions, applied and received permission to excavate the site on behalf of the British Museum.[139] This work commenced in early 1911 under Hogarth's direction. Subsequent seasons of excavation, led by Leonard Woolley, were carried out during 1912–14, as well as in 1920.[140] The British Museum excavations were reported in three lavish archaeological publications, most of the key findings dating back to the Neo-Hittite period, particularly from the ninth and eighth centuries BCE, when the city was greatly built up and embellished with a palatial *bit-hilani*, a temple, gates providing access to the inner town and citadel, and façades adorned with richly carved stone orthostats.[141]

The modern political border between Turkey and Syria, established in 1920, runs straight across Carchemish's outer town. The citadel mound and inner town, both of which are on the Turkish side of the border, have since 2011 seen renewed excavations by a Turkish–Italian archaeological team that continues to uncover and comprehend Carchemish's long settlement history.[142]

For many today, the significance of Carchemish lies not necessarily in its ancient remains but in its special connection to one of the most notable figures of the early twentieth century, T.E. Lawrence – 'Lawrence of Arabia'. This remarkable person, who would play a key role in the Arab Revolt against the Turks during World War I, participated in the archaeological excavations of Carchemish during the 1911–14 seasons. Working as a young archaeological protégé, first under the direction of Hogarth and his second-in-command, Campbell Thompson (1911), and subsequently under Leonard Woolley (1912–14) (Fig. 2.10), Lawrence assisted with the day-to-day operations of the project's excavations. His various tasks included copying ancient inscriptions, drawing sculpture fragments, measuring and cataloguing other artefacts and occasionally

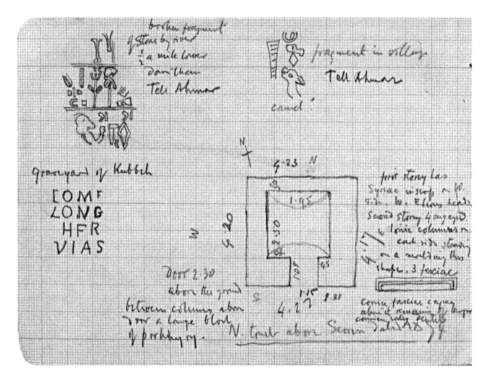

Fig. 2.9   A page from Bell's field notebook, showing her hand copies of two Neo-Hittite hieroglyphic inscriptions from the sites of Tell Ahmar (top right) and Qubbeh (top left, for which no further studies have yet been undertaken), a Latin inscription from a stone in the Qubbeh graveyard (lower left), and a sketch plan and notes of the north tower tomb at Serrin (lower right).

purchasing antiquities from locals in the neighbouring vicinities, where other ancient settlements and cemeteries were known to exist.[143] With his particular interest in ceramics, Lawrence was given specific charge over the pottery finds, producing drawings, photographs and written descriptions of the ancient vessels and their provenance.[144] Finally, he assisted with supervising the local labour force of diggers, the majority of whom were peasant-farmers from the nearby Arab village of Jerablus. Often comprising 100–250 men, unskilled and unfamiliar with the methods required to dig an ancient site, this workforce could sometimes be daunting to direct.[145] Nevertheless, Lawrence wholly enjoyed the task, entering into an amicable relationship with his workers, visiting them in off-hours in their homes, meeting their families and learning about their personal lives.[146]

Despite Lawrence's continuing engagement with the inhabitants of Jerablus, he did not make light of or forego his archaeological responsibilities.[147] On the contrary, he appears, on the whole, as a committed and conscientious contributor to the success of the Carchemish project. Recent assessments of Lawrence's field notebooks, sketches and other written reports have shown that he was a perceptive excavator who maintained detailed and accurate records of the archaeological finds, particularly the pottery.[148]

Carchemish was a critical training ground for Lawrence's own understanding of the Near East, not only its tumultuous past but its present, which was on the cusp of seismic socio-political change. He developed and perfected his skills in Arabic there, and through his close relationships with his workers and their families, he formed an appreciation for their values, traditions and beliefs, and sympathy for their poverty under a corrupt Turkish administrative system and a medieval-like feudal system dominated by tribal sheikhs.[149] Lawrence saw in these people – and especially in Dahoum, a Jerablus village boy with whom he developed a particularly close friendship – the qualities of an ideal Arab. With their relative isolation in a rural area of inland Syria, the people of Jerablus, in Lawrence's eyes, had not yet been tainted by the corrupting forces of European modernization that were overtaking the cities of the Near East. Lawrence admired their simple nature, humour and generosity.[150] It is said that Lawrence's affection for these people provided some of the stimulus for his active role in the Arab Revolt against Turkey in the war years that followed, this further culminating in his efforts to secure Arab self-determination in the aftermath of the fallen Ottoman Empire.[151]

It is remarkable that Gertrude Bell and T.E. Lawrence, two of England's most significant players in the theatre of Middle Eastern politics in the early twentieth century, both had an archaeological past, and that they would actually first meet in an archaeological setting, at Carchemish. Upon her return through eastern Anatolia from her second Mesopotamian journey in spring 1911, Bell decided to visit the site in the hopes of finding Hogarth there.[152] He had already left, so instead, Bell received a tour of the excavation work at the site from the two other expedition members, R. Campbell Thompson and T.E. Lawrence.[153] Lawrence's letter home provides an amusing account of the lively exchange that followed among the three. Comparing Carchemish to the impressive German diggings at Qal'at Sherqat (Assur), which she had visited earlier in April, Bell called the British operations 'prehistoric', whereupon Lawrence and Campbell Thompson felt obliged to temper her criticism with a 'display of erudition':

She was taken (in 5 minutes) over Byzantine, Crusader, Roman, Hittite & French architecture (my part) and over Greek folk-lore, Assyrian architecture & Mesopotamian ethnology (by Thompson); Prehistoric pottery & telephoto [sic] lenses, Bronze Age metal technique, Meredith, Anatole France and the Octobrists (by me): the Young Turk movement, the construct state in Arabic, the price of riding camels, Assyrian burial-customs, and German methods of excavation with the Baghdad railway (by

Thompson). This was a kind of hors d'oeuvre: and when it was over (she was getting more respectful) we settled down each to seven or eight subjects & questioned her upon them. She was quite glad to have tea after an hour and a half, & on going told Thompson that he had done wonders in his digging in the time, and that she thought *we* had got everything out of the place that could possibly have been got: she particularly admired the completeness of our note-books.[154]

To be sure, the standards of archaeological recovery undertaken by the British archaeological team at Carchemish fell below those of other archaeological projects working in other parts of the Near East by this time.[155] Bell, having visited the German projects at Babylon and Assur in both 1909 and 1911, had actually seen some of the finest excavation work of the early twentieth century, renowned for the thoroughness with which the archaeologists articulated and planned architectural structures and discerned the chronological position of the buildings through time (see Chapter 4). She was reasonably justified in her criticism of the diggings at Carchemish, whose primary goal appears to have been the collection of inscribed material and sculptured stones at the expense of stratigraphy and context,[156] although it was rather discourteous of her to say so to the site's own excavators. In any event, we know that Bell did not harshly condemn Thompson's or Lawrence's excavation efforts in her diaries, letters or elsewhere in writing, merely commenting on what they had found and that she had spent a pleasant day with them, and remarking that Lawrence was 'an interesting boy, he is going to make a traveler'.[157] Lawrence, in his letter to his mother, described Bell as 'pleasant: about 36 [Bell was actually 42 years old at the time], not beautiful, (except with a veil on, perhaps)'.[158] Such was the nature of this first, somewhat inconsequential meeting between Lawrence and Bell. Over the course of their eventful lives, they would cross paths many more times, not in the arena of archaeology but in the theatre of Middle Eastern war and politics, and it is to these two that we may attribute some of the most critical – and, in retrospect, controversial – political decisions about the Middle East, the repercussions of which are still being felt over a century later.

Serrin Tower Tombs

Archaeology continued to be Bell's principal focus as she travelled down the eastern bank of the Euphrates River, and she was intent upon visiting and recording the remains of all periods. Given her familiarity with Classical remains, from her earlier archaeological work at Binbirkilise in Anatolia, however, Greco-Roman artefacts and architecture continued to hold some fascination. Thus, she was quite excited to visit and record the remains of two Roman-period tower tombs about four hours down the river from Tell Ahmar, in the rolling hills behind

Fig. 2.10 T.E. Lawrence (left) and Leonard Woolley (right) in 1913, standing next to one of the carved stone orthostats from the Long Wall of Sculpture, at Carchemish.

the village of Serrin.[159] Bell already knew of the tombs' existence; Max von Oppenheim had visited them back in 1898 and had mentioned them in print.[160] Nevertheless, as Bell reported, his focus on one of the tombs' inscriptions meant that further observations of the buildings' architecture and other special features merited additional investigations and photographs.[161] Bell's resulting report on Serrin's tower tombs, which was included in *Amurath to Amurath* (pp. 36–8), was the most detailed architectural description of these monuments until a fresh study by R. Gogräfe appeared in 1995.[162]

The most valuable aspect of Bell's report is that when she visited the tower tombs in 1909, both were preserved to a significantly higher level than in 1992, when Gogräfe visited the site. Of the north tomb, the entire upper part of the second storey had fallen by his time (Fig. 2.11),[163] while in the case of the south tomb, nothing remained but a pile of fallen stone blocks.[164] Because of this, in his report Gogräfe relied heavily on Bell's photographs for the reconstruction of the northern tomb (along with the images made by Oppenheim and Pognon). He had to depend exclusively on Bell's photographs of the southern tomb, since they constituted the only record of that edifice.

Although Bell was writing almost a century earlier, her description of the tower tombs' features essentially resembles Gogräfe's. Of the two tombs on the ridge behind Serrin, the more northerly one was better preserved, consisting of a square tower of cut stone blocks, divided into two storeys. The top of the first storey was defined by a slightly projecting cornice, under which, on the east and west sides, were a pair of animal protomes.[165] On the west side was also a Syriac inscription, dated to 73 CE, which reported that the tomb was built by Ma'nu and was intended for him and his sons; this inscription survives.[166]

The entrance to the grave chamber, on the ground floor, was located on the eastern side through a small opening to the north side of the central axis.[167] The body or bodies of the deceased would have been accommodated in this chamber, as well as the one above it. The lower chamber would formerly have been blocked by a sliding rectangular basalt stone, which by the time of this author's visit in 2009 was lying on the ground in front of the entrance. The interior was simply defined by a barrel-vaulted chamber with benches on all four sides and a small slit of light piercing the back wall. The second storey also had a chamber, entered on the east side like below. In this case, its basalt blocking stone was still in place.[168]

Each side of the second storey of the tower tomb was decorated with fluted engaged columns, one in each of the corners. The tops of the columns featured Ionic capitals carrying an entablature comprising a three-fasciae architrave, dentils and a projecting cornice above.[169] The roof no longer existed in Bell's time, although she conjectured that it originally had been pyramidal.[170] Significantly, Gogräfe spotted a fallen stone block nearby that had a sloped side with a boss, and he concluded that it was one of the blocks of a pyramid-shaped roof.[171]

The second tower tomb behind Serrin, about 2 km south of the first one, was less well preserved. Only the south wall remained in Bell's time, and of this she noted that the lower storey was decorated with a shallow engaged pier in each corner and had an entrance opening. The upper storey was characterized by engaged columns, but they were not fluted. In place of a chamber opening was an arched niche, possibly for a statue.[172]

While she walked on the hillside near the north tower tomb, Bell noticed several rock-cut tombs, now filled with stones and earth, and conjectured that the hill had been the cemetery of the ancient settlement that had existed near the riverside below.[173] Gogräfe observed in 1992 numerous graves dug into the rock in the vicinity of the southern tower tomb.[174] This writer noted in 2009 the presence of what looked to be the top of a vertical *dromos* of a rock-cut tomb immediately to the south of the north tower tomb, as well as others nearby that had been recently robbed. Finally, it is interesting that in Bell's photographs of the north tower tomb, one can clearly see a mound of cut stone blocks to the south-west.[175] This could well be the remains of yet another tower tomb, a conjecture given further credence by Gogräfe's observations of what appeared to be the foundation stones of such a structure in that area.[176] In 2009, the bare remains of those foundations were also noted by this writer, while virtually all of the remaining stones of that structure had completely vanished. In summary, there was almost certainly a necropolis on the hill upon which the tower tombs were built, as Bell suspected, but sadly much of this ancient cemetery has been disturbed, particularly over the past 100 years.

Recent research on Near Eastern tower tombs shows that the Serrin tower tombs belong to a different category than the more simply adorned funerary towers popularly and abundantly used at Palmyra in central Syria, and which spread across the desert to Halebiye, Dura Europos and Baghouz further down the Euphrates (Bell visited the latter in February 1909).[177] Rather, the Serrin tower tombs seem to be more akin to tombs known to the north and north-east, many of which belonged to the kingdom of Edessa and incorporated stronger Greco-Roman elements than those from Palmyra.[178] The territory of Serrin itself may have been part of that Edessan kingdom.[179] While Bell did not have available to her the mass of evidence we do today, she appears to have been on the right track when she noted a distinction between the tower tombs at Serrin and those at Palmyra: the 'well-known tower tombs of Palmyra and the Hauran are not capped by a pyramid, nor is the face of their walls broken at any point by engaged columns' (like the tower tombs at Serrin).[180]

Euphrates Sites

Bell's writings convey the exhilaration she felt as she travelled below Tell Ahmar and then Serrin, working her way down along the course of the Euphrates and entering into the sparsely inhabited lands of inner Syria. Part of her excitement was due to the fact that she was now entering a region very infrequently travelled by Europeans. Neither Hogarth nor Oppenheim had ventured this far to the south, and other earlier travellers, like Colonel Chesney and his companion Ainsworth (1835), had merely seen the eastern bank from a boat on the river. Only further downstream, at Raqqa, would Bell's route pick up where others, such as Eduard Sachau, Friedrich Sarre and Ernst Herzfeld, had ventured before her.

Bell was also captivated by the landscape. The open, rolling hills stretching away from the river banks were empty save for the occasional tents of a group of pastoral nomads. The landscape conveyed a sense of unencumbered freedom and simplicity, of which she wrote:

> The thin blue smoke of the morning camp fires rose out of the hollows and my heart rose with it, for here was the life of the desert, in open spaces under the open sky, and when once you have known it, the eternal savage in your breast rejoices at the return to it.[181]

With only one village reported between Mas'udiyeh and Raqqa on the east bank of the Euphrates, Bell observed that the land was largely devoid of sedentary occupation and farming activities. Rather, it was the home of tribes of the Beni-Said, the 'Anazeh and the Weldeh, pastoral nomadic groups who moved with their flocks according to the availability of grazing lands and water sources during the different seasons.[182] Nevertheless, observing its potential for productivity and the abundance of ruined tell sites near the river, she guessed that this region had not always been lightly populated:

> The majestic presence of the river in the midst of uncultivated lands, which, with the help of its waters, would need so little labour to make them productive, takes a singular hold on the imagination. I do not believe that the east bank has always been so thinly peopled, and though the present condition may date from very early times, it is probable that there was once a continuous belt of villages by the stream, their sites being still marked by mounds.[183]

As Bell conjectured, this zone of inner Syria through which she was travelling had experienced considerable fluctuations in human settlement throughout its long history. During some periods, the eastern bank of the Euphrates had been thickly settled with sedentary farming villages and towns, while at other times, including the early twentieth century when she passed through, the region had been given over to the grazing lands of only a few scattered pastoral nomadic groups. Recent landscape studies have carefully tracked these settlement oscillations, taking into consideration historical reports as well as observations by Bell and other early travellers about local conditions, and accounting for changes brought about by socio-economic circumstances.[184] Between the seventeenth and early twentieth centuries CE, the sparse inhabitation of the Middle Euphrates can largely be explained by the Ottoman government's absence of security and administrative control in this region.[185] The marginal character of the region, induced by a suboptimal climate, has also been frequently summoned to explain fluctuations in subsistence strategies. Much of this Middle Euphrates region, particularly that part covered today by Lake Assad of the Tabqa Dam, is located in the so-called 'zone of uncertainty' of the Near East, where rainfall isohyets of between 200 and 300 mm per annum indicate a high risk of crop failure, and agricultural pursuits are not always successful.[186] Under particularly harsh climatic conditions, the local populations may adopt a pastoral nomadic form of economy with dependence upon sheep and goat husbandry instead of crop production. In all, the Middle Euphrates valley has had a varied history of growth and decline, and of prosperity and poverty, and Bell was among the first to note these striking contrasts through time.

Fig. 2.11a + b Bell's photo of the north tower tomb at Serrin (top), and the author's photograph of the same tower tomb in 2009 (bottom). The upper part of the second storey of the tomb, adorned with capitals carrying an entablature of archivolt and cornice, has completely disappeared over the past century, as has the stone masonry of a second tower tomb, seen in Bell's photograph on the left. A robber's trench into a possible third tomb is visible directly in front of the tower tomb.

Besides containing observations of the modern tribal groups she encountered, Bell's documentation of ancient sites and scattered artefacts becomes particularly detailed at this point in her written reports. She frequently recorded the names of mounded sites, traces of ancient remains spotted on them and their distance from one another. Through these reports, it is often possible to track her precise passage over long stretches down the river, and to compare what she observed with what is currently known about these places.

A great deal of our current knowledge about this Euphrates region's ancient past has been facilitated by the fairly intense archaeological survey and excavation work that has taken place here, especially since the late 1960s. Much of this work was conducted in anticipation of the construction of hydroelectric dams along the Euphrates River, and the fact that the lakes created behind these dams would fill large parts of the valley and permanently submerge the ancient settlements. The first dam, built at the site of Tabqa, 40 km above the town of Raqqa, was completed in 1975 and created a 35 km-long lake directly above the dam. A second dam, constructed at Tishreen to the north, was completed in 1999 and filled another large section of the river valley up as far as the site of Tell Ahmar, its acropolis mound being all that remains above water of this once extensively occupied site. The surveys and archaeological excavations of the river valley preserve a vital record of this ancient landscape, many of the ancient settlements now being located under scores of metres of water. Gertrude Bell's photographic panoramas of various stretches of the river valley in this region from over a century ago also provide valuable glimpses of what is now a completely transformed or vanished ancient landscape.

Some of the ancient sites that Bell passed by, such as Dja'de el Mughara (her 'Ja'deh')[187] and Mureybet (her 'Murraibet'),[188] were places of prehistoric occupation.[189] Mureybet's Neolithic remains, dated between 10,000 and 8700 BCE, reveal traces of round or oval semi-subterranean huts where the inhabitants lived for extended periods. People at both sites were experimenting with cultivating food plants and keeping flocks of sheep and goats, making them among the earliest farming communities in the world.[190]

Still other ancient sites – namely, the mound of Sheikh Hassan, which Bell passed just below Munbaqa, and the high promontory of Jebel Aruda, on the other side of the river (her 'Sheikh 'Arûd') – have yielded occupation evidence from as early as 3600 BCE.[191] Judging by their architecture, pottery and administrative objects (numerical tablets and cylinder seals), their populations consisted of colonists from southern Mesopotamia who were living in Syria, possibly to conduct trade along the Euphrates River.[192]

Of particular interest are sites reported by Bell that we now know marked places of occupation in the Early Bronze Age of the third millennium BCE. These include Qara Quzaq (her 'Ḳara Kazâk'), Tell el Banât, Shems ed-Dîn,[193] Tell eẓ Ẓâher,[194] Jerniyeh[195] and Halawa (her 'Ḥaliâweh').[196] Archaeological investigations of these sites and the territories around them have revealed a thickly inhabited riverine region consisting of farming villages and towns, and pasturelands extending out into the steppe lands beyond. Some of these settlements possessed urban-like features such as carefully planned and well-constructed city walls, bastions and fortified gates, spacious houses, large temple complexes and funerary monuments.[197] Evidence for long-distance exchanges – often found in the site's cemeteries and taking the form of copper and bronze weapons, fine imported pots, and jewellery made of gold, silver and semi-precious stones – also testifies to the prosperous, cosmopolitan character of the Euphrates River Valley during this period in antiquity.[198]

Of all the sites in the region, Bell seems to have been most drawn to Munbayah, with its grand size and the impressive ruins she noted on its surface. Bell considered Munbayah, along with the ruins at Jerniyeh, to be the two 'most interesting sites' she had seen between Tell Ahmar and Qal'at Jabbar, and she reports having been tempted to 'clear away the earth and see what lies beneath'.[199] Her interest in Munbayah is also attested by the numerous photographs she took of the site and the plan of its ruins she drew up in her field notebook.[200] She conjectured that the grassy ridges and lines of stones she had followed were the remnants of the settlement's city walls, while the spaces in between were the city gates, one of which she aptly named the 'water gate', given its location facing high above the Euphrates (Fig. 2.12).[201]

More than a century later, we are exceptionally knowledgeable about the site of Munbayah – today commonly referred to as Munbaqa – on account of the extensive excavations carried out there by a German archaeological team between 1969 and 1994.[202] Although Munbaqa was occupied as early as the third millennium BCE and has a Roman-Byzantine cemetery on its summit, its main period of habitation was during the Late Bronze Age of the second half of the second millennium BCE. During this period, the site, whose ancient name was Ekalte, was a thriving settlement of about 15 hectares, with extensive contacts all over the Near East. It housed several monumental temples, craft production facilities and neighbourhoods of large, well-appointed domestic houses.[203] The walls Bell endeavoured to plan proved to be those of the Late Bronze Age city, comprising the walls that enclosed the *Aussenstadt* (outer city), *Innenstadt* (inner city) and *Kuppe* (the top of the tell).[204] Bell correctly identified the places of the north and south gates leading into the *Innenstadt*. Although she believed she had identified the 'water gate' as the space between two high stone walls, in reality what she saw were the walls of two of the site's monumental temples *in antis* (Steinbau 1 and Steinbau 2), these positioned on the highest points of the *Kuppe*, overlooking the river below.[205] Altogether, investigations have confirmed the impressive nature of Munbaqa's settlement in antiquity, rightly justifying Bell's desire to 'clear away the earth' and 'see what lies beneath'.[206]

Qal'at Jabbar

Described in a letter to her mother as the 'most splendid castle of all Arab time', Qal'at Jabbar was one of the more spectacular Islamic period sites that Bell encountered as she moved down the east bank of the river valley. It stood over the river, guarding an important trade corridor up and down the Euphrates as well as a river crossing on a route that provided a vital link between Aleppo to the west and Mosul to the east.[207] As one approached from afar, its defences, towers and prominent central minaret could be seen rising up on high ground above the valley, as Bell's photographs testify (Fig. 2.13). Today, it is no less impressive, although the surrounding landscape has been completely transformed. The waters of the Tabqa Dam's artificial Lake Assad now surround it to its base, the castle standing as an island amid the blue, with only a narrow causeway linking it to the shore.[208]

Although established as early as the seventh century, Qal'at Jabbar reached its greatest importance as a formidable river fortress between the eleventh and fourteenth centuries, when it was controlled by a succession of Seljuks, Zengids, Ayyubids and Mamluks. It also experienced a brief Frankish occupation in the early twelfth century, when the crusaders of the principality of Edessa (modern-day Urfa) captured it. Under Nur al-Din (1146–74), the castle experienced significant rebuilding, and much of what is seen today, including its impregnable fortifications and interior minaret and mosque, are attributed to this ruler. The Mamluks ordered some restoration work at Qal'at Jabbar in the fourteenth century after the castle's devastation by the Mongols in the previous century, but it never regained its former glory or importance and seems to have been abandoned only shortly after.[209]

Bell actually knew little about Qal'at Jabbar when she visited in 1909; her diary notes and letters provide the briefest descriptions, and to be sure, few earlier European travellers or scholars had visited the castle or written about it to any extent. By the time of writing *Amurath to Amurath*, however, she was able to provide a short historical outline based on information she had derived from medieval historian-geographers such as Abu'l Fida, Yaqut and Benjamin of Tudela.[210] Her photographs of Qal'at Jabbar capture architectural details no longer preserved. Her long-distance views of the castle standing high above the river valley, now replaced by Lake Assad, are noteworthy. Also worthwhile is her photograph of the brick wall of a large, vaulted building located immediately above the fortified entrance gate at the south-west. The stepped diamond brick-pattern decoration on the exterior wall, known as *hazarbaf*, is particularly striking (Fig. 2.14).[211] By the latter part of the twentieth century, part of this wall had suffered a collapse such that today it is just over half the width that Bell saw a century earlier. Her photograph of the square-based cylindrical minaret next to the mosque in the centre of the castle, which can be ascribed to the reign of Nur al-Din (1170 CE) on the basis of its *nakshi* inscription near the top, captures its original state before it underwent restoration at the time of the French Mandate, its eroded brick construction now replaced by modern baked bricks and concrete.[212]

Hiraqla

More important Islamic-period sites were to follow shortly after Qal'at Jabbar on Bell's journey. A day-and-a-half's ride further down the river (50 km) took her to the enigmatic ruin of Hiraqla (her 'Haraglah'), which she described as a rectangular fortress surrounded by a ditch and circular enclosure and was distinguished by four corner towers and brick vaults that required centring for their construction.[213] Bell did not believe that Hiraqla could be Islamic in date, and on that topic she agreed with other scholars, particularly Sachau, who saw it as a Roman military camp or fort.[214] Investigations undertaken by Sarre and Herzfeld after their own trip down the Euphrates in 1907, however, proposed an alternative dating, during the Abbasid period, setting its construction solidly in the Islamic period of the early ninth century CE.[215] As Sarre and Herzfeld were able to ascertain from Arab historians' accounts, Hiraqla had in fact been built by the caliph Harun al-Rashid and represents the remains of an unfinished monument to a military triumph against the Byzantines at Herakleon, in Anatolia.[216] Although Bell's suspected date for the monument proved to be incorrect, architecturally she did properly recognize that the brick vaults of the structure had supported a platform above, upon which had stood an upper storey, an observation that Herzfeld himself would also make and with which all scholars concur.[217]

Raqqa

Bell reached Raqqa, near the confluence of the Euphrates and Balikh Rivers, another 8 km beyond Hiraqla, finding here a wealth of Islamic period ruins. As with Qal'at Jabbar, judging by her diary entries and letters from the time of her visit to the site, Bell did not possess a great deal of historical background about Raqqa.[218] Her subsequent account of the site in *Amurath to Amurath*, however, shows that she learned enough to make several educated observations about the remains she recorded and photographed there.

Bell correctly surmised that of the two main ruin fields at Raqqa, the more easterly of the two was the site of the oldest Classical period city, known variously as Nicephorium and Callicium.[219] Its earliest foundations extended back to the Hellenistic period, and she was able to find traces of these in the form of marble column fragments and capitals scattered in the area around a still-standing square minaret in the centre of the ruin field.[220] We now know that the minaret and the mosque to which it belonged stood in the midst of this city, renamed 'Raqqa' after the Arab conquest in 639–40. The city experienced an embellishment during the Umayyad period of the eighth century, when the caliph Hisham established a new market at Raqqa, built two palaces, commissioned a bridge over the river and dug a canal to supply water to the city.[221] Significantly, the square minaret, which Bell observed to be made of brick resting on a stone base, now no longer exists, and her photograph, along with one taken by Max Oppenheim, are the only visual records of this once grand structure (Fig. 2.15).[222]

Bell also correctly conjectured that the western ruin field at Raqqa represented the remains of Rafiqa (meaning 'Companion'), the city established by the Abbasid caliph al-Mansur around 771–2. This new foundation was further expanded and aggrandized by his grandson Harun al-Rashid between 786 and 808, serving for a time as the ruler's summer capital.[223] She observed the constructional details of Rafiqa's horseshoe-shaped double city wall, the mounded ruins of which would have been clearly seen amid the desert plain upon which they were set.[224] She did not record the cluster of ruins to the north of the city wall, however, which upon excavation proved to be the site of a complex of palaces built by Harun al-Rashid and his court.[225] Rather, she was drawn to the ruined buildings for which preserved parts could still be seen

Fig. 2.12 Bell's photograph of the 'Water Gate' at the site of Munbaqa (her 'Munbayah'). Many of the large stones in this area on the summit derive from two of the site's Bronze Age monumental temples.

above ground, these including the Baghdad Gate in the south-easterly corner of the Rafiqa horseshoe enclosure, the so-called Qasr al-Banat – a ruined palace within the walls to the north – and the congregational mosque and minaret in the centre of the city.

It is no wonder that Bell was impressed with the remnants of the Baghdad Gate, given its finely decorated brick façade (Fig. 2.16).[226] In truth, however, no other monument in the entire Islamic world has evoked such disputes concerning its date of construction. K.A.C. Creswell assigned this distinctive structure to the time of the caliph al-Mansur, seeing it as part and parcel of the fortified enclosure of Rafiqa built in the late eighth century.[227] R. Hillenbrand argued that its decorative features and arch type made it a much later construction, possibly attributable to the late eleventh or twelfth century, with parallels in the Seljuq architecture of the Zengid period.[228] L. Korn argued that its decorative similarities to the palace of Qasr al-'Ashiq at Samarra place its date in the late ninth or early tenth century.[229] Bell did not speculate on the date of the Baghdad Gate in her description in *Amurath to Amurath*, only noting that the Frenchman H. Viollet attributed it to Harun al-Rashid.[230] Nevertheless, even at this stage she seemed aware that some of its architectural features could be diagnostic indicators of later dates. She noted, for example, that the Baghdad Gate's 'flattened pointed arch' was comparable to a thirteenth-century building near Ukhaidir.[231] Significantly, it was this arch form that would lead others, such as John Warren, to question Creswell's eighth-century date of the Baghdad Gate and to ascribe the structure as a whole to a later time.[232] Today, the precise date of the Baghdad Gate's construction at Raqqa remains unresolved, although few would now ascribe it to the early caliphs of the Abbasid Era.[233]

Bell's photographs of the twelfth-century Qasr al-Banat of Rafiqa, described by her as 'the group of palace ruins near the east wall', nicely highlight the edifice's striking decoration.[234] Particularly noteworthy are her images of the palace's four-storey tower on the east side, where a rich plaster decoration had been applied thickly over the brickwork.[235] The two photographs that Bell took of the tower and its decoration are all the more valuable in that this impressive structure no longer exists (Fig. 2.17).[236] Also valuable is Bell's photograph of the south-western corner of the Qasr al-Banat, spanned by an elegantly adorned *muqarnas* vault and blind arches (Fig. 2.18).[237] A large portion of this vaulting had already fallen by the time Creswell visited the site and photographed it in the 1930s, and so we are fortunate that Bell took the time to document this impressive and beautiful part of the palace.[238]

Bell spent the greatest amount of her three-day visit to Raqqa in the centre of Rafiqa, inspecting and planning the city's congregational mosque. Despite its ruinous state, Bell could make out its mudbrick outer walls with round bastions and its central court, where a brick minaret stood above a stone square base. Given the minaret's distinctive form and dog-tooth ornament near the top, comparing

Fig. 2.13 Bell's photo of the Islamic-period castle Qal'at Jabbar, standing over the Euphrates River valley below. With the completion of the Tabqa Dam and the formation of Lake Assad behind it in the 1970s, the river valley was flooded, and the castle now stands as an island amid the lake's blue waters.

favourably with the minaret she had just seen at Qal'at Jabbar, she was correct in assigning its construction to the later Atebeg Nur al-Din, *c.*1165–6 CE.[239] Similarly, she rightly assigned one of the mosque's brick arcades, still preserved on the south side of the court, to Nur al-Din on account of a Kufic inscription over the central arch, which reported his renovations to the mosque.[240] Nevertheless, Bell suspected that Nur al-Din had essentially retained the original plan of the mosque through his repairs, a point further taken up by others such as Creswell, who fixed the original date of the mosque's construction to the Abbasid caliph al-Mansur around 772 CE.[241]

Bell's keen powers of observation picked up important details of the mosque, and these were described, planned or captured in her photographs. Her estimation of the number and position of entrances into the mosque interior comes impressively close to what has been confirmed by the most recent German probes of the structure.[242] Her photographs provide with clarity the details of the stucco capitals of the engaged columns that appear in Nur al-Din's arcade,[243] as well as a rounded pier with open-jointed brick coursing.[244]

Besides noting Raqqa's architecture, Bell showed an appreciation for the city's pottery, which she saw strewn about the ruins of both Rafiqa and Raqqa. Already by her time, 'Raqqa ware' had become highly prized for its beauty and skilful craftsmanship, and complete vessels found among the ruins by locals were being collected and sold to dealers in Aleppo, many making their way to European consumers.[245] In its own time, Raqqa had been well known throughout the Muslim world for its craft industries, especially pottery and glass, which continued to be manufactured for 500 years until the demise of production prior to the Mongol invasion of Syria in 1258–60.[246] Potters' workshops, which have been located in several zones within and beyond both Rafiqa and Raqqa, were producing a variety of glazed and unglazed wares, the most celebrated coming from the second half of the twelfth up to the mid-thirteenth centuries and

Fig. 2.14a Bell's 1909 detail of a baked brick façade above the gateway at the medieval castle of Qal'at Jabbar.

Fig. 2.14b In 2009, the author photographed the same feature shown in Fig. 2.14a, illustrating the damage sustained to the decorative pattern of bricks.

consisting of lustre-painted stonepaste wares, these traded widely throughout the Near East and reaching southern Europe.[247]

In all, the site of Raqqa left a distinct impression on Bell. Her visit had immersed her in Islamic-period remains, and she rightly recognized Raqqa's important place in the overall development of art and architecture, with its blend of both Syrian and Mesopotamian techniques, materials and designs. Raqqa was all the more intriguing given that only a handful of scholars before her had taken the time to study its remains, and she looked forward to the further research she would undertake upon her return to England. The significance of Raqqa to Bell is borne out in a letter written to her parents, in which she relates her plans for a future book that would study the art and architecture of Raqqa alongside those of Ukhaidir and Samarra, these latter sites being those into which she had poured her greatest energies during her 1909 journey.[248] In the end, she did not undertake this work – Ukhaidir became the site that would consume most of Bell's scholarly endeavours in Islamic-period archaeology – but she never forgot Raqqa, its architectural forms and decoration being utilized at the service of Ukhaidir, helping to establish that site's place and importance in the evolution of Mesopotamian architecture.

Fig. 2.15 Bell's photograph of the square brick minaret from the ruin field of Raqqa, dated to the Umayyad period of the eighth century, is one of the only visual records of this structure, which is no longer standing.

Below Raqqa to 'Anah

Bell's interest did not flag as she made her way along the east bank of the Euphrates below Raqqa and as far as 'Anah. She continued to stop to inspect ancient sites, amply present in this stretch of the river valley, photographing

Fig. 2.16   Bell's photo of the impressive Baghdad Gate of Raqqa, with its fine brick arched entrance, side niche with brick *hazarbaf* decoration, and an upper façade of tri-lobed niches resting on engaged collonnettes. The gate remnant stands at the south-eastern corner of the fortified enclosure of Rafiqa, built by the Abbasid caliph al-Mansur in the eighth century, although the gate itself is believed to represent a later Islamic-period construction.

their remains, speculating on their age, significance and ancient names. Highlights of this riverine region through which Bell now passed included the well-preserved and impressive fortress of Halebiye, standing opposite her track, on the right bank of the river, about 100 km south of Raqqa.[249] She would have been familiar with the history of this site. It had been fortified first in the third century CE by the famous queen of Palmyra, Zenobia, whose vast realm had once stretched over to the Euphrates River. After Zenobia rebelled, claiming her kingdom's independence from Rome, Halebiye was captured by the Romans shortly after they took Palmyra in 273 CE.[250] Henceforth, Halebiye served as an important part of Rome's eastern defences against the Sasanian kingdom to the east. Halebiye still acted as an important line of defence on the eastern frontier at the time of the Byzantine emperor Justinian I in the sixth century CE, and to him one may attribute some of the impressive ruins of the site that are still seen today, such as its massive stone city wall and gates, a three-storey *praetorium* built into the city wall, and a citadel on its western summit.[251] Bell did not cross the river to inspect this site more closely, rather settling on an inspection of the contemporary yet less impressive sister fortress of Zalebiye on the left bank of the river, about 3 km downstream from Halebiye. Although she did not plan Zalebiye, she gives a brief account of its towered walls perched high above the river below, its fortified entrance gate, and the remains of a town beyond the fort upstream.[252] Virtually no systematic excavation work has been carried out at Zalebiye, and Bell's photographs attest to the fact that its ruins look nearly the same now as when she visited the site. Similarly, the course of the Euphrates River, judging by Bell's photograph of it, looking upstream back towards Halebiye, is one of the few stretches to remain virtually unaltered.[253]

Significantly, both Halebiye and Zalebiye were strategically positioned at a place on the Euphrates where the river channel narrows between rocky outcrops. This special topography would have facilitated the means by which the ancient defenders of the two sites could have supervised riverine traffic while watching over the caravan crossing point on the river.[254] In the most recent past, this narrow channel was selected as the proposed place for the construction of yet another dam in Syria, originally slated to be completed by around 2012.[255] Both Halebiye and Zalebiye would have been affected by this dam, not to mention many other archaeological sites up-river, which would have been either partially or completely flooded. The recent political upheavals in Syria have brought a halt to this initiative – and so, at least for the time being, this ancient stretch of the Euphrates River and its magnificent walled guardians of another tumultuous era still exist.

Below the town of Deir ez-Zor, where Bell was able to procure provisions and rest the pack animals, she continued her journey, still visiting and recording the remains of ancient sites. Notable was the site of Buseirah near the confluence of the Khabur River with the Euphrates, the location of ancient Circesium, a frontier station founded by the Roman emperor Diocletian (245–311 CE).[256] Here she noted the existence of small chambers with walls of tiles and stones exposed by the locals, and possible traces of vaults, as well as a later building that the local inhabitants called a church, but she did not plan these features or linger at length to comprehend them more fully.[257] Further down the river at Werdi, opposite the town of Abu Kemal, Bell visited the standing tower tombs of Baghouz (her 'Irzî') high upon the cliffs behind the river valley. Her photograph of the best preserved tomb, this known elsewhere as the tower of Abu Gelal, is presented in *Amurath to Amurath*.[258] Observing their internal staircases and burial chambers beneath the bases of the towers and into the

bedrock below, Bell conjectured that the tombs dated to the first or second century CE. However, more recent studies of the tombs, and their resemblance to similarly arranged tower tombs at Palmyra, suggest an even earlier date, sometime in the first century BCE.[259]

The landscape was changing as Bell made her way down this stretch of the river. The stream itself was now characterized by numerous islands in its midst. The east and west banks, consisting of desert lands inhabited by the pastoral nomadic tribes of the Dulaim (Bell's 'Deleim'), Amarat and Jeraif, were now occasionally interrupted by cultivated fields, palm groves and fruit trees.[260] Bell also observed the presence of groaning wooden *norias*, water wheels that conveyed the river water up to the higher levels on the banks, providing irrigation for the fields and gardens.[261] This altered landscape prompted Bell to report that she had 'passed over an unseen frontier' into Babylonia.[262] Perhaps

Fig. 2.17a + b The four-storey tower of the Qasr al-Banat, a twelfth-century elite residence at Raqqa (opposite). The structure is noted for its rich plaster decoration over the brickwork, which included a frieze of keel-shaped hoods containing smaller, cusped blind arches. In between, deep triangular indentations ensured a strong contrast between light and shade (above). Bell's valuable photographs are some of the few images of this impressive structure, which has not survived.

not coincidentally, it was in this area, below the town of Abu Kemal and above 'Anah on the Euphrates, that the modern political border between Syria and Iraq was drawn up after World War I by European administrators, including Bell herself.

Arriving at the settlement of Rawa on the east bank of the Euphrates, Bell crossed to the opposite bank by ferry, thereby reaching 'Anah, a well-populated market town along the post road coming up from Baghdad. The town occupied a narrow strip of land by the water's edge, several kilometres long and characterized by mudbrick residences and market stalls, interspersed with gardens of palm groves. Not wanting to linger, however, Bell quickly found another ferry to take her to the island of Lubbad in the stream just opposite the lower end of 'Anah. The island was thickly strewn with archaeological remains,

Fig. 2.18a + b Bell's photo of a room corner in the Qasr al-Banat, featuring plaster decoration over the brickwork (top). An intact *muqarnas* vault stands above five-cusped blind arches on engaged columns and a dog-toothed string course. The vault has since collapsed, as shown by the photograph taken of the same corner of the palace in 2009 (bottom).

Fig. 2.19 Octagonal minaret of the twelfth century CE on the island of 'Anah, in the Euphrates River, present-day Iraq. Before the dam at Haditha flooded the island in the 1980s, the minaret was cut into sections and re-erected in the new town of 'Anah. The minaret no longer exists, having been destroyed by a bomb in 2006.

Fig. 2.20 Bell's photo taken from the top of the minaret on the island of 'Anah. The lush vegetation of the island to the north is visible, as are the remnants of the bridge that once joined the island with the town on the western bank of the river. With the completion of the Haditha Dam downstream, this island was completely flooded.

having been inhabited as early as the Old Babylonian period.[263] It was also known to have been occupied during the Neo-Assyrian period of the early first millennium BCE, of which Bell herself saw evidence in the form of a carved stone relief fragment.[264] Particularly prominent on the island, however, were remains from the later Islamic period, namely a distinctive brick minaret that had once stood alongside a twelfth-century congregational mosque. Bell's photographs of this tall minaret, with its octagonal form, broken by eight rows of niches with cusped arches, are singularly striking (Fig. 2.19), as are the views she photographed from its summit, which take in the island's lush 'paradise of fruit-trees, palms and corn' (Fig. 2.20).[265] Bell could not have predicted that this beautiful and ancient island would no longer exist by the end of the twentieth century. With the construction of the Iraqi Haditha Dam in the 1980s, the island at 'Anah was completely flooded, and a large lake now stands in its place.[266] The townspeople of 'Anah relocated the octagonal minaret to the modern town on the west bank in 1985, but sadly, this last remnant of the town's rich ancient heritage was destroyed by a bomb in June 2006.[267] Bell's photograph remains one of the loveliest and clearest images of that monument in its original island location.

Bell's arrival at 'Anah brings us to the end of the first major leg of her 1909 journey. She had by this point travelled 26 days since Aleppo, covered around 625 km and reported over a hundred archaeological sites.[268] She had taken just under 200 photographs, these images providing an invaluable record of the numerous ruins and landscapes she had passed along the way. Many of these photographs are all the more precious since their subjects have been dramatically altered or no longer exist. But these Euphrates exploits by no means marked the climax of Bell's long journey or the height of her achievements. A greater and more spectacular prize of ancient splendour was yet to come.

CHAPTER 3

UKHAIDIR – DESERT SPLENDOUR

The principal aim of Gertrude Bell's 1909 journey was to travel along lesser-known routes through Mesopotamia, encountering places and peoples about which other travel writers had written little. In addition, her expeditions had by now taken on a serious archaeological aspect. Bell did not content herself with a passing comment and the occasional photograph of an ancient site or monument of interest. Now she endeavoured to describe, plan and systematically photograph archaeological sites with their myriad artistic and architectural details, and to make inquiries as to their date and historical import. Bell was academically ambitious at this point; she hoped that her Mesopotamian journey and subsequent publications would make an impact in archaeological circles and that she would be recognized as a serious and accomplished scholar in her own right. Nevertheless, as she made her way into the heart of the lands of the Tigris and Euphrates, the formidable nature of her goal grew more and more apparent. Several accomplished scholars and explorers had already been along some of these paths and had published learned reports of the antiquities they had seen. It would not be enough to photograph and provide a detailed description of a known ancient site. To best achieve scholarly recognition, she would need to discover something completely new, something truly magnificent and unknown. She had to be able to claim this discovery for herself, and through her subsequent research and publications demonstrate her scholarly credentials to the world.

The castle of Ukhaidir provided everything Bell could have hoped for. It was impressive and elusive, and in its splendid isolation deep in the desert, few Europeans knew much about it, much less had made any kind of scientific investigation. At the same time, it was a complicated site with an unusual character, and considerable effort would be required to establish properly its date and true identity. These were precisely the intellectual challenges Bell sought, and she took on Ukhaidir with enthusiasm, determination and energy. As it turned out, Ukhaidir was such a tremendous and significant monument that it consumed much of the next five years of her life. Not only did it require her to make two trips to Mesopotamia to ensure that it was fully recorded to her satisfaction, but it entailed intensive research into existing publications on other similar structures, and extensive correspondence with scholars who had knowledge of other sites with comparable architectural characteristics and functional attributes.

Discovery and Documentation

Bell knew nothing about the existence of the Ukhaidir palace when she set out on her journey down the Euphrates into the heart of Mesopotamia in the early months of 1909. Nevertheless, she had already developed an interest in the desert region west of the Euphrates River, where Ukhaidir is located, and in particular the Sasanian-period settlements that were believed to exist there. Bell's interest in the Sasanian period, dated between the third and seventh centuries CE, can in part be traced back to her prior investigations of the roughly contemporaneous Byzantine Era and in particular to her extensive research of the late antique ecclesiastical art and architecture of Anatolia. Her probing into the origins of some of the architectural features, such as the vault and the dome, observed in the churches of Binbirkilise, for example, had drawn her attention to similar forms known from the contemporary lands of the Sasanians to the east in Mesopotamia and Persia.[1] Added to this was Bell's fondness for the work of Josef Strzygowski and his strong conviction that one should look for the origins of the artistic and architectural foundations of Western art in the East, many of these having emanated from the lands of Sasanian Mesopotamia and Persia. Particularly influential for Bell was Strzygowski's comprehensive treatment of the desert structure of Mshatta, which had appeared in a long journal article in 1904.[2] As already reported, Bell had reviewed this important work for Salomon Reinach's journal *Revue archéologique*.[3] Her careful reading of Strzygowski's clever and complicated assessment of Mshatta, a structure that stands in the western Syrian desert some 30 km south of Amman, had provided Bell with a strong dose of the art and architecture of the Late Antique, Sasanian and Early Islamic Near East. It also drew her into the raging debate over the date and identity of this complex, with its striking stone-carved façade, at that point only recently transplanted to the Kaiser Friedrich Museum in Berlin.[4] She would have been well acquainted with Strzygowski's own conviction about the site's Sasanian architectural character, his dating of it to the fourth to sixth centuries CE, and his opinion that the building was a palace intended for rulers of the Ghassanids, Christian Arabs who had occupied the western part of the Syrian desert and protected the eastern frontiers of the Byzantine Empire.[5] The Mshatta problem would also have made Bell familiar with the Lakhmids, another somewhat more elusive Arab group who occupied the Syrian desert, mainly in the regions alongside and to the west of the Euphrates River of southern Mesopotamia. First independent of Sasanian control, the Lakhmids were eventually absorbed into the Sasanian Empire and helped to protect its western frontier, particularly against the threat of Byzantine expansion.[6] Some scholars were arguing, *contra* Strzygowski, that the Lakhmids were responsible for Mshatta's construction.[7]

Besides Strzygowski, Bernhard Moritz seems to have been the other source for Bell's knowledge of and growing interest in the Sasanian-period sites of the Syrian desert. In the course of her travels in the East, Bell had made the acquaintance of this German Arabic scholar, who had been head of the Khedivial Library in Cairo between 1896 and 1911.[8] In addition to his extensive study of early Arabic inscriptions, Moritz had travelled widely in Egypt and the rest of the Near East, and he was familiar with the history and archaeology of Mesopotamia, having even taken part in Robert Koldewey's excavations at the Sumerian sites of Zurghul and al-Hiba.[9] Bell knew about Moritz and his work as early as 1905.[10] Consequently, during a visit to Cairo in January 1907 with her father and her brother Hugo, Bell met Moritz in person at the Khedivial Library and discussed with him – sometimes in the company of his colleague, the archaeologist Max Oppenheim – various topics, including Sasanian ornaments, maps and photographs. That Bell found a friend in Moritz at this time is reflected in her comment, 'Moritz and I are hatching great plans for exploring the Syrian desert together!'[11] The remark also demonstrates her developing interest in that desert region, and the castles and peoples who used to inhabit it.

In January 1909, when Bell was in Cairo and about to embark on her Mesopotamian journey, she met up again with Moritz, who suggested part of the route to take: 'Moritz advised me to go down the E side of the Euphrates from there [Carchemish] as there are a number of towns to be identified there and nothing has been done. So there I shall go.'[12] Over dinner the following evening, Moritz repeated his advice to travel down the eastern bank, then also recommended that further down the river she make 'an excursion from 'Anah to the Lakhmid castles'.[13] Moritz was referring to the desert region to the west of the Euphrates and below the town of 'Anah, where the finest of the Lakhmid sites were believed to be situated. Bell clearly took Moritz's advice to heart, for we know that she included both of his recommended routes in her Mesopotamian journey. Indeed, it was her passage through the desert area below 'Anah that led to her discovery of Ukhaidir. As Bell departed from Cairo, she wrote to her mother another letter relating her respect and friendship for Moritz:

> I have had 2 enchanting days at Cairo – enchanting and most useful for my future movements, thanks mainly to the advice and wisdom of the good Moritz [...] Next morning I went out early to the oldest and most

interesting of the mosques, where I took a number of photographs for which I have been wishing for a long time, and then to the Khedivial Library to see Moritz – he's the head of it, a learned mis-sticked [sic] little German who has quarreled with almost everyone, but is still a great friend of mine.[14]

By March 1909, Bell had followed the Euphrates River down as far as the town of 'Anah, and there she began to make inquiries in earnest about the Syrian desert region to the west of the river, and about the ancient ruins to be found there. According to her account in *Amurath to Amurath*, she first heard of Ukhaidir, or 'Kheidir' as it was known colloquially among the local Arabs, from Bedouin tribesmen of the Jeraif, whom she found camped with their flocks on the left bank of the river. She questioned these men about the northern corner of the Sasanian Empire, and an old man – distinguished by a bullet still lodged in his cheek from his travels in central Arabia – piped up that he knew that desert country well, and if Bell would give him a horse, he would take her to all of the castles therein: Khubbaz, 'Amej, Themail, Kheidir:

> 'Where is Kheidir?' said I, for the name was unknown to me or to Kiepert.
> 'Beyond Shetateh,' answered a lean and ragged youth. 'I too know it, wallah!'
> 'Is it large?' I asked.
> 'It is a castle,' he replied vaguely, and one after another the men of the Jeraif chimed in with descriptions of the road. The sum total of the information offered by them seemed to be that water was scarce and raids frequent, but there were certainly castles; yes, in the land of Fahd Beg ibn Hudhdhal, the great sheikh of the Amarat, there was Kheidir. I made a mental note of that name.[15]

The route to Ukhaidir would require Bell to depart from the well-watered valley of the Euphrates and enter the precarious desert, where wells were rare and the threat of raids required that she bring a reliable guard who also knew the way to the pre-Islamic castles she was seeking. But Bell was resolved to take this daring journey. Below 'Anah, at the town of Hit, known for its hot-pitch springs, Bell found her guide and made the decision to send her caravan on to Kerbela to wait for her while she and Fattuh and a much smaller donkey caravan, laden with supplies and a light tent, would make their way into the desert.

Travelling in a south-westerly direction away from the Euphrates, Bell included stops at several oasis towns. She also took the time to visit a number of ruined forts – Khubbaz, Themail and Bardawi – which she planned, photographed and judged to be either Sasanian or Islamic on the basis of their layout and architecture.[16] Six days after leaving Hit, they reached Shetateh, an oasis of 160,000 palms, willows, pomegranates and irrigation streams, only a few hours from Ukhaidir (Fig. 3.1).[17] They set out on the next day, their little party having now been augmented by a young English engineer, B.T. Watts, who had been surveying the region and was camped at Shetateh.[18]

Bell relates the excitement of her first sight of Ukhaidir:

> We had ridden to the south-east for about 3 hours, through a most uncompromising wilderness, when, in the glare ahead, we caught sight of a great mass which I took for a natural feature in the landscape. But as we approached, its shape became more and more definite, and I asked one of the zaptiehs what it was. 'It is Kheidir,' said he. 'Yallah, Fattuh, bring on the mules,' I shouted and galloped forward.[19]

As Bell neared Ukhaidir, its impressive size and excellent preservation increased her amazement at this edifice in the middle of the desert (Fig. 3.2). Her first

Fig. 3.1 Shetateh, an oasis about four hours' ride from Ukhaidir, seemed a paradise to Bell and her group, 'who had dropped out of the deserts of the Euphrates' (Bell, *Amurath*, p. 139).

Fig. 3.2 Bell's photograph of the site of Ukhaidir from the north-east. Approaching from Shetateh, this would have been among Bell's first views of the site. Her shadow appears in the lower right.

impressions of the castle are evocatively related in *Amurath to Amurath*. K.A.C. Creswell, who visited Ukhaidir in 1930 and also recorded its ruins, was no less affected by his first view of Ukhaidir in its desert loneliness, and admits that he could do no better than to repeat these words of Bell in his own work:[20]

> Of all the wonderful experiences that have fallen my way, the first sight of Kheidir is the most memorable. It reared its mighty walls out of the sand, almost untouched by time, breaking the long lines of the waste with its huge towers, steadfast and massive, as though it were, as I had at first thought it, the work of nature, not of man.[21]

Upon entering Ukhaidir, Bell found the castle inhabited by a group of Arabs who had come from the Nejd, dissatisfied with the politics of that region and desiring to pursue a more lucrative trade in camels and horses in Ottoman-controlled Mesopotamia. They were using Ukhaidir as their base. The families had camped within many of the rooms, finding the shelter within the castle walls 'more than sufficient for their needs [than] to the race at whose command it had been reared'.[22] Bell was not troubled by the group's habitation of the palace; indeed, to her Orientalist imagination, they enhanced the romantic quality of the place, bringing its ancient character to life. Bell describes Ali, the sheikh of the Jawf, as 'a splendid creature with black hair falling in plaits on either side of his face' who, with his brothers, 'passed like ghosts along the passages, they trailed their white robes down the stairways'.[23] At her most lyrical, Bell describes the Arab tribesmen gathered round their hearth in the evening in the great hall of the palace:

> where their forefathers had beguiled the hours with tale and song in the same rolling tongue of Nejd [. . .] The thorns crackled, a couple of oil wicks placed in holes above the columns, which had been contrived for them by the men-at-arms of old, sent a feeble ray into the darkness.[24]

One of their members, playing a single-stringed Bedouin *rebabah*, sang about a

> prince great and powerful, patron of poets, leader of raids, and recently
> overwhelmed and slain in battle; but old or new, the songs were all pages
> out of the same chronicle, the undated chronicle of the nomad. The thin
> melancholy music rose up into the blackness of the vaults; across the
> opening at the end of the hall, where the wall had fallen in part away, was
> spread the deep still night and the unchanging beauty of the stars.[25]

Bell, enchanted by the scene around her, offered up her own verse for Ukhaidir, a quote from the poet Labīd ibn Rabī'ah, which also served as the epigraph for *Amurath to Amurath*: 'We wither away but they wane not, the stars that above us rise; / The mountains remain after us, and the strong towers when we are gone.'[26]

Bell's letters and diaries, which record her first impressions of Ukhaidir, make it clear that she at first believed the palace to be a sixth-century Lakhmid construction, contemporary with the other Lakhmid towns known to be strung out over the Mesopotamian desert to the west of the Euphrates River. Given its assumed identity and her belief that no one had previously planned such a place, it was an exciting prospect to investigate an edifice about which nothing had been properly studied and published. She set to work immediately, endeavouring to carefully plan the structure in its entirety and to photograph its many elements, no doubt with the objective of completing a full, publishable description upon her return to England.

Bell's planning of Ukhaidir was rudimentary yet thorough. B.T. Watts, her travelling companion, had his surveying instruments, possibly a theodolite, and supplied her with measurements for the long outer and inner lengths of Ukhaidir's fortifications and castle within.[27] All other measurements at Ukhaidir, however, were made by Bell with a simple tape measure and foot rule.[28] Bell's measurements were duly marked in several pages of a field notebook, in which she produced sketch plans of the various sectors of the complex and their features (Fig. 3.3). The challenges of planning such an enormous and complicated edifice must have been formidable, but Bell was determined to get a complete and accurate record of the palace, spending two full days taking measurements of Ukhaidir's walls, towers and gates, and receiving the assistance of the men from her travel entourage (Fig. 3.4). They took turns holding her measuring tape and carrying her camera: 'In a day they have learnt exactly what it is I want and they are infinitely useful to me for I simply have to walk after them with my sketch book and write down the figures from the tape.'[29]

Once her measurements had been made, Bell drew the ground floor of the whole complex out to scale, lying on the floor of one of the cool, shady rooms of the castle's stable, her own tents too dusty during the daytime for such careful work.[30] She also measured the two upper storeys of the castle on the day before

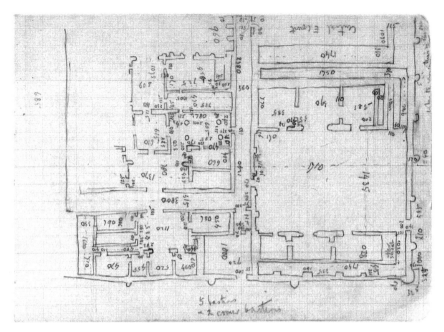

Fig. 3.3 A page from Gertrude Bell's field notebook, showing her sketch plan of the south-eastern sector of the Ukhaidir palace and her measurements. Bell is holding this notebook in Fig. 3.4.

her departure. In all, she completed the entire task with some pride, remarking that her plan worked out to within 40 cm of Mr Watt's measurements taken on the first day.[31] It was this plan that was reproduced in the first two of Bell's publications to describe her findings at Ukhaidir, these appearing in 1910 and 1911, respectively.[32]

In the early months of 1911, during her second journey to Mesopotamia, Bell included a short stop at Ukhaidir, staying three days to take additional measurements and photographs. By this time, the Jawf Arabs had left, replaced by the Zagarit – a sub-group of the Shammar tribe – whose tents were pitched nearby. During the day, when Bell was working on her measurements, the Zagarit would appear in the castle, sitting in a circle around her expedition's tents in the inner courtyard, sewing new shirts and watching her progress.[33] It would appear that Bell had possession of a plane table on this trip, for she mentions using it to make a plan of the castle and to assist with taking elevations, a task that consumed much of her time.[34] Even with this effort, however, she remained satisfied with her earlier 1909 plan, describing it as 'wonderfully accurate' and possessing only one or two mistakes.[35] For photography, she took shots of architectural features that she had missed in 1909 and used a telephoto lens for additional close-range details.[36]

Fig. 3.4 Bell recording one of Ukhaidir's walls in her field notebook. Her travelling companions are holding her measuring tape, rifles slung over their shoulders. Bell noted: 'nothing will induce them to leave their rifles in the tents. They are quite intolerably inconvenient; the measuring tape is forever catching round the barrel or getting up in the stock, but I can't persuade them to lay the damnable things down for an instant' (GB letter to her family, 29 March 1909).

Description of Ukhaidir

Bell provided descriptions of the location, layout and architecture of the palace and mosque of Ukhaidir in various publications, but her final report on the site, published in 1914, was the longest and most detailed.[37] Because the palace is made up of many interior rooms, corridors and open spaces, it was necessary for her to devise a system for distinguishing individual spaces and thus facilitate the matching of text descriptions of these spaces with associated plans and photographs. Bell appears to have abandoned her earlier, lettered room designations in favour of the numbered spaces employed by Oskar Reuther after he had visited Ukhaidir and published his own report in 1912.[38] Reuther's numbering system was also later adopted by K.A.C. Creswell,[39] and it is the system used here to locate and describe various spaces within the palace (Fig. 3.5). Given that Bell, Reuther and Creswell have all provided thorough, reliable descriptions of Ukhaidir's extensive architecture, mine is a much abbreviated report based mainly on Bell's description and plans. It is intended to highlight the palace's complexity and underscore Bell's remarkable achievement in recording it as accurately as she did in the few days she spent at the site. Creswell's own account of Ukhaidir, based on visits he made 21 years or more after Bell, does little to augment her architectural observations and descriptions, and his photos duplicate, sometimes

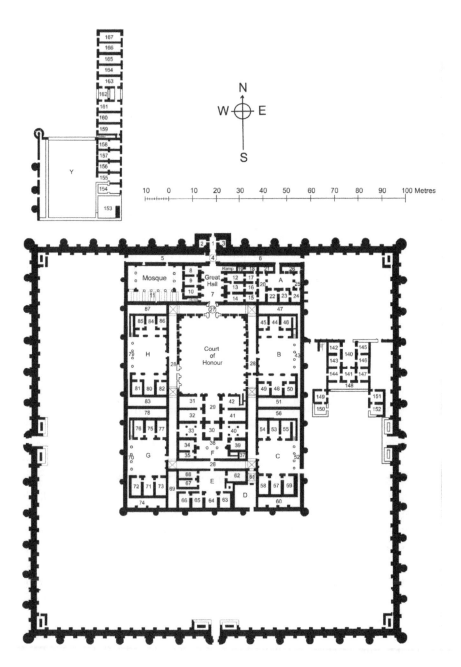

Fig. 3.5 Plan of Ukhaidir, adapted from Bell's published plan of the castle. The plan is based entirely on her own measurements and sketch plans undertaken at the site during her 1909 and 1911 visits. The numbers for the interior spaces, however, were adopted from Oskar Reuther's numbering scheme for Ukhaidir.

to lesser effect, her detailed and informative shots. The description of the layout of the complex provided here, along with its accompanying plan (Fig. 3.5), should also help to place Bell's architectural analyses, partially described later in the chapter, within a more comprehensible context.

Located about 45 km south-west of the city of Kerbela, the castle of Ukhaidir is situated in what is largely a lifeless desert, although the nearby Wadi al-Ubaid, which runs past the site, would have provided it with fresh water in antiquity.[40] Bell conjectured, probably correctly, that more favourable, moister environmental conditions in earlier times may have supported various fowl, boar and other wild animals, and that the residents of Ukhaidir would have found ample game to hunt.[41]

Ukhaidir itself consists principally of a large and high rectangular enclosure wall made of thin stone slabs and fortified with round towers, within which a palace structure and a smaller subsidiary building were set (Fig. 3.6).[42] Bell recognized the defensive character of the enclosure wall by features such as narrow window slits or loopholes, located in the towers and the wall in between, through which arrows or other missiles could be discharged.[43] She also noted gaps in the floor at each arrow slit – machicolations – which were another means by which missiles could be launched at the enemy standing at the foot of the wall.[44]

An arched gate on the northern side of the outer enclosure wall gave immediate access to the palace's main entrance, which was set almost directly inside the wall. The palace was itself furnished with towered walls and constructed of the same stone masonry as the outer enclosure, with baked brick used only for some of the vaults.[45] It has been pointed out that today the structure looks crude and inelegant, but one has to imagine that originally most of its interior wall surfaces would have been coated with a layer of smooth plaster and in some cases even raised stucco designs, providing a more polished, albeit somewhat sombre, opulence to the palace's interior.[46]

The focal point at the heart of the Ukhaidir palace interior was an open court, dubbed the 'Court of Honour'. One accessed this court through a series of domed and vaulted spaces[47] that led from the northern gate, the most impressive being the 'Great Hall' (Fig. 3.7). This grand two-storeyed space, the largest covered room in the palace, supported a magnificent, slightly pointed, brick vault whose construction greatly intrigued Bell and assisted in her proper identification and date of the palace as a whole (and about which more will be discussed later).[48] Of the central 'Court of Honour', Bell observed that its elegant façade consisted of blind arcades on all sides (Fig. 3.8).[49] While the east, west and south sides of the court were one storey high, the north side, from which one had entered through the front gate and the 'Great Hall', comprised an imposing three-storeyed block, each level equipped with various living spaces accessed by stairs or ramps accessed from the ground floor beside the 'Great Hall' (Fig. 3.9).[50]

Fig. 3.6 Bell's photograph of the south-eastern corner of the interior of Ukhaidir's enclosure wall, showing the remains of a staircase leading to an outwardly projecting corner round tower. On either side, blind, slightly pointed arches face the interior. The narrow windows above, accessed from a vaulted walkway that is no longer preserved in this corner, served as slits from which arrows or other missiles could be discharged. The square holes visible in the stonework mark the places where wooden ties once existed.

The façade in the south side of the Court of Honour led to some of the principal rooms of the palace. In the centre, a wide and tall arched doorway – possibly one of the earliest examples of a so-called *pishtaq* (a square framed archway, common in later Persian architecture, used to mark grand entrances)[51] – gave access to a deep, brick, barrel-vaulted chamber, which Bell dubbed an *iwan*, or principal reception hall (Room 29) (Fig. 3.10). Doorways on either side opened to flanking Rooms 31, 32, 41 and 42, placed at right angles to the *iwan*, while a doorway at the rear gave access to Room 30.[52]

With their elaborate stuccoed vaults, Bell observed that Rooms 31 and 32 were among the most important spaces within the palace as a whole. It is conceivable that these chambers were used as formal living rooms, where guests could sit on the floor on cushions, their backs against the wall, the centre of the back wall being the place of honour.[53] The vault in Room 31 featured a corrugated stucco pattern and a decoration of variously embellished square coffers in the ceiling, while blind windows marked the ends of the room.[54] Even more charming and original were the ceiling decoration and vaulting system of Room 32 (Fig. 3.11). As in Room 31, the barrel vaults, set between transverse arches, were embellished with stucco patterns, but here they comprised an even more elaborate arrangement of coffered designs and corrugations. Some of the vaults terminated against semi-domes, the corners of which were resolved by small recessed squinches or horizontal brackets.[55] On the wall between the arches, as well as at each end of the room, pairs of elaborately embellished blind windows further contributed to the distinctive character of this chamber (Fig. 3.12).[56]

Bell observed that the entire central block of spaces just described – namely, the Court of Honour, the principal *iwan* and flanking reception rooms, as well as additional chambers surrounding Room 30 at the rear – was enclosed by a narrow roofed corridor (Corridor 28).[57] The corridor created a physical divide between this central block of the palace, which clearly represented its ceremonial heart, and the remaining components. Of these remaining sections, four suites of living rooms – otherwise referred to as *baits* (from the Arabic for 'houses') – located on either side of the central ceremonial block filled much of the interior palace space. These units had central courts (B, C, G and H), at each end of which were long reception rooms flanked by living room chambers, referred to by Bell as 'liwan groups' (henceforth, '*iwan* groups').[58] Creswell conjectured that the groups of rooms facing the south would form the winter residence, while those facing north would be used in the summer.[59] To the north and south of the *iwan* groups, the *baits* were completed by the presence of rectangular chambers with barrel vaults pierced with terracotta pipes, and central open spaces (Rooms 47, 51, 56, 60, 74, 78, 83 and 87). It is highly likely these spaces served as kitchens.[60]

Fig. 3.7 Bell's photograph of the Great Hall (no. 7), facing north, with its recessed arched doorway in the centre leading back to the main gateway. Directly above, a shallow semi-dome is flanked by two niches. Even further above, three windows provide light into Room 88, located on the second storey of the palace.

Fig. 3.8 Bell's photograph of the north-western interior corner of the blind arcaded Court of Honour. The multi-storeyed northern gateway block rises up on the right at right angles to the single-level western side of the palace. In the foreground, tribesmen of the Zagarit, whom Bell encountered during her visit in 1911, are clustered around one of her tents. Bell's servant, Fattuh, is standing at the tent's entrance.

Bell determined that the arrangement of rooms in the north-western corner of the palace comprised the edifice's mosque (about which more will be said below). It consisted principally of a rectangular court surrounded on three sides by covered porticoes. On the north side were the principal doors into the mosque court (Fig. 3.13). The vaulting on the southern arcade was elaborately decorated with stucco, not unlike that observed in Rooms 31 and 32 in the palace.[61] Nine transverse arches carried across the southern side, each decorated with coffers of stepped lozenges, inside of which were smaller circular recessed coffers.[62] Between the arches, the vaulting was decorated in corrugated stucco. At either end of the vaulted arcade were two fluted semi-domes, each divided down the centre by a transverse arch decorated with stucco, while fluted squinches at the corners effected the curvature of the springing of the vault (Fig. 3.14).[63] In the centre of the south wall of the mosque was the *mihrab*, consisting of a rectangular niche covered by an undecorated semi-dome (Fig. 3.23).[64]

Bell observed and planned still other areas of the palace, including Court A in the north-eastern corner, surrounded by small chambers (Rooms 20–6),[65] and Court E at the southern end, this giving access to another *iwan* group (Rooms 63–5) and a kitchen to the west (Room 69).[66] To the south-east was Court D, accessed from Corridor 28 by a groined vaulted vestibule and also entered by a doorway from the palace yard outside.[67] A building known variously as the 'East Annex' or

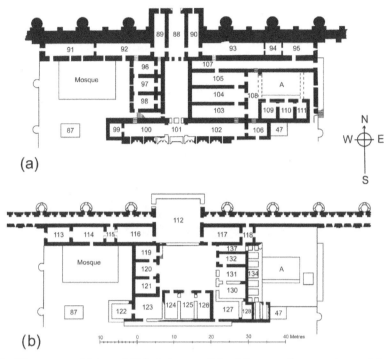

Fig. 3.9 The second (a) and third storeys (b) of the northern gateway block of the Ukhaidir palace, adapted from Bell's 1914 published plan.

'Inner Annex' existed to the east of the palace in the yard, within the fortified enclosure. Although this structure was probably a later addition, it shared much in common with the palace, so it was not likely to have been constructed much later.[68] As the internal arrangement of the rooms of the East Annex closely resembles the suite of rooms on the southern side of the Court of Honour (Rooms 140–7), it is conceivable that the East Annex functioned in a similar way to the palace's ceremonial suite, acting as the living and reception chambers of a person of honour.

Other structures existed outside the palace and beyond its enclosing wall. The Northern Annex is a complex of rooms located just to the north of the palace enclosure, one of its walls fortified with solid round towers, to the east of which is a large courtyard and 15 vaulted rooms.[69] A small, two-chambered bath, or *hammam*, was also found outside the enclosure, this located at some distance from the north-east of the palace. Although now entirely fallen, the bath's principal chamber would have been vaulted. Buttresses on the outside of the building helped to relieve the thrust of the vault, the only occurrence of this feature at Ukhaidir.[70]

A number of further walls enclose the Ukhaidir palace complex, these most clearly seen in an aerial mosaic provided by the Royal Air Force at the request of

Fig. 3.10 Reuther's drawing of the southern part of the Court of Honour shows his reconstruction of the *pishtaq*, the high rectangular frame set above the arched doorway leading into Room 29, the palace's principal *iwan*. It is surprising that none of Bell's photographs provide a complete view of the surviving stonework of this important southern façade; one must turn to either Reuther's or Creswell's reports for such images.

K.A.C. Creswell. Today these walls appear only as low mounded lines above the ground.[71] Bell observed many of these wall lines herself while standing on the top of the palace, and her own notes on these features probably provided the incentive for Creswell's later inquiries.[72] It is conceivable that the second, outer enclosure allowed camels to graze near the complex without risk of them escaping or being stolen.[73] The aerial view also discerned a number of rectangular enclosures between the northern wall and the edge of the Wadi Ubaid, these probably representing cultivated plots surrounded by low banks that would have helped to contain irrigated water.[74]

Other Early Twentieth-Century Visitors to Ukhaidir

Leaving Ukhaidir after her first visit in late March 1909, Bell felt triumphant, having carefully planned, described and photographed the magnificent castle and all of its facets. To be sure, other European travellers had passed by the castle before her, but she thought that she was the first visitor to take serious interest in its many architectural details and to produce a complete record of it. She would

Fig. 3.11 Reuther's reconstruction of the interior vaulting in the ceremonial Room 32, showing the vault to be divided down its length by four transverse arches. In between are three stuccoed barrel vaults, each treated differently and terminating against walls distinguished by semi-domes, squinches, coffered recesses and blind windows.

remain buoyant about her discovery of Ukhaidir until the very end of her Near Eastern journey in July 1909, by which time she had reached Constantinople and was preparing for her return to England. While dining with officials from various European embassies, Bell spoke with a French diplomat who knew that an individual by the name of Louis Massignon had visited the site of Ukhaidir only the year before and had published his findings in a short French journal article.[75] Although this unfortunate news may have come as a shock to Bell, who seemed so desperate to claim the honour of Ukhaidir's discovery for herself, her letters reveal no serious agitation. Her diary entries around this period in July do not even mention the fact that she had effectively been scooped. One might suppose

Fig. 3.12   Bell's photograph of the south wall, east end of Room 32. The blind windows are framed by engaged columns and accentuated by stucco mouldings of zigzags or simple fillets. Sunk into the centre of each blind window was the motif of an upright spear, while above was further decoration in the form of sunken rosettes or half-circles.

that she contented herself with the fact that she had produced complete, accurate plans of the Ukhaidir complex and intended to write a comprehensive report, something Massignon had not endeavoured. To be sure, on 31 March 1908, Massignon had visited Ukhaidir for just one hour because his group had come under attack by a group of Arab tribesmen. He managed to return again to Ukhaidir on 3 April with a larger escort, but, probably fearing further attacks, spent only a day taking a few measurements of the palace and photographing its remains. Not surprisingly, Massignon's reports and plans of Ukhaidir contain several inaccuracies and omissions, and his postulated date for the construction of the palace in the sixth century of the Sasanian period was ultimately proven incorrect.[76]

Massignon was not the only individual to erode Bell's sole claim on the desert castle. It seems that in her absence from Mesopotamia, between 1909 and her second visit to Ukhaidir in March 1911 to complete her plans and photographs, German members of the Deutsche Orient-Gesellschaft had visited Ukhaidir and were planning their own publication on the castle. Their report appeared shortly thereafter, in 1912, having been principally authored by Oskar Reuther but with the assistance of Friedrich Wetzel and Karl Müller, all members of the Babylon excavation team. Bell learned of the German visit in March 1911, when she met

Fig. 3.13 One of the principal doors into the mosque court of the palace, from the north. The door is set within a recess, while the archway above is embellished with a distinctive cusped pattern of stucco.

Reuther and Müller at the Babylon Expedition house just after her second visit to Ukhaidir.[77] Her letters and diaries make no mention of what again must have been a startling and disappointing revelation. Moreover, unlike Massignon on his brief visit, the Germans had spent several days at Ukhaidir, and with their highly developed architectural skills they had produced impeccable plans of the castle's every inch. Such a report would surely rival, if not surpass in its

Fig. 3.14   The south-eastern corner of the southern arcade of the mosque (no. 11), which was among the most highly decorated vaults in the palace. It consists of a quarter-dome formed by transverse arches and covered in a decorative stucco pattern of fluting, crenellated lozenges, recessed circles, a fluted corner squinch and flanking shallow semi-domes.

careful details, Bell's own record of the complex. Nevertheless, Bell remained surprisingly circumspect, at least in print. Her diary entry on 10 March 1911 simply notes that Reuther showed her his plans of Ukhaidir, and in a letter she writes that she found all the German team members 'as kind as could be'.[78] When her final report on Ukhaidir was published in 1914, she gracefully recalled that the Germans showed her their drawings and discussed with her Ukhaidir's details. She was grateful to be allowed to use some of their illustrations for her own publication and expressed her admiration for 'their masterly production'.[79]

Once more, Bell seems to have shown incredible restraint in the face of this stupendous scoop. To make matters even worse, she probably recognized that she had prompted the Germans' work in the first place. Back in 1909, just two days after having departed from Ukhaidir (on 30 March), Bell had made her first visit to the German excavations at Babylon. Still brimming with excitement over her discovery, she had not hesitated to announce her visit to Ukhaidir and was forthcoming about her plans and observations with the German team members, who included Friedrich Wetzel.[80] Her letter implies that the Germans had not known about the place and certainly had never seen it, much less were planning their own expedition there. Nevertheless, they were clearly impressed by its description, agreeing that it was, to use Bell's words, 'the most important building of its period that has yet been found'.[81] Bell was sufficiently proud of her discovery to write at the time: 'It's the greatest piece of luck that has ever happened to me. I shall publish it in a big monograph all to itself and it will make a flutter in the dovecotes'.[82] Such a statement surely reflects her impression of having a sole claim to the site.

We can only conclude that the Germans, having now heard through Bell of the magnificence of Ukhaidir, resolved to explore the place themselves. Ukhaidir was, after all, fewer than two days from Babylon, and a short excursion into the desert such as this would have been an entirely feasible, if not welcome, respite from long and arduous days of archaeological investigations in the mudbrick mounds of Babylon. Moreover, Reuther and his colleagues possibly felt they were capable of producing a more thorough and scholarly study than Bell, given their prodigious architectural skills and archaeological training, and so set out to publish their own report in a timely fashion. Bell, for her part, never reported what might have been construed as an underhanded scheme, nor, throughout her lifetime, did she ever express any bitterness over the incident. The only hint of her true feelings comes not from her own writings but from a speech penned after her death by her step-sister, Elsa (Lady Richmond). In this lecture on Bell's life and achievements, which was given to raise funds for the British School of Archaeology in Iraq, Lady Richmond recounts Gertrude's discovery of Ukhaidir and consequent publication.[83] She proceeds with the words: 'But it was a great disappointment of her that some German archaeologists who visited it after she did, brought out a book on it first before hers appeared.' Tellingly, a line was struck through that part of the sentence, indicating that Lady Richmond ultimately chose not to speak those words. We wonder whether, in the end, she also elected to preserve Bell's propriety over this disappointment.

There is no denying that Oskar Reuther's *Ocheïdir*, published on behalf of the Deutsche Orient-Gesellschaft, is a fine report. Particularly noteworthy is its focus on the architectural details of the Ukhaidir palace. Every room, court, doorway, arch and vault was carefully described, measured and exquisitely drawn. Considerable energy was also spent describing and visualizing the various construction techniques used. The report's greatest strengths are the splendid reconstructions of the desert edifice's various features, bringing the palace to life and impressing upon the reader its truly magnificent character when it was in use. It is hard not to be affected by the splendour of the Court of Honour as Reuther rendered it, with its dazzling, open space framed by arcades, the towering three-storey gatehouse walls at the back, and a peacock in the foreground, enhancing the court's noble character (Fig. 3.15). The solemn grandeur of the southern arcade of the mosque, with its stuccoed vaults and brick-columned portico, is evoked in another reconstruction.[84] Through such skilful recreations, the reader can enjoy the sensation of experiencing the palace in a way that plan drawings and even photographs of the present ruined mass can but hint at. Both Bell and Creswell, the latter visiting Ukhaidir in 1930, were clearly impressed by Reuther's publication and included several of his illustrations in their reports, thus acknowledging the clarity and experiential quality such images conveyed.

Bell's own published reports of Ukhaidir differ from Reuther's *Ocheidir* in several significant ways. For one, as she was not an architect and no doubt found the task of drawing and planning architectural features challenging, she endeavoured to compensate for this weakness by producing extensive photographic records of Ukhaidir's many structural features. She took something in the range of 164 photographs of the palace in 1909 and 1911, of which about 87 were included in her final report, and they enhance her architectural descriptions considerably, clarifying the manner and appearance of certain architectural features and providing an incontestable record of their state when she observed them. Bell rightly remarks:

> Accurate reproduction of detail is of the highest value, and one good photograph of a dome that stands is worth a thousand conjectures after it has fallen. It is therefore essential that those who have the opportunity of visiting ancient monuments should spare no pains in making a careful record of structural methods, and, judging from my own experience, however lavish they may be in the taking of photographs, they will always have subsequent occasion to wish that they had been more lavish still.[85]

Bell, however, was not simply satisfied by the task of producing a careful, detailed report of what she had seen and recorded. She was more ambitious than Reuther in that she wished to be able to *explain* Ukhaidir. She wanted to know who had occupied the palace, the date of its construction, and the range of architectural inspirations from both East and West that had affected its construction and end appearance. She was ultimately interested in Ukhaidir's place in the history of the architecture of the Near East and the Mediterranean world, and its relation to the cultural, religious and political developments of Late Antiquity and the Islamic period. To fulfil these ambitious aims, Bell felt the need to carry out research beyond Ukhaidir itself, incorporating not only information that she already had gained – in large part through her study of Late Antique ecclesiastical architecture – but also more recently acquired information from other Near Eastern archaeological and architectural reports. She also solicited the expertise and opinions of scholars working on the same issues and geographical region, to provide the most reliable, up-to-date reconstruction.

Fig. 3.15 Reuther's reconstruction of the Court of Honour, facing the northern gateway block. The northern façade, as also observed by Bell, had a second storey consisting of arched recesses, each separated from one another by piers made of clustered columns, while the arches themselves were decorated in plaster with a scalloped or lobed pattern similar to that which exists over the doors of the mosque. Within each of the arched recesses were two levels of blind niches. The upper storey was plain, with only two arched openings giving onto interior courts, while the top consisted of a band of shallow arched niches.

Bell's Architectural Analyses and Dating of Ukhaidir

Bell's first architectural investigations of Ukhaidir, which resulted in her proposal for the date of the palace, focused principally on several distinctive architectural features, which included its vaulting, the construction and employment of domed spaces, the use of masonry tubes and the presence of a mosque. These features were explored first in Bell's scholarly article 'The Vaulting System of Ukheidar', published in the *Journal of Hellenic Studies* in 1910.[86] The features subsequently formed the basis for further investigations of Ukhaidir that took place after Bell's second visit, in 1911, and were incorporated and expanded upon in her final publication on Ukhaidir, which appeared in 1914. Bell's observations and findings concerning these features are discussed briefly here, with special emphasis on their contribution to the dating and identity of Ukhaidir. Further research by Bell – which endeavoured to situate Ukhaidir temporally within the wider tradition of Near Eastern palatial constructions and summoned comparable materials from Mesopotamia and beyond – will be described in a later chapter after further investigations by Bell, both in the field and at home, have been considered.

Vaults

The vault, an architectural feature that abounds at Ukhaidir, was used to cover the majority of spaces within the palace, from the smallest galleries and narrow corridors to the grandest of hallways, such as the Great Hall (no. 7) with its impressive, intact, seven-metre-wide brick vault (Fig. 3.16), and the principal *iwan* (no. 29), the palace's ceremonial focal point. Bell observed that while much of the construction of the vaults in the Ukhaidir castle had been accomplished with uncut stones laid in a thick bed of mortar, some of the finer vaults, such as the Great Hall, had been built of brick tiles.[87]

Whichever material was used, Bell observed that the vaults had all been constructed using a time-honoured Mesopotamian technique known as the pitched vault. Such a construction was favourable because it was quite stable and did not require the placement of wooden centring beams in the vaults during the erection process, a quality much appreciated in timber-poor Mesopotamia.[88] Relying on A. Choisy and other earlier scholars' descriptions of the pitched vault technique, Bell describes the construction as often (but not always) consisting of walls that were first corbelled inwards on either side so as to reduce the space to be vaulted. Thus, the first few courses of brick or stone in the vault would have been laid lengthways, with each course receiving a slight inward projection. Above this, the bricks were set upright in concentric courses, or slices, thus forming the curve of the vault. The bricks were leaned at an angle against the head-wall at the back of the hall, so that each course of brick adhered to the course before it by means of a fast-drying mortar (Fig. 3.17). Slanting the bricks ensured that the succeeding course did not slip off before the mortar dried, and in this way the vault could be built without wooden centring beams. The result was a vault of ovoid or elliptical curve.[89] Bell noted that this technique of vault construction could be seen in buildings dating to the earlier Sasanian period. In particular, she observed such vaults set on slightly inwardly projecting courses of brick in the side chambers of the Taq-i Kisra at Ctesiphon.[90] The great vault of the Taq-i Kisra itself, which spans over 25 metres, was constructed using the same technique, although in this case there are no observable inwardly projecting courses to support it.[91]

Bell placed the origins of the vault technique back in the much earlier periods of Mesopotamian history, where it regularly appeared in brick.[92] In addition to its appearance among the Assyrian brick tombs at Assur, she reports a barrel vault with a span of four metres, found in the gateway of Sargon's Assyrian palace at Khorsabad and dating back to the eighth century BCE.[93] Actually, we now know that this type of construction dates even earlier in Mesopotamia. Vaults of pitched brick have been encountered at Tell al-Rimah in northern Mesopotamia, for example, the earliest examples dating back to around 2000 BCE.[94] They have also been found over brick drainage pits at Khafajeh and in Isin-Larsa levels at Nippur.[95] Whatever the precise date of the

Fig. 3.16 Bell's photograph of the pitched brick vaulted ceiling of the Great Hall in Ukhaidir's palace, looking south into the Court of Honour, where Bell made her camp during her visit to the site in 1911.

pitched brick vault's first appearance, current evidence does suggest that it originated in ancient Mesopotamia, and that by emphasizing these earlier instances, Bell correctly traced the vaults at Ukhaidir – not back to some Western architectural tradition but back to their direct ancestors in Iraq.

Besides the employment of pitched brick vaulting, Bell observed another distinctive vault construction at Ukhaidir, this taking the form of an intersecting or 'groin' vault. Bell noted eight examples at Ukhaidir, these occurring in the corners of Corridor 28, where the barrel-vaulted spaces meet at right angles. They also appear in the middle of the east and west arms of Corridor 28, where they were set between two transverse arches, and in Vestibule 61, the southern continuation of the corridor as it enters into the suite of rooms centred on Courts D and E.[96] Finally, she observed a groin vault in the square Room 141 of the East Annex.[97] These distinctive groin vaults were constructed of stone slabs cut to resemble the shape of bricks, the exception being the vault in Vestibule 61, which was actually made of bricks.[98] All of the vaults, regardless of their materials, were characterized by vertical courses, laid with a slight backwards inclination against the head wall or transverse arch and emanating from horizontally laid, corbelled springers that spanned the corners of the spaces to be covered (Fig. 3.18).[99] The groin vaults demanded little or no centring, and once constructed, they were covered over with plaster (Fig. 3.19).[100]

According to Bell, the groin vault originated to the west – first in Asia Minor (Anatolia) as early as the second century BCE – but developed more boldly in

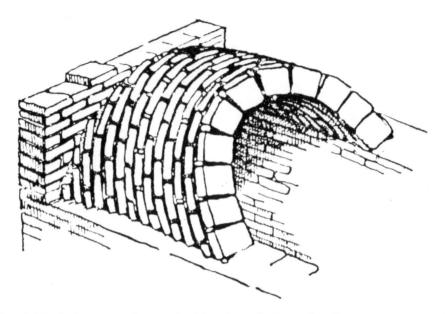

Fig. 3.17 A drawing of a pitched brick vault from the Neo-Assyrian site of Khorsabad, showing how each course of bricks was leaned at an angle against the head-wall of the room, providing the necessary support for the next course. This same time-honoured Mesopotamian tradition of vault construction was also employed within the palace at Ukhaidir, as observed by Bell.

Rome after that.[101] Its prolific presence is well documented in Constantinople during the Byzantine Era of the sixth century CE.[102] Nevertheless, it appears to have been unknown in Sasanian architecture further to the east.[103] This factor made Bell increasingly doubtful of a Sasanian date for Ukhaidir's construction, although many of her contemporaries, including the French scholar Marcel Dieulafoy, preferred this early period. Dieulafoy, a leading expert on Sasanian art and architecture who had excavated and recorded a great number of Sasanian-dated monuments in Persia, argued in a letter to Bell that the groin vault was the product of the many expeditions that Sasanian rulers had made around the eastern shores of the Mediterranean up to the beginning of the seventh century, and their exposure to the cultural traditions of Greece and Rome.[104] Bell, however, preferred hard physical evidence to this kind of conjecture, and for this reason she placed considerable stock in the work of A. Choisy, who had argued for an Islamic Umayyad date for the first appearance of the groined vault in Syria, based on his own survey of its known occurrences from this period.[105] Other data supporting an early Islamic date for the introduction of the groined vault, as reported by Bell, included its appearance at the hunting lodge of Qasr 'Amra on the western side of the Syrian desert (in present-day Jordan), just recently investigated in Bell's time and dated to the caliphs of the Umayyad Era in the first half of the eighth century.[106] Significantly, there is still no justification for the groin vault's presence in Sasanian-period architecture, underlining the reliability of some of Bell's early convictions concerning the spread and date of this distinctive feature in the East and her ultimate assertion that its appearance at Ukhaidir indicates an Islamic date for the complex.[107]

Domed Spaces

Considering when Bell's discussion of domed spaces was written, its depth and accuracy is considerable and its contribution to an understanding of Ukhaidir's architectural influences is not insignificant. Domed spaces were used sparingly at Ukhaidir. One dome, which is fluted on the interior and may have had an aperture at its summit, covers the small chamber (Room 4) between the North Gate and the Great Hall (Fig. 3.20).[108] Although not preserved, it is likely that a dome also covered the space (no. 27) between the Great Hall and the Court of Honour.[109] Last, Bell observed that the tower chambers in the *chemin de ronde* of the outer enclosure wall, none of which were found intact, were covered with ovoid domes.[110] Bell perceptively noted that many other spaces in the castle could have been domed, but instead the architect covered the space with barrel or groin vaults.[111] Moreover, of the spaces that *are* domed, none is particularly large – i.e., none is wider than about 3.1 metres.[112] Both of these facts suggest that the Ukhaidir builders were neither sufficiently experienced nor confident in their dome construction skills to make the dome a prolific element of the castle's architecture.

Bell's discussion probes the use of domed spaces in history, particularly from the perspective of the Near East and the development of the technology of dome construction through time in this part of the world. She points to early Mesopotamian examples of the dome, including an Assyrian carved relief image from the Kuyunjik mound at Nineveh, showing domed buildings dating back to the seventh century BCE.[113] She is probably correct to liken some of these Assyrian examples to contemporary mudbrick beehive houses known from parts of northern Syria and northern Mesopotamia, where the covered spaces are built of 'oversailing rings', or corbelling, and not true domes.[114] One may add to Bell's repertoire of Mesopotamian domes several other early examples encountered in excavations in parts of Mesopotamia over the past 100 years, some even going back into prehistory, but it remains to be proven that anything but small spaces were ever covered by such features.[115] Like vaults, domes over large spaces – such as would occur in monumental palaces or temples, for example – do not seem to have been present in ancient Mesopotamia.

Bell's discussion of Near Eastern domes relies on some of her earlier observations of such features, the product of her investigations of ecclesiastical

Fig. 3.18   Bell's photograph of the remains of a groin vault, located in the north-western corner of Room 141 in the East Annex. The corbelled springer in the corner is still preserved, although the rest of the groin has fallen in.

architecture in Anatolia, much of which appears in the 1909 work *The Thousand and One Churches*.[116] She brings in the evidence from the western part of the Near East, mainly the coastlands of Anatolia, where architects began to consider more seriously solutions for setting a spherical roof elegantly over a square plan. They accomplished this by introducing spherical pendentives, these basically consisting of curved triangular pieces of brick or stone masonry that rise up from the corners of a square substructure, transforming its angles into a circle upon which the dome can be set. Bell conjectures that the earliest examples of domes with pendentives date back even before the Age of Constantine (i.e., earlier than the third century CE), but that they became prolific in Western Anatolia and Syria in the Byzantine period of the sixth century and found their truest and most magnificent expression in the form of the massive dome of Justinian's Santa Sophia in Constantinople.[117] Bell also refers to an often cited dome at Jerash (in present-day Jordan) as a very early domed space with pendentives from Syria, although she hesitates to identify it with the

Fig. 3.19 Bell's photograph of the groin vault in the north-east angle of Corridor 28, with its plaster still intact. These types of intersecting vaults are rare at Ukhaidir, only appearing in eight examples in the palace and adjoining Eastern Annex.

pre-Christian Era; rather, she believes that it should be contemporary with Justinian's examples from Constantinople.[118]

In contrast to domes set on pendentives, Bell describes what she refers to as a more primitive form of dome construction, this prevalent among the inland Anatolian structures she had investigated, and dating to the fourth and fifth centuries.[119] Quite simply, the rectangular base of the space below was transformed into an octagon by placing horizontal brackets ('corbel stones') across the corners, and from this setting it was possible to construct a circular dome.[120] This type of dome construction remained quite prevalent in inner Anatolia and elsewhere in the inland parts of the Near East for several centuries.[121]

In addition to her examination of the Western development of the dome, Bell endeavoured to track the history of the dome in the East. In Persia, the Sasanians had arrived at their own solution for constructing a dome over a rectangular base. This involved using squinches, these being arched niches set over the corners of a room, serving to transform the angles into curves and thus allowing for the placement of the dome above.[122] Squinches enabled Sasanian builders to throw

Fig. 3.20 Bell's photograph of the south-western corner of the fluted dome in Room 4. The dome may have been originally furnished with a circular aperture at its apex. One can see the somewhat primitive way in which the dome has been set on brackets in the corners of the square room rather than with squinches or pendentives, which would have transformed the angles of the room into the curves of the dome more elegantly.

their domes over a span of up to 16 metres, a technique that can be observed at the site of Firuzabad, the earliest of the Sasanian palaces, and at Sarvistan, which was in Bell's time widely regarded as a good example of a Sasanian structure from the fifth century CE.[123] Bell also conjectured that several of the spaces within the 'small' and 'large' palaces at Qasr-i-Shirin also presumed to be of Sasanian date (the Palace of Khosrow and the Chehar Qapu), although no longer intact, had been domed with the use of squinches and had spanned up to 16 metres.[124]

When Ukhaidir's evidence for domes was considered in light of this amassed data, Bell noted that it could not be compared easily to the domes of the palaces to the east. While it is certainly true that Ukhaidir's architects were familiar with squinches, they never used them to construct true overhead domes. Rather, squinches were only employed to resolve angles between barrel vaults or corners.[125] One can observe such use, for example, in a corner of the second-storey gallery (no. 134) overlooking Court A at the north end of the castle (Fig. 3.21).[126] There are also examples of squinches in the southern arcade of Ukhaidir's mosque (no. 11), where they occur in the corners of semi-domes set between transverse ribs. One particularly well-preserved squinch in the mosque arcade is decorated with a fluted stucco pattern, flanked by shallow pointed niches (calottes), while above are concentrically recessed rosettes and crenellated brick patterns.[127] So there was certainly knowledge of the use of the squinch, whose idea the Ukhaidir architects may have borrowed from the architectural traditions of the East, but they do not seem to have been confident enough in their own skills to use the squinch to build true domes – certainly none with the wide spans of the monumental Eastern palaces.[128]

Of the domes at Ukhaidir, none exhibits the technique emanating from the West, described earlier, in which spherical pendentives rise from the corners of the angled spaces, allowing for the placement of a circular dome above. The Ukhaidir fluted dome depended instead on horizontal slabs placed obliquely across the corners of the square rooms, the other technique that we know emanated from the western part of the Near East but which is seen as a more primitive type of dome placement and figures prolifically in the earlier fourth- and fifth-century churches of inner Anatolia.[129] This feature might tempt one to postulate an early date for the domes of Ukhaidir as well, and yet geographical distance is conceivably the explanation: perhaps Western techniques had not yet reached the architects of Iraq.[130] In the end, the presence of the domes and squinches did not help Bell to fix a more precise date for the construction of Ukhaidir, but in the process of discussing these features, their points of origin and their specific manifestations within the palace, Bell drew attention to the complex, multi-directional nature of the inspiration and influences working upon its architecture. The recognition of Ukhaidir's multifarious character is quite significant; scholars both contemporary with and later than Bell frequently emphasize this diversity in the art and architecture of the Early Islamic period.[131]

Masonry Tubes

One other item relating to Bell's observations of the vaulting at Ukhaidir concerns somewhat unusual but practical features that occur several times, and which Bell describes as masonry tubes. They are hollow, vaulted galleries that run between adjacent chambers with parallel barrel vaults of the same height, as well as between vaults and straight walls.[132] The openings of these tubes are located high up in the spandrels between vaulted spaces, and their ends can often be seen in the façades of open courts, such as those of the *iwan* groups within the *baits* on the main floor of the palace (Fig. 3.22), and also in the façades of the *iwan* groups facing the open courtyard on the third storey of Ukhaidir's gatehouse.[133] The function of these hollow tubes would have been to relieve the enormous weight of the stone masonry of the vaults, although Bell suggests that they might also have served to keep the rooms cool by providing a belt of unheated air along the vaults.[134] For parallels to these tubes, Bell mentions their early presence at the Parthian site of Hatra, where they appear in some of the tombs.[135] On the other

Fig. 3.21 Squinch in one corner of Gallery 134 on the second storey of the palace's northern gateway block.

hand, Bell sighted masonry tubes at the thirteenth-century Khan Khernina above Tekrit and noted that this architectural tradition must have carried on for quite some time among Islamic builders.[136] She also suggests that these openings formed an essential part of the Islamic façade, transforming, for example, into windows and niches on either sides of arches in the façades of the mosque of Ibn Tulun in Cairo and the mosque of Abu Dulaf at Samarra.[137] In all, the presence of masonry tubes connected Ukhaidir to earlier supposed Sasanian antecedents, but to Bell it also underlined their continuing ubiquity in the early Islamic architecture of Mesopotamia, a period of which she was slowly taking greater notice as she considered Ukhaidir's architectural features as a whole and noted the great number of parallels they had to the structural attributes of that time.

Ukhaidir's Mosque
The north-western corner of the Ukhaidir palace – with its unique arrangement of open court and arcades decorated with stucco ornament, and doors framed

by elaborate cusped patterns – marked this section as special and distinctive. Bell's diary and letters of 1909, when she first visited Ukhaidir, provide no conjecture about this area, but already in her first scholarly publication on Ukhaidir, which appeared in early 1910, she raises the possibility that this might have been a mosque.[138] Significantly, the German scholar Ernst Herzfeld was quite struck by Bell's suggestion, reasserting this identity in his own article later in 1910, a piece on the date of the palace of Mshatta in the western Syrian desert. A similarly placed chamber in the Mshatta palace had led Herzfeld to conjecture the presence of a mosque there as well, thus suggesting an Islamic date for both desert palaces.[139] The only difference was that a niche in the south wall of the Mshatta chamber – ostensibly a *mihrab* – further strengthened its identity as a mosque, whereas this detail had not been reported at Ukhaidir.[140] In *Amurath to Amurath*, Bell returned to the issue of the identity of the north-western sector of Ukhaidir, offering a mosque as a possible function and citing Herzfeld's own findings, as well as his agreement with this idea.[141] But it seems that she was still undecided on the matter at this point, for alongside her suggestion of an early Islamic date for the time of Ukhaidir's construction she also offered an earlier Sasanian date.[142]

Not until Bell's final report on Ukhaidir, which appeared in 1914, did she put in print her absolute certainty about the matter. The reason: in the spring of 1910, Bell asked a French architect by the name of Henri Viollet, who was about to embark on a trip to Mesopotamia, to visit Ukhaidir and, while there, clear away the rubble from the centre of the south wall of the cloistered hall to see whether he could find a *mihrab* niche.[143] From one of Bell's letters to her mother, dated 5 January 1911, we know that it was while dining with Viollet and his wife in Paris upon the Frenchman's return from Mesopotamia that he told her news of his investigation at Ukhaidir. He had indeed found a concave *mihrab* in the place where she had told him to look (Fig. 3.23)! Bell's suggestion that this was a mosque and that Ukhaidir was Islamic in date was now firmly secured.[144] Interestingly, this was not the first time Bell had made a positive identification of a mosque. In the course of Ramsay and Bell's investigations of an early antique church at Binbirkilise in Anatolia in 1907, Bell recognized that a stepped platform in the church – previously regarded as a pulpit – was actually an Islamic *minbar*, and she then cleared away the wall beside it to reveal the *mihrab*. These features made it evident that the church had been converted into a mosque at some point. We are told that both Ramsay and the local Muslim workmen were deeply impressed and delighted by this discovery.[145]

The Proposed Date of Ukhaidir and Its Builder

While several scholars postulated dates for Ukhaidir after its details had been published, Bell was among the first to submit the most plausible date, in light of her own investigations and careful research. In his later report, Creswell details

Fig. 3.22   South side of central Court B in one of the *baits* along the eastern side of the palace, showing masonry tubes beside the central arched doorway into an *iwan* room (no. 48). Many of these masonry tubes likely would have been covered over with plaster.

the various deliberations over Ukhaidir's dating.[146] We need not repeat these data here, save to remark that many scholars, including L. Massignon and M. Dieulafoy, continued even into the 1920s to argue strenuously for a Sasanian sixth-century or early seventh-century date. Bell, meanwhile, had already insisted in 1914 that it must be Islamic and thus be dated after the Hijra (622 CE), given that one sector of the palace functioned as a mosque. Moreover, the finding of a concave *mihrab* suggested a date after 709 CE, when the first *mihrab* of this type appeared in the mosque at the prophet's home of Medina.[147]

It remained for Bell to decide precisely when in the Islamic period Ukhaidir's construction and occupation should be placed. Her copying and translation of an Arabic graffito, which was discovered in the passageway between Rooms 44 and 45 in the palace, offered few clues.[148] Assisted by two German Arabists, Bernhard Moritz and Enno Littmann, she determined the graffito to have been written around 1369–78 CE. The inscription reports the use of the well at Ukhaidir but does not give any indication as to the date of the structure's creation or its original owner.[149]

Ultimately, Bell appears to have stood by a date early in the Abbasid period, around the middle of the eighth century CE. Her reason for not placing the complex any later concerned the nature of the arches. While most were slightly pointed, a few examples were round, hearkening back to an earlier Sasanian tradition. This differed from the arches at Samarra, confidently dated by Herzfeld and others to the Abbasid period of al-Mansur in the late eighth century, which are all of the pointed variety. Ukhaidir's architects, therefore, had not adopted the widespread tradition of pointed arches, and thus had to have been designing them at a slightly earlier date.[150]

As for the identity of the individual who built Ukhaidir, Bell looked to the writings of the historian Yaqut, who mentions that a certain Isa ibn Ali ibn Abdullah, the great-uncle of the Abbasid caliph al-Mansur, had been responsible for demolishing a building in the desert called Qasr al-Muqatil and then subsequently rebuilding it.[151] She proposed that the newly rebuilt Qasr al-Muqatil was her Ukhaidir, and that its construction would have occurred around the middle of the eighth century (*c.*750 CE).[152]

Creswell had a different idea about the castle's builder and about the date. He noted, like Bell, that some of the architectural features, such as the concave *mihrab*, place its construction after 709 CE. He agreed with Bell that the pointed arch was not fully established at Ukhaidir, whereas it was at Samarra by around 849 CE. Thus, Ukhaidir must be earlier than this date. Creswell remarks that historically, the Abbasid caliphs did not lead the semi-nomadic lives of their Umayyad predecessors, who built residences for themselves on the Syrian side of the desert. On the contrary, they were town-dwellers and resided, at least after 764 CE, at Baghdad. Nevertheless, it was conceivable to consider other individuals from this general time period, and in this light Creswell proposes that Isa ibn Musa (ibn Ali ibn Abd Allah ibn Abbas), the nephew of as-Saffah and al-Mansur, was the builder of Ukhaidir.[153] Once the heir apparent to al-Mansur, Isa received a generous financial compensation for renouncing his claim to the throne and retired from public life around 775 CE. It is said that Isa retired to his estates, where he lived in complete isolation, 'only riding to Kufa once a week, during two months of the year to attend Friday prayers'.[154] As Creswell argues, Ukhaidir would fit Isa perfectly, as the palace could only have been built by a man with such wealth, and Isa is the only Abbasid prince known to have lived in isolation.[155] Furthermore, Ukhaidir's distance from Kufa is only around 80 km, which could have been covered in two stages, especially if one considers the use of the site of Khan 'Atshan as a resting post, given its location almost exactly halfway between Ukhaidir and Kufa.[156]

The precise identity of Ukhaidir's builder has not yet been confirmed, although many scholars continue to follow Creswell's highly plausible scheme

Fig. 3.23 Bell's photograph of the southern side of the mosque, the vaulting almost entirely fallen except for the south-western and south-eastern corners. In the centre of the south wall further down, peeking just above the pile of debris, is the semi-dome of the mosque's *mihrab*.

Fig. 3.24 The eastern façade of Ukhaidir's outer enclosure wall, with its blind arches set between semi-round and round towers. Bell's shadow figures prominently in the foreground centre of the photo.

and date.[157] Significant, however, is a different reconstruction, presented by Barbara Finster and Jürgen Schmidt. In the 1970s they undertook survey work in the desert east of Kerbela and probed in particular the ruins of Tulul al-Ukhaidir, a site only about 2.5 km to the north of Ukhaidir.[158] Following the earlier work of Werner Caskel,[159] their postulated reconstruction identifies Tulul al-Ukhaidir as Qasr Bani Muqatil, which was first built in the middle of the sixth century CE.[160] In the later Abbasid period, around 762 CE, Isa ibn Ali, the uncle of as-Saffah, pulled down the castle and rebuilt the new Qasr Muqatil at Ukhaidir.[161] One can see by this reconstruction that it nicely concurs with Bell's own attribution of Ukhaidir to Isa ibn Ali and her proposal that it was the rebuilt Qasr Muqatil, even if she knew nothing about the remains of the earlier Tulul al-Ukhaidir nearby. As remarked above, Ukhaidir's precise date and identity still cannot be established, but it is worth seeing that Bell's guesswork on these important issues falls closely in line with that of more recent scholars.

Assessment of Bell's Architectural Study of Ukhaidir, and Concluding Remarks

More will be said about the overall reception of Bell's work on the palace and mosque of Ukhaidir once her discussion of this complex as well as her consideration of the origins and evolution of the early Islamic palace in their entirety is discussed in Chapter 5. For now, suffice to say that her analysis of Ukhaidir's features such as vaults and domes, and her positive identification of the complex's mosque, was generally well received by many of her scholarly peers. Reuther, although producing his own work on Ukhaidir, acknowledged Bell's research of the site, including her correct identification of a mosque,[162] as did Herzfeld, who included her mosque proposal in his own brilliant article on the development of early Islamic art and architecture and the dating of Mshatta.[163] Slightly later, Creswell would himself visit the desert castle four times between 1930 and 1936 and produce his own detailed measurements, plan and photographs, all of which appeared as a full description and analysis in the second volume of his exhaustive *Early Muslim Architecture*.[164] Creswell's description would also appear, in an abridged format, in his *A Short Account of Early Islamic Architecture*.[165] Both would essentially become the standard references on Ukhaidir and are to this day the sources most frequently cited by scholars and students who have an interest in the desert castle and its place within the development of the architecture of the early Islamic period. Yet despite the publicity afforded to Creswell, the details he offers about Ukhaidir are essentially a synthetic treatment of the work presented earlier by Reuther and Bell. Creswell makes liberal use of Reuther's drawings and reconstructions and recounts the latter's fine points about various architectural forms and their methods of construction.[166] From Bell's work Creswell copies her discussion of the domed spaces and groined vaults within the palace,[167] her identification and suggested function of the masonry tubes,[168] her identification of the palace's mosque,[169] and her comparison of the layout and architectural features of Ukhaidir to those from Mar Tahmazgerd in Kirkuk, Firuzabad, Ctesiphon, Qasr-i-Shirin and Sarvistan.[170] Bell's erudite observations about pitched brick vaults, domes and pendentives are repeated in other sections of Creswell's work.[171] In sum, in its substance and organization, Creswell's treatment of Ukhaidir and his work on early Islamic architecture in general owes a tremendous debt to his predecessors, especially Bell.

By today's standards, it has to be admitted that Bell's description and architectural analysis of Ukhaidir falls rather short of what is expected of a comprehensive archaeological report. Particularly notable is its heavy emphasis on the layout and architectural forms of the castle at the expense of other recoverable artefacts, such as pottery, coins and other metal items, animal bones, botanical remains and micromorphological samples. It is certain that these types of evidence could have provided further valuable information about the life of the Ukhaidir complex, especially highlighting the particular activities that went on in and around the palace. We know that Bell, in the brief time that she was actually present at Ukhaidir, had neither the time nor the inclination to excavate or collect such artefactual material; her focus was almost strictly on what could be discerned of the complex's standing remains – namely, its architecture.

What seems especially missing from Bell's description of Ukhaidir (and from Reuther's and Creswell's accounts as well, for that matter) is a human element. With so much emphasis on brick constructions, domes, arches and vaults, it is as if Bell and the others had forgotten to consider at length the actual people who inhabited this desert complex. To be sure, Bell muses, somewhat romantically, on the ancient prince who inhabited this place, but she falls short of any serious considerations of what this individual, along with his court and entourage, did in its spaces, and how they experienced this marvellous place. How was their behaviour guided by the way in which Ukhaidir was laid out, furnished and adorned? Moreover, how did these things affect and direct their interactions with one another? The recent past's special emphasis on natural and built spaces, and of humans' experience with such spaces – often facilitated through digital technologies such as 3-D renderings, computer animations and virtual reality – would seem to be a particularly effective means of getting at those considerations, bringing the inhabitants of Ukhaidir back into their remarkable built space.[172]

At the same time, it would be wrong to overly disparage Bell's study, especially when one considers the context and time period in which it was carried out and its worth compared to other archaeological works that were being produced at approximately the same time. As reported already, Bell's study of Ukhaidir, with its attention to architectural details that were carefully described, measured, drawn and photographed, was equal to or in some ways exceeded the types of archaeological reports that her contemporaries were producing. Moreover, Bell's detailed observations and conclusions about the origins and development of the pitched brick vault, widely used at Ukhaidir, along with the presence of groin vaults, squinches, domes and masonry tubes, not only helped her and others to formulate a plausible date for Ukhaidir's construction, but also provided insight into the directions from which architectural traditions spread and evolved in late antique and early Islamic Mesopotamia. Bell's work on Ukhaidir was further enhanced by her brilliant identification of a mosque in the palace, along with her historical knowledge of the Sasanian and Early Islamic periods, which helped her to propose a possible builder for the palace and its true identity. In all, Bell's study of Ukhaidir was a remarkable achievement for its time, highlighting well the facility with which she was able to tackle and successfully present a complex, challenging archaeological subject.

Bell only returned to Ukhaidir once more in her later years, despite having become a resident of Baghdad and being well familiar with the countryside of southern Iraq. Moreover, there was now the convenience of a short motorcar trip to Ukhaidir, which compared comfortably to the long, dusty days on horses and camels that had defined her first expeditions to the desert palace. Bell made the final trip to Ukhaidir in April 1925, accompanied by companions from Baghdad, including her close friend and confidant, Ken Cornwallis. Despite her excitement to see Ukhaidir, however, the trip was a somewhat melancholy experience: additional parts of the palace had fallen in since her last visit, 14 years earlier, and she felt rather ghostlike to be there again, given the sad times that had elapsed in the interval.[173] Bell expresses a similar melancholy attitude in an earlier letter, written in 1921, when she passed through the town of Hit, the place from which she had first ventured into the western desert to seek Ukhaidir back in 1909. She recalls wistfully her earlier adventures:

> to me it's too full of the memory of rollicking journeys, of ghosts, which were once me, riding about on camels, before the world which was my world crashed together and foundered. I don't think I'll go there again. I don't like the look of those ghosts – they are too happy and confident. It's I who feel a ghost beside them.[174]

Bell's discovery and investigations of Ukhaidir seemed to hold in her memory a profound sweetness and somewhat naive, cheerful expectation that contrasted sharply with her later life and its graver professional achievements, as well as her sobering personal setbacks and heartbreak. After the bittersweet tone of these later reminiscences, it is heartening to return to the concluding lines of the preface to her 1914 monograph on Ukhaidir, which nicely reflect Bell's early captivation with the desert edifice:

> A subject so enchanting and so suggestive as the palace of Ukhaidir is not likely to present itself more than once in a lifetime, and as I bring this page to a close I call to mind the amazement with which I first gazed upon its formidable walls; the romance of my first sojourn within its precincts; the

pleasure, undiminished by familiarity, of my return; and the regret with which I sent back across the sun-drenched plain a last greeting to its distant presence. The unknown prince at whose bidding its solitary magnificence rose out of the desert, the unknown lords who dwelt in its courts, cannot at the time of its full splendour have gloried and rejoiced in their handiwork and their inheritance more than I who have known it only in decay; and, in the spirit, I part from it now with as much unwillingness as that which I experienced when I withdrew, further and further, from its actual protection.[175]

CHAPTER 4

ENCOUNTERS IN THE HEART OF MESOPOTAMIA

Fresh from the excitement of her scientific discovery of Ukhaidir, Gertrude Bell now embarked on the next important phase of her 1909 journey. Her route would take her into the heart of the Tigris and Euphrates alluvial plains of southern Mesopotamia, where she would encounter a host of ruined mounds and monuments testifying to the once-glorious civilizations that existed here in the ancient past. This region had given birth to some of the world's earliest cities and writing systems over 4,000 years ago. It had seen the rise and fall of kingdoms and empires. It had witnessed the exploits of charismatic rulers and conquerors, and had inspired generations of writers, poets and artists to commemorate the deeds of their nations' leaders, both great and grievous, through monumental, and sometimes poignant, works of art.

Bell's journey through southern Mesopotamia would expose her to all of these things. She visited the sites that had once served as the capitals of the Babylonians, Assyrians, Sasanians and Abbasids, and she often had the good fortune to experience, first-hand, efforts on the part of archaeologists to recover the art and architecture of those cities. Through her visits and the exchanges she had with other scholars who shared her fascination with the past, she developed a sophisticated understanding of the progress of human history through the ages and an appreciation for the best methods of recovering and chronicling its rich past. Bell's experience in southern Mesopotamia would have a lasting impact on her life and work. It would help her especially to refine her notions about the development of art and architecture in early Islam, and of Ukhaidir's place in this period of continuity and transformation. It broadened her connections within the scholarly world of ancient Near Eastern studies as a whole. It also instilled in her the importance of preserving the past through a careful program of archaeological recovery, documentation and conservation of ancient ruins for the benefit of future generations. All of these experiences would factor into Bell's later life, both in her scholarly achievements and in her future activities in the new country of Iraq.

Babylon

On 1 April 1909, having finished her records at Ukhaidir, Bell journeyed out of the desert and headed towards the Euphrates River. Her destination now was a group of mounds that make up the ancient city of Babylon. Bell's knowledge of its rich history made her eager to visit the site. Babylon was, after all, one of the most famous and frequently reported cities of the ancient world, documented by Classical authors as the place of the wondrous Hanging Gardens, and by the Bible as the location of the Tower of Babel and palace of the tyrannical King Nebuchadnezzar. But Bell's curiosity in Babylon was piqued by another factor as well: she knew that the ancient city's newest explorers, a team of German archaeologists, had been digging there since 1899. By 1909, they had brought to life many important aspects of the great city, and she hoped that they would be able to give her a personal tour of these discoveries.

Bell reached the German *Expeditionshaus*, which was nestled among a grove of date palms by the banks of the Euphrates. She was disappointed to learn that the expedition's director, Robert Koldewey, was unable to see her. Apparently Koldewey had taken ill, the price of his tireless energy working at the site – in particular, of toiling through the previous summer's punishingly hot months.[1] Nonetheless, she was received most kindly by Koldewey's assistants, Herr Buddensieg and Herr Wetzel, and shown to a lovely room in the house, with her servants camped comfortably beneath her windows under the palm trees (Fig. 4.1).[2] For Bell, this was to be the first of several visits to the dig-house at Babylon and its German archaeologists. In March 1911, after her second inspection of Ukhaidir, she returned to Babylon once more, this time received warmly by a healthy Koldewey. Later still, in the spring of 1914, she came to see Koldewey shortly after the conclusion of her journey to Arabia.[3] For Bell, her visits to Babylon were always exceedingly pleasant. Her diaries and letters report her delight at the clean, cool comforts of the dig-house, and the gracious, intellectually stimulating company of her German hosts.[4] Later, during World War I, when Bell was able to make frequent trips to Babylon from Baghdad, she would recall the pleasantness of her time with the Germans: 'They were all so kind to me, the German excavators, and no war can put an end to the affectionate esteem in which I hold Koldewey.'[5]

All of Bell's writings make it clear that she was particularly impressed with Koldewey, whom she found charming as a person,[6] and whose tireless efforts to make sense of the remains of this enormous site, where many of his predecessors had failed,[7] left a tremendous impression upon her (Fig. 4.2). To be sure, Koldewey was an experienced and skilled archaeologist. Trained in architecture and archaeology, by the time of his work at Babylon Koldewey had gained

Fig. 4.1 Gertrude Bell standing outside one of her tents at Babylon in April 1909.

much experience in the Mediterranean regions and the Near East. He had assisted with the German excavations of several sites in Greece, Sicily and Anatolia.[8] Koldewey had also excavated briefly at two large Sumerian-period tells in southern Mesopotamia (Surghul and Al Hiba, in 1887), where he had acquired the invaluable experience of uncovering and carefully tracing the remains of

Fig. 4.2 Bell's photo of Babylon's excavation director, Robert Koldewey, sitting on the upper balcony of the German dig-house during her visit in April 1914.

sun-dried brickwork.[9] His skill with mudbrick proved to be of the utmost importance for successfully excavating the mounds of Babylon, as much of the site's ancient architecture was composed of walls of crude sun-dried bricks. Such material had often eluded earlier excavators because of its close resemblance to the colour and texture of the earth fill that covered it.[10] Koldewey ensured that his workmen at Babylon were carefully trained in the art of tracing mudbrick, and having gained mastery over this excavation technique, they were able to delineate accurately the masses of brickwork that made up much of Babylon's ancient structures.

Koldewey's project was, without question, highly ambitious. Finding Babylon's buildings to be deeply buried, often under up to 21 m of soil, he employed between 200 and 250 workmen at any given time, and excavations were conducted over several months each year. The work continued between 1899 and 1917.[11] Attention was paid not only to the articulation of structures from one time period, but to evidence for progress through time, such as the construction of higher foundations, new floor pavements, changes in brick dimensions and new stamped brick inscriptions.[12] All of these important temporal observations he fastidiously recorded. Most importantly, Koldewey aimed to produce meticulously detailed architectural plans of the uncovered structures at Babylon, level by level, and this required countless hours of careful planning by him and his German assistants.[13] Thanks to these massive efforts, Koldewey was able to recover a great deal of Babylon's gates, defences, temples, palaces, streets and houses, and understand changes in these features through time. These findings were all carefully recorded and photographed, and the resulting plans produced by the German team are still considered masterful in their detail and completeness (Fig. 4.3).[14] Altogether, Koldewey's work at Babylon signified a radical transformation in the aims and objectives of Near Eastern archaeology. Excavation now became less concerned with the discovery of treasures and tablets, and more about uncovering all of the facets of an ancient city, chronicling its history and carefully documenting the lives of its ancient inhabitants, an aim that modern archaeologists still strive for today.

By the time of Bell's 1909 visit to Babylon, many of the site's key monuments had been exposed by Koldewey and his team. They had laid bare several structures of the period of Nebuchadnezzar, who had reigned over the city and the Babylonian empire from 605 to 562 BCE and had been responsible for greatly enlarging and embellishing the city. Bell was shown many of these excavated remains. She saw, for example, the Via Sacra, also referred to as the Processional Way, a long street that entered the Inner City of Babylon at its north end and passed through the centre of the city in the direction of the temple precinct of the city's supreme deity, Marduk.[15] As it approached the Inner City, the Processional Way was bordered by high, baked brick walls, and these were in turn embellished with processions of lions, produced in raised relief from moulded bricks and covered with coloured glaze.[16] Equally striking but perhaps more impressive was

Fig. 4.3 The German plan of Babylon, showing the architecture of the excavated areas. The Palace of Nebuchadnezzar and the nearby Ishtar Gate are visible above the centre of the plan on the left. Below centre on the left is the black square marking the place of the Marduk ziggurat ('E-Temenanki') and the city's principal temple ('E-sagila').

the gate at the northern end of the Inner City, through which this majestic avenue passed, named after Ishtar, the Babylonian goddess of love and protectress of the army. Bell called the Ishtar Gate the 'most magnificent fragment that remains of all Nebuchadnezzar's constructions', impressed as she was by its set of double towers, which reared 'their unbroken height in stupendous masses of solid masonry' (Fig. 4.4).[17] She likewise observed the decoration on the gates – alternating rows of bulls and dragons, cast in relief on moulded bricks (Fig. 4.5).[18] Bell's German hosts also showed Bell through the extensive brick ruins comprising the Palace of Nebuchadnezzar (also known as the Southern Palace), which lies to the west of the Processional Way and Ishtar Gate at the northern end of the Inner City. Bell observed the interior of the palace, which 'was a bewildering complexity of small courts and passages',[19] and took special note of the king's massive oblong throne room, the presumed setting of the Biblical story of Belshazzar's feast. Bell also saw earlier structures beneath Nebuchadnezzar's palatial structure, including the smaller palace of his father, Nabopolassar (626–605 BCE),[20] and fortified towers made of bricks stamped with the name of the Neo-Assyrian king Sargon II (721–705 BCE).[21] Her observations emphasized not only the tremendous labours of the German excavators to reveal these features – which were often found at great depths in the soil – but their keen sense of architectural stratigraphy and their diligent efforts to expose and record the history of Babylon's buildings in all of their remarkable detail.

Not until Bell's 1914 visit to Babylon does she mention one other notable feature of Nebuchadnezzar's Palace: a complex of vaulted chambers in the north-eastern corner. Koldewey apparently was available to give her a personal tour of the complex,[22] and in his opinion this was the location of the Hanging Gardens, known from ancient sources as the place where Nebuchadnezzar had built a luxuriant terraced garden for the pleasure of his Median wife, who missed the mountainous, tree-covered landscape of her home (Fig. 4.6).[23] The vaulted chamber complex, within which was found a well, was believed to have served as

Fig. 4.4 Bell's 1909 photo of the Ishtar Gate from the north (seen in the centre of the photo), and surrounding brickwork. The height of the excavated gate as seen in the photo gives some sense of the great depth of the German excavations in this sector of the city.

Fig. 4.5 Bell's detail of some of the moulded brick reliefs of bulls and dragons on the Ishtar Gate. These bricks were unglazed, belonging to earlier phases that subsequently became the underground foundations – up to 18 metres high – of later constructions of the gate as it was raised over time. The latest manifestation of the Ishtar Gate, which now stands reconstructed in the Vorderasiatisches Museum in Berlin, was covered with yellow and ochre-coloured glazed bricks set against a vivid blue background.

the below-ground foundations of an elaborate hydraulic system employed to convey water up to the level of the planted garden through a rotational system of buckets on waterwheels.[24] As tantalizing as this reconstruction is, however, many scholars disagree about this postulated location for the Hanging Gardens, preferring to place it in the quieter, private apartments of the king in the western sector of the palace, or in the larger building known as the Western Outwork, located beside the Euphrates River.[25] Even more drastically, others would like to place the gardens not in Babylon at all, but in the Assyrian city of Nineveh, where there is ample textual and physical evidence of ancient hydraulic systems for the watering of extensive palatial gardens.[26]

In the centre of the ancient city, Bell was directed to a massive vertical trench, where she was able to peer down some 21 m to the level of the remains of the E-sag-il, the 'House Whose Top Is High'.[27] Here had been the massive temple complex of Babylon's patron deity, Marduk. Across from it was the E-temen-anki, the 'Foundation Platform of Heaven and Earth' – the ziggurat of Marduk, equated with the Tower of Babel described in the Biblical book of Genesis.[28] Bell did not describe the E-temen-anki until her 1914 visit, when she was taken there by Koldewey.[29] Although some investigations of the ziggurat had been made earlier, it was only in 1913 that Koldewey's assistant Wetzel supervised the principal clearance of the area and was able to discern some of its essential features.[30] Of all the principal buildings of ancient Babylon, the ziggurat of Marduk had perhaps suffered the greatest destruction over the centuries. From ancient inscriptions, it may be reconstructed as a giant tower made up of multiple storeys, like a stepped pyramid, topped with a temple structure dedicated to Marduk, covered in dark blue glazed bricks.[31] All that remains, however, is the base of the tower's brick core, the enclosing baked bricks having been completely quarried throughout the centuries since antiquity. Today, the once-great monument, which would have been dazzling in Nebuchadnezzar's time and unparalleled in all of Mesopotamia for its size and height, now stands as a low heap of ruins in the midst of a square pond.[32]

The careful, patient investigation that Koldewey made of Babylon, along with his commitment to recording the site with detailed architectural plans, did not fail to impress Bell. She regarded Koldewey's archaeological work as among the most rigorous and up-to-date in the Near East. It was matched only by the German excavations at Assur – another site Bell would visit for the first time in 1909 – where she witnessed the same care in the recovery and meticulous documentation of the city's ancient remains, particularly its architecture. It is likely that the systematic excavation practices employed by these German teams continued to resonate with Bell in her later role as Iraq's director of antiquities and in her drafting of the country's first antiquities legislation. Using the German excavation teams at Babylon and Assur as a model of good scientific practice, in her legislation she made it a requirement

Fig. 4.6 Artist's view over the city of Babylon, as it would have looked in Nebuchadnezzar's time. The view incorporated archaeological information provided by the German excavators. In the centre one can see a procession through the Ishtar Gate. Above and to the right one can see the Hanging Gardens on top of the Palace of Nebuchadnezzar, while far beyond is the temple and ziggurat of Marduk.

that all archaeological missions have (i) equipment for making a photographic record and (ii) an experienced draughtsman, responsible for recording all of the site's ancient architecture.[33]

Bell's respect for Koldewey and his Babylon team may also have governed her later actions regarding the excavated materials from that site, a great deal of which had been left in the country at the onset of World War I. This included numerous crates full of glazed bricks from the city's Processional Way and Ishtar Gate, all of which had fallen into the hands of the British victors and were now seen as the property of the new Iraqi government. In the end, Bell authorized the delivery of the majority of the crates to Germany, with only the proviso that one reconstructed glazed lion be handed over to the new Iraq Museum, along with a selection of baked bricks and model reconstructions.[34]

In all, Bell's visits to Babylon and her encounters with the German excavators there, particularly Koldewey, would greatly impact her own understanding of and appreciation for Mesopotamia's ancient past, and impress upon her the importance of proper methods for uncovering and documenting its valuable remains. On a personal level, Bell appears to have had a genuine affection for her German host and revelled in his spirited company at Babylon. The sadness she felt when World War I had severed her ties to Koldewey and his German team is perhaps most poignantly emphasized in a letter she wrote upon her return to Babylon in January 1918, finding its dig-house deserted:

> On my way home yesterday (I came in by motor) I stopped at Babylon, having been asked by Sir Percy to advise on what we ought to do about the preservation of antiquities. Tempi passati weigh very heavy there – not that I was thinking of Nebuchadnezzar, nor yet of Alexander, but of the warm welcome I used to find, the good company, the pleasant days spent with dear Koldewey – it's no good trying to think of him as an alien enemy; and my heart ached when I stood in the empty, dusty little room where Fattuh used to put up my camp furniture and the Germans and I held eager conversation over plans of Babylon or Ukhaidhir. – What a dreadful world of broken friendships we have created between us.[35]

Ctesiphon

Following her rewarding visit to Babylon, Bell gathered up her caravan and headed northwards in the direction of Baghdad. Before proceeding to that city, however, she crossed over the Tigris River on a *guffah* – a bitumen-lined reed basket – some 35 km south of Baghdad to see the remains at Ctesiphon. In her accounts, Bell gave this name to what were actually several ancient cities on the east bank of the Tigris, located opposite the Hellenistic city of Seleucia-on-the-Tigris, the latter still unexplored in Bell's time. The Parthians had established their military presence at Ctesiphon, and this site eventually became the capital of the Parthian empire, which for a time stretched from Mesopotamia to the borders of India and even threatened Rome's political power and expansion into the East.[36] Parthia's enmity with Rome would result in Ctesiphon being thrice conquered by the Romans in the second century CE (by Trajan, Cassius and Septimius Severus) before it was taken over by the Persian Sasanians under their king Ardashir I (224–41 CE).[37] The Sasanian kings established their winter royal residence and capital of their empire in the area just to the south of Parthian Ctesiphon, in a place called Asbanbar. Here one finds the most well-preserved and striking monuments of the Sasanians, the so-called Taq-i Kisra, the monumental palace that contained the legendary vaulted throne hall of the Sasanian king of kings.[38] Under a succession of powerful kings, including Shapur I (241–72 CE) and Khosrow I (531–79 CE), Sasanian Ctesiphon enjoyed economic and political success, and the city was known across the entire Near East for its riches and splendour. During the reign of Khosrow II (591–628 CE), however, Ctesiphon experienced its ultimate defeat in the form of invading Muslim armies. Under the command of Sa'd ibn Abi Waqqas, the Muslim armies stormed the city in 637 CE and looted the palace, leaving the king and his court to flee.[39] Thereafter, the site declined in importance and was eventually abandoned.

Bell was no doubt drawn to Ctesiphon by her knowledge of its rich and eventful history, and like so many travellers before her, she was eager to see the Taq-i Kisra because of what remained of its imposing architecture. The great arched vault of the palace's throne room – the *iwan* – bears the distinction of possessing the widest span of any pre-modern brick building in the world (Fig. 4.7).[40] Made of slanting layers of brick set on edge without the use of centring beams, the parabolic vault, which tapers toward the top, stands 35 m high from the ground to its cornice and occupies a space over 42 m deep and more than 25 m wide.[41] The palace also boasts an impressive façade featuring four stories of blind arches, engaged columns and entablatures.[42] These parts of the monument were in a ruinous state, as attested by Bell's 1909 photographs, one of which shows the noticeable forward list of the south façade (Fig. 4.8). There was sufficient concern over the eventual collapse of this wall that in 1922, the Iraqi Department of Public Works added a reinforcing concrete base along the length of the façade.[43] In 1942, a tall buttress was added to the front of one end of the façade. In the 1970s, the Iraqi Antiquities Department tried to restore parts of the Taq-i Kisra, but this work was never completed; moreover, new cracks in the structure have since been observed.[44] Most recently, the site has suffered much neglect and damage as a result of the 2003 Iraq War, and in 2012, 'a slab about two metres in length fell off' because

Fig. 4.7   Bell's photograph of the Taq-i Kisra at Ctesiphon during her 1909 visit to that site, from the east. The northern side of the façade had collapsed in 1888, taking with it the front section of the central arch, so that by Bell's time, only the remaining central vault and the south façade survived.

of damp caused by heavy rains. The Iraqi government has launched a new initiative to repair the site.[45]

Back in 1909, through Bell's imaginative inclinations, all the realities of the ruin and continuing decay of the Taq-i Kisra were brushed aside, and she envisioned what the palace would have looked like in its splendid heyday during the sixth century. Her evocative image is largely based on the account of al-Tabari, a Persian historian of the late ninth to early tenth centuries:

In this hall, Chosroes held his court. It must have lain open to the rising sun, or perhaps the entrance was sheltered by a curtain which hung from the top of the vault down to the floor. The Arab historian, Tabari, gives an account of a carpet seventy cubits long and sixty cubits broad which formed part of the booty when the Mohammadans sacked the city. It was woven into the likeness of a garden; the ground was worked in gold and the paths in silver; the meadows were of emeralds and the streams of pearls; the trees,

Fig. 4.8 Bell's photograph of the exterior of the Taq-i Kisra from the south, showing the forward list of the surviving south façade, and eroded brickwork at the base. Despite various efforts to repair and restore the monument up to the present day, the Taq has continued to deteriorate at an alarming rate.

flowers and fruits of diamonds and other precious stones. Such a texture as this may have been drawn aside to reveal the Great King seated in state in his hall of audience, with the light of a thousand lamps, suspended from the roof, catching his jeweled tiara, his sword and girdle, illuminating the hangings on the walls and the robes and trappings of the army of courtiers who stood round the throne.[46]

Bell was largely interested in the Taq-i Kisra because it was a good example of surviving Sasanian palatial architecture, and she could see many points of architectural similarity between it and Ukhaidir, the desert palace she had investigated only a few weeks earlier in the spring of 1909. As described in the preceding chapter, for example, a fragmentary vaulted ceiling in one of the side chambers of the Taq-i Kisra had been set forward slightly from the face of the wall below; this sort of structure also existed at Ukhaidir (Fig. 4.9).[47] Bell also took careful note of the decoration of the niched arches, engaged columns and entablatures on the building's façade, with their marked Classical style; she then made a detailed comparison with the northern façade of the inner Court of Honour at Ukhaidir, which, although a later construction, shares some of the former's features and may have derived some inspiration from it.[48]

After the war, Bell continued to visit Ctesiphon frequently, given its proximity to Baghdad (where she was residing as a political officer) and the fact that its grandiose appearance never failed to make an impression on visitors. Her interest and role in the archaeology of the new Iraq also spurred her continued concern for the preservation of the Taq-i Kisra, as evidenced in one of her letters from 1921, in which she discusses with an architect (J.M. Wilson, the Director of the Department of Public Works) the prospect of putting 'a big wad of concrete against the foundations [...] which won't be pretty but ought to make the wall as safe as we can make it'.[49]

Bell was also aware of the importance of Ctesiphon not only for its architectural magnificence, but for its history and the potential for such history to reinforce the identity of Iraq and empower its new king. With this in mind, Bell took King Faisal to Ctesiphon in 1921, shortly after he had been crowned, and related to him the whole story of the site's illustrious past, ending with its conquest by the Muslim armies in 637 CE.[50] This was Bell's conscious attempt to impress upon the Arab king his own ties to Iraq and his legitimate place as its new protector. Bell, in her crucial political role in Iraq after the war, was certainly not above pressing an archaeological site into the service of the present and using it for political ends, as will be discussed further in this book's final chapter.

Baghdad

After Ctesiphon, Bell set her sights on Baghdad. She intended to rest there for a few days and to visit the British Consul-General, who had a lavish residence in the city. After crossing the Tigris River on a crowded pontoon bridge made of boats, Bell made her way to the British Residency, where she was given spacious and comfortable lodgings and enjoyed the friendly company of the Consul-General and his wife (Fig. 4.10).[51]

Fig. 4.9 Bell's photograph of the interior doorway and remains of a vault with 'oversailing' brickwork in the north-eastern corner of the south wing of the Taq-i Kisra at Ctesiphon. The scholar Ernst Herzfeld believed that this feature did not exist until the Islamic period. Bell's statement in her book *Amurath to Amurath* (p. 153, n. 1) that Herzfeld's opinion was erroneous further exacerbated the pair's combative relationship.

This would be the first of Bell's many visits to Baghdad, first in 1909, then in 1911 and 1914. Later, after the British forces moved up to Baghdad in 1917 and she became a political officer of the British government in Mesopotamia, Bell made Baghdad her principal residence and lived there until her death in 1926.

Baghdad would always hold a significant place in Bell's life, not only because of its antiquity, but because of its central position in present-day Mesopotamian affairs. From her very first visit in 1909, Bell found herself stimulated by the reports brought to the offices of the British Consulate and eager to lend her own assistance, given her first-hand knowledge of the lands through which she had just travelled. In many ways, Bell was more valuable than others in the diplomatic service, on account of her good knowledge of Arabic and the fact that so much of her travels entailed acquisitive conversations with local peoples and discussions about their affairs, both trivial and weighty. Thus, even at a time of her life when her interests were primarily geographical and archaeological, it is possible to see the early glimmerings of her future political career.

Bell had some knowledge of Baghdad's past, and in particular its time as the capital of the Abbasid caliphs, 'a period during which it had witnessed a magnificence as profuse and destruction as reckless as any others on the pages of history'.[52] Historical accounts have provided detailed descriptions of this early city, which was founded by the caliph al-Mansur back in 762 CE. Designed as a perfect circle, Baghdad was conceived as the navel of the universe.[53] Surrounded by high walls with four gates, the centre of the Round City featured the caliphal palace and congregational mosque, while military, commercial and residential quarters were segregated from each other and situated outside the circular enclosure.[54]

Unfortunately, virtually nothing remained of the initial city by the early twentieth century. Later Islamic-period remains diverted Bell's attentions, however, and she wandered around them as an enthusiastic tourist with her camera. She visited, for example, the Bab Talisman gate, built by the caliph al-Nasir in 1221 CE (Fig. 4.11), and the Tomb of Sitt Zubayda, a striking mausoleum constructed in the twelfth century and distinguished by a nine-layered *muqarnas* dome, not unlike the Imam al-Dur mausoleum she would later see at the northern end of Samarra.[55] She took in the elegantly ornamented minaret in the Suq al-Ghazi and walked around the old Mustansiriya.[56] She was refused entry into the thirteenth-century Palace of the Caliphs in 1909 because it was being used at that time as a military arsenal, but in 1911, she was given the opportunity to wander through its vaulted corridors and to photograph its exquisitely decorated, terracotta-panelled walls and ceilings.[57]

Altogether, Bell showed a fascination with Baghdad, past and present, and her visit to this city did much to revive her spirits and strengthen her resolve to know and document Mesopotamia as only a few other Western travellers had done before her. Going back to her first eager visit in 1909, however, it would be impossible to predict how all-consuming the affairs of Baghdad and its country would become for Bell later in her life. Baghdad would witness her greatest achievements and her darkest sorrows. Ultimately, it would know her in death and be her final resting place.

Fig. 4.10 Bell's photograph of the British Residency in Baghdad in 1911, with a paddle steamer in front, from across the Tigris River. Bell stayed with the Consul General and his wife here in both 1909 and 1911, finding her accommodations luxurious and comfortable.

Samarra

Bell departed Baghdad on 12 April 1909 and, having rejoined her servants and caravan, headed out of the northern side of the city, following the Tigris upstream. The natural countryside was flat and treeless above Baghdad, and a blustery wind made Bell think back wistfully to the comforts of the British Residency whence she had come. But there was much to divert her attention in the way of artificial mounds marking the places of ancient towns and villages. Bell's training in ancient history had made her aware of some of the momentous events that were believed to have taken place in these parts in pre-Classical and Classical Antiquity. These included the Battle of Opis, which brought an end to the Neo-Babylonian empire in 529 BCE, and the retreat of the emperor Julian's Roman army shortly before his death, in 363 CE.[58]

But another, later, era of antiquity was about to consume all of Bell's attentions, its traces already beginning to reveal themselves in the form of decorated Islamic period pottery sherds strewn thickly over the surface of heaped earthen mounds. Crossing to the other side of the Tigris on a *kelek* at Balad on 14 April,[59] and then passing over the dry cutting of an ancient canal, the Nahr el Kaim, Bell found herself surrounded by the vast ruin fields of the great city of Samarra, once the dazzling capital of the Islamic Abbasid dynasty in the ninth century CE, where 'bazaars and palaces stretched uninterruptedly along the east bank of the Tigris for a distance of twenty-one miles'.[60] Based on the history of Samarra – much of which was reported by ninth-century Islamic historians – it is known that the city had enjoyed only a brief period of magnificence, beginning with the caliph al-Mu'tasim (833–42),

Fig. 4.11 Bell's photograph of the thirteenth-century Bab Talisman in Baghdad, taken in 1909. When she returned in 1911, she took additional photos of this gate with a telephoto lens, capturing nicely the image above the doorway – a pair of winged serpent-dragons with a human figure sitting cross-legged between them. Bell's photographic record of the gate is valuable, as the Bab Talisman was completely destroyed by the Ottoman army when they withdrew from Baghdad in 1917.

who founded a new city that would accommodate not only the Abbasid court but the increasingly powerful and numerous Turkish army corps.[61] Four of al-Mu'tasim's successors would continue to inhabit Samarra, adding 'market to market, palace to palace and pleasure-ground to pleasure-ground'.[62] Finally, in 892, the caliph al-Mu'tadid returned to Baghdad, and the city declined rapidly thereafter:

> the walls of Samarra crumbled back into the desert from which they had arisen, and like the rose-scented clay of Sa'di's apologue when the fragrance had vanished, became once more the dust they had been. A glory so dazzling, so abrupt a decline, can scarcely be paralleled on any other page of history.[63]

The city of Samarra had been magnificent in its time, its massive piles of heaped earth that covered some 57 square km – probably the largest ruin field in the world – providing testimony to its once caliphal grandeur and extravagance.[64] While on the ground it only seems to feature shapeless masses of piled earth and broken bricks, from the air one can clearly discern the outlines of vast cantonments for the huge army corps, streets and broad avenues, horse-racing tracks and polo fields, congregational mosques and, above all, palaces with their monumental enclosure walls, numerous gateways, residential courts and grand audience halls.

Bell herself would have been aware of the existence of Samarra on the Tigris before the start of her Mesopotamian trip and would have ensured that she was generally apprised of any current knowledge of the site. Her preparations would have made her familiar with Islamic writers such as al-Ya'qubi and al-Tabari, who had recounted Samarra's history, and her more recent study of the early Islamic city of Raqqa and her discovery of Ukhaidir – the latter of which had many architectural parallels to Samarra – would have made her especially attuned to the site's distinctive details of construction.

Of recent archaeological investigations at Samarra, Bell seems to have known about those made by a French general by the name of Lucien de Beylié, who had visited Samarra in 1907 and had published his results in the same year.[65] Bell was also carrying with her a copy of a short book on the history and architecture of Samarra, which had been recently published by a young German scholar by the name of Ernst Herzfeld.[66] Herzfeld would go on to have a famed career because of his astounding achievements, especially in the fields of Iranian archaeology, history and religion. But in 1909, Herzfeld was still a young and relatively unknown 30-year-old Oriental scholar with a promising academic future. This would be an important year for Herzfeld, as he completed his masterful work on the desert palace of Mshatta, located south of Amman in present-day Jordan.[67] This article would present his controversial but correct opinion that Mshatta was an Islamic Umayyad construction of the eighth century, thereby overturning earlier arguments for its Sasanian, Ghassanid or Lakhmid dates, asserted by Strzygowski and others.[68] Even today, Herzfeld's Mshatta article, published in 1910, is considered a masterpiece among studies of Umayyad art because of its clear methodology, persuasive argument and broad frame of reference.[69]

Bell, with her own archaeological experience and confidence, felt entitled to criticize Herzfeld's efforts at Samarra. Upon arriving there and inspecting the Great Mosque, she wrote the following in a letter to her father:

> Now Samarra is the most important place in the world for early Mohammadan buildings. Two people have worked here, a Frenchman and a German. The good old Frenchman (he's a general with a taste for archaeology) published a short paper after a still shorter visit and gave

some very interesting information. The plans were not so good because he confessed that had lost his notes before drawing them out – rather an innocent admission![70] The German published a monograph with a great flourish of trumpets and was particularly pleased because he said his labours proved Strzygowski to be all wrong.[71] I confidently expected to find all the things he had done could not be improved on; I have only seen one of them as yet (one of the originals) and Herzfeld's plan, except as to the general outlines, is the creature of his fancy. I shall therefore have to do this one over again and I rather fear that the same will apply to the rest of his work. He's an architect. How an architect could spend an hour in that mosque and not see the extraordinarily interesting details of construction which escaped his notice, I can't imagine. Sometimes when I have occasion to go closely over the work of professional archaeologists, I think I'm something of an archaeologist myself – but of course that's going too far! At any rate one can always have enough respect for the things one is studying to reproduce them as they really are. And that's half the battle.[72]

In another letter a few days later, Bell wrote:

As I feared, all Herzfeld's work has had to be redone and I have been at it hard for 3 days and a half. However, it's all finished now and I don't regret it because one learns more about buildings when one goes over them brick by brick with the measuring tape than in any other way. Also (but this is an unworthy consideration!) I shall have a merry time showing up Herzfeld. He deserves it however.[73]

The letters demonstrate that Bell found the recent studies of Samarra's architecture, especially Herzfeld's efforts, to be lacking in detail and accuracy, and felt compelled to produce her own, authoritative architecture study, complete with photographs, descriptions and carefully prepared plans. As it turned out, the Great Mosque at Samarra was not her only objective. Bell was ambitious and seems to have been intent on making a record of several of Samarra's Islamic period monuments during the days of her visit in 1909. Thus, between 15 and 18 April, she set out to make plans, descriptions and photographs of the site of Qadissiyya (Fig. 4.12) and the ruins that constitute the famous Dar al-Khilafa, or the Palace of the Caliphate, a residence and principal place of caliphal government in Samarra (Figs 4.13 and 4.14).[74] On the opposite, western side of the Tigris, where there were additional ruins of Samarra, Bell planned and photographed the Qubbat al-Sulaybiyya (her Kubbet es Slebiyeh) – an octagonal building whose function is still debated – and further to the north, Qasr al-'Ashiq, a well-preserved palace of fired brick and gypsum, which was probably built by the caliph al-Mu'tamid sometime between 877 and 882 CE (Fig. 4.15).[75]

Bell seems, however, to have spent most of her time recording the formidable remains of the Great Mosque of Mutawakkil, this lying beyond the modern walled town of Samarra.[76] Constructed by the caliph al-Mutawakkil between 848 and 852 CE, this mosque was intended not only to serve the growing number of the faithful gathered in prayer in the midst of the city, but also to provide a grand stage for the caliph's entry during prayers on Fridays and major holidays.[77] The mosque featured numerous rows of brick and marble supports for the roof (long since removed), all enclosed within an immense rectangle of bastioned walls of fired brick, producing the largest mosque in the world.[78] It is perhaps one of the most famous Islamic mosques in Iraq, for its enormous size but also for its distinctive spiral minaret, known as the Malwiye, which stands to the north of the mosque. The Malwiye's cylindrical tower is distinguished by a sloping ramp that winds round the tower to the top, 50 m above the base. It provides a commanding view over the Great Mosque and the medieval city of Samarra beyond.[79]

Bell found Herzfeld's published plan of the Great Mosque 'woefully bad' and so set out to produce her own. The plan (Fig. 4.16) (reproduced in her book *Amurath to Amurath*) improves upon Herzfeld's 1907 effort, which included several notable errors. Bell was also careful to take good photographs, which provide interesting and important details of the architectural features she observed in the mosque and associated minaret (Fig. 4.17).

Heading north from Samarra along the east bank of the Tigris on 19 April, Bell encountered many other extensive Islamic period ruins and passed through the ruins of what was known in the Abbasid period as the southern sector of al-Mutawakkiliyya, the city that the caliph al-Mutawakkil set about constructing immediately to the north of Samarra around 859. The new city was intended to replace Samarra as the Abbasid capital and may additionally have satisfied some of al-Mutawakkil's kingly pride and voracious appetite for building.[80] Alas, al-Mutawakkil was to enjoy only nine months of glory before being assassinated by his Turkish generals during a nightly drinking bout in the palace that he had built for himself at the northern end of the city. Upon his death, much of al-Mutawakkiliyya was pulled down and demolished, and it was never again occupied.[81]

Travelling past the remains of many of the city's buildings, comprising broad avenues, houses, military cantonments, markets and *musallas* (open spaces for public prayers during festivals), Bell was most interested in reaching the mosque of Abu Dulaf, which she ended up spending almost five hours measuring and photographing. Once more, Bell had been dissatisfied with the reports of earlier visitors, especially in this case with those of General de Beylié, and felt compelled to produce her own detailed and complete record.[82] Like the earlier mosque of

Fig. 4.12 Bell's 1909 photograph of the massive octagonal enclosure of Qadissiyya from the south-east at Samarra, showing the remains of its round bastions. The site, which appears never to have been inhabited, probably marks the place of an unfinished city started by the caliph Harun al-Rashid in the eighth century.

al-Mutawakkil in Samarra, Abu Dulaf was a congregational mosque and possessed a similar layout and accompanying spiral minaret (Fig. 4.18). In place of the mudbrick interior supports of the Great Mosque, which had either disintegrated or been removed in their entirety, the interior of the Abu Dulaf mosque was well preserved, its internal rows of rectangular and square piers having been built entirely with fired brick. In contrast, the exterior wall was constructed of mudbrick, and its consequent deterioration over the centuries made precise recording of details difficult.[83] Nonetheless, Bell made a valiant attempt to record the mosque, and her resulting photographs, description and plan are commendable for their accuracy and details.[84]

Moving beyond the northern limits of al-Mutawakkiliyya, Bell reached the town of Dur, where she stopped to visit and record a mausoleum, known as the Imam al-Dur, dedicated to a Shi'ite holy man and built by a prince of Mosul during the dynasty of the 'Uqaylids in the eleventh century.[85] Striking in form

Fig. 4.13   Bell's 1909 photograph of the triple-vaulted Bab al-Amma Gate of the palace of Dar al-Khilafa at Samarra, *c.*836 CE. It lay on the main axis of the southern palace, the Dar al-Amma, which ran from west to east. This was the formal gatehouse through which visitors, coming up from the river to the palace, would arrive. According to the textual sources, the Bab al-Amma was also a location for public punishments and executions.

and decoration, the mausoleum was topped by a *muqarnas* dome of five superimposed octagonal zones of squinches, decreasing in height towards the top (Fig. 4.19). The interior of the tomb featured an elaborate honeycombed stucco decoration, typifying the Samarran 'rococo' style that appeared in Iraq under the 'Uqaylids.[86]

Bell relates that upon arriving at the Imam al-Dur, she noted an Arabic inscription engraved on a marble slab by the doorway of the shrine, where she read the date 871 AH (1466 CE) after a villager had scraped away some of the whitewash that covered it at the bottom. This date would become the source of some disagreement between Bell and Herzfeld; Herzfeld had inspected the inscription in 1908 but had not seen the date. The ensuing correspondence between Bell and Herzfeld between 1909 and 1911 contains much discussion of this Imam al-Dur inscription, over the course of which the eminent Arabic philologist Max van Berchem also weighed in on the issue.[87]

Fig. 4.14 Bell's 1909 photograph of fragments of stucco work, presumed to come from the Dar al-Khilafa at Samarra, collected and placed outside Bell's tent. The stucco pattern seen here is of the so-called Samarra 'Style C', which developed in the ninth century CE. A copy of this photograph can be found among Herzfeld's papers, now housed in the Freer and Sackler Galleries of the Smithsonian Institute in Washington, DC. It was probably enclosed in a letter that Bell sent to Herzfeld in 1910.

This controversy among Bell and her colleagues in the early twentieth century, however, seems trifling compared to the recent reports that the Imam al-Dur mausoleum was blown up and completely destroyed by the Islamic State (IS), probably in October 2014. This act was part of IS's aggressive destruction of Shi'a monuments and material culture.[88] The beautiful mausoleum, with its remarkable dome – the first of its kind in Iraq – which was respected and untouched by both Sunni and Shi'a Muslims alike for almost one thousand years, exists no more.

With her copious notes, plans and photographs, Bell no doubt wanted to make something of her days at Samarra, aspiring to publish her findings together with her work on Raqqa and Ukhaidir. These ambitions are expressed in a letter that she wrote in April 1909:

Fig. 4.15   Bell's 1909 view of the brickwork on the western side of the northern façade of the Qasr al-'Ashiq at Samarra, believed to have been built by the caliph al-Mu'tamid *c.*877–82 CE. Blind niches and polylobed arches were set between semicircular buttresses. The niches were partially blocked with bricks at a later date, since their back walls were too thin and had collapsed.

> I'm planning a book now; it's to be called 'Khethar, Samarra and Rakka: a study in Mesopotamian architecture.' What do you think of that? And all the pottery fragments and the plaster work and the Rakka pots will come in too. It would be wonderfully interesting to write, but it will take a long time. I feel very much excited about it however. The only drawback is it won't pay! but don't mention that to Heinemann – nor to my bankers.[89]

Her ambition to publish Samarra in a big way seems to have continued upon her return to England later in the year, for she began to probe further the state of research on the site, gathering additional information about each monument that she had inspected. Through such probes, she learned that a French scholar by the name of Henri Viollet had been to Samarra in 1908 and had recorded the remains of the Dar al-Khilafa, the Great Mosque and the Qasr al-'Ashiq,

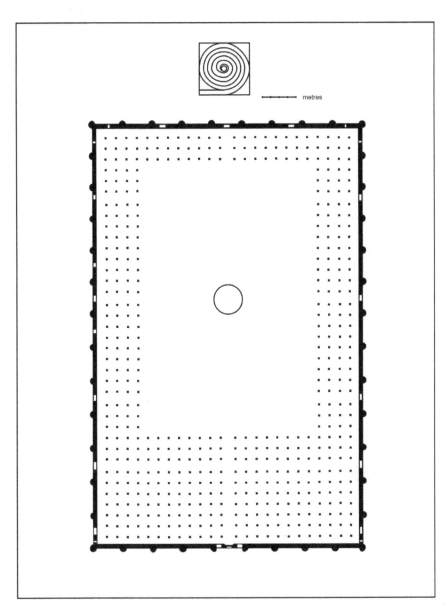

Fig. 4.16 Bell's 1909 plan of the Great Mosque of Samarra (*c.*847–61 CE) and its spiral minaret (the Malwiye), which was included in her monograph *Amurath to Amurath*. With this effort, Bell sought to improve upon an earlier plan of the mosque published by Ernst Herzfeld. Herzfeld would himself produce a much-corrected plan of the mosque in the same year.

Fig. 4.17 Bell's 1909 photo of the surviving brickwork of the entrance to the Dar al-Imara on the south side of the *qibla* wall of the Great Mosque of Samarra, next to an outer semicircular tower. It matches well the description provided by Herzfeld, who reports a brick frame that formed part of the entrance to the Dar al-Imara on the west side; this was removed in the course of the post-war restoration of the mosque and stabilization of the *qibla* wall. Bell's photograph of the unusual brick pattern of five horizontal layers alternating with one layer of vertically set bricks remains the best visual record of this now vanished feature.

publishing his work in 1909.[90] It seems that Viollet also had plans to return to Samarra the following year to carry out excavations, the eventual outcome of which would be his further report on some of the details of the Dar al-Khilafa.[91]

In England, Bell also made the decision to write to Herzfeld (Fig. 4.20), whose 1907 report on Samarra she had consulted in the field. One of her

Fig. 4.18   Bell's photograph of the spiral minaret of the Abu Dulaf mosque at the northern end of Samarra, built by the caliph al-Mutawakkil, *c.*847–61 CE. The minaret is similar in plan to the Malwiye of the Great Mosque at Samarra, although it is less than half of that mosque's height.

principal inquiries concerned Herzfeld's 'woefully bad' plan of the Great Mosque at Samarra. She may have written to him in the hope of getting further clarification on the structure's architectural details, or perhaps she wanted to present her own corrected version for his consideration. After all, she had earlier written that with her new, improved plan of the Great Mosque, she would 'have a merry time showing up Herzfeld'. Whatever the motivation for her writing, she received in return from Herzfeld a great deal of valuable

Fig. 4.19 Bell's photograph of the mausoleum of Imam al-Dur at the northern end of the Samarra ruin fields, built in the eleventh century CE. At the time of the photo, in April 1909, the distinctive lobed domes of the structure's roof were topped by several storks' nests. Sadly, this lovely Shi'a structure no longer exists, having been destroyed by the Islamic State in October 2014.

information about Samarra and its monuments. Most significantly, Bell learned that Herzfeld had been back to Samarra with Friedrich Sarre in 1909, and that a more comprehensive report on the site was about to be published that would do much to improve on his earlier – and somewhat cursory – Samarra report. She also learned that Sarre and Herzfeld were returning to

Samarra, and were planning a full exploration of the site and its monuments on behalf of the Kaiser Friedrich Museum in Berlin.

In light of this information and the investigations already carried out by Viollet, Sarre and Herzfeld, and despite some of the objections she had to their work, Bell appears to have abandoned her plan to publish Samarra's art and architecture in a grand fashion. In the end, her short excursus on the site, which is included in *Amurath to Amurath* – accompanied by some of her photographs and plans of buildings, such as the Great Mosque, the Qasr al-'Ashiq, the Qubbat al-Sulaybiyya and the Abu Dulaf mosque – comprise the sum total of her published investigations of the place. One suspects that Bell, having seen the work of the other Samarra scholars and learning that further intensive investigations were about to commence, realized that this spectacular site and its valuable remains were now in the hands of people who had more time and effort to commit to it than she. In the end, it would seem that Bell was content to dedicate herself to Ukhaidir, resolving to make that site the subject upon which she would leave her lasting scholarly mark.

The correspondence between Bell and Herzfeld continued for about three years (1909–12) and reveals a lively exchange between two individuals who shared a similar interest in Samarra's art and architecture, as well as other topics pertaining to the archaeology of the Near East.[92] The letters written by Herzfeld to Bell have been located and studied, and they are extraordinary for the wealth of archaeological details they contain, highlighting especially Herzfeld's prodigious learning and the rapacious interest he took in practically every ancient site and monument he visited and studied. Of Samarra, Herzfeld's letters contain extensive comments about: the layout, construction and building materials of the Great Mosque and the mosque of Abu Dulaf, along with enclosed plans of these structures; a discussion of the stucco decoration from the Dar al-Khilafa; his identification of the Samarra cubit; his discovery of the palace of Mutawakkil at Balkuwara and notes about its layout and architecture, including the disposition of its mosque in comparison to mosques found at Mshatta and Ukhaidir; and his own work on the Imam al-Dur mausoleum, with comments about its architecture, decoration and the content and palaeography of its inscriptions. Beyond Samarra, Herzfeld's letters also make reference to Coptic art, Syrian and Anatolian Christian architecture, Sasanian pottery and architecture, the development of arch and vault construction – with reference to Ctesiphon, Sarvistan, Qasr-i-Shirin, Ukhaidir, Mshatta and Raqqa – and his own views (which differed from Bell's) on the proper location of the ancient sites of Thapsakos and Opis. The sheer breadth of Herzfeld's interests is clearly apparent from this manifest of topics, which fill page after page of his letters. This compendious information was not wasted on Bell. She would have been the one who queried many of the topics upon which

Fig. 4.20 Photograph of Ernst Herzfeld as a young man. After Bell's visit to Samarra in 1909, she and Herzfeld engaged in a spirited correspondence. Despite whatever initial objections Bell may have had about Herzfeld's scholarship, she became highly influenced by his work, adopting especially many of his ideas regarding the development of early Islamic art and architecture.

Herzfeld commented. There is no question that Bell was an eager recipient of the knowledge contained in Herzfeld's letters, and his influence on her scholarship should not be underrated.

Besides their astonishingly learned character, Herzfeld's letters to Bell are also interesting for the glimpse they provide of the often turbulent environment of Oriental scholarship at the time, and the maelstrom of jealousies, disagreements and back-stabbing that frequently churned among European academics. Neither Herzfeld nor Bell were completely removed from or blameless in this acrimonious environment, as revealed in the letters, and much of the conflict centred around the controversial figure of Josef Strzygowski. In contrast to Bell's long-standing positive regard for this scholar's work, Herzfeld frequently disagreed with Strzygowski, calling into question the methods by which he tracked artistic developments through time and space, and his dogged insistence on the Eastern origins of all important early Islamic artistic and architectural developments. Herzfeld, in contrast, emphasized the multiplicity of directions from which early Islamic art and architecture was inspired and the fact that older forms indigenous to a particular place of construction were often emulated and built upon. Unlike Strzygowski, Herzfeld acknowledged the complex, entwined manner in which influences were utilized and melded into novel forms to create the new art of Islam.

Although Bell and Herzfeld held different views about Strzygowski, the two were unanimous in their highest esteem for another scholar of repute, Max van Berchem (Fig. 4.21). Unlike Strzygowski, whose churlish behaviour frequently antagonized other scholars, van Berchem had a likeable personality and was universally respected by everyone with whom he came into contact.[93] Born in Geneva and having studied in Stuttgart and Leipzig, by the opening of the twentieth century, van Berchem had gained a reputation as a leading European scholar in Arabic epigraphy as well as Islamic art and archaeology. One of his major projects was the *Corpus Inscriptionum Arabicarum*. Initiated in 1893, this involved an international collaboration of scholars to collect and publish Arabic inscriptions found on Islamic monuments from around the Middle East. Van Berchem himself contributed to this ambitious project with epigraphic materials from Egypt, Jerusalem, Syria and Anatolia, these appearing in several volumes of *Matériaux pour un Corpus Inscriptionum Arabicarum* between 1894 and his death in 1921.

Ernst Herzfeld had frequent contact with van Berchem through his own contributions to the *Corpus Inscriptionum Arabicarum*, frequently sending van Berchem copies of inscriptions, photographs and notes from his extensive travels through Syria, Mesopotamia and Anatolia.[94] In return, van Berchem wrote the epigraphic section of Sarre and Herzfeld's four-volume work *Archäologische Reise im Euphrat- und Tigris-Gebiet*, which surveyed and charted Islamic monuments in Mesopotamia.[95]

Interestingly, Bell also developed a close personal relationship with Max van Berchem, probably the result of their mutual interest in Islamic period monuments and the fact that Bell had visited or was planning to travel to many places from which van Berchem was seeking inscriptions. They began to exchange letters around 1909, the year of Bell's first Mesopotamian journey, and she appears to have seen him in person on at least two occasions.[96] Significantly, Bell and van Berchem shared a friendly relationship with the ever-problematic Strzygowski, resulting in their scholarly contributions to his *Amida*, a study of the medieval architecture, art and epigraphy of the region of Diyarbakir and the Jazireh.[97] Like Herzfeld, Bell sent van Berchem materials collected from her travels, namely architectural plans and photographs of the sites that she had visited and inscriptions she had seen, these all gratefully received by van Berchem, who praised Bell for the care and precision with which she carried out her research.[98] Van Berchem must have been a welcome correspondent to Bell, who had few colleagues with whom she could share her scholarly interests so completely and unreservedly. Moreover, van Berchem's unsurpassed knowledge of Arabic history and culture, which he imparted generously, was matched by his kind-hearted attentiveness. He conveyed keen interest in Bell's travels and research and flattered her with praise for her achievements. Consider here the exchanges between the two:

(van Berchem to Bell, 18 October 1911, in French): It's largely thanks to you, your plans and your splendid photographs that I was able to give him such precise instructions, because your documents are much better than those of other investigators (with the exception of Mr. Sarre). It seems to me that most investigators are too rushed. They want to see too much in too short a time, and they just use their Kodaks and take rapid notes. But later when you want to make use of their documents, you find that you have to go back on site to complete them yourself.

Your photos are so beautiful that one wouldn't in any case want to use any others, and your plans as far as I can tell are as precise as those of Rivoira. While we are on this subject, I'd like to ask permission to keep these beautiful photographs. I consider them so precious that I wouldn't know how to do without them, and they currently constitute the most solid basis of the future Corpus Inscriptionum Arabicarum for the section on Mesopotamia.[99]

(Bell's response in a letter dated October 1911, in English): Of course you must keep the photographs and I must, moreover, send you those which give the architectural details... But you must please clearly understand that

Fig. 4.21 Max van Berchem, the prominent Swiss scholar of Islamic art and archaeology and Arabic epigraphy, with whom Bell developed a close friendship because of their shared scholarly interests. The photograph, taken in Cairo in 1913, shows a seated van Berchem, while the individual to the right is believed to be Ali Bahgat, an Egyptian scholar of Islamic archaeology with whom van Berchem regularly worked.

it is a pleasure and an honour to send you photographs and you must always ask me for any that you want.[100]

(van Berchem's next letter to Bell, dated 28 October 1911, in French): I can't thank you enough for your very kind letter and your generous offer for me to keep the beautiful photos you sent. I do believe, all things considered, that I am obliged to accept, because, as an old French poet once said, 'A woman's wish is God's pleasure.'[101]

Van Berchem clearly knew how to navigate wisely and graciously among his friends and associates. To be sure, the fact that he had a long-time friendship with Strzygowski – given the latter's absolute genius for making enemies – speaks volumes about the Swiss scholar's personal qualities.[102] He was a good judge of character and had a knack for reconciling others' differences, as evidenced in a letter in which he endeavours to temper Bell's fierce loyalty to Strzygowski and her critical opinion of Herzfeld:

I haven't yet really read Herzfeld's article on *Amida*. I had a quick look at it, but these unending arguments between the Germans really put me off so much that I haven't had the heart to read it in detail. I already gave you my opinion on Strzygowski; I fear that with his uncompromising approach, he only makes difficulties for himself. If you're going to get on your high horse with people, you'd better be sure of what you're arguing about. Still, in *Kunstgeschichte*, you can never be completely sure you're right and unfortunately, for all his brilliant qualities, our friend definitely has a weakness for crazy theories which don't have a lot to do with science. If I admire Herzfeld, it's not for his theories on the history of art (I told him they don't interest me much), it's because he's very good at collecting material, maybe a little too fast, it's true, but nevertheless fast and with an abundance of detail! He sends me something interesting almost every week. Quite a while ago, he wrote to me that the mysterious building on the citadel at Diyarbekr was of no great value; I'm curious to know what exactly he thinks of it.

As for *your* theories, they still interest me because you are clever but cautious; and you document things so well![103]

Bell's relationship with Herzfeld did not remain strained forever. Perhaps she took van Berchem's perceptions to heart, or possibly she was swayed by the indisputable erudition of Herzfeld's scholarship. Whatever was the case, by 1912, the two appear to have reached a respectful, friendly accord. This culminated in a pleasant and productive visit by Bell to Berlin to see Herzfeld in person and to discuss their mutual interests. They pored over their photographs and plans of Samarra and Ukhaidir, and Bell even had the pleasure of meeting members of Herzfeld's family, whom she deemed 'nice people'.[104] In light of this rapprochement, it is not surprising to find Herzfeld's scholarship well reflected in Bell's 1914 publication on the site of Ukhaidir. Later, amid the turbulence of war in 1915, Bell managed to convey a letter to Herzfeld through van Berchem, inquiring after him and her other German friends such as Koldewey and Andrae and reminding him that 'friendship is stronger than war'.[105]

World War I and its aftermath did not bring an end to Bell's relationship with Ernst Herzfeld and the site of Samarra, although circumstances certainly altered these associations. Now, besides her archaeological knowledge of Mesopotamia, Bell was also a British colonial officer in that country, and part of her responsibility in this new capacity was the governance of the country and its cultural property. The issue of Samarra came up in 1917, after Britain's Mesopotamian Expeditionary Force had found at that site numerous cases of antiquities that had been left by Herzfeld's German archaeological team from before the war.[106] There was considerable debate within the War Office and India Office back in London as to who should ultimately take possession of these antiquities and where they should go.[107] Were the Samarra antiquities to be considered trophies of the war against Germany and hence go to Britain to fill its national museums? Alternatively, and especially in light of post-war sentiments about state-building and the right of each nation to its own culture and identity, should the objects remain in their natural home and be housed in some future museum of Iraq? Bell herself inspected the antiquities in her office in Baghdad. Wearing her hat as a loyal daughter of the British Empire and probably swayed by her knowledge of Samarra and its value to the understanding of early Islamic art, she recommended that the cases of Samarra antiquities, which included examples of stucco, frescoes, glass and pottery, be shipped to Britain, where they might augment the Islamic collection of the Victoria and Albert Museum.[108] This proved to be a controversial proposal – there was a great deal of opposition to removing antiquities from their country of origin – but in the end, most of the cases wound up in the hands of British authorities in London.[109] In 1921, it was decided – under the consultation of T.E. Lawrence and, interestingly, Ernst Herzfeld – that the items were to be parcelled off to museums in Europe, North America and the Middle East, with the British Museum and the Berlin Museum receiving the choicest pieces.[110] Part of the agreement was that a representative selection of the antiquities should return to the Iraqi government, free of charge, once 'they are prepared to receive it'.[111] Regrettably, not until 1936 was some of the Samarra material returned to its native country, and by then, the share 'had deteriorated and was hardly representative of the overall collection'.[112] Given this final outcome, it is hard not to be critical of Bell and her part in this Samarra affair. While she would become a champion of the new Iraq and an ardent defender of its cultural property, particularly as Iraq's Antiquities Director, there were also times, as here, when her actions seemed at odds with her ideals. This unusual contradiction in Bell's behaviour will be addressed again in further detail in this book's last chapter.

As for Ernst Herzfeld, he did not excavate again in Samarra until 1930. His principal attentions after the war were focused on Persia, and most of his energies were dedicated to the archaeology of important sites in that country, such as Pasargadae and Persepolis.[113] In 1923, however, Herzfeld did pass through Iraq on his way to Iran and received a warm welcome there from Bell, who was now Iraq's Director of Antiquities.[114] Bell describes a motor excursion that she took with Herzfeld to Hillah, Babylon and Kish, the last being the site of recent excavations. In letters to her parents, Bell refers to Herzfeld as 'an archaeological friend' and mentions the fact that she has loved being 'with a learned German again'.[115] Clearly, her old differences with Herzfeld were long forgotten.

Returning again to 1909 and Bell's four-day visit to Samarra, it is hard to anticipate the significance the place would have in her life and achievements. Samarra opened up a new world to Bell. It added greatly to her knowledge of the early Islamic period and galvanized her interest in the art, architecture and history of that era. It was instrumental in her assessment of Ukhaidir's date and architectural context. Most importantly, Samarra exposed Bell to the wider world of European scholarship, facilitating her connection with other important researchers who were engaged in the still-fledgling study of Islamic art and archaeology. Through connections with scholars such as van Berchem, Viollet and Herzfeld, and the exchange of valuable data with them, Bell earned her own right to be counted among this learned cohort of individuals and their advancement of the field of Mesopotamian late antiquity. The experience that Bell gained from knowledge of Samarra and its remains would ultimately factor into her later political life, governing her actions both as an officer of Britain and as one charged with Iraq's antiquities.

Assur

After Samarra, Bell's next destination in Mesopotamia would prove to be the happiest of her entire 1909 journey. Her aim was the ruinous mound of Qal'at Sherqat, the place of the ancient city of Assur, where she knew that another team of German archaeologists was hard at work uncovering its ancient brickwork. The site is located on the western bank of the Tigris River, on a rocky promontory rising some 40 m above the floodplain. In its strategic position overlooking the Tigris, Assur would have controlled all commercial boat traffic travelling up and down the river. It also lay on a vital east–west route that connected the resources of the highlands of Iran to the markets of the Euphrates and of the Mediterranean coast to the west.[116]

Upon approaching Assur, Bell was favourably impressed with its striking appearance, especially of the tall remains of its ancient ziggurat, or temple tower:

> As you ride over the ridge of barren hills that skirt the Tigris to the south of Kal'at Shergat, your eye is caught by a great formless pile standing up on the high ground by the river's edge. It is the pyramid, the *zigurrat*, to give it its proper title, that marked the temple of Assur, tutelary god of Assyria. Few deities have been endowed with a shrine more favourably placed. From the summit of the *zigurrat* the god could survey the cradle of the race that did him service. The Tigris washes the foot of his temple mound; far away to the north rises the snow-clad barrier of Kurdish mountains, whence its waters flow, a barrier which nature set in vain against the valour of the armies of Assyria, and across the river the plain stretches away in long undulations to where Arbela lies behind low hills. It would, indeed, be difficult to exaggerate the commanding beauty of the site.[117]

As soon as she arrived at the site, Bell was taken to the expedition house near the edge of the river, where she was warmly received by the four German excavators.[118] Bell instantly took to this group of archaeologists, who were 'keen as mustard', but above all she was drawn to the 'big, shy, silent' director of the expedition, Dr Andrae, who gave her a tour of the diggings and was most forthcoming with his findings and conclusions (Fig. 4.22).[119]

Bell's esteem for Andrae is not surprising. A man of extraordinary abilities, Walter Andrae was almost universally regarded with admiration and respect by those who knew and worked with him,[120] and by the time of Bell's visit in 1909, he had become an archaeologist of the highest order. Trained as an architect in Germany, Andrae had his first experience in the field of archaeology with Robert Koldewey in the early years of the excavations at Babylon, between 1899 and 1903. Under Koldewey's expert guidance, Andrae quickly learned the vital skills of exposing and delineating mudbrick architecture, and of transposing these remains with infinite detail and precision into architectural plans. Andrae was not only a superb excavator and draughtsman, however; he was a talented artist who revelled in capturing the qualities of light, shadow, colour and texture of the Mesopotamian landscape and its ancient remains in striking watercolours and pastels.[121] He also endeavoured to reconstruct, through his artwork, ancient buildings or cityscapes as they would have appeared in their heyday in antiquity. Andrae himself may never have branded his own artistic output as anything more than a 'hobby' or healthy pastime, but for us today, his paintings and sketches provide a valuable record of the ruins of the ancient sites, the surrounding countryside and the life ways of its inhabitants.[122] More than 100 years later, much of this south Mesopotamian environment has now vanished. Furthermore, Andrae's reconstructions bring to life the splendour and monumentality of the ancient cities and their grand structures, these often appearing in the present day as unimpressive, shapeless mounds of earth and rubble.[123] Andrae's reconstructions of Assur and its numerous architectural components in the city's prime during the Middle and Neo-Assyrian periods are particularly numerous and noteworthy and enliven many of his published reports (Fig. 4.23).[124]

Confident in his young protégé's abilities, Koldewey entrusted Andrae with the directorship of the excavations at Assur, which he initiated on behalf of the Deutsche Orient-Gesellschaft in 1903.[125] Once in this position, Andrae set about disclosing the ancient city's rich history, a task that he would undertake practically every year, with only two returns to Germany, until 1914.[126] As it turned out, the site was remarkable for its longevity, having been more or less continuously inhabited for approximately 2,000 years. Its earliest discernible remains dated back to the middle of the third millennium BCE, when the settlement clearly had links to the cities of Sumer in southern Mesopotamia. But it experienced its greatest surge in power and wealth during the latter part of the second millennium BCE, often referred to as the Middle Assyrian period. Within Assur, building projects proceeded, often on a monumental scale, as its rulers sought to highlight the magnificence of their achievements, their cosmopolitan status and their unwavering dedication to their patron god, Assur. After a short interlude of political weakness and fragmentation in the tenth century BCE, the kingdom of Assyria rose to prominence once again, transforming into a powerful Near Eastern empire (883–612 BCE). Although Assur lost its status as the administrative capital of this Neo-Assyrian realm, being replaced by other imperial cities to the north, it remained an important ceremonial and religious centre for the god Assur until its demise in 614 BCE, when it was looted and destroyed by the invading Medes. Finally, Assur flourished between the first century BCE and around 230 CE; in the latter period, it became the seat of local Parthian administrators and was characterized by private housing, a temple and the palatial residence of the Parthian satrap.[127] After the destruction of the Parthian city in the third century CE, the site was never again reoccupied.[128]

The architecture that Andrae and his team unearthed at this amazing site went through countless buildings, rebuildings, restorations and additions, producing several levels of stone and brickwork set higher and higher above the naturally elevated plateau upon which the first settlement was established. Often found in association with all of this architecture were incised clay tablets and other inscriptional material, which provided clues as to age and the events that had taken place in the city.

All of Assur's long, rich history was conveyed to Bell by Andrae, whose knowledge of the site and its countless architectural remains, artefacts and texts was unsurpassed, and whose commitment to shedding light on every aspect of this large

Fig. 4.22   Bell's 1909 photograph of Assur's excavation director, Walter Andrae, feeding a gazelle. Bell had a fondness for this 'big, shy, silent' man and greatly respected his archaeological methods and achievements at Assur.

city, no matter how small or seemingly insignificant, was unparalleled. Bell was clearly aware of Andrae's dedication to the site and his detailed approach, for she writes: 'There is no guess-work here and no scamping, but observation so minute that nothing can escape it, and the true respect for ancient monuments and ancient art which makes no toil seem too long or too heavy.'[129]

The archaeological work at Assur was praiseworthy, and – along with the work at Babylon – Andrae's achievements at this site are regarded by many scholars today as forming the foundations of modern, scientific archaeological exploration in Mesopotamia. As with Koldewey at Babylon, Andrae's focus on obtaining a good architectural record of Assur was paramount, and he sought to record in detail and with accuracy all of the ancient buildings unearthed, down to their individual bricks and stones. Such an achievement in architectural planning is all the more impressive when one considers the vast size of the areas that were opened for excavation – exposed with the assistance of teams of hundreds of local labourers – and the resulting number of structures within the city of Assur that were actually excavated and recorded from 1903 to 1914.

Fig. 4.23 Andrae's charcoal-and-chalk drawing of the cityscape of ancient Assur, looking from the top of the Assur ziggurat down to the Old Palace and Anu-Adad Temple behind, with its twin ziggurats. Beyond the city walls, at the right of the drawing, is the Festhaus, which stood in a specially planted and watered garden. This was the so-called *bit akitu*, a sacred building where religious ceremonies that celebrated the renewal of the king's reign and the favour of the god Assur were performed during the annual New Year's Festival.

Andrae also made a concerted attempt to understand the different temporal phases of Assur's long history through systematic, stratigraphically controlled excavations. Such an investigation was carried out in the area of the Ishtar Temple in the north-west part of the upper city, where a continuous sequence of cult buildings from the mid-third to the mid-first millenniums BCE – a period of some 2,000 years – could be obtained.[130] In the end, by a process in which the architecture of each temple phase was carefully delineated, recorded and then partially destroyed to get down to the next phase below, Andrae and his team of excavators revealed no fewer than eight principal phases of the Ishtar Temple (phases A–H) through time. Each phase represented either completely new temple structures or already existing buildings that had been renewed and redecorated. For the early twentieth century, this endeavour to chronicle the complicated life of this sacred complex was archaeological practice at its very best, and the resulting published reports, which occupy several volumes, testify to the care and thoroughness that went into such an enterprise.[131]

The Assur excavations that Bell witnessed in 1909 were in full swing, and her diary entries reflect her determination to understand and record everything that Andrae and his colleagues showed her as they led her around the site. She must have been a rather intense visitor, overwhelmingly eager for knowledge and tireless with her questions. In his memoirs, composed later in his life, Andrae writes: 'She wanted to know absolutely everything and crept with me tirelessly into every hole and corner of the excavation.'[132] Bell herself writes of her days at Assur:

> I spent the first day and a half going over the excavations inch by inch with Dr. Andrae. During all the time I was there, every moment when we were not actually looking at ruins we were deep in unpublished photographs and plans, and at lunch and in the evening Dr. Andrae, Mr. Jordan and I eagerly discussed the conclusions at which they are arriving.'[133]

Among Assur's ancient remains, Bell was led to the great ziggurat – a massive tower with a temple structure on its summit – which lies near the northern edge of the city, occupying a large area and made of stepped brickwork, still preserved to a height of 30 m.[134] She was also shown the double temple and ziggurats of Anu and Adad, the Mesopotamian gods associated with heaven and the storm. She reports having seen several of the trial trenches that Andrae had dug across wide expanses of the site, in an effort to expose all aspects of the settlement of Assur, not just monumental architecture associated with elite royal and religious activities. In some cases, the trenches had probed quite deeply, exposing very ancient, partially visible houses and streets.[135] Bell writes evocatively of the effect of peering into one of these trenches:

> The houses are in an unusually perfect state; their walls, preserved not infrequently to a height of several feet, enclose little cobbled courtyards with narrow cobbled streets between. These worn and ancient ways, emerging from under the steep sides of the trench and disappearing again into the earth at its further limit, give the observer a sense as of visualized history, as though millenniums had dropped away that separate him from the busy life of the antique world.[136]

Last, Bell was shown Assur's Parthian-period remains, which were found over much of the site; the Germans spent considerable time planning for and comprehending these.[137] Bell describes the Parthian remains enthusiastically in her diary entries and a letter to her parents. She also took several photographs showing various Parthian-period details, in the form of columns, capitals, colonnades and sculptural decoration.[138] As Bell noted, much of the later Sasanian and early Islamic architectures with which she was preoccupied, especially at Ukhaidir, derived their inspiration from earlier Parthian forms.

Bell's interest in such developments would figure especially in her 1914 work on the Ukhaidir palace, during which she traced many of Ukhaidir's features, particularly the open-sided *iwan*, back to the Parthian period.[139]

Bell's photographs from Assur are particularly numerous and capture several aspects of the site and its peoples. Besides her predilection for recording the artistic and architectural details of ancient remains, so often reflected in other photographs of her Mesopotamian journey, Bell was also capable of appreciating Assur from a wider perspective. This finds expression in her panoramic photographs, several of which highlight the impressive setting of the site, with its location high above the Tigris River.[140] The panoramas also emphasize well the incredibly broad exposures of some of the excavations, revealing the foundations and wall remnants of entire building complexes, such as the so-called Festhaus outside the city walls,[141] or the massive brickwork of the city fortifications at the western Tabira Gate.[142] In a few cases, Bell also endeavoured to capture the vertical scale of the excavations, as in her photograph showing the Assur ziggurat from the east, which takes in the height of the ziggurat, as well as the massive ruins of brickwork descending as far as the Tigris floodplain below (Fig. 4.24).[143] In another photograph, taken from the level of the floodplain, one sees not only the towering fortifications of the ancient city, but also the enormous sloping layers of debris that represent the German excavators' spoil heaps, the by-product of their prodigious diggings.[144]

Together with the images of cleared and well-articulated architecture, some of Bell's photos of the Assur excavations are enlivened with the presence of the local labour force responsible for the physical clearance of these ancient structures. They are seen standing in the midst of the operations or resting to one side, while being directed on high by a German supervisor (Fig. 4.25).[145] Still other photographs feature Assur's *Expeditionshaus*, where the payment of workers was being carried out on a table pulled to the middle of the courtyard.[146] The contrast between the German archaeologists sitting upright in their neat suits – one white, one with the appearance of a military uniform – and their un-queued group of variously clad workers highlights well the perceived unequal relationship between the two parties (Fig. 4.26). It is interesting that Bell chose to capture these particular scenes. On the one hand, one could argue that she was simply making a record of an archaeological project that she thoroughly admired, with all of its organization, industry and efficiency. On the other hand, her photos could reflect her underlying colonial attitude and her belief in the intellectual superiority of the foreign team of archaeologists in contrast to the unnamed, uneducated, local labour force at Assur.[147]

Bell was intrigued by just about everything she was shown at Assur and appreciated not only Andrae's profound knowledge of the history of the site and its architecture, but his personality, too. She was touched by his friendly behaviour towards her and his generosity. Even when she returned to Assur in 1911, Andrae was in her view the perfect host and colleague:

> I found this year, as I found 2 years ago, great profit from endless talks with Dr. Andrae. His knowledge of Mesopotamian problems is so great and his views so brilliant and comprehensive [...] He put everything at my disposal, photographs and unpublished plans and his own unpublished ideas. I don't think that many people are so generous.[148]

Bell's photographs further reflect her esteem for Andrae, who appears in several of her shots, on site, in the company of his fellow archaeologists and in two charming photographs where he crouches down to feed a gazelle (Fig. 4.22).[149] Last, with her German colleagues at dinner in the Assur *Expeditionshaus* – in a rare image of Bell from this time – we see her smiling, wearing a fine dress and leaning slightly into Andrae, seated directly to her left (Fig. 4.27).[150]

Above all, Bell seems to have been captivated by Andrae's abilities to bring the past to life through his colourful reconstructions, and with this she found in him a kindred spirit. Although she does not mention his drawings or artwork, she recalls his ability to describe the past in a vivid way that echoed her own penchant for imagining history in all of its rich colour and vividness. Her imagination, so inspired by Andrae, is best reflected in a passage from *Amurath to Amurath*:

> As Dr. Andrae led me about the city, drawing forth its long story with infinite skill from wall and trench and cuneiform inscription, the lavish

Fig. 4.24 Bell's 1909 composite photograph of Assur from the east, showing the ziggurat and the masses of exposed brickwork extending down to the river valley below.

Fig. 4.25 Bell's 1911 photograph of excavations in progress at Assur, showing workmen and a German archaeologist in the foreground (possibly Conrad Preusser).

cruel past rushed in upon us. The myriad soldiers of the Great King, transported from the reliefs in the British Museum, marched through the gates of Asshur; the captives, roped and bound, crowded the streets; defeated princes bowed themselves before the victor and subject races piled up their tribute in his courts [...] Human victims cried out under nameless tortures; the tide of battle raged against the walls, and, red with carnage, rose into the palaces. Splendour and misery, triumph and despair, lifted their head out of the dust.

Fig. 4.26 Bell's 1911 photograph of Assur workmen being paid at a table set up in the centre of the German expedition dig-house courtyard. Seated are two members of the German team, Paul Maresch (facing the camera) and probably Conrad Preusser.

One hot night I sat with my hosts upon the roof of their house. The Tigris, in unprecedented flood, swirled against the mound, a waste of angry waters. Above us rose the ziggurat of the god Ashur. It had witnessed for four thousand years the melting of the Kurdish snows, flood-time and the harvest that follows; gigantic, ugly, intolerably mysterious, it dominated us, children of an hour.

'What did they watch from its summit?' I asked, stung into a sharp consciousness of the unknown by a scene almost as old as recorded life.

'They watched the moon,' said Dr. Andrae, 'as we do. Who knows? They watched for the god.'

I have left few places so unwillingly as I left Kal'at Shergat.[151]

Bell's later publication on Ukhaidir contains numerous references to the findings made at Assur and Hatra, another site whose excavations were directed by Andrae (see Chapter 5). Bell also liberally cites Andrae's opinions regarding key Near Eastern architectural developments through time, again reflecting well her admiration for the man's intellectual qualities. Above all and most telling is the fact that of all the people in Bell's life to whom she could have dedicated her book on Ukhaidir, her most mature and scholarly archaeological report, she chose Andrae:

> To my friend, Dr. Walther Andrae. In grateful recollection of happy and profitable days spent in the first capital of Assyria which has been revealed by his labour and recreated by his learning.[152]

As already discussed in the context of Koldewey's work at Babylon, Bell's antiquities legislation in her later role as Iraq's new Director of Antiquities, which called for more scientific procedures in the field, is almost certainly a reflection of what she had witnessed at both Babylon and Assur. At the same time, Bell's friendly relationship with Andrae was put to the test in the years after the war. Earlier in 1920, Bell had taken an opposing stance to Andrae regarding the problematic 'Lisbon Collection', some 448 cases of Assur antiquities that had been apprehended in Lisbon at the outbreak of the war and were now considered a war prize. Despite Andrae's pleas for the objects' safe delivery to Berlin, Bell claimed that the antiquities rightfully belonged to the 'future Mesopotamian State' and its new museum in Baghdad.[153] Fortunately for the Germans, most of this collection ended up in their hands. Furthermore, as has been discussed, the bulk of the antiquities from Babylon that had been left in Iraq during the war were also authorized to go to Germany around the same time, this latter action clearly reflecting Bell's much-softened attitude towards her old German archaeological friends and their treasured antiquities.[154]

Fig. 4.27   Dinner in the German *Expeditionshaus* on the eve of Bell's departure from Assur, 6 April 1911. Seated from left to right: Walter Bachmann, Paul Maresch, Gertrude Bell, Walter Andrae and Conrad Preusser. Julius Jordan, the other German team member, is absent from the group and is probably the photographer.

Andrae, recalling late in life his relationship with Bell, showed appreciation for her passionate interest in archaeology and her competence as a scholar but never forgot the key role she had played in Mesopotamian political affairs.[155] He suspected that even at the time of her early visits to Mesopotamia, she was on a 'diplomatic mission' (i.e., that she was acting as a spy).[156]

When we return once more to Bell's own writings from 1909 and 1911, it is impossible to discern any motives other than her intense passion for travel and archaeology, this especially evident during her visits to Assur. Her words, laden with superlatives, remind us of the impact that this site and its excavators made upon her:

> I spent at Assur the most delightful days of my whole journey. [...] Yes, these have been wonderful days. I was very very sorry to come away and they pressed me to stay, but I thought if I once began staying there was no reason why I should ever leave off.[157]

> K. Shergat was looking its best, all clothed in grass and flowers. I love it better than any ruined site in the world, but perhaps that is

mainly because of the gratitude and affection which I feel towards my hosts there.[158]

Nimrud

Following the Tigris River on its northerly course, Bell approached another ancient site with spectacular remains from the same period as Assur. This place, however, left a starkly different impression on Bell, given its state of neglect. The site was Nimrud, its vast mounds marking the place of ancient Kalhu, known from the Bible and numerous ancient sources as one of the great capital cities of the Neo-Assyrian Empire. Situated at the confluence of the Tigris and the Greater Zab rivers, the city was founded by King Assurnasirpal II in 878 BCE. During his reign, Assurnasirpal built a lavish palace, temples and a ziggurat on the high mound by the river. Later kings would add to the city with further palaces and temples and a massive arsenal, the place for the king's military equipment and booty. Although the mudbrick walls of these edifices had decayed, the materials within them – including innumerable inscribed clay tablets, stone statuary and exquisitely carved wall panels – were often found intact, and they reflect well the prosperity of Assyria and the formidable imperial power once wielded by its ancient kings.[159]

Bell would have been familiar with Nimrud on account of the well-publicized excavations that had been carried out there in the previous century by the English adventurer-archaeologist Austen Henry Layard.[160] Layard's probes on the acropolis mound at Nimrud had unearthed the treasures of Assurnasirpal's palace (known today as the Northwest Palace), and he had overseen the shipment of many of its lovely sculptures to London, where they became housed, amid considerable fanfare, in the galleries of the British Museum.[161] Layard would go on to dig also at the Assyrian site of Nineveh, opposite Mosul to the north, and find there several other palaces and their precious tablets and sculptures. Today, the Assyrian artefacts of the British Museum, which are largely the product of Layard's and his successors' prodigious diggings in Mesopotamia in the mid to late nineteenth century, constitute a key collection of that institution.[162]

In contrast to the Nimrud antiquities' revered state in the British Museum, however, Bell found the ancient remains at the site itself much neglected. Layard's old excavation pits and holes were 'filled to the brim with grass and flowers', and it was virtually impossible to trace the lines of the ancient Assyrian structures that stood here.[163] Bell found it distressing that several excavated sculptured stones, which had not been previously removed, lay half-exposed in the ground and had been subjected to vandalism and damage from the elements. The British Museum still held the permit for the excavations of this site, but it had not taken the steps to conserve and protect these antiquities that it had left in the ground. Bell remarks in particular on a large statue of an Assyrian god whose upper half was exposed above ground. His nose and ears had been much defaced.[164] She also photographed a pair of stone-carved, human-headed, winged lions (*lamassu*), leaning into the ancient doorway they once would have guarded (Fig. 4.28).[165]

Fresh from her visit to the Germans' neat excavations trenches at Assur, and having witnessed the care with which all of the antiquities were being exposed, documented and removed, Bell found Nimrud's neglect all the more pronounced. She responded by publishing what she saw, carefully contrasting the responsible diggings of the Germans at Assur with the neglectful attitude she had witnessed at Nimrud, and she appealed to the British Museum to pay to have the exposed antiquities either removed or reburied so they would no longer be subjected to damage.[166]

Despite her published reports, however, nothing appears to have happened immediately with the exposed pieces at Nimrud, although in 1926, probably at the instigation of Bell as Iraq's Director of Antiquities, some of the sculptures were brought to the Iraq Museum.[167] The massive statue-in-the-round of a god, now known to be from the Nabu Temple and dated to the reign of the Assyrian king Adad-Nirari III, stands in the Assyrian gallery of that museum.[168] The two *lamassu* that Bell photographed are human-headed, winged lion-centaurs, each holding a goat. Their heads were smashed at some point after 1909, but they were restored to their upright position in 1955. They continued to guard one of the main doors to the throne room of the Northwest Palace of Assurnasirpal II at Nimrud until recent tragic events, perpetrated by IS militants; a video released on 11 April 2015 shows that much of the Northwest Palace's *in situ* contents were vandalized and smashed, after which the militants used barrel bombs to destroy large parts of the palace.[169] Much of the grand and highly celebrated palace of the Assyrian ruler, 'king of the four quarters of the world', for which Bell showed so much concern over a century ago, has been obliterated. A giant field of debris marks its once proud place on the site.

Mosul and Beyond

Our narrative and discussion of Bell's archaeological investigations pertaining to her first Mesopotamian journey comes to a close with her arrival in the city of Mosul on the Tigris River in late April 1909. To be sure, Bell would continue to take a deep interest in many of the ancient sites and monuments of the lands through which she passed right up to the end of her journey in June, when she reached Constantinople, but it is at Mosul that one sees a shift in her principal attentions. Pre-Classical, Parthian, Sasanian and Islamic-period sites and monuments, which had dominated the landscape and Bell's attentions since her entry to the Tigris-Euphrates Valley of southern Mesopotamia back in early

Fig. 4.28 Bell's photograph of her servant, Fattuh, on the right, and another man, standing next to a pair of leaning human-headed winged lion-centaurs, these once upright and guarding one of the entrances to Assurnasirpal II's throne room at Nimrud, *c.*883–59 BCE. Excavated and then reburied by A.H. Layard in the 1850s, by the time of Bell's visit in 1909, they had become partially exposed to the elements and were subject to vandalism. Bell contrasted the state of neglect at Nimrud 'to the pious care with which the German excavators were uncovering the ruins of Assur'. The entire palace of Assurnasirpal II was destroyed by the Islamic State in April 2015, so it is presumed that these stone statues no longer exist.

March, now took a back seat to the multitude of early Christian remains that characterize the rolling hills and mountainous regions of northern Mesopotamia and Anatolia. Beginning with the antique churches and monasteries in and around Mosul, and continuing up through eastern Anatolia, Bell committed herself to reporting and extensively photographing the early ecclesiastical art and architecture she passed. Her focus on churches would culminate in her visit to the Tur-Abdin, a remote, rugged region of south-eastern Anatolia between Diyarbakir and Nusaybin, where Christian communities existed as early as the third century and continued to thrive, with unbroken traditions, for at least

1,000 years.[170] As it transpired, Bell's fascination with these churches, as well as those in the surrounding districts of northern Mesopotamia, resulted in their publication – not only in her 1909 travel account, *Amurath to Amurath*, but in a chapter of a monograph by M. van Berchem and J. Strzygowski.[171] Finally, after another journey to Mesopotamia and a visit to the Tur-Abdin in 1911, during which time Bell carried out additional investigations and made extra observations, she published a substantial report as a journal article.[172]

Other scholars have done an admirable job of bringing together Bell's research and analysis of late antique ecclesiastical architecture and underlining the significance of her work in the grand scheme of contemporary research on late antique Christian material culture.[173] More recent scholarship has also brought attention to the fact that many of the buildings of the Tur-Abdin that Bell documented have been lost through destruction and rebuilding, making Bell's notes and photographs an invaluable source of information about this unique region.[174]

Many of the churches that Bell examined were constructed around the same time as the Sasanian and early Islamic-period structures and assisted her in tracking certain Near Eastern artistic and architectural trends through time, particularly those that were shared by Persian and Islamic artisans. In all, her work on these churches further underlines the incredible scope of her knowledge and the ambitiousness of her research.

CHAPTER 5

FURTHER TRAVELS AND ARCHAEOLOGICAL RESEARCH, 1910–14

Bell emerged as a fully committed and capable archaeological scholar after her return from the Near East in 1909. For the next four years she plunged into archaeological research, immersing herself in the study of Classical and Near Eastern art and architecture, and travelling almost solely with archaeological objectives in mind. While many of her interests continued to be Byzantine churches, she also gave herself over to the study of the Sasanian and Early Islamic periods, acquired through her recent travels and her special discovery of Ukhaidir. The culmination of her work on these time periods was the publication of *Palace and Mosque at Ukhaidir* in 1914.[1] The monograph combined many of her recorded observations from her Near Eastern trips and represented her most mature and erudite treatment of an archaeological subject. In terms of its methodology and conclusions, it took into account the scholarship of colleagues such as Josef Strzygowski, Ernst Herzfeld and Walter Andrae. The work also reflected what Bell had learned from her Classical archaeology colleagues and what she had gained from her own experiences in Italy and the Dalmatian Coast, these affecting in particular her thinking about Classical influences on early Islamic architecture. In all, the years 1910–14 were incredibly productive for Bell and led to her most significant and commendable work in the field of archaeology.

First Publications after Bell's 1909 Near Eastern Trip

Back in England, one of Bell's first aims was to publish an account of her journey, just as she had accomplished with her earlier travels through the Levant, *The Desert and the Sown* (1907). She now had field notebooks, diary entries, letters and photographs with which to put together this work, and after some effort, it was submitted to the publishers at the end of 1910. This book – carrying the somewhat obscure title *Amurath to Amurath*[2] – has a more distinct scholarly character than *The Desert and the Sown*. The book contains lengthy deliberations over the dates of ancient events and the identification of place-names, detailed architectural descriptions of archaeological sites, and references to ancient historians and modern scholars who had commented on the places visited.[3]

Amurath to Amurath also contains discussion about the region's modern peoples and the current political climate of the East. These subjects engaged the ever-inquisitive Bell, often with the same intensity as that which she applied to the area's antiquity. The book's dedication to Bell's friend Lord Cromer[4] is particularly noteworthy for its political content, describing the reformist coup of the Young Turks, who had successfully deposed the despotic sultan of the Ottoman Empire in April 1909 and introduced an ambitious set of new, liberal reforms designed to bring the empire and its government into the twentieth century.[5] Travelling through the East in 1909, Bell had been surrounded by news of the Young Turks' actions and had taken note of the reaction to the dissemination of their progressive ideas among the Arabs of Mesopotamia, notably the little-understood notion of 'liberty'.[6] Bell found herself encouraged by these developments and urged Cromer to help her raise sympathy in England for the Young Turks movement.[7]

Despite all of Bell's good intentions to produce an interesting work that mixed both current affairs and archaeology, *Amurath to Amurath* never found a good audience upon its publication in 1911. It did not fit well within the genre of travel writing because of its detailed exposé of archaeological sites, and its overview of current events was too scattered and impressionistic to be regarded as a true political commentary. When it was released, the book sold fairly well, possibly on account of the success of *The Desert and the Sown* and of people's continuing fascination with Bell as an intrepid woman traveller, but it didn't receive the same critical praise and public fanfare as the earlier work. One reviewer complained of its 'detailed descriptions of ruins', which were 'apt to be skipped even by a conscientious reviewer'.[8] Bell's friend David Hogarth commented that with its 'maturer science', the book possessed less of the 'careless rapture' of her first travel book.[9] In spite of its mixed reception, however, *Amurath to Amurath* demonstrated Bell's abilities as an unparalleled observer of all things modern and ancient in the Near East, and of her ability to record them in all of their richness and diversity.

Besides *Amurath to Amurath*, Bell produced several scholarly works during these years. She wrote a long article for the *Geographical Journal*, describing her journey down the east bank of the Euphrates River,[10] and contributed an important chapter on the churches of the Tur-Abdin in Anatolia to a book entitled *Amida*, which her mentor and friend Strzygowski was putting together with her other scholar-friend Max van Berchem.[11] Of particular importance to Bell, however, was the castle of Ukhaidir and her efforts to ascertain its date and influences, principally on the basis of certain architectural features found within it, like vaults. The outcome of her research was an article in the *Journal of Hellenic Studies* that appeared in 1910,[12] much of whose content has already been discussed and assessed in Chapter 3.

Rather than bringing an end to her work on this desert palace, however, Bell's Ukhaidir report in the *Journal of Hellenic Studies* only whetted her appetite. Ukhaidir had too many unanswered questions, and she wanted to be the one to answer them. To be sure, with Ukhaidir's complex blend of inspiration from the worlds of Greece, Rome and the Near East, she may have felt particularly well suited to taking on this project, given her considerable knowledge of all of these regions. Whatever the case, it was clear that further field research was necessary, and so even by the end of 1909, Bell was hatching plans for more ventures abroad. Two trips, in 1910 and 1911, not only entailed a second journey to Mesopotamia – including a brief but exciting excursion into the Persian frontier; they also included travel to inspect archaeological remains in Italy and the Dalmatian Coast. Upon her return from these trips, Bell spent much time corresponding and conferring with other scholars about the ancient remains she had seen, as well as formulating and writing up her conclusions.

Italy and the Dalmatian Coast, 1910

'Dearest Mother. I have begun life as a student [if you do not recall me] and have been working all day long at a palace, partly at the German Institute and partly in the Palatine. It has been delightful beyond words.'[13] Such were Bell's sentiments upon writing home from Rome in February 1910. Never content to travel for pure, unfocused pleasure, even in a place which offered as many varied cultural delights as the Eternal City, Bell set herself to learn as much as she could about the Roman architectural remains and absorb what she could from the cadre of eminent Classical scholars residing there.

Although none of Bell's extant letters indicate specific reasons for coming to Italy, her archaeological interests at the time – which primarily concerned the palace of Ukhaidir in Mesopotamia and its architectural elements that derived inspiration from Greco-Roman traditions – must have been her primary motivation. Bell had by this time just recently completed her article on the vaulting systems of Ukhaidir, which she had submitted to the *Journal of Hellenic Studies*,[14] and she still had foremost in her mind the vaults' possible connection to Rome and the West, something she had only cursorily explored thus far.

It is evident that while in Rome, Bell wished to spend more of her time with archaeologists than with any other friends or acquaintances, for the former are frequently mentioned in her letters both before and after the departure of her father, who had been her travelling companion in Rome for at least ten days in February.[15] When Bell remained on her own in Rome for the rest of February and into March, her education in Roman-period architecture and ornament seems to have intensified, particularly after a lecture that she gave, probably at the British School at Rome. She reports that it was attended by 'a very distinguished audience of professors'.[16] It is likely that on this occasion Bell lectured about her findings at Ukhaidir, and that she received helpful and enthusiastic feedback from the attendees.

Present at Bell's lecture, and probably the person who had organized the talk, was a long-time friend of Bell, Eugénie Strong, at that time the assistant director of the British School at Rome (Fig. 5.1). Working in that capacity until 1925, Strong helping to transform the institution into a major scholarly and cultural centre.[17] Strong was a well-connected individual in Britain, having moved in London high society in her youth, and then having benefitted from her marriage to Sanford Arthur Strong, a scholar of Oriental languages and literature and an art historian, who served as Librarian to the Duke of Devonshire at Chatsworth House in Derbyshire.[18] Eugénie herself would assume this post for four years upon her husband's death in 1904. She was also a well-trained and skilled scholar of Classical art and archaeology. She had been educated at Cambridge, the British School at Athens, and Munich, where she studied under the Classical archaeologist Adolf Fürtwangler and the philologist Ludwig Traube.[19] Her interests gradually shifted from Greek to Roman art, and during her time in Rome, where she lived until her death in 1943, she published widely on Roman art – particularly sculpture – and Roman religion.[20]

By the time of her trip to Rome in 1910, Bell had known Eugénie Strong for some time. They had moved in the same circles of English society, and their families were acquainted.[21] Bell was also connected to Sanford Arthur Strong, who had offered to teach her Persian in 1892 before her departure to Persia.[22] Later, in 1896, she received instruction in Arabic from him in London, where he had been appointed Professor of Arabic at University College, and he had read over her translations of the Persian poet Hafiz.[23] After Eugénie and Arthur married in 1897, Bell's relationship with both of them continued, and then with Eugénie alone after Arthur's death.[24] While in Rome in 1910, Bell saw Eugénie frequently, especially after her father's departure. Strong's connections with the scholarly community of Rome made it easy for Bell to move about in this society, meeting Strong's colleagues in the British School at Rome, listening to lectures – including one delivered by Strong – and wandering with her around the Palatine Hill, Forum and Baths of Caracalla.

Bell also became acquainted with the director of the British School at Rome – and Strong's closest working colleague – Thomas Ashby. Appointed to the British School in 1906, Ashby spent most of his adult life in Rome, becoming a

Fig. 5.1 Photograph of Eugénie Strong, a friend of Gertrude Bell, working as Librarian at Chatsworth House (1904–9), shortly before taking up her post as the Assistant Director of the British School at Rome. Well liked and well connected to the scholarly community of Rome, Strong introduced Bell to experts of Classical antiquity such as Thomas Ashby, Esther Van Deman and Richard Delbrück.

foremost researcher of the topography and monuments of the city and of the surrounding Campagna.[25] He hiked and biked tirelessly around the Roman countryside, investigating and recording all extant inscriptions and Roman remains and endeavouring to place these finds within their proper historical context.[26] With Thomas Ashby as director and Eugénie Strong as assistant director, the British School at Rome possessed an academically robust and balanced team that would bring the school into its heyday of success and prestige. While Ashby was the expert on Rome's topography and countryside, Strong's specialization was the Roman art in the galleries.[27] Moreover, while Ashby was painfully shy and lacked social graces, Strong was socially confident and brought to her position a developed network of connections, which not only bolstered the British School's relationship with other important Italian and European researchers but helped to bring necessary funding.[28] Bell does not mention any of Ashby's shyness in her letters, only remarking that he spent much of his time 'trotting around with us'.[29] On at least one occasion, she reports having an immensely pleasurable motor outing in which Ashby showed her and her companions the ruined villas around the hills of the Campagna.[30]

Of special interest is Bell's acquaintance with the American archaeologist Esther Van Deman, a 'nice little plain American woman', as Bell describes her in a letter (Fig. 5.2).[31] It is conceivable that Van Deman met Bell in the British School at Rome, and she possibly attended Bell's lecture, being counted among the 'distinguished audience of professors' at that event.[32] Bell's letters reveal that the two spent a considerable amount of time together, inspecting Roman ruins within the city, including the Palatine Hill and the Forum, the Pretorian Camp, Trajan's Baths and the Baths of Caracalla. Van Deman also accompanied Bell on her outing with Thomas Ashby to the Campagna, where they visited ruined villas. Later, she and Bell went to Tivoli to see Hadrian's Villa.[33]

Bell found in Van Deman not only a friendly companion but an impressive scholar of Roman archaeology. By 1910, Esther Van Deman, who was in her forties and living in Rome, had earned a scholarly reputation for her extensive, detailed work on Roman construction, particularly the uses of concrete and wall-facing techniques, subjects on which she is now regarded as a pioneer.[34] She used the appearance and size of brickwork facings and concrete mortar to date Rome's buildings, a method presented in her monograph on the imperial Atrium Vestae, which she published in 1909.[35] This work was followed by two important articles in the *American Journal of Archaeology* (1912), which dealt also with the dating of Roman buildings through their bricks and mortar.[36] While Van Deman's dating method ultimately proved to be flawed, her work is still praiseworthy for its close observations and its scope. Moreover, many of her publications were expertly illustrated with exact architectural plans and crisp, detailed photographs.[37]

Fig. 5.2   Photograph of the American archaeologist Esther Van Deman, and a Roman brick construction. During her visit to Rome in 1910, Bell saw much of Van Deman and visited several Roman-period sites with her. She was probably influenced by Van Deman's interest in ancient materials and construction techniques, and the assiduous manner in which she recorded such details in her archaeological research.

By 1910, Van Deman had become well acquainted with Thomas Ashby, and in her letters to Bell it is clear that she held him in high esteem. Van Deman's and Ashby's scholarly relationship would later culminate, between 1924 and 1931, in a profitable collaboration on all of the surviving aqueducts in and around Rome, establishing their building histories and mapping their routes into the city.[38]

Van Deman also knew and liked Eugénie Strong[39] and admired the Ashby–Strong teamwork at the British School. In a letter to Bell, we get her fascinating assessment of that partnership:

My own work is not exciting – though I've found a number of new facts recently. I am working up the levels on the Palatine and in the Forum, and find there is much of value for my 'brick'. I think Mr. Ashby has my 'brickwork scheme' with him, but he has not yet sent it to Mrs. Strong or to Mr. Stuart-Jones, I hear. I so wish that same gentleman and Mrs. Strong were to change places, for he does not like the public duties and wishes her to do them, while she does them so well. But if any must be over her, I hope there may be no change, for they go admirably, and he is so very loyal and nice to her in every way – all men would not be so lovely. And he is a sound, good scholar and is honored everywhere for his real ability and good work. With her here, the School seems ideally managed only I hope they may let Mrs. Strong have more time to work next year – she cannot be rude, but it is hard to see so many people constantly, for it saps one's vitality, especially in our climate.[40]

Bell must have been impressed by Van Deman's scholarly drive and diligence, and no doubt saw a little of herself in this unique woman, who often conducted her research alone in the field and yet managed to collect a tremendous amount of detailed architectural data, just as Bell strove to do. She would have witnessed first-hand Van Deman's fastidious, focused approach to archaeological remains. On one occasion in Rome, with her father in tow, Bell remarks that 'we considered every separate brick in the Forum with her one morning'.[41] On another occasion, Bell recounts how she joined Van Deman at the Baths of Caracalla 'and worked at them all the afternoon'.[42] Rather than finding these close observations of Roman ruins tedious, Bell describes them as 'most interesting'. Her comprehension of these complex constructions enlivened her, as is evident from her comments about her visit with Van Deman to the Baths of Caracalla: 'what a delightful sensation it is to begin to understand these things. I feel so excited about them that I can scarcely bring myself to come in for lunch!'[43]

In Bell we see a similar drive to provide clear and detailed observations of construction methods and technical considerations in her descriptions of ancient buildings (Fig. 5.3). This is nowhere more evident than in her letter written to Van Deman from the Dalmatian Coast, where she travelled from Rome in April 1910, with the aim of taking in Roman ruins and learning about their schemes outside Italy. Given Van Deman's own penchant for exactitude, Bell felt no need to hold back in her description, as she might have when writing to her parents. Moreover, Van Deman would have been genuinely interested in her observations. Bell's details from the palace of Diocletian at Split (Spalato) include the following:

Now the vestibule dome was built of rings of tufa a. brick, not very regular, a course or two of brick, then, 3 or 4 of stone; with mortar. No filling, the brick a. stone structure goes right through. The bricks are rectangular, indeed exactly square, 32c–35c square x 2–4c thick. The mortar 4–5c thick.[44]

Fig. 5.3 Bell's photograph of one corner of the Hall of Doric Piers at the Villa of Hadrian, Tivoli (Italy). Her effort to photograph this architecture probably was inspired not only by her own interests in brick constructions, but those of Esther Van Deman, her travelling companion, who would have pointed out to her the net-like *opus reticulatum* brickwork, and the vertical and horizontal brick bands around the doorway.

Van Deman warmly received Bell's letter, even if the details supplied fell outside of the construction schemes she was familiar with in Rome:

> I was *much* interested in Spalato and under great obligation to you for writing me all these interesting facts. After the Basilica in Trier, which is solid brick, & of square bricks too, I am less astonished at anything my Romans may do, but I'm sorry they try so *many* new schemes.[45]

In Bell's own published works, direct evidence of Van Deman's influence upon her is not readily apparent, although one can perhaps detect it indirectly. Bell's coverage of the palace at Ukhaidir, with her careful observations, measurements, descriptions of brick, arch and vault constructions, as well as her detailed notes on structures elsewhere, emulate Van Deman's emphasis on such matters.[46] Specific techniques – such as the construction of archivolts, and arch constructions with wooden centring – although copied from O. Reuther's own detailed observations at Ukhaidir, reflect Bell's appreciation for such subjects, possibly in the wake of having witnessed Van Deman's careful observations in Rome.[47] Lastly, Bell's goal to record construction details, not only in her plans and notebooks but also through her photographs, may be credited in part to Van Deman, whose photographic records of brickwork in wall facings were abundant and meticulous.[48]

Over the course of their eventful lives, Bell and Van Deman crossed paths only once, during those happy days in Rome in 1910, and their correspondence was brief. Nevertheless, their letters show a clear attitude of friendliness and respect. Bell included Van Deman among her 'bosom friends' in Rome, and Van Deman, who could be aloof and brusque with some, expressed her admiration for her friend by signing her letters 'affectionately'[49] and 'very sincerely and affectionately'.[50] Her sense of having found another kindred spirit who revelled in the exploration of ancient ruins, away from the bustle of city life, is conveyed by her remarks to Bell: 'How I wish you were here to go off into these wild hills with me'[51] and 'I wish you were here to take a few more wild runs after vaults, for our hills remain lovely.'[52] One wonders what sorts of achievements these two extraordinary women might have accomplished had they combined their professional talents. But they were both fiercely independent, and the marks they ultimately made in their respective careers were achieved largely by 'going at it' alone.

Of all of her connections in Rome, Bell's relationship with Richard Delbrück (1875–1957), a noted German expert on Hellenistic and early Republican Roman architecture, seems to have made the greatest impact on her research pertaining to Ukhaidir and early Islamic architecture.[53] Once in Rome, Bell did not waste any time tracking down Delbrück, who at the time was the First Secretary of the Deutsches Archäologisches Institut, in Rome. Delbrück appears to have been flattered by Bell's intense but nonetheless intellectually inquisitive and attentive nature towards him, and willingly made himself available to her. Especially after the departure of her father, Bell spent a great deal of her time in the company of Delbrück – visiting sites in Rome, attending lectures, discussing topics such as vaults or simply reading books he recommended in the German Institute.[54] Delbrück also advised Bell of other places to visit in Italy, giving her a guidebook to Spoleto and providing her with introductions to the Director of Antiquities in Split, on the Dalmatian Coast.[55] The intensity of their relationship and the mutual admiration each felt for the other is evident in a letter that Bell wrote to her mother:

> Yesterday morning I spent 3 hours with Delbrück who gave me the most wonderful disquisition I have ever heard on the history of architecture. It was a regular lecture; he had prepared all his notes and all his books to illustrate what he was saying. He is a very remarkable man and as he talked I got the hang of things that had always remained mysteries to me. He ended by saying that it was absurd that I should be so ignorant of the Roman monuments and by telling me that I ought to come here for 6 weeks to study.[56]

With so much time spent in each other's company, one wonders whether a more personal attachment evolved between Bell and Delbrück, although there is no evidence that anything of that nature transpired.[57] In any event, Bell's continued scholarly esteem for Delbrück is reflected in her 1914 monograph on Ukhaidir, in which she addresses the subject of Early Islamic architectural forms, materials and construction techniques, and the inspiration they received from the architecture of Rome. Practically all references pertaining to the transmission of Hellenistic forms to Roman Italy, notably vaults and wall decorations such as arched and columned niches, and their consequent transference to the Near East – now on a grander and more ubiquitous scale – are to Delbrück's *Hellenistische Bauten in Latium*.[58] Bell regarded this monograph as the authoritative work on the subject, and she found in Delbrück a scholar whose efforts to trace the evolution of architectural forms through time and across space were a good match to her own methodological emphasis on this process – this being a critical feature of her discussion of the genesis of the Islamic palace.

The last part of Bell's 1910 trip to Italy included a short excursion to the Dalmatian Coast of Yugoslavia across the Adriatic, where she wanted to see archaeological sites of Roman and Late Antique date. Her interests were no doubt precipitated by her continuing research into the transmission of architectural features between East and West during these periods, spurred on not only by her work on the early Islamic period in Mesopotamia but also by her ongoing study of Late Antique Anatolian churches. She left Rome on 27 March, spending two nights in Spoleto in east Umbria before reaching Ancona and crossing the Adriatic. Once at the city of Split (Spalato) on the Dalmatian Coast on 30 March, Bell made a speedy inspection of the ruins on her wish list: the palace of Diocletian at Split, the cathedral and Venetian fortresses at Šibenik (Sebenico), early Christian basilicas at Solin (Roman Salona, where Diocletian was born), the walled medieval town of Trogir (Trau) further up the coast, Zadar (Zara) and Pola. From Pola, Bell journeyed to Trieste and then carried on back into Italy to Udine and Ravenna, reaching the latter on 7 April.

Although venturing alone on this trip to Dalmatia, Bell made the acquaintance of several people along the way, many of whom were archaeologists. These included Max Dvořák – a leading art historian of the Vienna School of art history and an opponent of Josef Strzygowski – and Emil Reisch, Director of the Austrian Archaeological Institute.[59] Bell also made the acquaintance of the German archaeologist Georg Niemann, well known for his research and fieldwork in Greece and Anatolia, as well as his careful architectural study of Diocletian's palace at Split.[60]

The care with which Bell made architectural observations of ancient buildings continued on this journey, as evidenced by her letter to Van Deman, quoted above, in which she provides detailed comments about the building materials and construction methods at the palace of Diocletian. Bell's photographs of the sites she visited, mostly of vaults, columns, capitals and carved friezes, betray her continuing interest in architectural ornament, styles and building techniques.[61] All the while, she observed the impact made by the East on the region's architecture, noting in the palace of Diocletian, for example, that 'suddenly the East steps in, bends the architraves into arches, sets new and fantastic decorations on every cornice, brings even the plan of a Syrian camp on which to build the house of a king'.[62] On her visit to Trogir, she remarked that the cathedral's system of vaulting was taken 'straight from Byzantium'[63] and that a tiny domed basilica in that town was a type peculiar to the Levantine coast.[64] At Zadar, she looked at a ninth-century church 'of oriental type'.[65] These hints of the East also reminded Bell of the pleasure she felt exploring its lands, and they reawakened her desire to see it once more. Still in Italy, Bell wrote, while visiting Spoleto:

> I climbed a hill outside the town, walking through brushwood full of primroses, hepaticas, anemones and violets, and at the top there was a ruined church, very lonely and beautiful – I felt again as if I must be back in the East and half wondered why Jusef was not there to carry my camera and Fattuh to hold my measuring tape.[66]

Such reflections clearly indicate that the East had taken hold of Bell. She would not stay away much longer.

Mesopotamia and Persia, 1911

'I have not heard anything of politics – not thought of anything but archaeology. It's so enchanting to plunge into it again.'[67] Such were Bell's sentiments upon arriving in Cairo and spending two days with her old friends, the scholars Bernhard Moritz and Enno Littmann, having talked 'ceaselessly about the origins of Moslem art – interspersed with much gossip about the people who are researching into them'.[68] This was the start of Bell's trip to the East, shortly after which she would sail to Beirut, and then journey overland to Damascus. From Damascus, her intent was to carry out an intrepid camel ride straight across the Syrian desert, approaching her beloved Ukhaidir from the west (Fig. 5.4).

Although Bell was going to be travelling to many of the places she had visited in 1909, her 1911 undertaking was different in character. This was not so much a journey of exploration as it had been in 1909, when Bell travelled off the beaten track into remote regions simply for their own sake. Now, she had a list of specific places that she wanted to visit and particular objectives to be carried out at each of them. She was focused on the things that needed to be seen, planned and photographed, and she did not waste much time in between.

In light of such determined motives, which are borne out in Bell's letters and diaries, we will address what others have conjectured about this stage of her life, and the nature of her pre-war interest in the East, particularly Mesopotamia, the principal objective of her travel in both 1909 and 1911. Since Mesopotamia was the country in which Bell would chiefly focus her intelligence activities during the war that was to follow only a few years later, there has been speculation that the true nature of Bell's pre-war travels involved gathering information for the British government. One can certainly discern her interest in the current political affairs of the country – amply evident, for example, in *Amurath to Amurath*, which features long commentaries about modern Mesopotamia and the Ottoman Empire's control over it. Moreover, even the book's dedication, as has been noted, had a markedly political overtone in its address to Lord Cromer. Adding to this impression are the opinions of others who knew Bell at the time, such as Walter Andrae. Andrae would later write in his memoirs that he suspected Bell had been a spy when she came to visit him at Assur in 1911.[69] Considering the degree of esteem in which Bell held Andrae, the amount of his work she endeavoured to emulate in her own scholarship, and the fact that her Ukhaidir account – indisputably the scholarly achievement of which she was most proud – was dedicated to Andrae, this remark seems surprisingly inapposite. But Bell's later political career was of such a remarkable and all-pervading nature that for many, it was difficult to recall that she had once *not* been an agent of the British government in Mesopotamia.

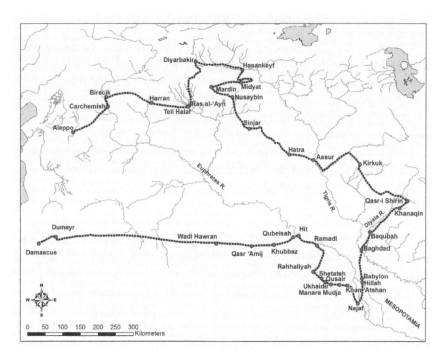

Fig. 5.4   Map of the Near East, showing the route of Bell's 1911 journey, which included visits to Ukhaidir and the Persian frontier before heading through northern Mesopotamia and across Anatolia.

Bell's 1911 travel itinerary dispels any notions concerning her intelligence-gathering aims and activities. Although she passed through Damascus and Baghdad, where the politics swirled around her, she spent more time in the desert – following, for example, the old caravan route across the Syrian desert to Ukhaidir, or eastwards from Baghdad, where she intrepidly crossed over into the Persian frontier to visit the ruins at Qasr-i-Shirin. Bell also took in the ruins at Assur and Hatra, then swiftly made her way up to the Tur-Abdin to complete her survey of the Christian churches in that remote area of south-eastern Anatolia. All of these places were far removed from the political and economic centres of the Ottoman administration. But they interested her archaeologically and were relevant to her research either on Ukhaidir or on late antique ecclesiastical architecture.

Constructions around Ukhaidir, Early March 1911
Bell's planned trip across the Syrian desert from Damascus was hampered by severe cold and snow, which detained her for many days.[70] She eventually left the city on 9 February, but even still, her progress was slow, and it took the remainder of the month to cross the cold and wet desert with her caravan of

guides, guards and camels before she reached the town of Hit on the Euphrates River (23 February) and then Ukhaidir to the south (1 March). Upon arriving at the castle, Bell set herself to re-measuring and planning some of its architectural features, taking additional notes about its construction and layout and photographing features that she had neglected to record during her first visit in 1909 (see also Chapter 3).

By this second trip to Ukhaidir, Bell was also curious about the palace's surroundings and the geographical and historical context in which Ukhaidir may have grown and developed; she thus took some time to visit and record sites that were thought to be contemporary with Ukhaidir and related to it in some way. Among these was the site of Qusair (Bell's Qṣair), about seven km (4.5 miles) north-west of Ukhaidir, to which Bell rode one day to inspect and photograph it, and where she observed a few houses, along with rectangular tanks.[71] She conjectured that at Qusair had been obtained the gypsum to make the mortar that held together the masonry of the Ukhaidir palace, and that it also had provided lodgings for the gypsum workers.[72] Investigations of this site in more recent times, however, have shown that it was a Late Sasanian-period settlement containing the remains of two Christian churches.[73] The site should thus be dated earlier than Ukhaidir, and there is no evidence that it manufactured gypsum, as Bell had postulated. Nevertheless, Bell's photographs of the standing architecture at Qusair have proven valuable. An archaeological survey conducted later in the twentieth century found that some of this architecture had subsequently crumbled and disappeared.[74]

Once her work at Ukhaidir was finished, Bell took the time to visit some of the ruins that lay in the desert between Ukhaidir and Najaf and the Euphrates River to the east. One of the sites, reached after about three to four hours' ride from Ukhaidir over sandy desert (roughly 25 km), was a ruined, round brick tower called Manara Mujda (Bell's Mudjḍah). At the time of Bell's visit in 1911, the zone of recessed niches with rectangular heads above the level of the doorway was fully preserved all the way around the tower, as were even higher courses of plain brickwork and a course of dog-tooth brickwork (Fig. 5.5).[75] When Creswell passed by the tower in the early 1930s, several courses of brickwork at the top had disappeared in places. By the time of Finster and Schmidt's visit in 1973, up to ten courses of brickwork had crumbled.[76] Today, the zone of recessed niches is more than half-destroyed in places, regrettably demonstrating its significant deterioration over the past 100 years.[77]

With no ruins in its vicinity, the Mujda tower appears to have stood on its own. Bell conjectured that it functioned as a landmark for caravans passing over this flat expanse of desert from Najaf over to 'Ain al-Tamr, a short distance to the north-west of Ukhaidir, where there was an oasis.[78] Bell hesitated to give a firm date for Mujda, save to say that on the basis of its primitive arch construction, it should be earlier than comparable minarets assigned to the thirteenth century CE.[79] Later scholars who visited this remarkable tower agree that it functioned to mark the way across the desert towards Ukhaidir or 'Ain al-Tamr, and that it would have served as part of the 1400-km Darb Zubayda, the Muslim pilgrim route that linked the religious centre of Kufa, at Najaf, with Mecca and Medina in the Hijaz.[80] Some scholars have further noted that its inspiration may have come from the watchtowers constructed in this area during the Sasanian period, which served to guard southern Mesopotamia's western frontier.[81] Mujda is now postulated to be contemporary with Ukhaidir, or perhaps earlier in the Umayyad period, before the settlement in the area around 'Ain al-Tamr had begun to decline.[82]

After a few more hours of riding across the flat desert away from Mujda, in the direction of Najaf, Bell and her entourage reached Khan 'Atshan, a ruined caravanserai, where Bell stopped to camp and took the time to plan and photograph (Fig. 5.6). Bell was actually the first European to visit and properly plan this structure. She noted its square, defensive appearance, with thick walls strengthened by projecting round towers, and a fortified gateway.[83] Inside, a courtyard with a water tank gave access to covered chambers, one of these having the appearance of a vaulted *iwan* (no. 5).[84] She observed that several of 'Atshan's architectural details – notably the plan of its fortified gateway, the method of vault and semi-dome construction (in Room 6), and the decoration of engaged columns and arched niches – could also be found in the palace at Ukhaidir, suggesting a proximate date.[85] Moreover, 'Atshan's location, about halfway between Kufa and Ukhaidir, with the Mujda tower to mark the halfway point to Ukhaidir, suggested to her that it must have been part of the same route system that connected all of these places in the same time period or slightly later.[86] Creswell, in his own investigation of 'Atshan, concurred that the site was contemporary with Ukhaidir.[87] Further, he conjectured that with its vaulted *iwan* and a nearby room that had a distinctively elegant semi-dome of concentric brick rings (Creswell's Room G and Bell's Room 7), it did not serve as a regular khan but rather would have been used by someone of princely stature, like Isa, nephew of al-Mansur, the possible builder of Ukhaidir, who would have treated 'Atshan as a stopping place on his occasional trips to Kufa for Friday prayers.[88] As convincing as Creswell's interpretation may be, a more recent study of 'Atshan by Finster and Schmidt has drawn attention to certain architectural details (more rounded archways and rounded door wings) and pottery that must be dated earlier than Ukhaidir, and the authors therefore postulate a pre-Abbasid date for the ruin.[89]

Bell's photographs indicate 'Atshan's extreme state of dilapidation; long cracks were clearly visible in the brickwork of the structures, and much of the superstructure and roofing had long ago caved in.[90] By the time of Creswell's visit,

Fig. 5.5 Bell's photograph of the tower of Manara Mujda, near Ukhaidir, in southern Iraq. Although much diminished from its original height, this brick tower's fluting, dog-tooth ornament and rectangular niches are still preserved in its lower courses. The tower probably functioned to mark the way across the desert as part of the Muslim pilgrim route to Mecca and Medina in the early Islamic period.

Fig. 5.6 The caravanserai of Khan 'Atshan, in the desert near Ukhaidir, with its outer round towers. The building is believed to be earlier than Ukhaidir, although the two places share similar architectural features. Bell's photographs of the building, taken in 1911, bear testimony to long cracks in the brickwork and a much-crumbled superstructure and roofing. Today, the site is even further ruined.

some 20 years after Bell's, the height of the enclosure wall to the east of the main entrance had diminished just over two metres, apparently due to brick robbing.[91] By the time of Finster and Schmidt's visit in the 1970s, deterioration from the elements had led to a further crumbling of the elliptical barrel vault in Room 6.[92] Today, 'Atshan is not a well-preserved site but instead a pale echo of its once-princely state in the desert more than one thousand years ago.

Bell's visit and plans of these desert structures around Ukhaidir represent the first concerted attempt to record their ruins and situate them in the wider context of the desert east of the Euphrates, their possible relationship to Ukhaidir, and peoples' movements in the region when Ukhaidir was occupied. Later research would expand upon or refine Bell's earlier suppositions, particularly about postulated dates, but it is still generally agreed that both 'Atshan and Mujda served within a system of way-stations or markers on a route that led away from Kufa into the desert, and that Ukhaidir itself was also linked to this route. Bell's description and plans of Qusair, Mujda and 'Atshan, reported in full in her 1914 publication *Palace and Mosque at Ukhaidir*,[93] are all basically correct, and her photographs preserve a useful record of structures that have since fallen into further disrepair or have disappeared altogether.

Qasr-i-Shirin

A daring aspect of Bell's 1911 journey was her venture beyond the borders of Ottoman-controlled Mesopotamia, into the Persian frontier to the east. The objective of this particular trip was Qasr-i-Shirin, an ancient site located in the Kermanshah province of Persia. Her interest in this site was prompted by her study of Sasanian palatial architecture, its influence on the site of Ukhaidir, and her knowledge that the ruins of at least one Sasanian palace were believed to exist there. According to literary tradition, one of the residences of the last Sasanian king, Khosrow II (590–628 CE), had been established there in honour of his beloved queen, Shirin.

Qasr-i-Shirin had been previously investigated by the French archaeologist Jacques de Morgan, who had briefly stopped by the ruins in 1891 and had published his plans of the principal buildings he had observed, in his *Mission scientifique en Perse*.[94] Bell was aware of de Morgan's report of the site but did not have the French plans with her, and thus she could neither confirm nor reject some of the architectural elements that de Morgan had indicated, many of which she suspected to be conjectural.[95] Her visit aimed to obtain a fuller description of the site and to assess the degree to which its postulated Sasanian design may have inspired later Islamic period palaces, such as Ukhaidir.

After leaving Baghdad on 19 March 1911, Bell travelled in a north-easterly direction, roughly following the course of the Diyala River, before crossing the hills of Jebel Hamrin and reaching the town of Khaniqin, on the Alwand River, on 22 March.[96] From there she moved into the Persian frontier, beyond the Ottoman border, reaching Qasr-i-Shirin on 23 March. She would remain at the site until 26 March, during which time she measured, planned and photographed the site's ruins. Upon her departure, she headed in a north-westerly direction towards the Turkish-Persian border, crossing over and travelling up to Kirkuk, which she reached on 31 March and where she inspected the unique church of Mar Tahmazgard. Afterwards, Bell travelled west, back over to the Tigris, reaching the site of Assur on 3 April.

At Qasr-i-Shirin, Bell was struck by the picturesque setting in which she now found herself: green grass and wildflowers growing all around and within the ruins, and the snow-covered mountains of the Zagros rising up in the distance to the east.[97] Despite the appearance of tranquil beauty, this region of Persia had become lawless, with local groups of Kurds managing their own affairs relatively free of official government interference. According to Bell's account, the Kurds were engaged in various forms of brigandry, extorting heavy levies on individuals and baggage animals passing through their territory.[98] Even more unnerving was that just about every person was armed and spent much of their time at rifle practice. Bell began in earnest to plan the Qasr-i-Shirin ruins, only to find bullets whizzing above her head, and so she had to set her camp within the courtyard of a khan in the nearby village, under the protection of the local Kurdish chief

(Kerim Khan), he himself being 'the worst brigand of the whole frontier'.[99] Despite the hazards, however, Bell's letters and diaries provide a colourful and happy account of her time spent at Qasr-i-Shirin; these no doubt reflect her enjoyment of both the places and the people she encountered here,[100] and her satisfaction with her archaeological work – finding, for example, that the big palace was 'far nearer to Ukhaidir than de Morgan shows'.[101] Bell worked for four days at Qasr-i-Shirin (two full days, and a few hours on the first and last days), planning out the ruined remains that were visible on the surface and taking many photographs. The end product of her work was a plan and detailed description of the Palace of Khosrow. She sometimes referred to this in her diaries and photographs as the 'big palace' or the 'Great Palace', while the remainder of her work was occupied with the plan of the 'small palace', otherwise known as Chehar Qapu, which was located a short distance to the south of the Palace of Khosrow.

Glancing through the photographs that Bell took of the ruins at Qasr-i-Shirin, one is struck with wonder as to how anything could be properly discerned and planned, particularly without the aid of excavation. Almost all upper parts of the buildings were in a severely ruinous state, having tumbled long ago and appearing as heaps of stone and brick rubble strewn about the ground, with grass growing thickly over the heaped ruins. Nonetheless, Bell patiently made careful observations of the architecture and room arrangements of these edifices, endeavouring to discern their general plans, reporting on significant details of construction and conjecturing as to their function and significance. In the end, her amassed data from Qasr-i-Shirin appear in their final form as an important chapter in her published work *Palace and Mosque at Ukhaidir*.[102]

The Palace of Khosrow (Fig. 5.7)

Of the ruin which was said to mark the place of the Palace of the Sasanian king Khosrow II (Bell's Khusrau), Bell observed that it was constructed mainly of coursed undressed stones laid in thick gypsum mortar, with a core of stone rubble and concrete.[103] Brick appears to have been used occasionally for columns, vaults and arches, but unfortunately, only a few of these features were found standing.[104] The palace was built upon a massive raised platform of earth, recalling earlier Achaemenid and Assyrian palaces (i.e., Persepolis and Khorsabad), which were also built on elevated platforms.[105] Three sets of double ramps or stairways, also recalling those of earlier Achaemenid palaces, provided access to the top of a large, open court devoid of structures at its eastern end. The monumental palatial complex, comprising an axial arrangement of grand ceremonial reception rooms and massive open courts, with surrounding corridors and private apartments, rose magnificently to the west.[106]

Of the two edifices at Qasr-i-Shirin, Bell felt that the Palace of Khosrow had the greatest similarities to Ukhaidir. She was struck by the use of barrel vaults to cover most of the interior spaces, as at Ukhaidir, not to mention evidence of similar vault types, including those with a slight outset from the wall at the level of the springing, which she compared to similar offset vaults at Ukhaidir.[107] Bell could also observe similarities in room forms and arrangements, particularly striking among the so-called *iwan* groups in the Palace of Khosrow, which took on the same appearance as those found within the *baits* of the palace at Ukhaidir.[108] The central part of the palace itself – with its large, open court in front, monumental *iwan* porch (no. 1),[109] antechamber (no. 2) and lavish audience hall (no. 3) (Fig. 5.8),[110] where the Sasanian 'king of kings' himself may have held court – provided the general scheme that would be adopted by the early Islamic architects in their planning of Ukhaidir's ceremonial core, with its open court, *iwan* porch and square hall of audience in behind. Last, and especially significant to Bell, was the overall layout of Khosrow's palace, in which the ceremonial rooms were placed in the centre of the palatial complex, separated from the rest by narrow corridors,[111] and then flanked on either side and at the back by the private apartments or *baits*, with their *iwan* groups (Fig. 5.9).[112] It is possible that these room groups represented the accommodations for the harem and other members of the royal court.[113]

At the same time, Bell was aware of some of the differences between the badly preserved Palace of Khosrow and Ukhaidir, and she did not use the latter to fill in the missing parts of the former.[114] Lionel Bier's wry accusation regarding Bell's Qasr-i-Shirin palace plan – that it is a prime example of 'how Sasanian architecture can be influenced by early Islam' – seems somewhat unreasonable in light of the architectural differences Bell describes.[115] Her reconstructed scheme, in which a latitudinal chamber (no. 2) appears between the porch (no. 1) and domed hall of audience (no. 3) in the ceremonial core of Khosrow's palace, for example, differs from Ukhaidir's arrangement, in which the principal *iwan* or porch (no. 29) gives immediate access to the hall of audience (no. 30). Furthermore, the strong defensive character of Ukhaidir, with its fortified outer enclosure wall and fortified gatehouse, can be contrasted with the unfortified nature of the Palace of Khosrow. Although the entire royal complex and large pleasure-grounds of Qasr-i-Shirin would have been surrounded by walls, the palace itself was resolutely undefended, standing in the centre of a capital of the Sasanian empire and not in some remote desert locale.[116] Where Bell did see parallels between Khosrow's Palace and Ukhaidir – namely in the axial arrangement of the principal ceremonial rooms and the flanking *iwan* apartments – such features can often be corroborated by photographs of the still-standing structures she took on the spot and by her field notebook, in which her plans and measurements of such architectural features were carefully recorded.

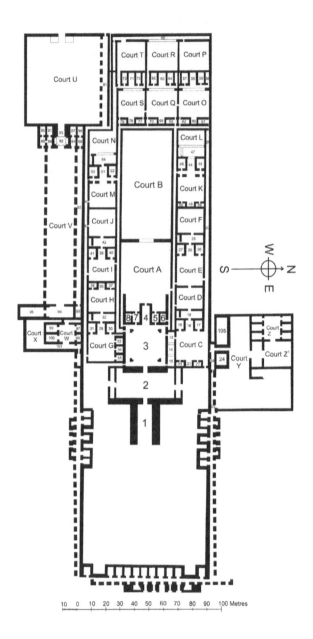

Fig. 5.7 Bell's plan of the Palace of Khosrow at the site of Qasr-i-Shirin (modern western Iran). The building, with its numerous corridors, courts and chambers, was actually built on two levels, the area of the central rooms and courts (Courts A–J and Halls 1–3) rising higher than the remaining parts of the structure.

Fig. 5.8 Hall 3 in the Palace of Khosrow, Qasr-i-Shirin, facing south-west. Bell regarded this space as a vast domed 'hall of audience'. The remains of an adjacent rectangular vaulted *iwan* (no. 4) can be seen on the right side of the photograph. Qasr-i-Shirin's other pre-modern structure, Chehar Qapu, can be seen in the distance beyond the palace.

The German scholar Oscar Reuther offered the only other fully reconstructed scheme of the Palace of Khosrow at Qasr-i-Shirin, this appearing in his often-cited report on Sasanian architecture, in Arthur Upham Pope's magisterial, multivolume series *A Survey of Persian Art*, published in 1938. Ever the skilful architect, Reuther not only produced his own version of the plan of the palace,[117] but he drew a lovely reconstruction,[118] which has become widely accepted as the definitive form of the structure.[119] As L. Bier has pointed out, however, Reuther himself probably never visited Qasr-i-Shirin, and his plan is simply an amalgam of de Morgan's and Bell's reconstructions, along with some postulated reconstructions derived from more recently excavated sites.[120] Reuther's plan deviates from Bell's principally in the palace's central block, where de Morgan's columned entrance porch or *iwan* is added to Bell's straight walls,[121] and Bell's subsequent latitudinal chamber is replaced by a domed hall that is flanked by vaulted side chambers.[122] Behind this arrangement is an open, arcaded court with *iwan* at the back, taking the place of Bell's domed space. This reconstruction is far more conjectural than Bell's, and in truth, if anything can be seen as a copy of later Islamic palaces, it is this – although admittedly, it also corresponds favourably with the interior arrangements of other presumed Sasanian palaces, such as those at Firuzabad and Sarvistan.[123] Ultimately, whichever reconstruction we choose to accept as the more faithful representation of Qasr-i-Shirin's magnificent complex, it is fair to conclude that Bell's primary motivation was to produce an honest plan of the structure. Her reconstructed scheme does appear to have been derived only from observations of surviving structures she encountered on the ground at Qasr-i-Shirin and not from preconceived notions as to what this palace *should* look like.

Fig. 5.9   A view towards the chambers (*iwan* groups) at the western ends of open courts Q and S, near the back of the Palace of Khosrow at Qasr-i-Shirin. These spaces are conjectured to have served as private apartments, with accommodations for members of the royal family and court.

Some of the debate concerning the date of the Palace of Khosrow can now be put to rest, given the most recent work on the ruins by Iranian archaeologists who have found compelling evidence in the form of pottery, coins and thermoluminescence dating for the early Islamic Abbasid age of the palace.[124] If this dating is accepted, the monument's place within the evolution of the eastern palace, as formulated by Bell, must be rejected. Nonetheless, Bell's original observations of the intriguing parallels between this palace and Ukhaidir can still be supported, not because one building inspired the other, but because they were roughly contemporary edifices and would both have been informed by similar architectural concepts circulating around the Near East at the time of their construction.

Chehar Qapu (Fig. 5.10)

Besides her detailed description of the Palace of Khosrow, Bell's report on Qasr-i-Shirin includes a description of the 'Smaller Palace', or Chehar Qapu, which covered a large rectangular area[125] just over half a kilometre to the south-west of the Palace of Khosrow (Fig. 5.11). According to Bell's observations, the building was accessed by a main entrance gateway, this flanked by courts and small chambers.[126] The gateway opened into a long, open courtyard, Court D, with a further gate (no. 15) at its western end. On either side of Court D, and accessible to it by vaulted passageways at the court's western end, were groups of courts and associated rooms (Figs 5.12–13).[127]

At the western end of the Chahar Qapu, in an area much ruined, stood Hall 54, a large, square chamber over 16 m^2 in area, with 3.90 metre-thick walls (Fig. 5.14). This particular feature dominated the whole complex.[128] It was believed to have carried a dome constructed of brick and set upon squinch arches.[129] Arched doorways gave access to the interior domed chamber on all four sides, these too being built of bricks and surmounted by small, round-headed windows.[130] A few ruined chambers were observed to the north-west and south-west of Hall 54, but little else was preserved in this sector.[131]

In her description of Chehar Qapu, Bell never stated that the domed Hall 54 stood separate and detached from other structures around it; she merely said that she was not able to discern the exact form of the nearby structures on account of their ruined state, nor could she determine whether they had any relation to the hall.[132] Nevertheless, her plan does render Hall 54 in a discrete state in the larger building,[133] and in her published discussion of Qasr-i-Shirin, she pronounced it to be 'isolated'.[134] On the basis of this distinctive arrangement, she raises the possibility that the hall functioned as a fire temple, and she compares it to other structures with proposed fire temples, such as the square western annex of the 'palace' at Hatra.[135] Bell's concluding remarks convey her opinion that on account of Chehar Qapu's lack of symmetry and irregularity in the arrangement of the rooms, and its conspicuous square hall at one end, it is not similar to Ukhaidir.[136] Bell herself was convinced of the building's Sasanian date and saw it as sacred, with a fire temple 'wherein the holy element burned with a perpetual flame'.[137]

It is striking the degree to which Bell's observations and conclusions about Chehar Qapu have held sway over the literature, and few scholars, until recently, have further clarified this structure. Bell's plan, description and photographs have thus far been the most extensive record of Chehar Qapu, and her report has been used as the basis of all later scholarly interpretations. Thus, other scholars, such as K. Erdmann, E. Herzfeld and G. Gullini, regarded Bell's rendering of the isolated place of the domed Hall 54 accurate, and this led to their agreement that the hall functioned as a fire temple.[138] Reuther, in his much-quoted chapter on Sasanian architecture, adopted Bell's plan, only adding an ambulatory around Hall 54 and remarking that amid the ruins, this feature could have been missed.[139] He also noted that the recess in the outer stonework between the arched doors and the windows above[140] could have supported the springing of a lower vaulted walkway.[141] He, too, favoured the hall's identity as a fire temple.[142]

J. Schmidt was one of the first to seriously challenge Chehar Qapu's function as a fire temple, citing early Arab descriptions of the settlement at Qasr-i-Shirin, none of which make any mention at all of a fire temple there.[143] Schmidt suggests, alternatively, that the building as a whole may represent a palace, and

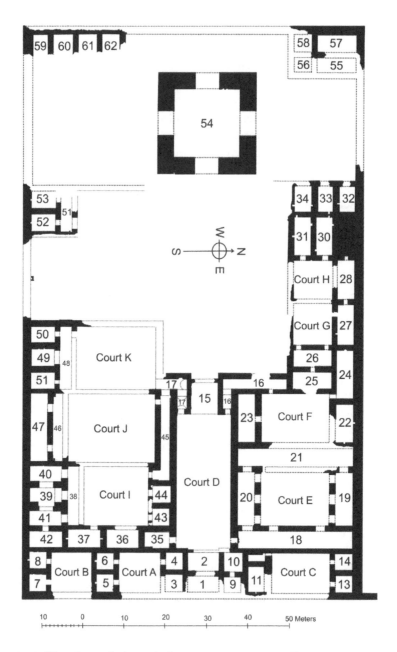

Fig. 5.10 Bell's plan of the Chehar Qapu at Qasr-i-Shirin. Many scholars, including Bell, have postulated that the building functioned as a Sasanian fire temple on account of the large square Hall 54 near the back. It is more likely, however, that this was a palace from the Islamic period.

Fig. 5.11   A general view of the ruins of Chehar Qapu at Qasr-i-Shirin from the south-east, showing the remains of vaulted spaces and of the massive square Hall 54, to the right of centre.

that it is remarkably similar in its internal layout to the Abbasid palace at Ukhaidir.[144] Bier also recognized the two palaces' similar outer dimensions and elaborate entrance complexes, which comprise a long hall terminating in small vestibules at both ends.[145] The second vestibule in both palaces gives access to an open court beyond. The disposition of *baits* around the central part of the palaces is also regarded as similar. Last, Bier equates the square, domed Hall 54 of Chehar Qapu to Room 30 at Ukhaidir, regarding both as the principal focus of the building (audience chambers) and noting their similar position towards the back of the palace.[146]

Perhaps the most striking parallel between the two palaces, and one that has not yet been noted in print, is the uncannily similar position and plan of a rectangular court to the right of the entrance complex, which is surrounded on two or three sides by covered porticos.[147] Since this complex at Ukhaidir has been unanimously accepted as the palace's mosque, it is tempting to assign the same function to the arrangement at Chehar Qapu, and thus to argue for the building's Islamic – not Sasanian – date, something already suspected by Bier.[148] It is interesting that Bell herself never observed these striking parallels, preferring the Palace of Khosrow as the better parallel to Ukhaidir, and pointing to the lack of a symmetrical arrangement in Chehar Qapu as being the ultimate factor negating its identity as a palace and its similarity to Ukhaidir.[149]

Since Bell's and Reuther's time, probes around Chehar Qapu have shown that Hall 54 was not completely isolated but rather was part of a complex surrounded by other chambers, making its identity as a fire temple less likely.[150] Moreover, recent Iranian investigations have found evidence for columns surrounding Hall 54 on all four sides, giving the arrangement the form of a pavilion.[151] Lastly, a great deal of Islamic pottery has also been found in and around the complex, lending credence to a later Islamic date.[152]

Fig. 5.12 Within the ruined spaces of Chehar Qapu, Bell could often make out interesting architectural features, such as this corner squinch in Room 14, which would have helped to resolve the angle between the square space of the room below and its domed roof. Parts of the plastered fillets of the squinch are still preserved.

In the end, we are still not in a position to state definitively the date and function of Chehar Qapu, although an Islamic date seems highly plausible, given the evidence described above. Whatever the case, Bell's drawn plan of the complex is still the most complete record in existence of this building, and it has continued to be that from which almost all reconstructions, comparisons and interpretations are made.

Hatra

As Bell had long known about the site of Hatra and its importance for comprehending the development of architecture in the Near East, her 1911 Mesopotamian trip would have been incomplete had she not been able to visit this magnificent desert site and take in some of its impressive ruins. Although not the first to record Hatra, Bell took careful note of several of its remains, these consequently figuring prominently in her scholarly work on Ukhaidir and her discussion of the development of Oriental palatial architecture.

First settled in the Late Hellenistic period (second to first centuries BCE), Hatra became the seat of a local Arab dynasty, gaining its economic livelihood as a caravan stop and trading centre on several vital trade routes through the desert steppe of northern Mesopotamia.[153] Hatra also lay near the border between the Parthian kingdom and the territories controlled by the Romans and became for a time a buffer state that checked the advance of the Romans.[154] Hatra would continue to be closely linked to the Parthians up to the second century CE, and its art and architecture bears the strong imprint of Parthian culture and religion. The site withstood several Roman attempts at capture during the reigns of Trajan (116/117 CE) and Septimius Severus (198/199 CE), but after the collapse of the Parthians in the early third century, Hatra became allied with Rome and housed one of its legionary garrisons. The city was eventually captured by the Sasanians under their leader Ardashir and his son Shapur I in 240–1 CE and fell into decline thereafter, becoming deserted by the mid-fourth century CE.[155] Hatra remained an abandoned, ruined site, infrequently visited, until the beginning of the twentieth century, when investigations by the German archaeologist Walter Andrae on behalf of the Deutsche Orient-Gesellschaft were carried out.[156] The site underwent further excavations by Iraq's Directorate General of Antiquities and restorations later in the twentieth century, and was added to UNESCO's World Heritage List in 1985.[157] Today, Hatra's future is most precarious, having fallen victim to Islamic State (IS) and suffering from deliberate, devastating acts of vandalism and destruction (reported further below).

Gertrude Bell's interest in Hatra may originally have been sparked in early 1909 by Bernhard Moritz, who mentioned the site to her when she visited him in Cairo before her first journey into Mesopotamia.[158] Later, upon arriving at Assur in early April of the same year, Bell learned from Andrae about his own investigations of Hatra, which he had begun in 1906 and was carrying out in tandem with his more

Fig. 5.13 Room 31 in Chehar Qapu, with an ovoid, offset vault, and a small arched niche in the back wall. Bell compared vaults such as these at Qasr-i-Shirin to those at Ukhaidir, although different construction materials (stone versus brick) had been used.

extensive excavations at Assur.[159] From Bell's diary entry we know that Andrae showed Bell photographs of Hatra when she was at Assur in April 1909, and that she was fascinated by the site's ample display of carved ornaments, which adorned the lintels and jambs of doorways.[160] Hatra was also part of an animated discussion of vaults, domes and niches that took place over dinner in the Assur dig-house that night, along with the subject of the place of Parthian architecture – including that from Hatra – in the long evolution of architectural traditions in the Near East, which continued to the time of Ukhaidir's construction.[161] Altogether, Bell could see, from this early stage in her thinking about Ukhaidir, that Hatra played a pivotal role in her understanding of the architectural traditions from which the makers of her desert palace had received inspirations and influences.

Bell's interest in the Parthian architecture at Hatra did not wane upon the completion of her 1909 trip, for she questioned Andrae further about the impact of Western art and architecture on Hatra in a letter she wrote to him in 1910.[162] Andrae's reply, in a letter dated 20 June 1910,[163] expresses uncertainty as to the specific lines of Western influence upon Hatra, suggesting that they came via Rome and Hellenistic forms already transposed in the Near East. He asserts, nonetheless, that it is difficult to find direct descendants at Hatra, since everything already appears there in hybrid form, with a curious melding of Eastern and Western traditions. The complex, entwined nature of Near Eastern

Fig. 5.14 Hall 54 of Chehar Qapu from the south, showing the partially preserved vaulted roof of Room 62 on the left. The arched doorway in the centre of the south wall of Hall 54 is made of horizontally laid bricks. A small, round-headed window appears above the doorway. Hall 54's interior space is believed to have been covered by a massive dome set upon squinch arches, the latter of which are still preserved in places in the interior.

art and architecture that Andrae emphasizes is a prominent and persistent theme in much of Bell's scholarly writing pertaining to late antiquity and the early Islamic period, and it is probable that Andrae – along with Herzfeld, who also emphasized this theme in much of his work – provided the strongest influences in her thinking on this subject.

Clearly inspired by Andrae's account of his work at Hatra, and their conversations about the site, Bell made her actual visit in April 1911, after she had departed from Assur and a happy reunion there with the German excavation team. It seems that she had long intended to visit Hatra, for already in Andrae's letter to Bell in 1910, he was giving her directions concerning her arrival there.[164] Hatra lies just over 51 km due west from Assur, and she records that it took her caravan 11 hours to reach Hatra, passing over rolling steppe the entire way and crossing the Wadi Tharthar, a salty seasonal stream.

Upon arriving at Hatra, Bell was immediately impressed by the size and grandeur of the ruins, particularly the 'palace' that stood in its midst, which could be seen from a five-hour distance on every side, and whose 'immense stone built halls, roofed with huge vaults' were decorated with 'the strangest carved ornaments that have ever grown out under oriental chisels' (Fig. 5.15).[165] Perhaps equally exciting to Bell, however, was the fact that the site had become the base of the Turkish army's military operations and was currently accommodating some 300 men, encamped in tents. Apparently, the army had been dispatched to bring the Shammar Bedouin to order, and the Turkish commander, Riza Beg, had done admirably in levying the tribes, getting them to pay taxes and settling all of their grievances. Rather than being annoyed or intimidated by the ample display of soldiery in this remote desert place, Bell writes happily and glowingly of her interactions with the Turkish soldiers, heaping praise on their achievements and showing particular admiration for their commander, whom she deemed a 'very remarkable man'.[166] Before her departure, the whole army – cavalry, infantry and artillery – paraded before her, and she took the opportunity to photograph the spectacle, much to everyone's satisfaction.[167]

It is interesting to read Bell's description of the Turkish military presence at Hatra, and her appraisal of their work, in a letter to her parents:

> The whole business has been brilliantly well done and I think that if the government has a few more men like Riza Beg (which it has) and knows how to use them, the whole desert will shortly be as safe as any city. I shall write a long article for some leading journal when I get home and call it 'The Pacification of the Desert', for it should be known how well and wisely the Turks are handling matters here [...] The immediate future of the Turkish empire depends, to my mind, entirely on what the soldiers are like, for it is carefully to be remembered that the whole work of government is at this moment military, and will be for some time to come, that is till the country is internally at peace.[168]

Bell's description of these affairs reflects well her interests beyond matters relating to ancient relief decoration and monumental stone architecture, as spectacular as they would have been at Hatra. Indeed, they presage her work in Middle Eastern political affairs, which would eventually consume her life, particularly after the war. It is noteworthy that in 1911, she felt genuine esteem for the Turkish army and only wished, innocently, to publicize its positive achievements in some 'leading journal'. Such sentiments clearly highlight her extreme interest in current affairs, as well as her perceptiveness and desire to weigh in on such matters.

Of Hatra's ancient remains, Bell repeatedly commented on the bizarre nature of the design and placement of their carved ornaments, with their unusual mélange of Greek, Roman and Oriental elements, deeming them 'pretty mad', 'a nightmare' or 'quite barbaric'. Her photographs nicely capture many aspects of this unusual art, as they focus on specific elements of ornament located on architraves, door jambs and the underparts of lintels (Fig. 5.16). Bell's images are also valuable for preserving a record of the original ruins of Hatra and these distinctive ornamental details before they underwent significant restoration later

Fig. 5.15 Gertrude Bell's camp in front of the ruins of the Temple of the Great *Iwans*, Hatra.

in the twentieth century.[169] Far worse, however, have been the recent actions of IS in its efforts to destroy pre-Islamic idols and 'false gods'. Damage to Hatra's antiquities appears to have started in February 2015 with the smashing of statues, many of them representations of Hatrene kings, housed in the Mosul Museum.[170] Video footage from early April 2015 documents IS individuals chipping and smashing sculpture at Hatra with pickaxes and sledgehammers. A trio of carved human heads that Bell photographed in 1911 was shot at with an AK-47 rifle (Fig. 5.17). Such wanton acts further underscore the value of Bell's photographic images, since the latter are a permanent record of Hatra's antiquities, which now simply no longer exist or are damaged beyond repair.[171]

Of Hatra's architecture, Bell was drawn in particular to the Temple of Shamash (also known as the Great Temple or the Temple of the Great *Iwans*), which stands on the western side of a large, rectangular *temenos* enclosure in the centre of the city, and which at the time of her visit was considered a palace. Its principal constituents are several lateral rectangular chambers roofed with lofty vaults. Bell took the time to observe carefully the form and technology of these vaults at Hatra, and she devotes considerable space to their description in her 1914 final report on Ukhaidir.[172] Particularly interesting to her, in this report, is the place of Hatra in the history of the development of the vault, this feature first being observed in ancient pre-Hellenistic Mesopotamia and then continuing prominently right up to the Islamic period at locales such as Ukhaidir, as will be discussed further below. The other principal architectural feature of the Temple of Shamash in which Bell took a great deal of interest was the *iwan* – this room-type with its open end facing a courtyard in front, which characterizes the main lateral chambers covered by the high vaults just described.[173] The persistence of the *iwan* – from its early origins in ancient Mesopotamia, up through the Parthian and Sasanian periods and into the architecture of the early Islamic period – represents a critical aspect of Bell's grand narrative concerning the development of the early Islamic palace, as at Ukhaidir, as will also be discussed further below.

Bell had the opportunity to return to Hatra one more time, in 1922, when she was most active as a political officer of the British government in the newly founded kingdom of Iraq. She was on a tour of the northern polities of Iraq, and time allowed her – accompanied by other British officers – to visit the ancient sites of Assur and Hatra.[174] Travelling now by car over the same 'glorious rolling steppe' she had traversed on horseback in 1911, Bell found Hatra remained captivating. In a letter to her father, she describes with almost lyrical prose the strangeness of the carved ornaments and the loftiness of the vaults. Reflecting the dramatic turn of events brought about by the war and the downfall of the Ottoman Empire, Bell also reports the presence of the Shammar camel-guard who now presided over the site, where before their overlords the Turks had tried to tame them. Despite such changes, however, Bell – peering down at the camels and horses of the guard within the courts and seeing the smoke of the Shammar Bedouin tents beyond the ancient city walls – was struck by the timelessness of her surroundings: 'It was a scene in which past and present were so bewilderingly mingled that you might have looked down upon it like any evening for twenty centuries.'[175] Sadly, one cannot make that claim now in the twenty-first century. Recent events in Iraq have been most unkind to ancient sites, including spectacular Hatra.

The Genesis of the Islamic Palace, 1911–14

Upon the completion of her travels, first to Italy and the Dalmatian Coast, then to Mesopotamia and Persia, Bell had amassed sufficient data to write her most ambitious scholarly report ever. Her work on this volume carried through 1912 and 1913 and was completed just as she embarked on her monumental trip to Arabia, at the end of 1913. Appearing in print in 1914, *Palace and Mosque at Ukhaidir: A Study in Early Mohammadan Architecture* represented in many ways the culmination, and largely the endpoint, of her scholarly pursuit of archaeology.

As already described in the chapter concerning Ukhaidir, Bell's monograph provided a detailed and learned discussion of the castle's architectural forms and the sources of its creators' inspiration. The work also offered an informed proposal for the desert palace's date. Yet, it was evident that Bell was not merely content in this book to devote herself to these descriptive and temporal matters about Ukhaidir. Another complete report on Ukhaidir had already appeared, by

Fig. 5.16 The left side of the North *Iwan* of the Temple of the Great *Iwans* at Hatra, showing the remnants of a flanking engaged column and arch decoration, consisting in part of sculpted human heads. Bell's photograph captures the appearance of this complex before later twentieth-century excavations and reconstruction work restored the temple façade to its full height.

Fig. 5.17 Bell's photograph of a group of three sculptured heads or masks on the interior wall of the South *Iwan*, in the Temple of the Great *Iwans*, with arched doorway below. These incurred damage in early 2015, when they were targeted by IS gunfire.

the German scholar Oscar Reuther in 1912, and Bell could hardly improve upon this publication's detailed plans and illustrations, which highlighted beautifully the palace's distinctive architectural characteristics.

For Bell's report to stand apart from Reuther's effort, it required a broader, more substantive scope. She attained this by situating Ukhaidir's 'oriental' palace and mosque within the wider context of the architecture of the Near East and of the ancient world as a whole, tracking its features back to their earliest origins and discussing the multitude of cultures and architectural traditions that had inspired their development up to their appearance in the early Islamic period. In the end, such investigations constitute three extensive chapters within the Ukhaidir monograph. Two cover the Classical and 'oriental' inspiration for the three-storeyed north façade of Ukhaidir's 'Court of Honour' and the earlier Islamic antecedents of Ukhaidir's mosque.[176] The third and longest chapter (67 pages), 'Genesis of the Early Mohammadan Palace',[177] traces the Ukhaidir palace form back to Classical and ancient Near Eastern prototypes, some existing as early as the second millennium BCE. The chapter forms the central piece of the monograph and is particularly ambitious, given its temporal range and geographical scope, which go far beyond a mere consideration of Ukhaidir in and of itself. It reflects Bell's wide learning from over a decade of research on late antique ecclesiastical architecture and early Islamic monuments. In particular, it highlights her knowledge of the broad sweep of Near Eastern antiquity, much of this acquired through her Mesopotamian journeys, where she was exposed to ancient sites and monuments extending from the earliest periods of high civilization up to those thought to have existed only shortly before Ukhaidir's construction, like Qasr-i-Shirin in Persia. The chapter additionally underlines Bell's exposure to the artistic and architectural innovations of Greece and Rome, which had also left their mark on Ukhaidir. Her knowledge of Classical traditions derived from her earliest studies of the ancient world as well as her recent visit to Italy. All of these subjects were informed by Bell's self-directed studies and by knowledge obtained from other scholars with whom she engaged in extensive and fruitful correspondences, or with whom she developed close personal relationships. It is indeed remarkable the extent to which, in the chapter, Bell highlights her acquaintance with these scholars and draws on their expertise. In so doing, she demonstrates her capacity for intensive research while simultaneously impelling her readers to acknowledge her deserved place among her academic peers.

In its method and ambitious scope, 'Genesis of the Early Mohammadan Palace' continues to bear the imprint of her early mentor, Josef Strzygowski, whose work frequently consisted of broad sweeps and grand narratives that situated architectural and artistic traditions within the wider history of the ancient or pre-modern world and traced them to their roots. Bell's attempt to take components of the Islamic palace back to their 'genesis', for example, clearly echoes Strzygowski's style in finding the earliest manifestations of particular formal characteristics. Moreover, the fact that Bell was able to locate the origin of the heart of the Islamic palace, the *iwan*, in the 'Orient', and not in Greece and Rome (as discussed below), fell in line with Strzygowski's insistence on the eastern, non-Classical origins of nearly all important architectural forms of late antiquity and the Islamic period.[178] Like Strzygowski, Bell gave priority to the style and form of art, especially architectural features, and tracked similarities through time and space using comparative analysis. Her objective was to demonstrate a clear and convincing path of cultural diffusion that spread out from one point of origin. This method did not place much emphasis on other factors that may have affected the development of certain characteristics, such as the social and political contexts in which architectural traditions had developed, or the choices and peculiar tastes of individual human agents. Bell's comparative, formal analysis clearly had its shortcomings, but it was deemed an acceptable and effective approach in its time, and was attractive to scholars of the ancient world in Europe and North America who no longer wished to or could not give primacy to the philological, textual evidence, this having long dominated studies of antiquity up to that point.

I suspect that besides Strzygowski's influence, Bell's 'Genesis of the Early Mohammadan Palace' bears the imprint of another individual, Ernst Herzfeld, whose scholarship she also greatly admired at the time of writing the chapter. Bell was familiar with Herzfeld's 1910 article, 'Die Genesis der islamischen Kunst und das Mshatta-Problem', which comprised his masterful study of the art and architecture of the desert palace of Mshatta, located south of Amman in present-day Jordan, and his controversial – but correct – opinion that this was an Umayyad Islamic construction of the eighth century CE.[179] Even today, this article is considered a masterpiece among studies of early Islamic art because of its clear methodology, persuasive argument and broad frame of reference.[180] There is perhaps a touch of irony in the fact that Herzfeld's 'Genesis' article triumphantly overturned the hypothesis of Bell's mentor, Strzygowski, who had argued for a pre-Islamic date for Mshatta.[181] Moreover, Herzfeld had accomplished this coup de grâce largely by employing Strzygowski's own comparative formal methodology, thus beating him at his own game.[182] As we have already seen through Bell's early correspondence with Herzfeld (see Chapter 4), his bitter rivalry with Strzygowski was the cause of some antagonism and resentment at first, but by the time she was completing her Ukhaidir monograph in 1913, Bell was on amicable terms with Herzfeld and had come to respect, even admire, his phenomenal knowledge and his knack for getting things right.[183] Knowing these circumstances, it is hard to resist the idea that the title of Bell's chapter may well echo that of Herzfeld's article; her attempts to highlight all the cultural influences that affected the construction, style and layout of Ukhaidir in the eastern Syrian desert arguably emulated Herzfeld's treatment of Mshatta in the western desert.

To discuss and assess the entire contents of Bell's chapter on the genesis of the early Islamic palace in her Ukhaidir monograph would require a lengthy report going well beyond the limits of this work. Presented here, therefore, is an overview of one of the principal architectural features of the Islamic palace: the ceremonial reception room, known as the *iwan*, which Bell traced back to its origins. The overview is intended to give the reader some sense of the scope of the research Bell carried out through her reading, her correspondence and discussions with other archaeologists and scholars of antiquity, and her own astute deliberations on the subject. One can also see how her archaeological fieldwork and observations factored into her work and constituted a critical aspect of her overall conclusions.

At Ukhaidir, the most notable *iwan* was Room 29, open to its full width at one end. Deep in the centre of the palace, it was reached only after the visitor had passed through the complex's elaborate gatehouse and grand gallery, led through a magnificent interior open courtyard. The *iwan* was grandly vaulted, serving to highlight its function as the palatial complex's principal reception room, and it gave access to other important reception chambers in the palace. Although this particular *iwan* was the most notable at Ukhaidir because of its ceremonial character, this distinctive type of room occurred elsewhere within the palace. Its form could also be located in the private suites, or *baits*, situated on either side of the central ceremonial block. In these *baits*, the open-ended *iwan* was flanked by more closed, private chambers and in this context probably served as the main living room for the occupants of the suite and the place where visitors were received.

According to Bell, the *iwan* originally derived from the lands of the Hittites of northern Syria, Anatolia and northern Mesopotamia.[184] Her proposal advanced a theory of the German archaeologist Robert Koldewey. Although mostly known for his excavations at Babylon, Koldewey had previously excavated at the Neo-Hittite settlement of Zinjirli in Anatolia, and had outlined in that site's archaeological report the development of the two-chambered, towered Hittite gateway into the palatial *bit hilani*. Several examples of the *bit hilani* palace were observable at Zinjirli, dating back to the beginning of the first millennium BCE, and according to Koldewey they contained within them the antecedents of the *iwan*, taking here the form of a covered portico flanked by two towers, which in turn gave access to an inner hall with a small chamber at either end.[185] Bell relates that Assyrians subsequently adopted this *bit hilani* arrangement for their own palaces in the succeeding centuries, and then the arrangement reappeared in Achaemenid architecture, where it took the form of two towers flanking a columned portico, with a hall of audience in behind.[186] The Achaemenid builders of the palaces of Pasargadae, Persepolis and Susa carried out the scheme in colossal dimensions: the *iwan* was now a deep, latitudinal, columned portico, while the hall of audience was greatly expanded into a massive, quadrangular chamber, and its roof was supported by a 'forest of columns'.[187]

Because Bell had met Koldewey during her visit to Babylon in 1911, it is conceivable that the subject of the Neo-Hittite *bit hilani* came up in their talks. Bell's diary entry from her visit to Assur in 1911 reveals, however, that it was probably Walter Andrae, Assur's excavation director, who first drew her attention to the *bit hilani* scheme and to Koldewey's discussion of its origins and development.[188] The notion that this form passed into Achaemenid architecture seems to have found the support of Ernst Herzfeld, with whom Bell had an active correspondence at the time of her research on Ukhaidir and whom she cites as having suggested that the *bit hilani* was transmitted to the Achaemenids through Media.[189]

Andrae appears again as the brainchild for the next stage in the evolution of the *iwan*, as outlined by Bell in her chapter. This development appears in the art and architecture of the Parthians, and it is manifested clearly at Hatra, another site that Andrae had excavated and which Bell herself had taken the time to visit in 1911 (as described above). The spread of Hellenism and Roman expansion into the Near East brought Classical artistic conceptions to the art and architecture of the Parthians. Thus, Parthian buildings often bear Ionic-style columns and capitals, and Greek-inspired geometric mosaics, plaster ornaments and stucco wall fragments, not to mention Greek architectural units, like the square peristyle court.[190] As Bell explains, however, certain architectural features in this period continue to bear a Near Eastern imprint, and nowhere is this continuity more apparent than with the *iwan* arrangement, which she perceives as the Parthian interpretation of the *bit hilani* scheme.[191] In Parthian architecture, the portico and audience chamber are transformed into one room, the *iwan*. It became a longitudinal rectangular chamber, walled on three sides, with the fourth distinguished by an arched opening taking up most or all of its width.[192] According to Bell, the columns of the former *bit hilani* portico simply decorate the walls that flank the archway of the *iwan*.[193] Most significantly, the Parthian *iwan* became roofed with a barrel vault. The original scheme of the vault was a Mesopotamian innovation executed in mudbrick, which can be traced back, for example, to Assyrian palace corridors and gateways.[194] Nevertheless, by the time the vault was incorporated into the Parthian architecture at Hatra in the first century CE, it had passed from Greece and Rome to the west, where it had been transformed from brick into stone.[195] Moreover, it was from the west that the vaulted room was elevated from its place in minor side passageways and shallow chambers to its use in regal reception halls, given its ability to emphasize the room's height and longitudinal axis.[196] At Hatra, Bell illustrates the Parthian vaulted *iwan* arrangement in the central Temple of the Great *Iwan*s, believed in her time to be a royal palace. The building was characterized by two large central *iwan*s, 21 metres in width, each of which was roofed with barrel vaults and flanked by a row of smaller *iwan*s (Fig. 5.18).[197]

The next phase of the evolution of the eastern palace takes Bell to Persia, where she begins her investigation of the architecture of the Sasanians, whom she argues had adopted the *iwan* arrangement from the Parthians or the Achaemenids for their own palatial buildings. At Ardashir's third-century palace at Firuzabad – the earliest of the buildings from the Sasanian period known in Bell's time – one finds a deep, vaulted *iwan*, providing access to a domed audience hall in behind.[198] To counteract the main thrust of the vaulted *iwan*, the side chambers were placed at right angles to it instead of running parallel, as at Parthian Hatra, for example.[199] Bell also describes the architecture of the well-preserved building at Sarvistan, believed to date to the fifth century CE, with an arched-entrance *iwan* that provided access to a domed audience hall behind.[200] Turning to the sixth-century Palace of Khosrow at Qasr-i-Shirin, Bell draws attention to the central part of the palace, with its large, open court in front and its monumental porch (Room 1). The *iwan* took the form of a closed antechamber (Room 2), this leading to a lavish hall of audience in behind with its own deep *iwan* (Rooms 3 and 4).[201] This was the latest realization of the *bit hilani*, already recognizable at earlier Firuzabad, although less magnificently, and providing the general scheme that would be adopted by the early Islamic architects in their planning of Ukhaidir's ceremonial core, with its open court, *iwan* and square hall of audience in behind. As has already been noted, Bell was also struck by the so-called *iwan* groups in the Palace of Khosrow, these taking on the same appearance and arrangement within the palace as the *baits* within the palace of Ukhaidir.[202] To Bell, Ukhaidir was closely linked to this remarkable palace at Qasr-i-Shirin in many ways, the latter providing much of the inspiration for her later Islamic complex. She must have felt that her efforts to visit this place in person and to carefully plan it were among her most worthwhile endeavours.

In Iraq itself, the *iwan* also appeared to have been adopted into elite architecture during the Sasanian period. Bell was particularly intrigued by reports of the desert *hira*s of the Lakhmid princes, Arab allies of the Sasanians, who had lived in the Mesopotamian desert between the third and seventh centuries.[203] Indeed, it was the mention of these elusive palaces, where princes could escape the confines of their urban courts and return to the simpler lifestyles of their desert nomadic forebears,[204] that had drawn her to the region west of the Euphrates River in the first place and led to her discovery of Ukhaidir. Although none of these Lakhmid *hira* complexes was very well known in Bell's time, having never been systematically explored – or even positively located, in some cases – later Islamic historians had written about them, describing them as palaces comprising a central audience chamber for the king (the centre or 'breast') and two wings that lay to the right and left, in which were lodged the king's courtiers and the special stores of the royal wardrobe and wine.[205] Bell believed she could see some resemblance of this layout at Ukhaidir, with its central *iwan* being the principal audience chamber for the princely occupant, flanked by private apartments. An additional and tantalizing parallel could also be found within the early Islamic palace of Balkuwara at Samarra, excavated by Ernst Herzfeld in 1911, with its central block of monumental gates, cruciform domed reception hall and opposing *iwans*, flanked by wings on either side for residential quarters, storage facilities, parade grounds and stables.[206] Both cases further bolstered the notion that important architectural features in early Islamic palatial architecture had earlier Sasanian-period antecedents, including those that had developed in Mesopotamia.

Finally, Bell could not ignore the monumental use of the *iwan* in the Sasanian Taq-i Kisra at Ctesiphon in central Iraq. The massive *iwan*, open to its full width on one side, occupied pride of place in the centre of the palace, where it served as the king's ceremonial audience hall. It was flanked on either side by five vaulted chambers and was covered by an enormous pitched-brick barrel vault, the largest of its kind in any pre-modern brick building. While this large audience hall is not particularly akin to the comparatively modest scale of the *iwan* at Ukhaidir, it could still be regarded as having developed from earlier palatial schemes with their open-ended audience halls, realized now through a massive vaulted roof and vast space underneath.

Overall, in describing these architectural examples from the pre-Islamic periods, Bell effectively underlined the strength of Ukhaidir's pre-Islamic influences, these having emanated largely from ancient Mesopotamia and Persia. Presumably, these earlier constructions, with their frequent – and often lavish – use of the *iwan* within palatial contexts, would have been well known to the architects of the early Islamic period who were constructing their own sumptuous palaces, such as Ukhaidir, in the same regions. Much of Ukhaidir's distinctive interior arrangement, and the centrality of its own *iwan*, then, was clearly situated within a long line of palatial schemes firmly at home within eastern traditions.

Commentary on Bell's Scholarship on the Development of the Iwan

Bell's tracing of the *iwan* back to its Hittite origins, and her following it through its Assyrian, Achaemenid, Parthian and Sasanian manifestations, was an ambitious endeavour, and few scholars today would carry out such a bold scheme, given the span of centuries, the cultural groups and the morphological transformations undergone by this particular type of reception hall. Particularly problematic today is the place of the palaces at Sarvistan and Qasr-i-Shirin in her ambitious evolutionary scheme. Bell regarded these as representing notable Persian Sasanian antecedents that inspired later Islamic architecture, as at Ukhaidir. Recent scholarship has argued convincingly, however, that these edifices are probably not Sasanian at all, but rather are early Islamic. Thus, the points of similarity among these structures can be explained by their contemporaneity. On the one hand, Bell may be credited for properly recognizing these parallels, but on the other hand, because of their revised date, her evolutionary scheme, in which Sasanian architecture played such an important role in the transmission of architectural principles, is weakened.

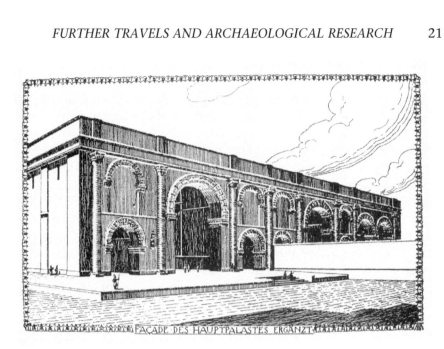

Fig. 5.18 Andrae's reconstruction of the Temple of the Great *Iwans* at Hatra, Parthian Era, highlighting the open-ended North and South *Iwans*; these were believed to have inspired similarly planned reception halls in the later Sasanian and Islamic periods, and they are well represented in the palace at Ukhaidir.

Most scholars today, nevertheless, would agree that the Islamic *iwan* does hearken back to Parthian times, where it was well known at Hatra in the first century CE but also recognized in, among other places, the Parthian palace complex at Assur and the north quadrant of the Parthian fortress at the site of Nippur.[207] Interesting, the latter complexes are characterized by a four-*iwan* arrangement, with the halls grouped around a central courtyard.[208]

A continuing debate concerns, however, the origins of the *iwan*. Some argue that its open-ended form with mudbrick barrel vault was an eastern take on the Hellenistic flat-roofed, columned portico, this replacement most readily evidenced in first-century architecture at the Mesopotamian site of Seleucia-on-the-Tigris, where Parthian exchanges with the cultures of Greece and Rome were particularly strong.[209] Alternatively, it might have been an adaptation of the Roman house's *tablinum* in the architecture of Iran and Mesopotamia.[210] Still others have preferred an entirely Eastern inspiration for the *iwan*, positing Iranian origins or even venturing that it was an adaptation of the huts of the marsh inhabitants of southern Mesopotamia, in which the barrel-like roofs were built out of bent bundles of reeds covered with matting.[211]

Few scholars of Parthian, Sasanian and Islamic antiquity today seem to accept that the Neo-Hittite *bit hilani* lies at the root of the much later *iwan*, although interestingly, this notion has had its proponents. F. Oelmann took up

Koldewey's idea in a lengthy article in 1922.[212] Reuther, in his discussion of the existence of the *iwan* in Parthian architecture, refers back to Oelmann's article and treats as a possibility the resemblance between the *iwan* and an element of the Hittite palaces at Zinjirli.[213] In his discussion of Ukhaidir in the more recent past, R. Hillenbrand proposes that in addition to the palace's Syrian Umayyad character, it is overlain with features rooted in native Mesopotamia, like the *bit hilani* of Syro-Hittite temple architecture, although Hillenbrand does not pursue this identification further.[214]

In defining what is meant precisely by the Neo-Hittite *bit hilani* and its adoption by Neo-Assyrian kings in their palaces, the Near Eastern art historian Irene Winter considers the possibility that the *iwan* might be the latest manifestation of this ancient form. Particularly compelling to her is the apparent multifaceted nature of the *bit hilani*, whose form in Neo-Hittite and Neo-Assyrian contexts was associated with a gate complex, a palatial reception hall or a private suite, much like the later Parthian, Sasanian and Islamic *iwan*s functioned within this variety of contexts.[215] She finds further tantalizing the fact that the Neo-Hittite *bit hilani* suites of rooms are sometimes grouped around a central courtyard, as at the site of Zinjirli or in the Neo-Assyrian palace of Sennacherib at Nineveh, just as one finds three or four *iwan*s arranged around a central courtyard in various building complexes in the later periods.[216] While incomplete evidence for a direct continuity of the *bit hilani* to the *iwan* over such a long period of time prevents us from confirming such a relationship between the two forms, Winter's compelling parallels do urge one to consider more seriously the impact of architectural forms from the pre-Parthian-Sasanian and pre-Islamic Near Eastern worlds into the later periods.[217] Moreover, her observations, which essentially fall in line with Bell's own arguments concerning the origins of the *iwan*, discourage one from quickly dismissing Bell's bold scheme.

While the development of the palatial *iwan* constituted the principal architectural feature investigated by Bell in her lengthy and complicated chapter on the genesis of the early Islamic palace, she did not ignore other architectural elements and cultural influences that made their way into palaces like Ukhaidir. Of particular note is her consideration of Ukhaidir's fortified exterior appearance, with its high walls and rounded towers, and her argument that such defensive architecture could ultimately be traced back to the fortified camps established by the Romans along their Arabian desert frontier or *limes*.[218] She consequently showed how these fortified camps provided the essential blueprint for the defences of elite desert residences of the early Islamic Umayyad period (660–750 BCE). Bell particularly emphasized two Umayyad castles in present-day Jordan with which she was most familiar, Qasr Kharana (Bell's Kharaneh) – which she would end up visiting and recording in 1914 (Fig. 5.19)[219] – and Mshatta, lying only a few more kilometres to the west of Qasr Kharana, in the western desert (Fig. 5.20).[220] Both of these castles' defensive character, characterized by their high walls and rounded towers, recalled the early Roman forts and at the same time provided direct inspiration for the fortified appearance of the slightly later Abbasid castle at Ukhaidir, on the eastern side of the Syrian desert.

Through her discussion of these features and their diverse origins, Bell was ultimately emphasizing the unique, hybrid character of early Islamic architecture. While the interior arrangements of palaces such as Ukhaidir had clearly been affected by traditions emanating from the East – with their central *iwan* schemes and flanking apartments, not to mention some of their technological elements and materials, which were born of local traditions – other architectural features could often be traced back to Rome and the West. The key to early Islamic architecture, therefore, was understanding its unique blending of Eastern and Western traditions. Bell's research, so comprehensively reported in *Palace and Mosque at Ukhaidir*, astutely traced the multidirectional nature of Ukhaidir's influences. With such observations, Bell moved beyond the more simplistic assertions of scholars such as Strzygowski, who with their polemicizing stance were determined to locate and isolate only one vital source of inspiration that defined the essence of an artistic or architectural monument, be it from the East or the West. Bell, in her scholarly maturity, accepted the complexity with which ideas and influences had been exchanged and intermingled in the early years of Islam, when old traditions were combined with new elements to give rise to a novel and distinctive cultural style.[221]

Palace and Mosque at Ukhaidir: *Flutter in the Dovecotes?*

Palace and Mosque at Ukhaidir, the work into which Bell poured all of her archaeological field investigations, her correspondences and discussions with other scholars, and her own extensive research, was lavishly published by Oxford's Clarendon Press in 1914. It featured oversized pages, fold-out plans, maps and an abundance of cleanly reproduced black-and-white photographs. The book's sumptuous form was an appropriate medium for this ambitious project, with its detailed, well-illustrated treatment of Ukhaidir, not to mention its review of all of the architectural forms, through the ages, that had provided the inspiration for Ukhaidir's palatial layout and mosque.

At long last, Bell had completed her most ambitious and complicated work that had continued to absorb her attentions from the time she had first laid eyes on the spectacular castle of Ukhaidir in early 1909. But did it ultimately meet her expectations as a researcher and scholar? When she had first excitedly announced her discovery of Ukhaidir back in 1909, she thought she had found the most 'important building of its period' and vowed that she would 'publish it in a big monograph all to itself' that would make 'a flutter in the dovecotes'. But in the end, was this the significant scholarly contribution she had striven for, and did it achieve the recognition for which she might have hoped?

A definitive 'yes' or 'no' cannot be offered. The reception of Bell's work was very mixed and remains so. Many of the reviews that appeared back in 1914 were not overly effusive in their praise. While most were clearly impressed with Bell's scholarship, many disliked the ponderous writing style, and her adoption of what one called the 'German method of throwing crude note-books undigested at the head of your readers'.[222] It must be admitted that 'few will take the pains to wade beyond the first ten pages',[223] as Bell is 'throughout severely technical'.[224] As was rightly observed, if one is looking forward to the 'romance of travel', with the 'vivid descriptions of manners and records of Eastern chat which made "Desert and the Sown" so fascinating', one will be disappointed by the dense, scholarly content of this monograph. Even still, it must be admitted that the patient reader will find 'a great harvest of information'.[225]

Such drawbacks aside, it is impossible to ignore the prodigious learning that Bell's book evinces, particularly its comparative materials, which Massignon's and Reuther's earlier reports of Ukhaidir do not present so exhaustively. Bell was also praised for her ability to support her arguments with 'a solid mass of monumental evidence'.[226] Few scholars criticized the content of the work, the exception being Marcel Dieulafoy, who in a lengthy review still disagreed with Bell's proposed Islamic date for the palace, believing that her identification of a mosque at Ukhaidir was unconvincing; he remained firm in his belief in the pre-Islamic date of the complex.[227] But even he admired Bell's clear writing, her rich evidentiary documentation and the abundance of comparative sources she had been able to collect.[228]

Unlike in German and French academic circles, where many were acquainted with Gertrude Bell and her archaeological research, English-speaking scholars knew little about her, as in the early decades of the twentieth century, Bell's was practically the sole English voice in the study of the architecture of the Sasanian and Early Islamic periods.[229] She had few colleagues who possessed the background knowledge or interest in the subject to take an informed critical stance on her work. Of scholars of antiquity who reviewed *Palace and Mosque*, one was clearly a Romanist, who predictably highlighted her investigations on the influence of Roman imperial architectural forms on Ukhaidir.[230] The other notable reviews came from Creswell, who although still a relatively unknown scholar in 1914, recognized Bell's achievement, noting that 'under each heading Miss Bell, with the whole available material at her finger tips, exhausts her subject, and that the book is a model for all time of the scientific method'.[231]

Anyone doubting Creswell's positive regard for Bell's research needs only look through the pages of his *Early Islamic Architecture*, published a few decades later, to see how extensively he appropriated many of her facts and conclusions. As noted earlier, in Chapter 3, although Creswell himself visited Ukhaidir, his discussion of particular architectural features from the complex, their origins and development and their comparison to those from other pre-Islamic and Islamic-

Fig. 5.19 Interior of Qasr Kharana, an early eighth-century Islamic fort (in present-day Jordan). Bell saw within it many architectural affinities with the palace of Ukhaidir. She took this photograph at the beginning of her Arabian journey in January 1914. Bell actually spent three days at the castle, taking photographs, drawing plans, copying Kufic inscriptions and overall doing 'much more at it than anyone else'.

period sites often repeated or expanded upon what Bell had already discussed. But while such borrowing underscored Creswell's tremendous respect for Bell's work, it ultimately drew attention away from the latter. With everything now subsumed in his widely available and comprehensive opus, there was little reason for readers to consult earlier reports. In this way, Bell's monograph faded into relative obscurity while Creswell's came to be regarded as the authoritative report, widely read and extensively cited.

Today, more than a century after the publication of *Palace and Mosque at Ukhaidir*, it is still possible to find praiseworthy aspects of Bell's archaeological research. Even if many of her evolutionary schemes concerning architectural features such as the vault and *iwan* may be incorrect or overly simplistic, one is still impressed by the vast knowledge of Classical and Near Eastern art and architecture that Bell had amassed, and her ability to bring this vast knowledge to bear persuasively upon her discussions. As has been pointed out, some of her conclusions, such as her interpretation of the Chehar Qapu as a fire temple, have continued to hold considerable sway in the archaeological literature. Her analogies between Ukhaidir and other palatial complexes such as Mshatta and the Palace of Khosrow are remarkably astute and still valid. Bell also must be

Fig. 5.20 The beautifully carved façade of the eighth-century Umayyad castle of Mshatta, photographed by Bell in 1900 shortly before it was subsequently removed and taken to the Kaiser Friedrich Museum in Berlin, where it is still housed to this day (now the Museum für Islamische Kunst, Pergamonmuseum). Bell proclaimed Mshatta to be 'the most princely of *hirahs*, wrapped round by the grass-grown Syrian desert, mild and beneficent in winter; and the flocks of the Sukhur resort to it as kings resorted of old' (Bell, *Palace and Mosque*, p. 188 n. 1). Mshatta would figure prominently in Bell's research of the early Islamic castle of Ukhaidir and her efforts to trace earlier buildings from which it derived inspiration.

praised for her perceptiveness and tenacity in the field, even in the most difficult and dangerous of conditions, qualities that helped her to produce detailed, accurate plans of archaeological monuments. Such plans, like those of the Palace of Khosrow and the Chehar Qapu at Qasr-i-Shirin, have yet to be completely corrected and improved and are still consulted.

Finally, as emphasized many times over the course of this and previous chapters, Bell's continued dedication to photography meant that her *Palace and Mosque at Ukhaidir* includes a wealth of images of that remarkable complex and others sites that figure in her account. Several of the photographed monuments and architectural details no longer exist, and her images are often the only record we possess of these remarkable ancient features. In light of this fact, even if the remainder of her scholarship is ultimately judged to be imperfect, Bell's photographic achievement – lavishly proven by the almost 100 pages of clear, detailed photographs that appear in *Palace and Mosque at Ukhaidir* – is enough to merit her inclusion in the cohort of the early twentieth century's most important and accomplished Near Eastern archaeologists.

It is regrettable, in light of its quality, that few today take the time to consider the merits of *Palace and Mosque at Ukhaidir*, Bell's final work. Robert Hillenbrand comes close to an explanation when he remarks that although Bell's account of Ukhaidir is 'magisterial', her other interests 'prevented her from following her vocation as an Islamic art historian with the full vigor of which she was capable'.[232] Those other interests were significant, and they quickly followed on the heels of Bell's scholarly activities. She had actually just completed the subject index for *Palace and Mosque at Ukhaidir* while on board a ship bound for Cairo in late 1913,[233] and her next journey would take her into the heart of Arabia and immerse her in the current affairs of that country, with its bitter rivalry between the powerful tribal houses of Ibn Rashid and Ibn Saud. This was a decidedly different trip, and although some of Bell's interests along the way were archaeological in nature, they would be strongly overshadowed by her courageous, eventful journey to the desert capital of Hayil and her report on the treachery of the house of Ibn Rashid. Bell would henceforth be remembered for the current news she brought back to Britain, and her bold wanderings in Arabia would earn her the Founder's Medal of Britain's Royal Geographical Society.[234]

The outbreak of war just shortly after Bell's Arabian journey led her even further away from archaeology. By November 1914, she was working for the Red Cross in Boulogne, locating missing or wounded soldiers.[235] This was followed in April 1915 by further work with the Red Cross in London. Bell's grief upon learning, at the end of April, of the death of her much-loved Dick Doughty-Wylie at Gallipoli was crushing, and many months would pass before she recovered from the shock.[236] Thus, it must have been some relief when in November, Bell's old friend and colleague David Hogarth summoned her to help with the war effort in the British Office of Military Intelligence in Cairo, soon to be renamed the Arab Bureau. Now, her life found a new and urgent purpose. Because of her first-hand knowledge of the countries of the Middle East and their peoples, she served as a useful set of eyes and ears for the British, helping to analyse the power and politics of local Arab leaders, evaluate their links to the enemy Turks and judge their potential loyalty to the British. Her archaeological investigations, which had been the prime motivations for her earlier travels to Mesopotamia, were no longer of direct relevance or importance, given the more pressing matters of the war. As Bell accepted her post in Cairo, her life's direction was inextricably altered. Now that she had plunged deeply into the affairs of the modern Middle East, her older persona as scholar of the past dropped away almost entirely, replaced by her role as a 'woman of the hour' with a remarkable part to play in the shaping of things to come.

CHAPTER 6

MESOPOTAMIA AND IRAQ – PAST AND PRESENT ENTWINED

The final chapter of Gertrude Bell's incredible life, from 1915 up to her death in 1926, has been described and discussed by several biographers and historians. Their published works have chronicled Bell's involvement in Britain's effort in the Middle East during World War I, first with her service in the Arab Bureau in Cairo, and thereafter with her move to Basra and finally Baghdad, where she was appointed Oriental Secretary to the British High Commissioner. They also describe her important role in the creation of the new state of Iraq, the drawing up of its borders and the selection of its first king.[1] The details of this eventful period in Bell's life need not be repeated here. Rather, this final chapter seeks to articulate the relationship between Bell's scholarly endeavours in the archaeology of Mesopotamia up to 1914 and her political and administrative activities after that point. To be sure, Mesopotamia was the common ground for all of Bell's work: she had invested the greatest energies in understanding its past architecture and history, and with her war-time activities and post-war efforts to build the state of Iraq, Mesopotamia continued to be her principal focus. But whereas her former endeavours strove to shed light on Mesopotamia's remarkable antiquity, her later efforts were largely bound to its present conditions, current inhabitants and the nation's continued success into the future. Given these separate and distinct foci in her life – one strongly connected to the past, the other absorbed with the present – we may ask what relationship existed between the two?

I will try to show that the experiences and knowledge that Bell acquired during the years in which history and archaeology played a central part in her life and work had a significant impact on her later political activities. Her early engagement with the archaeology of the Near East, particularly with the archaeology and history of Mesopotamia, gave her a unique understanding of this part of the world. It significantly influenced her ideas about how the region should be governed, and her own place within that scheme. Throughout the discussion, I take into consideration Bell's romantic proclivities, which were evident even in her earliest Near Eastern travels and encounters with the past, and which especially encouraged her vision of Mesopotamia's past being played forward to the present.[2] Her belief in the possibility of Iraq's self-rule seems to have been particularly influenced by her romantic notions of its past achievements, but it was also guided by her comprehensive knowledge of the history of the Near East and by her unique perspective, which recognized the creative power of the Near East independent of Western influence or intervention.

As a final topic of discussion, I will consider Bell's work as Iraq's honorary antiquities director and founder of the country's national museum, and the degree to which her decisions and responsibilities in those roles were also deeply affected by her earlier archaeological experiences and achievements. Altogether, what emerges is an accentuation of Gertrude Bell's remarkable yet complex character. Her combination of intelligence, imagination, sense of authority and tirelessness worked together throughout her life, bringing about notable achievements wherever she focused her energies. At the same time, the very qualities of her character that led to her triumphs also made her deeply aware of the transitory nature of power and of her own short-lived place within the world that she had created.

Romance with the Past

Before delving into Bell's political activities in her later life, and the particular ways in which her past experiences seemed to inform those activities and decisions, it is important to discuss a few key aspects of Bell's unique character and how they affected and intersected with her attitudes towards the past. One important facet of Bell's personality that must be considered alongside her other character attributes is her romanticism. This sensibility gave her a particularly unique and intense engagement with the past which persisted throughout her travels to the Near East, and which seemed particularly potent during her visits to archaeological sites and monuments in the Near East.[3] Her romantic inclinations pervade much of her writings and even her most scholarly inquiries. Thus, it is not possible to discuss the impact of Bell's archaeological past on her later political activities without taking into account this special aspect of her character.

Despite the outer image which she frequently projected of herself – as a pragmatic realist guided by rational inquiry and scientific analysis rather than emotion – Bell was at heart a person with profound and intense sensibilities. Her step-mother, Florence, who knew her well, wrote:

> In truth the real basis of Gertrude's nature was her capacity for deep emotion. Great joys came into her life, and also great sorrows. How could it

be otherwise, with a temperament so avid of experience? Her ardent and magnetic personality drew the lives of others into hers as she passed along.[4]

Such sensibilities explain Bell's love of poetry, to which she was drawn at an early age,[5] and they find ample reflection in her writings, which often convey, in highly expressive language, her reactions to places and peoples encountered, and experiences enjoyed or deplored. Bell certainly found that travel and exploration awakened such emotions in the most powerful way. Her journeys to unfamiliar lands, with the demands they placed on her physical endurance, bravery, mastery of languages, and skills in map reading, photography and cartography, heightened the sense of adventure and gave her a heady feeling of accomplishment.[6] She also revelled in these voyages because they were an escape from the routine and confining existence of daily life and gave her an enlivening sense of liberty. This emancipatory feeling was enjoyed by many Western travellers to Eastern lands, especially women, many of whom sought travel as a means of avoiding the restrictive conventions of European society at home, and Bell was no exception.[7] In her travelogue, *The Desert and the Sown*, Bell lyrically expresses her feeling of liberation at the onset of a journey:

> To those bred under an elaborate social order few such moments of exhilaration can come as that which stands at the threshold of wild travel. The gates of the enclosed garden are thrown open, the chain of the entrance of the sanctuary is lowered, with a wary glance to right and left you step forth, and, behold! The immeasurable world! The world of adventure and of enterprise, dark with hurrying storms, glittering in raw sunlight, an unanswered question and an unanswerable doubt hidden in the fold of every hill.[8]

As has been remarked upon earlier, Bell was particularly enamoured with the Near East, and her writings, especially in the years between 1900 and 1914 – when she was travelling in the Levant, Turkey, Mesopotamia, Persia and Arabia – are positively bursting with glowing, emotive assertions of the wonder or fascination of many of the places she visited and the peoples she met. Her descriptions endeavour to evoke the vivid colours, textures, smells and tastes of the places she experienced, amply testifying to the sense of elation brought about by travel in the foreign lands of the East. Travel also seems to have activated Bell's rich Orientalist imagination, frequently leading her to embellish, exalt or exoticize many of the predicaments or places in which she found herself. The romance of travel felt by Bell is reflected well in one of her essays from 1914, titled 'Romance', this testifying to her particular captivation with the lands of southern Mesopotamia – or 'the 'Iraq', as it was often referred to before World War I:

I have written of politics and of commerce, of steamships and of locomotive engines, but I have not pronounced the word which is the keynote of the 'Iraq. It is romance. Wherever you may look for it, you will find it. The great twin rivers, gloriously named; the huge Babylonian plains, now desert, which were once a garden of the world; the story stretching back into the dark recesses of time – they shout romance. No less insistent on the imagination, and no less brilliantly coloured are the later chapters in the history of the 'Iraq. The echoing name of Alexander haunts them, the jewelled splendours of the Sasanian King of Kings, the clanging fame of the Mohammedan Khalifate, the tragic dissolution of the Mongol invasion, and last (to English ears not least) the enterprise, the vigour, the courage of our seamen and merchants who forced their path through the gates of the 'Iraq and brought the Pax Britannica into the torrid seas of the Persian Gulf.[9]

Besides underscoring her unbridled admiration for British imperialism, the passage also highlights how the romance of a particular place was particularly enhanced by its rich history. In the case of southern Mesopotamia, the rivers of 'the 'Iraq' were great because they were inexorably associated with an eventful past that stretched back for centuries. For Bell, being aware of or exposed to that glorious past was largely what made travel so thrilling. Already we have observed this excitement even in her earliest journeys – for example, in Greece in 1899, when the sight of 4,000-year-old pots shown to her by the archaeologist David Hogarth made her 'mind reel'.[10] In her subsequent travels in the Near East, where she encountered ancient monuments and sites at every turn, her sense of wonder for the past seems to have become especially amplified. *The Desert and the Sown*, in which she recounts her 1905 journey through Palestine and Syria, frequently captures her enchantment with places where the distant past feels acutely accessible, as in the late antique 'Dead City' of el Barah, located south of Aleppo:

It is like a dream city which children create for themselves to dwell in between bedtime and sleep-time, building palace after palace down the shining ways of the imagination, and no words can give the charm of it nor the magic of the Syrian spring. The generations of the dead walk with you down the streets, you see them flitting across their balconies, gazing out of windows wreathed with white clematis, wandering in palisaded gardens that are still planted with olive and with vine and carpeted with iris, hyacinth and anemone.[11]

Writing from the Sasanian palace remains of the Taq-i Kisra at Ctesiphon in Mesopotamia in 1909, Bell transports us into the past with her beautiful description of the throne room, no doubt inspired by the present magnificence of its still-standing parabolic vault, but also by her active imagination. She writes of the richly bejeweled carpet that would have hung from floor to ceiling, which, when drawn aside, revealed:

> the Great King seated in state in his hall of audience, with the light of a thousand lamps, suspended from the roof, catching his jeweled tiara, his sword and girdle, illuminating the hangings on the walls and the robes and trappings of the army of courtiers who stood round the throne.[12]

Bell was not unique in her predilection for evoking the East's history, often in romantic terms. In fact, she was preceded by a long line of European artists, poets, historians and experts in Oriental languages who had endeavoured to capture, through writing or the visual arts, some of the romance and exoticism of the East, both present and past.[13] Mesopotamia, the Near Eastern land with which Bell would become most intimately associated, was not exempt from this treatment, its tumultuous past being conjured up by many artists, even before archaeological investigations had revealed any of the region's real antiquities. In art, rousing examples of Mesopotamia's torrid history included, for example, the English painter John Martin's image of the *Fall of Nineveh* (1830), or the famous *Death of Sardanapalus* (1827–8), painted by the French artist Eugène Delacroix.[14] These paintings depict with considerable imagination the destruction of Babylon and Nineveh and the defeat of its kings, brought about by excess and decadence. The artists relied on Classical Greek histories or Biblical accounts to formulate the settings for ancient Babylon and Assyria and their infamous rulers, and their negative portrayals of the Mesopotamian cities and their tyrannical despots are in line with these accounts.[15] After all, Babylon was 'the mother of all whores, and of every obscenity on earth', according to the Bible (Rev. 17.5), while the Assyrian city of Nineveh was 'the bloody city, all full of lies and booty' (Nah. 3.1).[16] Mesopotamia did not fare much better among Classical historians. While admiring Assyria's political, military and architectural achievements, Greek and Roman historians still stressed its rulers' brutality and decadence.[17] Overall, the images within these paintings, as with many other eighteenth- and nineteenth-century European works of art that portrayed the ancient Near East, comprised a strong moralizing tone, serving to illustrate the much-deserved, devastating endings brought about by greed, corruption and the tyrannical behaviour of ancient Oriental despots.

Besides the highly embellished, exoticized images of the ancient East produced in romantic literature and art, travel reports of Westerners who had ventured into the remote parts of the Near East, including Mesopotamia, often contained historical accounts of the places through which they passed. Many travellers sought to learn about the ancient magnificence that had once existed in various places they visited, much as they had while travelling through the antique lands of Greece and Italy on the Grand Tour. When confronted with the reality of a ruined Babylonian or Assyrian site in Mesopotamia, however, few writers could bring themselves to say anything remotely pleasing about the ruins themselves or the landscapes in which they were located. The parched, sun-baked plains of Mesopotamia were a far cry from the lush, pastoral landscapes of Greece and Italy, and decaying brickwork hardly matched the beauty of Greece and Rome's ruined stonework.[18] Austen Henry Layard, the English adventurer whose archaeological investigations in northern Mesopotamia led ultimately to the fantastic discovery of two of Assyria's grandest ancient capitals, Nimrud and Nineveh, expressed well the contrast between Classical and Mesopotamian ruins:

> The graceful column rising above the thick foliage of the myrtle, the ilex and the oleander; the gradines of the amphitheatre covering the gentle slope, and overlooking the dark blue waters of a lake-like bay; the richly carved cornice or capital half hidden by the luxuriant herbage; are replaced [in Mesopotamia] by the stern shapeless mound rising like a hill from the scorched plain, the fragments of pottery and the stupendous mass of brickwork occasionally laid bare by the winter rains.[19]

There is no 'visual delight' in this Mesopotamian landscape. Layard goes on:

> The scene around is worthy of the ruin he is contemplating; desolation meets desolation; a feeling of awe succeeds to wonder; for there is nothing to relieve the mind, to lead to hope, or to tell of what has gone by.[20]

To some, the current desolation of an ancient site served to underscore the long temporal distance between a city's once glorious past and its thoroughly decayed present. Further, this reality could be seen to affirm the just outcome of Mesopotamia's past wickedness. The bleak, indistinguishable masses of ruined brickwork testified well to the price that the people of Assyria and Babylonia had paid for their sins and greed, conveying in a sense the same moralizing subtext as the paintings of Martin and Delacroix. Finally, it didn't help that Mesopotamia's modern occupants didn't seem to be remotely aware of or interested in any of the histories of their country's venerable past. They were perceived as being completely ignorant of the past; only Western ingenuity and enterprise, possessed by individuals such as Layard, could reveal the grand palaces and monumental gates which had lain completely unknown beneath the feet of the local inhabitants for their entire lives.[21] Any romanticism was to be found not so much in the ancient ruins themselves as in the picture of the enterprising Western archaeologist in Oriental garb, or the turban-wearing Arabs, who gazed in horror and fascination as human-headed bull colossi emerged from the rubble before their eyes.[22]

It is worth comparing Bell's own histories of the East, especially of Mesopotamia, to the works of other Western artists and travel writers such as those just described. For one, Bell's works rarely carried moralizing undertones that were influenced, for example, by stories drawn from the Hebrew Bible, in which Mesopotamia's past civilizations paid the price for their decadence, as testified by their present ruined, desolate state. Gertrude's indifference to such moralistic attitudes is due to the fact that she, like most other of her Bell family members, with the exception of her brother Hugo, were 'happily irreligious' and not particularly predisposed to assessing their lives and actions in terms of righteous conduct.[23] If Bell had an interest in the Bible, it was for its valuable information about the history of ancient Mesopotamia, not because it was a repository of divine treatises on good and evil behaviour. Bell pronounced few moral judgements on historical figures, such as the Babylonian king Nebuchadnezzar, for example, despite the Bible's infamous portrayal of him as a tyrannical, ruthless despot. In Bell's own references to this king, Nebuchadnezzar is respected for his greatness as a prolific builder and conqueror, and he is grouped together with other such important figures who graced the history pages of Mesopotamia's past, such as Alexander the Great and Harun al-Rashid, irrespective of the moral character of their deeds.[24]

We have outlined contemporary writers' tendency to accentuate the striking contrast between Mesopotamia's glorious past and its present reality of desolation amid a degenerate, ignorant population. Even David Hogarth, a friend and mentor of Bell and fellow archaeologist, was known to have stated that the antiquities of the Near East 'conspicuously exalt the past at the expense of the present'.[25] In contrast, Bell was more often prone to discern remarkable similarities between past and present realities. The landscapes through which she travelled, with their haunting ruins, took hold of her senses and powers of imagination, this most amply demonstrated in her evocative descriptions, quoted above, of the Syrian 'Dead City' of el-Barah and the palace of Ctesiphon. Through her eyes, one can vividly access the past in these impressive remains. It is also significant that Bell often wrote of ancient places and peoples as if they were but links in a long, unbroken sequence through time. The traditional ways of doing things and ancient behaviour were still very much present in today's inhabitants, in Bell's view. This sense of continuity is nicely conveyed when she describes the bitumen-producing town of Hit on the Euphrates, through which she passed in mid-March 1909:

> The sun was setting as we came down to the palm-groves by the river. The fires under the troughs of molten bitumen sent up their black smoke columns between the trees; half-naked Arabs fed the flames with the same

bitumen, and the Euphrates bore along the product of their labours as it had done for the Babylonians before them. So it must have looked, this strange factory under the palm-trees, for the last 5,000 years, and all the generations of Hît have not altered by a shade the processes taught them by their first forefathers.[26]

While this melding together of past and present produced a thrilling sensation, it also elicited within Bell a kind of uneasiness. On the one hand, she could feel the excitement of being in a place so evocative of the past that it was easy to imagine ancient Babylonians engaged in the same task as Arab workers today, or perhaps even to envision Alexander the Great and his soldiers striding forward across a dusty plain. On the other hand, the unchanging quality of the landscape and its inhabitants over millennia accentuated to her the transitory, futile endeavours of humankind. What significance can be attached to any past action or achievement if, even after centuries, nothing has changed? Bell seems to have been particularly conscious of this paradox when she composed *Amurath to Amurath*, the account of her 1909 journey through Mesopotamia. Even the title, which references the succession of the Ottoman rulers of the same name,[27] not only conveys the fact that the history of the land through which she was travelling was once governed by Turkish rulers of great power, but also draws attention to the fleeting nature of their power: they were merely a succession of kings of the same name, one after the other, through time. This image is similarly evoked in the book's preface:

[those with] experience of the East, have learnt to reckon with the unbroken continuity of its history. Conqueror follows upon the heels of conqueror, nations are overthrown and cities topple down into the dust, but the conditions of existence are unaltered and irresistibly they fashion the new age in the likeness of the old. [...] past and present are woven so closely together, the habitual appreciation of the divisions of time slips insensibly away. Yesterday's raid and an expedition of Shalmaneser fall into the same plane; and indeed what essential difference lies between them?[28]

This emphasis on the futility of human achievements is a recurring trope in Bell's writings and occasionally injects a pessimistic flavour into her otherwise lively imaginings of antiquity. It also hints at her somewhat conflicted attitude, believing on the one hand that humanity was capable of positive change, while at the same time doubting that this was really possible. While Bell appears to be referencing the Middle East in this specific case, other writings suggest that she often found the West equally incapable of enlightened, 'progressive' behaviour, thus highlighting her pessimistic outlook on life in general.

Nowhere is Bell's writing more evocative of the past than when she writes of an ancient site that she herself spent time recording, or which had been excavated by others but presented ample traces of its rich past for her to view. As we have seen, Bell was particularly caught up by the romance of the desert castle of Ukhaidir, whose architecture she had planned and recorded with tremendous effort in 1909 and 1911. Its monumentality and impressive preservation made it easy to imagine what it would have looked like in its original state. The castle's present Arab occupants also served to re-animate its lofty spaces, according to Bell. Some of her most stirring writing in *Amurath to Amurath* describes Ukhaidir's residents as the inheritors of the castle's greatness: They 'lived and starved and died in this most splendid memorial of their own civilization'; they 'passed like ghosts along the passages, they trailed their white robes down the stairways' and at night 'gathered round the hearth in the great hall where their forefathers had beguiled the hours with tale and song in the same rolling tongue of the Nejd'. To Bell, their songs of past powerful princes were 'all pages out of the same chronicle, the undated chronicle of the nomad'.[29] Far from being a distant cry from the past noble residents of this palace, the present Arab occupants were Ukhaidir's true descendants and rightful inheritors, belonging to one and the same race as its first owners. Such an effect rendered Bell's readers closer to rather than further away from Ukhaidir's magnificent past.

No less evocative of a rich past to Bell were the sites of Babylon and Assur, where contemporary German excavators had revealed traces of their monumental edifices and occupants, transporting her vividly back into their ancient days. When Bell writes of these cities, her descriptions are replete with colourful visions of their past and how they are entwined with her present reality. She hears the nightingale singing at Babylon and muses that the same sound would have been heard by Nebuchadnezzar and even Hammurabi.[30] While gazing at the excavated brickwork of the city before her, she is fascinated to be able to locate the places where soldiers slept and where Alexander lay dying.[31] At Assur, Bell is at her most lyrical when she imagines, as we have already noted, the 'lavish cruel past' rushing in on her, with Assyrian soldiers marching through the gates, bound captives crowding the streets, and defeated princes and subject races bowing to the victorious king and piling up their tribute before him. 'Splendour and misery, triumph and despair, lifted their head out of the dust.'[32]

The fact that Bell was visiting Babylon and Assur just at the time when the massive brickwork of their ancient buildings was being freshly uncovered no doubt heightened the sensation of being transported back to the time of their original use. Further, one should not ignore the effect which the excavators themselves had on Bell's sensibilities. Physically present at Babylon and Assur during her visits, and taking the time to show her around their diggings, Robert Koldewey and Walter Andrae possessed tremendous knowledge about every aspect of the ancient cities, and they appeared to have willingly conveyed many of these details to Bell. Besides their superlative historical knowledge, their talent for evocatively summoning the cities' pasts and great kings appealed tremendously to Bell's romantic proclivities. Bell records Koldewey as having said of Alexander the Great, who died at Babylon, 'the perpetual drunkenness, the blood he spilt – he was mad with wine, love and power. And must he not be mad who conquers the world? There is no other way.'[33] The fact that Bell found this passage appealing is indicated by its repetition in more than one of her writings.[34] She was no doubt thrilled by its haunting quality, but we suspect that its appeal also related to Koldewey's beguiling narrative manner. One gets a similar sense of Bell's sensibilities being enlivened when she was in the presence of Walter Andrae, the excavator of Assur. Bell relates that she sat with her German host on the dig-house roof one evening and took in the form of the mighty, ancient ziggurat of Assur towering above them. When she asked Andrae what people would have watched for from the ziggurat's summit, he responded, 'They watched the moon, as we do. Who knows? They watched for the god.'[35] This pronouncement left Bell, as she remarks, most unwilling to depart from the site. The passage serves again to underline the thrill she felt when confronted with Mesopotamia's vivid past. At the same time, it hints at another layer of her romantic sensibilities, kindled through the act of sharing this remarkable past with an intelligent German man whom she deeply admired.

Eastern Outlook

Beside her romantic sensibilities, particularly in her encounters with the richness of Mesopotamian antiquity, it is also important to consider the importance that Bell placed on her acquired knowledge of Mesopotamia's past – achieved through her intensive travels in that country and study of its ancient remains – and the fact that much of her knowledge pertained to periods of time other than Classical Antiquity. Through her relationships with Koldewey and Andrae, for example, she had become familiar with the archaeology of the famous pre-Hellenistic cities of Babylon and Assur. Her own investigations of Sasanian and Early Islamic edifices such as Ukhaidir, Ctesiphon and Samarra had made her an expert on the periods post-dating the Classical Age. The art and architecture of these sites was all largely the product of indigenous development, born of traditions that ultimately sprang from the lands between the Tigris and Euphrates rivers. Bell's scholarship, therefore, was largely acquired through the perspective of Mesopotamia's own history and culture. The fact that she had closely followed the scholarship of Josep Strzygowski from an early stage in her academic research may also have been responsible for this distinctive Eastern viewpoint. Like him, she had learned to appreciate the creative power of the Near East in its own right and sought to trace many of its traditions back to Mesopotamian origins rather than emphasizing the pervasive influence of Greece and Rome.

Given her Eastern knowledge and perspectives, Bell was fairly unique among experts of Near Eastern antiquity in her time, the majority of whom came to know the Near East principally through their studies of Greek and Roman culture. A case in point was Bell's colleague David Hogarth, who over the course of his academic career became well acquainted with the archaeology and history of the ancient Near East. But he was initially drawn to this part of the world through his familiarity with ancient Greece and Rome, and the positive, powerful impact these Western civilizations had made upon the Near East through either conquest or cultural influence.[36] It is interesting to consider the possible effect this Classical, Western perspective had on Hogarth's subsequent involvement in the political affairs of the Near East. It might explain in part, for example, his consistent denigration of the modern populations of the East – they were hostile, unappreciative and culturally degenerate – compared to the people of the West.[37] Hogarth portrayed the East's modern inhabitants as childlike or adolescent in character, their sole hope for future survival being the motherly assistance of Britannia and the peace and good government that only she could provide. Hogarth even compared Britain to the ancient Romans, claiming the present British Empire was moving in the same direction in its efforts to 'incorporate' and 'assimilate' various disparate regions and populations under its sway, and in the process bring stability, justice and a sense of political and cultural unity.[38] The strong Orientalist tone in Hogarth's writings, with its subtext of Western imperialist motives and its desire to control the East, has been pointed out by post-colonial critics such as Edward Said.[39] Bell may occasionally be charged with the same underlying sentiments, noted, for example, in her unrestrained commendation of 'Pax Britannica' in her 'Romance' manuscript, quoted above. It seems that she could not always escape in her mind from the fact that she too was an agent of a colonial power. At the same time, however, her greater familiarity with the people and lands of the East, especially Mesopotamia, on their own terms, and her expert knowledge of their indigenous cultural heritage, frequently tempered these patronizing attitudes, revealing themselves in her writings far less frequently than those of her colleague Hogarth.

Knowledge, Authority and Ownership of the Past

It is important to emphasize yet one final aspect of Bell's attitude towards the past, and that concerns the importance she placed on having an expert knowledge of a place and its antiquity, and the authority that such knowledge accorded. To Bell, a passing acquaintance with the history and culture of a particular place or people did not suffice; her own travel books, such as *Amurath to Amurath*, or her study of Ukhaidir demonstrate her requirement for a comprehensive investigation of the ancient textual sources, artefacts and architecture of a particular site, and her feeling that only after all of this exertion had she truly come to 'know' that place. Her admiration for others, particularly for the excavators Walter Andrae and Robert Koldewey, is largely on account of the expertise with which they commanded the past. They had the authority to speak eloquently and evocatively of the past because of their prodigious efforts to understand the histories of Assur and Babylon through their years of investigations and careful, detailed probes. Moreover, her own appreciation for these sites could only be effected if she too gained a solid command of their long histories. As has been noted, at both Babylon and Assur, Bell crept tirelessly with their excavators 'into every hole and corner of the excavation',[40] asking a myriad of questions and taking extensive notes. With this full command of the past, she deemed permissible any romantic musings on historical figures such as Alexander the Great; they merely provided a colourful narrative to empirically acquired historical facts. Bell could in the same way justifiably romanticize her beloved Ukhaidir, given the exertion she had applied to know all of its form and function. Her informed knowledge of the past gave authenticity to the recreations and augmented their truthfulness.

Given the physical and mental efforts required to achieve a comprehensive knowledge of the past, it is not surprising that Bell developed a kind of proprietary attitude towards archaeological sites and their antiquities. The site of Assur, although founded by the Assyrians, became very much bound to Andrae and his German excavators, just as Ukhaidir had become 'her castle'. Further, all of the information acquired through the study of that ancient site – its political history, its inhabitants, the general time period in which it existed – also became linked to the scholars who had endeavoured to obtain it in the first place. In a sense, these researchers of ancient Mesopotamia, and by extension the countries from which they hailed, became owners of the past and had just as much a stake in their sites' antiquities and ancient heritage as the country within whose borders they were acquired. It is not difficult to see the implications of this kind of proprietary attitude playing out in Bell's political career, and also in her later work as Iraq's honorary Director of Antiquities.

Mesopotamia and Iraq: Past and Present Entwined

Having reviewed a number of significant attitudes which Bell had towards the past, particularly the ancient Near East, let us now see in particular how such attitudes may have impacted her political activities and views about the current state of Mesopotamia, and its future governance.

In British-occupied Mesopotamia both during and immediately after the Great War, one of the key issues confronting Bell as a political officer, as well as the other members of the colonial administration, was the form of Mesopotamia's future governance. Was it possible for Mesopotamia ever to achieve self-rule, or must it remain mandated to a European power, namely Britain? There were a number of conflicting opinions about this question in the wake of the war. While some clung tenaciously to the pre-war notions of empire, others now had increasingly cynical notions about empire's advantages and effectiveness and were becoming beguiled by the liberalizing notion of Woodrow Wilson's self-determination, which was sweeping like wildfire across many of the world's nations.[41] Bell's own opinions seem to have fluctuated greatly. As a member of the British colonial enterprise herself, she believed in the positive effects of Britain on the governance of Mesopotamia,[42] but as her experience with Mesopotamia grew and she too embraced the notion of autonomy, she began to express a more conflicted position, seeing less the advantages of foreign rule and more an optimism for it as an ultimately self-governing Arab state.[43] There were numerous complexities involved in uniting the present inhabitants of Mesopotamia – a truly disparate mix of tribes, towns, Sunnis, Shi'as, Kurds, Jews and Christians – and many saw this as an unrealistic vision. And yet Bell was often optimistic that such a country could eventually become stable and self-governing. While this objective was probably the product of Bell's extensive first-hand experience with the modern issues of the country and its people – her being 'on the spot', as it were – one can also argue that part of this optimism seems to have been informed by her knowledge of Mesopotamia's history, and her awareness that in many periods of antiquity, the country had been brought together under a single, indigenous political administration. Strong rulers had governed justly, and with their energies and charisma had succeeded in uniting the disparate ethnic groups and peoples into a single state.

Through her knowledge of Mesopotamia's history, Bell knew that the Assyrians and Babylonians had, for example, achieved large empires that covered all of northern and southern Mesopotamia during the first millennium BCE. She also knew that the Abbasids of the early Islamic Period had created a remarkably long-lived empire. In 750 CE, the Abbasid caliphs, who claimed descent from the Islamic prophet Muhammad's youngest uncle, had replaced their Umayyad predecessors and had moved the imperial capital from Damascus eastwards to the old Sasanian heartland in Mesopotamia, where they constructed the city of Baghdad.[44] Mesopotamia, with Baghdad at its heart, quickly emerged as the centre of an empire that spread, for a time, all the way from Spain to Afghanistan. The civilization of the Abbasids drew inspiration from the earlier cultures of Greece, Byzantium and Persia.[45] The Abbasid caliphs themselves promoted a cosmopolitan and inclusive society, welcoming at their court 'not only Muslim scholars, poets and artists but also Nestorian Christian and Jewish physicians, astrologers of all faiths, and pagan philosophers'.[46] And this flowering of Islamic civilization was not confined to the halls of the caliphs' palaces; it spread to all Muslims, who now conceived of themselves as members of a single community. Their feelings of common identity and solidarity 'were reinforced by the presence of Quran reciters, storytellers and poets who repeated the tale of Muhammad's life and doings and sang of the feats of the Arabs in the new *lingua franca* of Arabic in mosques, marketplaces and military camps' across the vast empire.[47] This had indeed been a glorious era in which political and cultural unification had spread far and wide, and it was, too, an imperial power that had developed from within Mesopotamia itself, not as part of a conquering force from the outside. The Abbasid Empire was, in many ways, the perfect metaphor for Bell's own vision of the new Iraq, and to her it was not beyond the realm of possibility to resurrect that empire's past glory.

Along with her vision of self-government, so easily imagined because of her knowledge of Mesopotamia's past, Bell was also quite receptive to the idea that the new nation should be ruled by a king. She first began to support this idea of kingship around the time of the 1919 Paris peace talks, when she travelled to Paris and met for the first time the charismatic Faisal, the Hashemite prince of Central Arabia who had helped the British defeat the Turks during the war and now expected to be compensated for his wartime efforts by being given territories over which to rule. Bell also attended the Cairo conference in March 1921, when it was decided that Faisal should be made the first king of Iraq. And she was most visibly present in Baghdad later that year, when Faisal entered the city and was crowned as the country's ruler. Thenceforward, Bell became a close advisor to Faisal.

Bell's support for Faisal was certainly influenced by her realistic understanding that he was the best candidate on the scene, and that his pro-British leanings made him an ideal Arab leader for Mesopotamia, which would remain mandated to the British until 1932. At the same time, one can also argue that Bell's support was affected by her romantic ideal of Arab unification in the Middle East, and her vision that part – or all – of the region should be governed by a magnetic Arab prince of ancient noble blood. In Faisal's case, it helped that by belonging to the Hashemite family, he could trace his ancestry back to the house of Muhammad himself.[48] Ever historically minded, Bell also knew that the Abbasid rulers presented themselves as representatives of the Hashemites, since they claimed descent from the uncle of Muhammad, who had been the chief of the Hashemites. To Bell, Faisal's links with the founder of Islam and the caliphs of the Abbasids fully legitimated him as the new king of Iraq, and raised the possibility that the nascent Iraq could reach the same glorious heights through its new ruler as the Islamic caliphs had achieved in the country several centuries before. Bell's writings during the year of Faisal's arrival and coronation in Iraq are replete with images which offer this positive vision of a newly regenerated Arab kingship. Her description of Faisal's reception at Falluja by the desert Bedouin tribes of the Dulaim and Anazeh typifies her romantic imagining of the kingly Faisal, inspired as she was by the 'converging images of traditional and modern Iraq'.[49] On this occasion, masses of individuals on horses and camels showed up to catch a glimpse of Faisal, who looked splendid in his white robes, black mantle, gold belt and dagger, and flowing white headdress bound with a silver rope. He spoke like a 'chieftain of tribesmen in the sonorous language of the desert, with command and injunction and question to which his audience gave deep-tongued answer. So it has been in such gatherings since the earliest days of Arab civilization.'[50] She also observed that it had been '700 years since an Arab king walked among his Mesopotamian subjects, a longer interval even here where we reckon history by millenniums'.[51]

One event in particular emphasizes most strongly Bell's vision of Mesopotamia's glorious past and its link to the present, as well as her desire to impress upon the new king of Iraq his own rightful place in this magnificent history. This was Bell's organization of a trip with Faisal to the ancient site of Ctesiphon, taking place in August 1921, only shortly after he had been crowned king (Fig. 6.1). As noted already, Bell knew well the history and architecture of Ctesiphon. She had first visited the site back in 1909 and had taken notes on the architectural elements of the façade, arch and side chambers of the Taq-i Kisra, the massive surviving arched *iwan* of the impressive palace of the Sasanian king Khosrow I, which had been a byword for imperial splendour throughout the Middle East back in the sixth century CE. Bell had been fascinated at the time of her first visit to Ctesiphon by Sasanian traditions and their possible influence on the architecture of her prized discovery, the Palace of Ukhaidir. Significantly, some of the features of the Taq-i Kisra – notably, its method of brick vaulting, which is paralleled at Ukhaidir – influenced Bell's choice of an early date for the latter structure's construction.

Several pages of *Amurath to Amurath* are devoted to describing Ctesiphon and its history, much of the information deriving from the writings of the famous al-Tabari, a late ninth- to early tenth-century Persian historian and exegete of the Qur'an who wrote a multivolume history of the Muslim world and the Middle East. From al-Tabari's account, Bell fashioned her own evocative image of Ctesiphon during its heyday, with its king and his dazzling throne room, which has already been quoted. Bell also recounts al-Tabari's description of the Arabs' taking of Ctesiphon under the banner of Islam, led by Sa'd ibn Abi Waqqas, and in particular of the first fording of the Tigris by 600 volunteers, who successfully crossed the river on horseback despite resistance by Sasanian horsemen.[52]

When Bell brought King Faisal to Ctesiphon in 1921, the history that she presented to him must have been quite similar to what she related in *Amurath to Amurath*. Describing the occasion to her father in a letter, she wrote:

It was wonderfully interesting showing that splendid place to Faisal. He is an inspiring tourist. After we had reconstructed the palace and seen Chosroes sitting in it, I took him into the high mounds to the south, whence we could see the Tigris, and told him the story of the Arab conquest as Tabari records it, the fording of the river and the rest of that magnificent tale. It was the tale of his own people – you can imagine what it was like reciting it to him. I don't know which of us was the more thrilled.[53]

The purpose of Bell's visit to Ctesiphon with Faisal was not only to present to him one of the country's most magnificent testimonies to ancient royal authority, but also to impress upon him that these were *his* monuments as an Arab king, and that the events that had unfolded among them were his to possess and by which to feel empowered. When Bell related that 'it was tale of his own people', she was reminding Faisal that he was descended from the Arabs who had conquered this site. Just as they had taken it from the Persian Sasanians, Faisal, as the new king, was taking his country back from the Ottoman Turks.

Bell's potent act cogently reflects many of her attitudes to Mesopotamia's history. It especially highlights her propensity for summoning the past to give meaning and purpose to the present. Her romantic evocation of al-Tabari's account of Arabs conquering the most powerful, glittering symbol of the Persian occupation – the great palace at Ctesiphon – was done carefully and consciously to parallel Faisal's own authority to rule Iraq after centuries of the foreign Turkish occupation of Mesopotamia, emphasizing that what had once taken place in history was being repeated. It is further significant that Bell's choice of this particular chapter from Ctesiphon's history involved kings and conquerors hailing entirely from the Near East; her appreciation for the Near East's venerable history in and of itself, devoid of Western influence or imposition, was evoked through this example in an effort to augment its potency for the new king of Iraq.

It is difficult, however, to ignore the fact that it was Bell herself telling this vital historical tale to Faisal, and we doubt that the king would have been unaffected by her presence. On one level, Bell's presence symbolized Britain's powerful influence and, indeed, authority over the newly created nation of Iraq. On another level, what emerges is Bell's own authority and power, not simply as a voice for Britain but in her own person and forceful identity. After all, no other officer of the British colonial service in the new Iraq, and few among the country's indigenous inhabitants, had a greater command of Ctesiphon's glorious history. She had acquired this knowledge prodigiously through her own intensive research of the art, architecture and cultural history of the Sasanian and Early Islamic periods. It was this learning and the feeling of authority that it accorded to her personally that justified her reporting this event to the new king of Iraq. One might even suggest that on a subconscious level, given Bell's sense of proprietorship over the past, she felt that she was

Fig. 6.1   Gertrude Bell with Faisal, King of Iraq (second from the right), at a picnic at Ctesiphon in 1921, shortly after Faisal's coronation.

conferring her own personal ownership of Mesopotamia's past onto Faisal. If we accept all of these motivations, a more spectacular act of hubris is difficult to summon in Bell's political career, and yet its timing was favourable. Bell was at her most politically potent when she staged Faisal's visit to Ctesiphon in 1921. In her entire lifetime, her influence over the events and individuals of the new Iraq would never be as formidable as when she was standing with Faisal on that hill at Ctesiphon, describing to him that impressive story of Iraq's past imperial splendour.

Iraq's Antiquities Director and Museum Founder

As a final example of the impact which Bell's experience and achievements in the history and archaeology of Mesopotamia had upon her later career, we can turn to her position as honorary Director of Antiquities for Iraq and her role in establishing the country's first museum. King Faisal asked Bell to head up the antiquities directorate in 1922 because of her extensive knowledge of Iraq's archaeology.[54] In that capacity, she drew up the country's first legislation regarding its antiquities, which passed in June 1924. The new law followed standard antiquities legislation then prevalent in most countries, particularly in Europe, except that it still permitted a large share of the excavated objects to be rewarded to the permit holders.[55] Thus, the Director of Antiquities in Iraq was given the authority to select objects that were necessary 'for the scientific completeness of the Iraq Museum',[56] but the remainder of the objects could be freely exported back to their sponsoring institutions outside of the country rather than remaining the property of the state of Iraq.[57] This particular aspect of the antiquities legislation clearly was formulated by Bell to benefit the Western archaeological establishment, encouraging their continued archaeological activities and research in Iraq and promoting the development of their own national collections, such as the British Museum.[58]

One can also see Bell's personal imprint in a few other articles of the Iraq antiquities legislation – for example, Article 19(i), which states that excavation work must be accompanied by adequate equipment for making photographic records as well as architectural plans of the remains.[59] These stipulations especially reflect Bell's earlier archaeological background, namely her personal penchant for taking an abundance of photographs at archaeological sites and her realization that such images capture freshly cleared artistic and architectural details most effectively. Her recognition of the importance of making architectural plans of the excavated remains no doubt derives from her exposure to some of the most comprehensive, detailed plans of any archaeological projects in Mesopotamia before the war: those of Robert Koldewey at Babylon and Walter Andrae at Assur.

In her capacity as honorary Director of Antiquities of Iraq, Bell took her job seriously, issuing excavation permits only to individuals and institutions she considered qualified and fiscally capable of carrying out the prodigious task of excavating an ancient site in Iraq.[60] During her tenure, she also visited archaeological projects throughout the countryside and was present at sites for the division of the finds, which took place at the end of each field season. Wearing her official hat as Iraq's Director of Antiquities, Bell would select from among the excavated objects those that she felt were a representative sample of the site's archaeological remains, keeping them for Iraq's new national museum, while the remainder could be claimed by the excavation director. Her letters report in particular her visits to the ancient city of Ur, where, under the direction of the British archaeologist Leonard Woolley, a joint venture sponsored by the British Museum and the University of Pennsylvania was excavating some of the most exciting finds of the entire twentieth century in Iraq, including an incredibly rich 'royal' cemetery dating back to the Sumerian period of the third millennium BCE. Bell and Woolley spent many difficult hours negotiating over the division of Ur's extensive finds.[61] At the excavations of the multi-period ancient site of Kish, Bell and the director of the joint mission of Oxford and the Chicago Field Museum often settled the division of the finds by spinning a coin.[62]

Bell's second important activity relating to Iraq's antiquities concerned her creation of a museum in which to house the country's archaeological treasures. First established in 1923, this was a modest affair, consisting of a room in one of the government offices in Baghdad, but in 1926, it was transferred to its own building in the northern part of the city and was officially opened by the king in a special ceremony.[63]

On the one hand, the new museum, which was a place to display the country's heritage to its people, testifies to Bell's efforts to link Iraq's glorious past with its present, hopeful future. On the other hand, the museum's emphasis on pre-Islamic artefacts and history – those of a most ancient past – rather than the country's more recent Islamic-period remains, falls short of its ability to inspire modern Iraqis, the majority of whom would have found the Islamic past particularly relevant and meaningful.[64] This disregard for Islamic-period remains is all the more striking when we remember that Bell's own knowledge of ancient Iraq derived in large part from her archaeological research of the early Islamic periods, and that she was well aware of the political potency of that history. She had, after all, used this more recent history to empower King Faisal at Ctesiphon.

Bell's attitude towards the establishment of a museum for Iraq does not appear to be particularly politically minded beyond her belief – shared by most British politicians charged with overseeing Iraq's creation – that Iraq should have a national museum like other advanced states in the modern world.[65] Rather, for her the most important function of the new museum was one of practical necessity: a large quantity of antiquities was beginning to pile up as a result of archaeological excavations in the country, and the need for a place where these items could be housed was becoming increasingly urgent. In this way, in its earliest stages, the Iraq Museum was principally regarded as a safe repository for the country's ancient treasures and archaeological records and was not formulated as a display of 'a metanarrative of the Iraqi nation'.[66]

As for the pre-Islamic content of the new museum, this too was very much associated with the reality of the archaeological excavations that were taking place in Iraq. The excavations were invariably run by Western foreign missions whose principal interests tended to be ancient cultures of the very distant past. Much of their focus continued, like that of their nineteenth-century predecessors, to be on the peoples and cultures of ancient Mesopotamia which could be linked in some way to the Bible. Despite the increasing scientific interest in the history of ancient Mesopotamia for its own sake, the fact remained that Western audiences were still hugely enthused by antiquities that could be related to the stories of the Bible, and thus archaeological missions in Iraq still strove to satisfy those public interests. It is also important to remember that most successful archaeological investigations in Iraq were those financed by generous funding sources coming from the West, and that those funds usually supported the digging of ancient sites of the Biblical period. In the end, it is fair to submit that the new museum's lack of Islamic-period artefacts was simply the product of Western antiquarian interests and associated economics, and that Bell largely conceded to those interests in her position as the museum's director.

If, in her capacities as museum director and Iraq's Director of Antiquities, Bell maintained an attitude of deference to Western excavators, this was also due to her tendency to bestow authority and ownership upon those with learning. She acknowledged that the directors of the foreign archaeological missions, by virtue of their intensive investigations, were important shareholders in the past, and that they ultimately should have a large say in the destiny of the artefacts they had so carefully extracted from the sites that they had brought to light. Bell's attitude explains especially her lenient behaviour at the divisions of the finds, where the directors of foreign archaeological missions received a generous share of the antiquities they so greatly prized, and were permitted to take them home to their sponsoring institutions. They rarely felt that their most precious discoveries had been grabbed by Bell for her Iraq museum.[67] Having confidence in and respect for the excavators and their prodigious efforts to know the past, Bell rewarded their achievements accordingly.

Bell's lenient attitude towards Iraq's antiquities garnered opposition from a number of Iraqi officials, particularly Sati' al-Husri, a leading proponent of Iraqi nationalism. King Faisal had appointed this individual as Director General of Education; during his tenure, al-Husri had been active in promoting Arab and Islamic history within the Iraqi school curriculum, especially Iraq's role as the centre of the Abbasid Caliphate.[68] Later, as Director of Antiquities in the 1930s, al-Husri would continue to strengthen recognition of Iraq's Islamic past, directing funds and energies towards the restoration of Islamic monuments, overseeing the writing and publication of several guidebooks pertaining to Arab monuments and antiquities, and sponsoring official archaeological excavations such as the site of al-Wasit, this having been a prominent Islamic city during the Umayyad and Abbasid dynasties.[69] Lastly, al-Husri was instrumental in the establishment in 1937 of the Museum of Arab Antiquities, which contained objects solely from Iraq's Islamic era, in a famous covered market in Baghdad, the Khan Murjan.[70] With such noble aims to empower Iraq's modern inhabitants with their rich past, it is not surprising that al-Husri opposed Bell's proposed antiquities legislation, which still permitted the export of much of Iraq's precious cultural heritage. Indeed, according to Bernhardsson, who has tracked the progress of Bell's proposed antiquities legislation, it was largely due to al-Husri's opposition to the bill within the Iraqi cabinet that its passage took almost two years.[71]

One might consider it puzzling that Bell did not show more support for al-Husri, given his noble aspirations, with the interests of Iraq guiding his objectives, as well as their shared knowledge of and interest in the Islamic period. Rather, she seemed to dislike him intensely, referring to him as a 'dry, little stick of a man'.[72] It is likely that some of this animosity toward al-Husri may also have come from the fact that he was one of Faisal's political appointments and not whom the British administration had recommended, and that his anti-British leanings made him an unfavourable individual with whom to collaborate. At the same time, Bell's own attitude of authority must be taken into account, along with the underlying understanding that policy was to be carried out principally on her terms. Given her own proprietary hold on the past, Bell may have believed that al-Husri was usurping what she considered to be her own particular area of expertise and felt threatened by his interference in what was largely being guided, in an official capacity, by her own special knowledge of Iraq's history. In the end, it was *her* version of the country's past that held the greatest authority and authenticity in the new state of Iraq. As it transpired, as long as Bell was the Director of Antiquities in Iraq, al-Husri's impact over the museum and antiquities legislation was minimal. It was only after her death, when he assumed the position of Director of Antiquities himself, that his own particular vision and pedagogy with respect to Iraq's history took a prominent place in the country's cultural life.

It is perhaps one of the most notable, and yet human, aspects of Bell's personality that she often found herself deeply conflicted with respect to her own actions and opinions. Thus, alongside her attitude of self-assurance and authority, she had at the same time serious doubts and uncertainties about her responsibilities. These qualms often found expression in her writings, especially in her letters to her parents. Of her role as antiquities director, Bell openly admitted that the task of dividing the archaeological finds at the end of each excavation season between the Iraq Museum and the foreign mission that dug was often 'difficult' or 'agonizing', given her competing roles of rewarding a foreign mission for their exertions and taking into consideration the requirements of building a representative national collection for Iraq.[73] Moreover, as Bernhardsson has observed, as museum director she often showed uncharacteristic anxiety over how museum objects should be arranged and exhibited.[74]

Nor in the sphere of politics did Bell show any more self-assurance or confidence in her actions. Indeed, Rory Stewart has observed that Bell is remarkable among her contemporaries for her propensity to admit in candidly honest terms, without dressing them in jargon and platitudes, the uncertainties of making policy in the new state of Iraq.[75] She and her colleagues had to contend with a myriad of practically irresolvable complications, among them the corrupt and weak nature of the previous Ottoman administration, the persistence of the country's tribal system, the divisions between urban and rural areas, and the varied ethnic composition of its inhabitants. In this way, according to Stewart, Bell's strength lay not in her political success but 'in the clarity and imagination with which she explored failure'.[76] Bell's letters to her parents are replete with her conflicted attitude, many of these expressing her doubts about the success of the involvement of the West, particularly Britain, in Iraq:

We're near to a complete collapse of society – the end of the Roman empire is a very close historical parallel. We've practically come to the collapse of society here and there's little on which you can depend for its reconstitution. The credit of European civilization is gone. Over and over again people have said to me that it has been a shock and a surprise to them to see Europe relapse into barbarism. I had no reply – what else can you call the war? How can we, who have managed our own affairs so badly, claim to teach others to manage theirs better? It may be that the world has now to sink back into dark ages of chaos, out of which it will evolve something, perhaps no better than what it had.[77]

Fewer than two weeks earlier, she had written:

All this adds to my general feeling of uncertainty as to the future. In the light of the events of the last 2 months there's no getting out of the conclusion that we have made an immense failure here. The system must have been far more at fault than anything that I or anyone else suspected. It will have to be fundamentally changed and what that may mean exactly I don't know. I suppose we have underestimated the fact that this country is really an inchoate mass of tribes which can't as yet be reduced to any system. The Turks didn't govern and we have tried to govern – and failed.[78]

Despite her lifelong attachment to Iraq, both to its rich past and to its difficult birth as an independent state in the modern era, Bell ultimately remained doubtful about the real wisdom of the nation-building effort and her own part in it. Ever historically minded, she, above everyone else, was aware of the fleeting nature of power, and she was also conscious that her own encounter in this foreign land, as a Westerner and outsider, was to be brief and ultimately devoid of distinction. It is perhaps worthwhile to recall an excerpt from a letter Bell wrote to her father back in 1909, when she was sitting on a rise that commanded a wide view of the rolling hills stretching away from the Tigris River, below the great ancient city of Nimrud:

I sat on the hill top for half an hour and considered the history of Asia that was spread out before me. Here Mithridates murdered the Greek generals, here Xenophon began his command, and just beyond the Zab the Greeks turned and defeated the archers of Mithridates, marching then on to Larissa, the mound of Nimrud, where Xenophon saw the great Assyrian city standing in ruins. Nimrud stood out among the cornfields at my feet. A little further east I could see the plain of Arbela where Alexander conquered Asia. We people of the west can always conquer, but we can never hold Asia – that seemed to me to be the legend written across the landscape.[79]

In our presumed enlightened state today, we feel justified in criticizing Bell's emphasis in this passage – as in several of her other writings – of the West's dominant position as a conqueror of the East and the assumption of its moral superiority. At the same time, however, Bell's recognition of the futility of this action tempers its superior claim. More than 100 years later, when this very landscape within which Bell stood continues to be a raging battleground of clashing nations and ideologies, marked by ongoing and damaging interference from the outside, is anyone really justified in claiming higher enlightenment?

NOTES

Introduction

1. GB letter to her mother, 30 November 1915, Gertrude Bell Archive. Janet Wallach, *Desert Queen* (New York, 1996), p. 146.
2. Elizabeth Burgoyne, *Gertrude Bell: From Her Personal Papers, 1914–1926* (London, 1961), pp. 30–1. Liora Lukitz, *A Quest in the Middle East: Gertrude Bell and the Making of Modern Iraq* (London, 2008), pp. 107–9.
3. See especially Lukitz, *A Quest*; but also H.V.F. Winstone, *Gertrude Bell* (London, 1978); Wallach, *Desert Queen*; and Georgina Howell, *Gertrude Bell: Queen of the Desert, Shaper of Nations* (New York, 2006). For a more critical perspective on Bell's part in the creation of Iraq, and the long-term consequences of Britain's involvement with Iraq in the 20th century, see Kwasi Kwarteng, *Ghosts of Empires: Britain's Legacies in the Modern World* (London, 2011), pp. 11–85.
4. Gertrude L. Bell, *Palace and Mosque at Ukhaidir* (Oxford, 1914), p. 1.
5. Wallach, *Desert Queen*, p. 87.
6. Howell, *Queen of the Desert*, p. 124. Wallach (*Desert Queen*, p. 364) notes that Bell's find of the palace had been 'usurped and written about by French archaeologists before she had had a chance to publish her work'. This seems to confuse the efforts of the German team in 1910 with those of the Frenchman L. Massignon in 1908. See also Winstone, *Gertrude Bell*, p. 108.
7. Julia M. Asher-Greve, 'Gertrude L. Bell (1868–1926)', in Getzel M. Cohen and Martha Sharp Joukowsky (eds), *Breaking Ground: Pioneering Women Archaeologists* (Ann Arbor, 2004), p. 143.
8. Bell's dedication in *Palace and Mosque* reads, 'To my friend Dr. Walther Andrae, in grateful recollection of happy and profitable days spent in the first capital of Assyria which has been revealed by his labour and recreated by his learning.'
9. E.W. Andrae and R. M. Boehmer, *Bilder eines Ausgräbers. Die Orientbilder von Walter Andrae 1898–1919/Sketches by an Excavator*, 2nd enlarged edition, English translation by Jane Moon (Berlin, 1992), p. 140.
10. Ibid., p. 140.
11. GB letter, 2 April 1905, Gertrude Bell Archive.
12. GB letter to her father, 15 April 1909, Gertrude Bell Archive.
13. GB letter, 2 April 1909, Gertrude Bell Archive.
14. GB letter to her father, 18 April 1918, Gertrude Bell Archive.

15. Bruce Trigger provides an overview of the kinds of approaches prevalent in the early days of archaeological practice, including the concept of diffusionism and a typological method for ordering and dating artefacts (including architecture), which were largely employed by Bell and her contemporaries; see Bruce G. Trigger, *A History of Archaeological Thought* (Cambridge, 1989). For useful overviews of the practice of archaeology in the latter part of the twentieth century and up to the present, and especially the kinds of analyses of artefacts undertaken, see Kevin Greene and Tom Moore, *Archaeology: An Introduction*, 5th edition (London, 2010); Colin Renfrew and Paul Bahn, *Archaeology: Theories, Methods and Practice* (London, 1991).

16. William M. Ramsay and Gertrude L. Bell, *The Thousand and One Churches* (London, 1909), reprint, with a new foreword by Robert G. Outsterhout and Mark P.C. Jackson (Philadelphia, 2008); Mark P.C. Jackson, 'A critical examination of Gertrude Bell's contribution to archaeological research in central Asia Minor', in Charles Tripp and Paul Collins (eds), *Gertrude Bell and Iraq – A Life and Legacy Conference Publication* (London, in press); Gertrude Bell and M. Mundell Mango, *The Churches and Monasteries of the Tur 'Abdin* (London, 1982); M. Szymaszek, 'The lost screens of the churches of Mar Cyriacus in Arnas and Mar 'Azaziel in Kefr Zeh (Tur 'Abdin, Turkey)', *Eastern Christian Art* 9 (2012–13), pp. 107–18.

17. Particularly notable is Bell's abandonment of her plans to produce archaeological reports of the sites of Raqqa and Samarra, both the subject of considerable investigation during her 1909 Mesopotamian journey (see Chapter 4). We can only guess that after the publication of F. Sarre's and E. Herzfeld's *Archäologische Reise im Euphrat- und Tigris-Gebiet* (Berlin, 1911–20) (which provided considerable coverage of Raqqa and Samarra), and then Herzfeld's subsequent, intensive fieldwork at Samarra, Bell realized that other scholars were producing learned reports of these sites that in many ways exceeded her own.

Chapter 1 Early Life and First Steps in Archaeology

1. Geoffrey Tweedale, 'Bell, Sir (Isaac) Lowthian, first baronet (1816–1904)', *Oxford Dictionary of National Biography* (Oxford, 2004), available at http://www.oxforddnb.com.ezproxy.library.ubc.ca/view/article/30690 (accessed 29 July 2015).

2. Ibid.; Janet Wallach, *Desert Queen* (New York, 1996), p. 7.

3. Wallach, *Desert Queen*, p. 7.

4. Tweedale, 'Bell'; Wallach, *Desert Queen*, p. 7.

5. Julia M. Asher-Greve, 'Gertrude L. Bell (1868–1926)', in Getzel M. Cohen and Martha Sharp Joukowsky (eds), *Breaking Ground: Pioneering Women Archaeologists* (Ann Arbor, 2004), p. 145.

6. Tweedale, 'Bell'.

7. Wallach, *Desert Queen*, p. 7; Asher-Greve, 'Gertrude L. Bell', p. 145.

8. Wallach, *Desert Queen*, p. 25; Asher-Greve, 'Gertrude L. Bell', p. 147.

9. Many aspects of Gertrude Bell's early travels can be reconstructed from her letters. Good accounts of her experiences abroad in Europe and Persia can also be found in H.V.F. Winstone, *Gertrude Bell* (London, 1978), pp. 22–31; Wallach, *Desert Queen*, pp. 26–37; Georgina Howell, *Gertrude Bell: Queen of the Desert, Shaper of Nations* (New York, 2006), pp. 42–59. Elizabeth Burgoyne's lightly biographical

work, *Gertrude Bell: From Her Personal Papers 1889–1914* (London, 1958) also gives valuable background details to Bell's letters and other writings from the period of her early travels.

10. Bell's mountain-climbing escapades are described in Wallach, *Desert Queen*, pp. 58–65; Howell, *Queen of the Desert*, pp. 74–93.

11. Bell's diary entries and letters sent to family members provide a valuable source of information about these world tours. The second world tour is also documented through numerous photographs taken by Bell. See GB diaries and letters, December 1897–June 1898 and November 1902–July 1903; GB photographs, Albums RTW, vols 1–5, 1902–3, Gertrude Bell Archive.

12. Wallach, *Desert Queen*, p. 32; Asher-Greve, 'Gertrude L. Bell', p. 150.

13. Wallach, *Desert Queen*, pp. 32–7; Asher-Greve, 'Gertrude L. Bell', p. 151.

14. Lady (Florence) Bell (ed.), *The Letters of Gertrude Bell*, vol. 1 (London, 1927), p. 29.

15. Asher-Greve, 'Gertrude L. Bell', p. 151.

16. Numerous entries in Bell's letters and diaries attest to the energy she exerted learning Arabic. See GB letters and diaries, December 1899–March 1900, Gertrude Bell Archive.

17. See GB letters and diaries, March–June 1900 for the details of these journeys, as related by Bell herself, Gertrude Bell Archive.

18. Gertrude Bell, *The Desert and the Sown* (London, 1907), reprint, with a new introduction by Rosemary O'Brien (New York, 2001), p. 1.

19. Bell employed Mikhail, a native of Jerusalem who had formerly travelled with Mark Sykes, as her cook. See Bell, *Desert and the Sown*, p. 3. Towards the end of her trip, while in Cilicia in Anatolia, however, Bell picked up Fattuh, an Armenian from Aleppo, and he would continue to be her cook on all subsequent trips; see GB letter, 24 April 1905, Gertrude Bell Archive.

20. Anonymous, Review of Gertrude L. Bell, 'The Desert and the Sown', *The Academy* (2 March 1907), p. 210.

21. Anonymous, Review of Gertrude L. Bell, 'The Desert and the Sown', *The Spectator* (16 February 1907), p. 17.

22. Ibid., p. 17.

23. Bell, *Desert and the Sown*, pp. x, xiii and 228.

24. Edward Said, *Orientalism* (New York, 1978), pp. 229–31; Bell, *Desert and the Sown*, pp. viii–ix; Andréa Elizabeth Schnell, *Gertrude Bell: An Orientalist in Context* (MA thesis, McGill University, 2008), pp. 32–40.

25. Bell, *Desert and the Sown*, p. xxi.

26. Schnell, *Gertrude Bell*, p. 37; Billie Melman, *Women's Orients: English Women and the Middle East, 1718–1918* (London, 1992), p. 9.

27. Schnell, *Gertrude Bell*, p. 37; Melman, *Women's Orients*, pp. 308, 310 and 315.

28. Bell, *Desert and the Sown*, pp. 160–8; 198–209.

29. Ibid., p. 176.

30. Ibid., p. 235.

31. Ibid., p. 238.

32. Ibid., pp. 241–2.

33. Ibid., p. 256. The Princeton archaeological expedition that Bell encountered was directed by Howard Crosby Butler (1872–1922). First a student, then a faculty member of Princeton University, Butler undertook three archaeological expeditions to Syria: one in 1899, a second in 1904–5 (when Bell met up with him), and a third in 1909. He and his team travelled through northern and southern Syria, measuring, drawing and photographing buildings, inscriptions and

sculpture. Most praiseworthy was Butler's exploration, mapping and photographs of the area of the Dead Cities in the Limestone Massif of Syria between the Orontes and Afrin Rivers. Agricultural life had flourished here during the Roman and Byzantine periods, reaching a peak in the fifth and sixth centuries CE. Literally hundreds of 'Dead Cities' occupy this region, their livelihood having been largely drawn from the production of olive oil, which was exported all over the Mediterranean world. Bell would have been familiar with Butler's work, *Architecture and Other Arts* (New York, 1903). For a short biography of Butler, see 'Butler: Catalogue of Photographs', *Research Photographs of Princeton University* (Princeton, 2015), available at www.princeton.edu/researchphotographs/archaeological-archi ves/butler/ (accessed 29 July 2015).

34. Bell, *Safar Nameh: Persian Pictures* (London, 1894), p. 31.
35. GB letter to her mother, 11 April 1899, Gertrude Bell Archive.
36. GB letter to her family, 6 December 1899, Gertrude Bell Archive.
37. GB letters to her mother, 28 February and 3 March 1902, Gertrude Bell Archive.
38. GB letters to her mother, 6, 7 and 8 March 1902, Gertrude Bell Archive.
39. GB letters to her mother, 17 and 19 March 1902. See also Asher-Greve, 'Gertrude L. Bell', pp. 164–5, and p. 191 endnotes 163 and 164. Asher-Greve notes rightly that Bell simply watched over these archaeological excavations as opposed to actually participating in them, as previous biographers had often assumed.
40. GB letter to her family, 29 March 1900, Gertrude Bell Archive.
41. GB letter to her family, 20 May 1900, Gertrude Bell Archive.
42. GB letter to her family, 22 May 1900, Gertrude Bell Archive.
43. Bell, *Desert and the Sown*, p. 167.
44. She learned this fact only after writing the chapter on this region for her book, *The Desert and the Sown*; see Bell, *Desert and the Sown*, p. 276 fn.
45. Ibid., p. 278.
46. Stephen L. Dyson, *Eugénie Sellers Strong* (London, 2004), pp. 59–60; Aron Rodrigue, 'Totems, taboos, and Jews: Salomon Reinach and the politics of scholarship in fin-de-siècle France', *Jewish Social Studies* 10 (2004), p. 5.
47. Dyson, *Sellers Strong*, p. 60; Rodrigue, 'Totems', p. 5.
48. Claude Schaeffer, 'Salomon Reinach: Born 29 August 1859: Died 4 November, 1932', *Man* 33 (1933), p. 51. A complete list of the works published by Reinach was itself published as a book; see Arthur E. Popham, *Bibliographie de Salomon Reinach* (Paris, 1936).
49. The date of Bell's first meeting with Reinach is inconsistent in the latter's writings. In his obituary of Bell, written in 1926, Reinach notes that through a letter of introduction from Eugénie Strong, Bell saw him in Paris towards the end of 1905, eager to show him her photos and drawings from her trip to the Levant and Anatolia; see S. Reinach, 'Gertrude Bell', *Revue archéologique* 24 (1926), p. 265. In Bell's own letters, however, it is evident that she became acquainted with him one year earlier, in November 1904, and it was at that time that he invited her to write her piece on Mshatta for the *Revue archéologique*. Nevertheless, Bell did also visit Reinach on at least two occasions in 1905, one briefly in January and another in October, after she had returned from her Near Eastern journey with plans and photographs. One can only suppose that Reinach had forgotten about that earlier meeting in 1904.
50. Dyson, *Sellers Strong*, p. 89.
51. Ibid., pp. 60, 99.

52. GB letters to her mother, 7, 8, 10 and 11 November 1904; 24 October 1905, Gertrude Bell Archive.

53. Pascale Linant de Bellefonds, 'Vogüé, (Charles-Jean-) Melchior de', *Grove Art Online. Oxford Art Online* (Oxford, 2007–15), available at www.oxfordartonline. com.ezproxy.library.ubc.ca/subscriber/article/grove/art/T090069 (accessed 29 July 2015). In actuality, Bell tried to visit, but never managed to see, de Vogüé while in Paris with Reinach; he was away at the time. See GB letter to her mother, 8 November 1904, Gertrude Bell Archive. Nevertheless, she was familiar with his work and travels in the Hauran and the region of the Dead Cities of Syria, herself passing by the same sites in these areas in 1905 and making reference to his publications. See Bell, *Desert and the Sown*, pp. 76, 125, 131, 244 and 297.

54. Édouard Dhorme, 'René Dussaud (1868–1958)', *Revue de l'histoire des religions* 153 (1985), pp. 149–53. Bell was able to meet Dussaud, 'the Syrian traveller', during a visit to Reinach in Paris in October 1905, having a 'most delightful hour's talk'. See GB letter to her mother, 24 October 1905, Gertrude Bell Archive. As with de Vogüé, Bell retraced some of the steps that Dussaud had taken in Syria, although she additionally hoped to explore places he had *not* yet visited. See, for example, GB letters to her family, 17 and 18 February 1905, Gertrude Bell Archive, in which she expressed interest in visiting a site since it had not yet been explored by a European, only to decide, after learning that Dussaud had in fact visited it, not to go there. Later, when reporting her desire to visit the Nejd, she urged herself to hurry, for Dussaud meant to go there too! See GB diary, 1 March 1905, Gertrude Bell Archive.

55. Schaeffer, 'Salomon Reinach', p. 51; see also GB letter to her mother, 8 November 1904, Gertrude Bell Archive: 'He does nothing but work – never goes out, never takes a holiday except to go and see a far away museum. And the consequence is he knows everything.'

56. Reinach wrote these words about Bell to their mutual friend, Eugénie Strong; see Dyson, *Sellers Strong*, p. 89 (from the Girton College Archives: S. Reinach/ES 1905, note 53, p. 226).

57. GB letter to her mother, 10 November 1904, Gertrude Bell Archive.

58. Bruno Schulz and Josef Strzygowski, 'Mschatta', *Jahrbuch der Königlich Preussischen Kunstsammlungen* 25 (1904), pp. 205–373.

59. Gertrude L. Bell, Review of B. Schulz and J. Strzygowski, 'Mschatta', in *Revue archéologique* 5 (1905), pp. 431–2.

60. Gertrude L. Bell, Review of Karl Holzmann, 'Binbirkilise: Archäologische Skizzen aus Anatolien. Ein Beitrag zur Kunstgeschichte des Christlichen Kirchenbaues', in *Revue archéologique* 7 (1906), pp. 219–20; G.L. Bell, 'Notes on a journey through Cilicia and Lycaonia', *Revue archéologique* 7 (1906), pp. 1–29, 385–414; 8 (1906), pp. 7–36, 225–52, 390–401; 9 (1907), pp. 18–30.

61. Josef Strzygowski, Review of Gertrude L. Bell, 'Notes on a journey through Cilicia and Lykaonia' (in *Revue archéologique* 1906 and 1907), *Byzantinische Zeitschrift* 16 (1907), p. 381. This French passage was translated into English by Asher-Greve, 'Gertrude L. Bell', p. 167. See also Maciej Szymaszek, 'Josef Strzygowski in the letters and diaries of Gertrude Lowthian Bell', in P.O. Scholz and M.A. Dlugosz (eds), *Von Biala nach Wien: Josef Strzygowski und die Kunstwissenschaften zum 150. Geburtstag von Josef Strzygowski* (Vienna, 2015), pp. 104–5.

62. See endnote 60, above.

63. GB diary and letter to her family, 16 May 1905, Gertrude Bell Archive. William M. Ramsay and Gertrude L. Bell, *The Thousand and One Churches* (London, 1909),

reprint, with a new foreword by Robert G. Outsterhout and Mark P.C. Jackson (Philadelphia, 2008), p. ix; for a biographical sketch of Ramsay, see pp. xi–xiv.

64. GB letter to her family, 28 May 1907, Gertrude Bell Archive; Ramsay and Bell, *Thousand and One Churches*, p. 9; Mark P.C. Jackson, 'A critical examination of Gertrude Bell's contribution to archaeological research in central Asia Minor', in Charles Tripp and Paul Collins (eds), *Gertrude Bell and Iraq – A Life and Legacy Conference Publication* (London, in press).

65. Ramsay's contribution is essentially to be found in Parts I and IV of *Thousand and One Churches*, while Bell's constitutes Parts II and III.

66. Jackson, 'A critical examination'.

67. Ramsay and Bell, *Thousand and One Churches*, pp. 13–15; Jackson, 'A critical examination'.

68. Ramsay and Bell, *Thousand and One Churches*, pp. 298–302; Jackson, 'A critical examination'.

69. Ibid.

70. Ramsay and Bell, *Thousand and One Churches*, p. x.

71. Robert G. Ousterhout, *John Henry Haynes: A Photographer and Archaeologist in the Ottoman Empire 1881–1900* (Hawick, 2011).

72. Ramsay and Bell, *Thousand and One Churches*, p. x; John Winter Crowfoot, 'I. Binbirkilise (Madenschehr)', in J. Strzygowski, *Kleinasien. Ein Neuland der Kunstgeschichte* (Leipzig, 1903), p. 2; Jackson, 'A critical examination'. Jackson mentions earlier explorers who observed the attrition of the standing remains.

Chapter 2   Euphrates Journey

1. Gertrude L. Bell, *Amurath to Amurath* (London, 1911), pp. 1–3.

2. Ross Burns, *Monuments of Syria: An Historical Guide* (London, 1992), p. 28.

3. David Gill, 'Hogarth, David George (1862–1927)', *Oxford Dictionary of National Biography* (Oxford, 2004), available at www.oxforddnb.com.ezproxy.library.ubc. ca/view/article/33924 (accessed 29 July 2015); David Hogarth, *Accidents of an Antiquary's Life* (London, 1910), p. 6.

4. Hogarth, *Accidents*, pp. 7–11.

5. Gill, 'Hogarth'.

6. David Hawkins, 'Karkamiš', *Reallexikon der Assyriologie und Vorderasiatischen Archäologie* (Berlin, 1976–80), p. 434; Gill, 'Hogarth'.

7. C.R.L. Fletcher, 'David George Hogarth, President R.G.S. 1926–27', *The Geographical Journal* 71 (1928), p. 333; Gill, 'Hogarth'.

8. See especially Hogarth's travels in Cyprus, described in *Devia Cypria: Notes of an Archaeological Journey in Cyprus in 1888* (London, 1889) and in *A Wandering Scholar in the Levant* (New York, 1896); see also Adam Hill, *Stepping Stones in the Stream of Ignorance: D.G. Hogarth as Orientalist and Agent of Empire* (MA thesis, Southern Illinois University Edwardsville, 2008), pp. 32–46.

9. Hogarth's work *The Nearer East* (New York, 1902), for example, describes the topography, climate, environment, population groups, economies and lines of communication in the Balkans, the Near East and Egypt. See also David Hogarth, 'Geographical conditions affecting populations in the east Mediterranean lands', *The Geographical Journal* 27 (1906), pp. 465–77.

10. Hogarth, *Accidents*, p. 2; Hill, *Stepping Stones*, p. 31.

11. Hogarth, *Accidents*, p. 2.
12. Gill, 'Hogarth'.
13. David George Hogarth, *The Life of Charles M. Doughty* (London, 1928). The work would be completed by Hogarth's son after his death. See also Jeremy Wilson, *Lawrence of Arabia* (New York, 1990), p. 816, in which T.E. Lawrence's cancelled introduction for this work is discussed.
14. Fletcher, 'David George Hogarth', p. 330.
15. Bell's letters and diary entries, April 1896 and April 1899, Gertrude Bell Archive.
16. GB letter to her mother, 11 April 1899, Gertrude Bell Archive.
17. David Hogarth, 'Problems in exploration: I. Western Asia', *The Geographical Journal* 32 (1908), p. 556.
18. Bell, *Amurath*, p. 29, fn. 1; Gertrude L. Bell, 'The east bank of the Euphrates from Tel Ahmar to Hit', *The Geographical Journal* 36 (1910), p. 513.
19. GB letter to her mother, 8 October 1909, Gertrude Bell Archive; David Hogarth, 'Carchemish and its neighbourhood', *University of Liverpool Annals of Archaeology and Anthropology* 2 (1909), pp. 165–84 – see especially pl. 40: 1, 2 and 4, which are Bell's photographs, as are all of the images on pls. 41–42. In addition, four letters sent from Hogarth to Bell between 1902 and 1911 are housed in the Gertrude Bell Archive of Newcastle University, Miscellaneous Item 13. One (dated January 1911) provides details about the Tell Ahmar inscriptions, and Hogarth describes a lecture which he heard on imperialism, delivered by their mutual acquaintance, Lord Cromer.
20. See GB letter to her father, 2 March 1917, Gertrude Bell Archive, in which she says that after the war, she wants to cross the Arabian desert but will come home first to get a theodolite and other equipment.
21. See Bell's letters to her parents, 31 March, 1 April, 23 and 26 May 1900, Gertrude Bell Archive, in which she first expresses her interest in Ibn Rashid.
22. David Hogarth, 'Obituary: Gertrude Lowthian Bell', *The Geographical Journal* 68 (1926), p. 366.
23. Hogarth, 'Problems', pp. 556–7.
24. Ibid., pp. 562–3. See also Hogarth's obituary of Bell, 'Gertrude Lowthian Bell', p. 365. He reports that 'for a good part of the long east-bank track from Rakka to Anah she [Bell] remains our only authority.'
25. One can also note that the choice of journal for her account of the leg of the journey that proceeded down the eastern bank of the Euphrates was *The Geographical Journal*, this having recently printed two of Hogarth's own reports, namely 'Geographical conditions' and 'Problems'.
26. Bell, *Amurath*, p. 23, fn. 4; p. 24, fn. 3; pp. 54, 62, 76, 79, 113 and 200. Ammianus Marcellinus (330–95 CE) was a Latin historian who participated in Julian's campaign in Persia and provided an account of it in his history, *Ammianus Marcellinus*, Books 22–5. John F. Matthews, 'Ammianus Marcellinus', in Simon Hornblower and Antony Spawforth (eds), *The Oxford Classical Dictionary*, 3rd revised edition, online version (Oxford, 2005), available at www.oxford reference.com.ezproxy.library.ubc.ca/view/10.1093/acref/9780198606413.001. 0001/acref-9780198606413-e-361?rskey=Oqh5jT&result = 363 (accessed 29 July 2015).
27. Bell, *Amurath*, pp. 16, 18, 24, 73, 82 and 114. Xenophon (*c.* 430 BCE) was a Greek Athenian, celebrated for his part in the expedition of the Persian prince Cyrus against his brother Artaxerxes II, king of Persia, in 401 BCE. Xenophon's account is provided in the work *Anabasis*. Bell frequently mentions the route of

the long march of Cyrus' expeditionary forces, which included 10,000 Greek auxiliary troops, to the Battle of Cunaxa near Babylon, and the route of their retreat to the Black Sea. See Christopher J. Tuplin, 'Xenophon', in Hornblower and Spawforth, *The Oxford Classical Dictionary*.

28. Bell, *Amurath*, pp. 10, 22, 23. Strabo was a Greek geographer (64 BCE–c. 21 CE), responsible for producing two lengthy works, one entitled *Geographica* (in 17 books), which describes the physical geography of the chief countries of the Roman world, their historical and economic developments, and other features of their customs, animals and plants. Strabo's 16th book is dedicated to the geography of the land of the Near East. See Nicholas Purcell, 'Strabo', in Hornblower and Spawforth, *The Oxford Classical Dictionary*.

29. Bell, *Amurath*, p. 21. Lucian (115–80 CE), who was born in Syria and travelled in Asia, Greece, Italy and Gaul, is credited with writing *De Dea Syria*, which includes a description of parts of Syria. See Linda Dirven, 'Author of "De Dea Syria" and his cultural heritage', *Numen* 44 (1997), pp. 153–79; Kenneth Snipes, 'Lucian', in Alexander P. Kazhdan (ed.), *The Oxford Dictionary of Byzantium* (Oxford, 1991); an updated version is available online at www.oxfordreference.com.ezproxy.li brary.ubc.ca/view/10.1093/acref/9780195046526.001.0001/acref-9780195046526-e-3209?rskey=eMTOu3&result = 3209 (accessed 29 July 2015).

30. Bell, *Amurath*, pp. 28, 38, 44 and 113–14. Ptolemy was a celebrated astronomer who lived in Alexandria in the second century CE. Besides his astronomical and mathematical endeavours, he also worked on geographical issues. His *Geography* contains tables of the positions of all the principal places in the world as then known. The work was provided with maps, some of which have survived. See Andrew D. Barker, 'Ptolemy', in Hornblower and Spawforth, *The Oxford Classical Dictionary*.

31. Bell, *Amurath*, pp. 23, 200; the Peutinger Table was a map created in the second century CE or earlier, representing the inhabited world from Spain and Britain in the west to India in the east. See Nicholas Purcell, 'Peutinger Table', in Hornblower and Spawforth, *The Oxford Classical Dictionary*.

32. Bell, *Amurath*, pp. 23, 28, fn. 1; the document is a written collection of roughly 225 routes along the road system of the Roman Empire. For each, the start and destination are provided, as well as the total distance and the relating distances between each of the main stopping points. See Nichols Purcell, 'Itineraries', in Hornblower and Spawforth, *The Oxford Classical Dictionary*.

33. Bell, *Amurath*, pp. 108–14; Isadore of Charax was a geographer who lived between the first century BCE and the first century CE. His best-known work, *Parthian Stations*, is an itinerary of the overland trade route from Antioch to India, specifically the caravan stations maintained by the Arsacid government as they existed around 26 BCE. See Rüdiger Schmitt, 'Isidorus of Charax', in *Encyclopedia Iranica* XIV/2 (2007), pp. 125–7; an updated version is available online at http://www.iranicaonline.org/articles/isidorus-of-charax (accessed 29 July 2015).

34. Adam Silverstein, 'Ibn Khurradadhbih', in J.W. Meri (ed.), *Medieval Islamic Civilisation: An Encyclopedia* (London, 2006), pp. 359–61. Living in the ninth century CE during the time of the Abbasid Caliphate, he is known primarily for his geographical treatise on Muslim lands (*Book of Routes and Kingdoms*). The work includes itineraries of the caliphal road system, descriptions of overland and maritime routes, as well as information on the revenues collected from

various regions of the caliphate. It also describes non-Muslim countries, including China, Byzantium and the region of the Indian Ocean.

35. For Istakhri, see Marina A. Tolmacheva, 'Geography', in J.W. Meri (ed.), *Medieval Islamic Civilisation: An Encyclopedia* (London, 2006), pp. 285–6. Living in the tenth century CE, Istakhri composed reference works pertaining to Islamic geography. Information was provided about various regions' topography, administrative data, commercial and postal routes, descriptions of boundaries and information about the languages and peoples of these regions.

36. David Morray, 'Ibn Jubayr, Abu'l-Husayn Muhammad B. Ahmad', in Meri, *Medieval Islamic Civilisation*, pp. 358–9. Ibn Jubayr was an Andalusian traveller and author, born in 1145 CE, known for an account of his travels, entitled *Rihla* (Journey) through Mesopotamia, the Levant, and Egypt, and his pilgrimage to Mecca.

37. Claude Gilliot, 'Yaqut', in Meri, *Medieval Islamic Civilisation*, pp. 869–70 (the full article is pp. 284–8). Yaqut (al-Rumi al-Hamawi) was a twelfth-century slave by birth, who was purchased by a merchant of Hama in Syria and, who, over the course of his life, travelled to many places in the Middle East. He wrote several learned works, one being the *Geographical Dictionary*, which contains useful detailed geographical and historical information about place names in the Islamic world.

38. Daniella Talmon-Heller, 'Abū l-Fidā', al-Malik al-Mu'ayyad 'Imād al-Dīn', in G. Krämer, D. Matringe, J. Nawas and E. Rowson, *The Encyclopaedia of Islam, Three* (Leiden, 2008), 2008/1: pp. 39–40. Abu'l-Fida was a Syrian Ayyubid prince of the thirteenth to fourteenth centuries CE, known for his learned treatises pertaining to the history of humankind and world geography.

39. The site of Thapsacus, for example, which figures in Xenophon and the Greek army's crossing of the Euphrates in 401 BCE, is now almost unanimously located at Zeugma above Birijek, not at Dibseh as reported by Bell (*Amurath*, pp. 18, 22, 24 and 47). Bell's location of Thapsacus at Dibseh is based on the suggestion provided by her friend Bernhard Moritz (ibid., p. 18). For recent scholarship regarding Thapsacus' location at Zeugma and the possibility of there being a lower Thapsacus at Halebiyeh-Zalebiyeh as well, see Michal Gawlikowski, 'Thapsacus and Zeugma: The crossing of the Euphrates in antiquity', *Iraq* 58 (1996), pp. 123–33.

40. For example, frequent mention of the place-name Europus on the Euphrates River in the Classical accounts of Appian, Lucian, Ptolemy, Procopius and the Peutinger Table led Hogarth to conclude that this was the Greco-Roman name of Jerablus, the place of the ancient mound of Carchemish; Hogarth, 'Carchemish and its neighbourhood', pp. 167–9. Actually, if one must look for the original source of inspiration for Bell's investigations into matters of historical geography – and Hogarth's too, for that matter – one must turn to William Ramsay, the scholar with whom they were both familiar. As reported, Hogarth had accompanied Ramsay on his epigraphic travels through Anatolia in the 1880s, while Bell worked with Ramsay at Binbirkilise in Anatolia. Both would have become well acquainted with Ramsay's method for the study of ancient geography, amply presented in works such as his magisterial *The Historical Geography of Asia Minor* (London, 1890). The work took into consideration a myriad of ancient sources, both epigraphic and archaeological, from all periods of history, and combined them with his own careful observations of the topography of the lands through which

he travelled. As a Classical scholar par excellence, Ramsay had an unparalleled command over ancient textual sources, but even he recognized the importance of actually seeing and moving over the landscapes being described in those ancient texts. 'Topography is the foundation of history,' Ramsay wrote. Hogarth – and Bell even more so – could hardly agree more, their own research being heavily informed by their physical presence in a given Near Eastern region, and their own journeys, either on foot or on horseback, through its varied landscapes.

41. Gill, 'Hogarth'.
42. Hill, *Stepping Stones*, p. 9.
43. Wallach, *Desert Queen*, pp. 145–6.
44. Ibid., p. 16, quoting from T.E. Lawrence, *Seven Pillars of Wisdom* (New York, 1991), p. 58.
45. Margaret Olin, 'Art history and ideology: Alois Riegl and Josef Strzygowski', in Penny S. Gold and Benjamin C. Sax (eds), *Cultural Visions: Essays in the History of Culture* (Amsterdam, 2000), pp. 162–3.
46. Suzanne Marchand, 'The rhetoric of artifacts and the decline of classical humanism: The case of Josef Strzygowski', *History and Theory* 33 (1994), p. 110.
47. Marchand, 'Rhetoric of artifacts', p. 121.
48. Talinn Grigor, '*Orient oder Rom?* Qajar "Aryan" architecture and Strzygowski's art history', *Art Bulletin* 89 (2007), p. 564.
49. Marchand, 'Rhetoric of artifacts', p. 118; Jás Elsner, 'The birth of Late Antiquity: Riegl and Stzygowski in 1901', *Art History* 25 (2002), pp. 375–6.
50. Marchand, 'Rhetoric of artifacts', pp. 109–11, 123.
51. Ibid., p. 116.
52. Ibid., p. 120.
53. Ibid., p. 126; Robert Hillenbrand, 'Creswell and contemporary Central European scholarship', *Muqarnas* 8 (1991), pp. 27–8.
54. Olin, 'Art history and ideology', pp. 164–5; Elsner, 'Birth of Late Antiquity', p. 372.
55. Olin, 'Art history and ideology', p. 167.
56. Elsner, 'Birth of Late Antiquity', p. 361.
57. GB letter to her mother, ? February 1896, Gertrude Bell Archive; Maciej Szymaszek, 'Josef Strzygowski in the letters and diaries of Gertrude Lowthian Bell', in P.O. Scholz and M.A. Dlugosz (eds), *Von Biala nach Wien: Josef Strzygowski und die Kunstwissenschaften zum 150. Geburtstag von Josef Strzygowski* (Vienna, 2015), p. 101.
58. Bruno Schulz and Josef Strzygowski, 'Mschatta', *Jahrbuch der Königlichen Preuszischen Kunstsammlungen* 25 (1904), pp. 205–73.
59. Bell, Review of 'Mschatta', pp. 431–2; Szymaszek, 'Josef Strzygowski', pp. 102–4.
60. Marchand, 'Rhetoric of artifacts', pp. 124–5; Thomas Leisten, 'Concerning the development of the hira-style revisited', in Ann C. Gunther and Stefan R. Hauser (eds), *Ernst Herzfeld and the development of Near Eastern studies, 1900–1950* (Leiden, 2005), p. 373.
61. See Chapter 4; Lisa Cooper, 'Archaeology and acrimony: Gertrude Bell, Ernst Herzfeld and the study of pre-modern Mesopotamia', *Iraq* 75 (2013), pp. 143–69.
62. Marchand, 'Rhetoric of artifacts', p. 119.
63. Ibid., p. 120.
64. Allan Marquand, 'Strzygowski and his theory of early Christian art', *Harvard Theological Review* 3 (1910), pp. 361–2.

65. Bell, 'Notes on a journey', p. 30 n. 19. GB's letter from 13 May 1905 indicates that she used Strzygowski's book as a reference guide to the architecture of the churches at Maden Shaher (Binbirkilise); William M. Ramsay and Gertrude L. Bell, *The Thousand and One Churches* (London, 1909), reprint, with a new foreword by Robert G. Outsterhout and Mark P.C. Jackson (Philadelphia, 2008), pp. xx and xxix; Szymaszek, 'Josef Strzygowski', p. 104.

66. Ramsay and Bell, *Thousand and One Churches*, pp. xx–xxi.

67. GB letter to her parents, 2 April 1909, Gertrude Bell Archive; Szymaszek, 'Josef Strzygowski', p. 108.

68. GB letter to her mother, 18 April 1909, Gertrude Bell Archive; Szymaszek, 'Josef Strzygowski', p. 108.

69. GB letter to her mother, 5 November 1904; GB letter to her father, 14 June 1907; GB letter to her father, 26 July 1907; GB letter to her mother, 7 July 1909; GB letter to her parents, 1 June 1911, Gertrude Bell Archive.

70. GB letter to her mother, 15 February 1909, Gertrude Bell Archive.

71. See, for example, GB photos J_121, K_023, K_053, K_218, L_052 and L_168, Gertrude Bell Archive.

72. Jim Crow, 'Gertrude Bell – Fotografin und Archäologin', in Charlotte Trümpler (ed.), *Das Grosse Spiel. Archäologie und Politik zur Zeit des Kolonialismus (1860–1940)* (Essen, 2008), p. 599.

73. Ibid., p. 605.

74. Ibid., p. 605; see GB photos K_232, K_239 and L_001 for panoramic views of Ctesiphon, and K_086–090 for panoramas of Ukhaidir, Gertrude Bell Archive.

75. Ibid., p. 605; see especially Bell's panoramas of Ukhaidir, K_088 and K_089, in which her shadow is particularly clear.

76. See, for example, GB's pace measurements of the ruins at Munbaqa, in field notebook GLB12, Royal Geographical Society (London).

77. See GB letter in October (date uncertain) 1913, Gertrude Bell Archive, where she relates her instructions for observing the stars and taking bearings for a map by someone from the Royal Geographical Society in London. See also GB letter to her mother, 3 November 1913, Gertrude Bell Archive. GB diary entries for 4 and 7 December 1913, Gertrude Bell Archive, report on work with the theodolite in Damascus. Her diaries and letters also contain numerous references to bearings taken over the course of her Arabian journey in 1913–4. Last, Bell's notebook for that trip, GLB 14, housed in the Royal Geographical Society in London, contains her written calculations for obtaining latitudes.

78. GB letter to her mother, 2 February 1909, Gertrude Bell Archive; GB diary entries for 16 and 17 February 1909, Gertrude Bell Archive, provide elevations above sea level. She refers to the instrument as her 'aneroid' or the 'barometer'.

79. Bell makes references to Kiepert maps during her travels in Palestine in 1899, in western Syria and Anatolia in 1905, and in Anatolia again in 1907; GB diary entries for 21 and 26 March 1905 and for 17, 22 and 27 April 1905; GB letters 13 December 1899, 21 March 1905 and 3 May 1907, Gertrude Bell Archive.

80. Ute Schneider, 'Die Kartierung der Ruinenlandschaften. Späte Würdigung', in Trümpler, *Das Grosse Spiel*, pp. 46–7.

81. F.R. Chesney, *The Expedition for the Survey of the Rivers Euphrates and Tigris, carried on by order of the British government, in the years 1835, 1836, and 1837; preceded by geographical and historical notices of the regions situated between the rivers Nile and Indus*, 4 vols (London, 1850); W.F. Ainsworth, *A Personal Narrative of the Euphrates Expedition*, 2 vols (London, 1888).

82. Richard Kiepert, 'Syrien und Mesopotamien zur Darstellung der Reise des Dr. Max Freiherrn von Oppenheim von Mittelmeere zu Persischen Golf, 1893, Westliches Blatt und Östliches Blatt', in M. von Oppenheim, *Von Mittelmeer zum Persischen Golf* (Berlin, 1899–1900).

83. GB diary entries 27, 28 January 1909, and GB letter 29 January 1909, Gertrude Bell Archive.

84. See Bell's diary entries for 21 and 22 February 1909, Gertrude Bell Archive, in which she refers to 'villages marked by Oppenheim' and 'Oppenheim's road', together with descriptions of the tower tombs above Serrin that Oppenheim had recorded and the mosaic pavements at nearby Mas'udiyyeh. Bell also came to learn of Oppenheim's investigations at Tell Halaf at this time – she reports in her diary entry for 27 January 1909 that she purchased his publication of the site (Oppenheim's *Der Tell Halaf und die verschleierte Göttin*, Berlin, 1908). See also her reference to Oppenheim's 1899 trip across the Euphrates at Qalat en-Nejm and then on to Serrin, in Bell, 'The east bank', p. 515, fn. ‖. Bell's relationship with Max von Oppenheim, a fascinating and colourful German who figured prominently not only in Near Eastern archaeology but also in German–Ottoman politics before World War I, had its highs and lows. For more information on the life and activities of Max von Oppenheim, see Gabriele Teichmann, 'Max Freiherr von Oppenheim – Archäologe, Diplomat, Freund des Orients', in Trümpler, *Das Grosse Spiel*, pp. 239–49. She was first introduced to Oppenheim through her friend Moritz in 1907, when she was in Cairo with her father (GB letters 8 and 10 January 1907, Gertrude Bell Archive). As has been indicated, she had frequent exchanges with him in 1909, all of which were friendly and helpful. In 1911, when she made another trip into Mesopotamia and Anatolia, she had planned to meet up with Oppenheim while he was excavating at Tell Halaf, but failing to find him there would instead see him in Aleppo. Her letters provide a much harsher opinion of him at that point:

> (On board the Niger) The next day was mostly occupied in winding up affairs, selling my horses and paying off my people. I went to tea with Mme Koch and presently there came in Oppenheim who was still in Aleppo preparing for his expedition to Ras al 'Ain – where you remember I went expecting to find him already established. Oppenheim is really awful, the most shocking little vulgar Jew – blatant now, you might think he had taken all Mesopotamia into his wise keeping to hear him talk! He is much worse than he was in Egypt when he was well kept under. I prophecy that none of the architects and people he is taking out with him will stay with him – he is too dreadful. (GB letter to her mother, 29 May 1911, Gertrude Bell Archive)

Anti-Semitic remarks about Oppenheim were also made by David Hogarth and T.E. Lawrence, both of whom would have met Oppenheim in Syria before World War I. These are rather surprising given that Oppenheim never identified himself as a Jew. His mother was Christian and his father was only half Jewish. See Lionel Gossman, *The Passion of Max von Oppenheim: Archaeology and Intrigue in the Middle East from Wilhelm II to Hitler* (Cambridge, 2013), pp. 325, 330. Gossman suspects that Oppenheim's adversaries may have exploited anti-Semitic prejudice in order to present an even blacker picture of a fairly formidable foe. Oppenheim, after all, was not only an archaeologist before the war but a dangerous intelligence agent of the German Kaiser (ibid., p. 331); Scott Anderson, *Lawrence in Arabia* (Toronto, 2014), pp. 37–9. It must be questioned, however, the degree to which individuals like Lawrence and Bell were fully aware of Oppenheim's political motives and activities as early as 1911.

85. Bell, *Amurath*, p. 3.
86. Ibid., pp. 3–10.
87. Burns, *Monuments*, p. 28.
88. Bell photograph J_085. Bell refers to the location of this stone as the Jami' Elkikan, or mosque of Ḳiḳân; GB diary entry for 6 February 1909, Gertrude Bell Archive; Bell, *Amurath*, p. 11; Burns, *Monuments*, p. 38. The Hittite stone in question is a foundation document that records the building of the temple of the gods Hebat and Šarruma by the Hittite vice-regent Talmi-Šarruma around 1300 BCE; David Hawkins, *Corpus of Luwian Inscriptions. Volume 1: Inscriptions of the Iron Age* (Berlin, 2000), p. 388.
89. GB letter to her mother, 9 February 1909, Gertrude Bell Archive; Bell, *Amurath*, p. 11, Fig. 2.
90. This is Bell's Jâmi' el Ḥelâwîyeh; Bell, *Amurath*, p. 11, Fig. 6; Burns, *Monuments*, p. 35.
91. This is Bell's Jâmi' esh Shaibîyeh; Bell photos J_88–92, Gertrude Bell Archive; Bell, *Amurath*, p. 12. The mosque is also known as the Mosque al-Tuteh; see Burns, *Monuments*, p. 38.
92. This is Bell's Jamiet et Tawarki, GB diary, 10 February 1910, Gertrude Bell Archive. Bell photographs, Album J_075–080; J_076 is her photograph of the minaret. See also http://monummamluk-syrie.org/Fiches/Alep/HLB_mos quee_Tawashi_Jawhar.htm for recent images of the mosque, including the minaret before its destruction.
93. GB photo J_053, Gertrude Bell Archive.
94. Robert Hillenbrand, *Islamic Architecture* (New York, 1994), p. 359.
95. GB photos J_61 and J_62, Gertrude Bell Archive; H.Z. Watenpaugh, *The Image of an Ottoman City: Imperial Architecture and Urban Experience in Aleppo in the 16th and 17th Centuries* (Leiden, 2004), pp. 192–3.
96. GB photo J_059, Gertrude Bell Archive.
97. GB photo J_058, Gertrude Bell Archive; Watenpaugh, *Image*, p. 194.
98. Watenpaugh, *Image*, p. 194.
99. GB letter to her mother, 15 February 1909, Gertrude Bell Archive.
100. Bell, *Amurath*, pp. 17–18.
101. Ibid., p. 16.
102. Ibid., p. 27; GB letter to her parents, 17 February 1909, Gertrude Bell Archive.
103. Bell, *Amurath*, p. 28.
104. Ibid., p. 515.
105. Hogarth, 'Carchemish', p. 179.
106. Bell, 'The east bank', p. 513; Bell, *Amurath*, p. 29, fn. 1; GB letter to her parents, 17 February 1909, Gertrude Bell Archive.
107. GB diary, 17 February 1909, Gertrude Bell Archive.
108. Bell, *Amurath*, pp. 28–30; GB diary 17–18 February, 1909; GB letters to her parents, 17–18 February 1909, Gertrude Bell Archive.
109. Bell's visit to Hogarth in Oxford to go over her squeezes and photographs is reported in a letter to her mother, 8 October 1909, Gertrude Bell Archive.
110. Hogarth, 'Carchemish', pl. 39.

111. Ibid., p. 179.
112. For GB's visit to this site, see her diary entry, 9 June 1909, and letter to her mother, 10 June 1909, Gertrude Bell Archive.
113. Hogarth, 'Carchemish', pp. 180, 182; pls. 40: 1, 2, 4; 41: 1–6.
114. F. Thureau-Dangin and M. Dunand, *Til-Barsib* (Paris, 1936); A. Roobaert and G. Bunnens, 'Excavations at Tell Ahmar-Til Barsib', in G. del Olmo Lete and J.-L. Montero Fenollós (eds), *Archaeology of the Upper Syrian Euphrates: The Tishrin Dam Area* (Barcelona, 1999), pp. 163–78; G. Bunnens, *Tell Ahmar: 1988 Season* (Leuven, 1990); G. Bunnens, 'Looking for Luwians, Aramaeans and Assyrians in the Tell Ahmar stratigraphy', in S. Mazzoni and S. Soldi (eds), *Syrian Archaeology in Perspective: Celebrating 20 Years of Excavations at Tell Afis* (Pisa, 2013), pp. 177–97.
115. Guy Bunnens, *A New Luwian Stele and the Cult of the Storm-God at Til Barsib-Masuwari* (Louvain, 2006), pp. 103–4; Bunnens, 'Looking for Luwians', p. 184.
116. Peter Akkermans and Glenn Schwartz, *The Archaeology of Syria* (Cambridge, 2003) p. 382.
117. Lisa Cooper, *Early Urbanism on the Syrian Euphrates* (London, 2006), pp. 230–2; Guy Bunnens, 'A third-millennium temple at Tell Ahmar (Syria)', paper delivered at the 9th International Congress on the Archaeology of the Ancient Near East, Basel, 12 June 2014.
118. F. Thureau-Dangin, 'Tell Ahmar', *Syria* 10 (1929), p. 198 and pls. 28–31; Hawkins, *Corpus*, TELL AHMAR 1 Stele, p. 239.
119. Earlier, in Ariyahinas's time, a competing family dynasty had taken the opportunity to usurp the throne and install its own king. The son of that usurping king was called Hamiyatas, and he apparently promised that upon his death, the heir of Ariyahinas, the usurped king, would be restored to power. When this did not happen, and Hamiyatas's own son tried to keep power, the legitimate heir seized power forcibly and was able to recover his heritage. See Bunnens, *A New Luwian Stele*, p. 103; Hawkins, *Corpus*, pp. 225–6; Guy Bunnens, 'Assyrian empire building and Aramization of culture as seen from Tell Ahmar/ Til Barsib', *Syria* 86 (2009), pp. 67–82, here p. 75.
120. Bunnens, *A New Luwian Stele*, p. 33.
121. Bunnens, 'Looking for Luwians', p. 183.
122. Bunnens, *A New Luwian Stele*, p. 1.
123. Ibid., p. 1.
124. Ibid., p. 85.
125. Ibid., pp. 103–8.
126. Or possibly a bull, according to Bunnens, *A New Luwian Stele*, p. 6; Bell, 'The east bank', p. 515; Bell, *Amurath*, p. 30; GB photograph J_135, Gertrude Bell Archive.
127. Bunnens, *A New Luwian Stele*, p. 6.
128. Ibid., p. 6.
129. Bell, *Amurath*, p. 31.
130. Ibid., pp. 31–2.
131. Ibid., p. 33.
132. Hawkins, 'Karkamiš', p. 429.
133. Ibid., pp. 428–34.
134. J.D. Hawkins, 'Carchemish', in E.M. Meyers (ed.), *The Oxford Encyclopedia of Archaeology in the Near East* (New York, 1997), p. 424; Trevor Bryce, *The World of the Neo-Hittite Kingdoms* (Oxford, 2012), pp. 89–98.
135. Bryce, *World*, pp. 83–4.

136. Ibid., p. 84.
137. Ibid., p. 84.
138. Hawkins, 'Karkamiš', p. 434; Hogarth, 'Carchemish', pp. 169–71 and pls. 35 and 36:1; Bell, *Amurath*, p. 34; GB photographs, Album J_145 and J_146, Gertrude Bell Archive.
139. Wilson, *Lawrence*, pp. 70–3 and *passim*. This biography of T.E. Lawrence provides a splendidly detailed timeline of the Carchemish excavations.
140. Hawkins, 'Karkamiš', p. 434.
141. David Hogarth, *Carchemish. Report on the Excavations at Jerablus on Behalf of the British Museum I: Introductory* (London, 1914); C.L. Woolley, *Carchemish. Report on the Excavations at Jerablus on Behalf of the British Museum II: The Town Defences* (London, 1921); C.L. Woolley and R.D. Barnett, *Carchemish. Report on the Excavations at Jerablus on Behalf of the British Museum III: The Excavations in the Inner Town, and The Hittite Inscriptions* (London, 1952); Hawkins, 'Karkamiš', pp. 436–8.
142. Nicolò Marchetti, 'Karkemish on the Euphrates: Excavating a city's history', *Near Eastern Archaeology* 75 (2012), pp. 132–47.
143. Wilson, *Lawrence*, pp. 81, 86, 96, 104, 116–17, 118–19, 122; Paola Sconzo, 'Bronze Age pottery from the Carchemish region at the British Museum', *Palestine Exploration Quarterly* 145 (2013), pp. 334–8.
144. Lawrence James, *The Golden Warrior: The Life and Legend of Lawrence of Arabia* (London, 1990), p. 47; Wilson, *Lawrence*, p. 80.
145. Ibid., p. 79.
146. Anderson, *Lawrence in Arabia*, p. 33.
147. Even one of L. Woolley's essays about T.E. Lawrence, written in later years, tends to make light of Lawrence's efforts on the project, giving the strong impression that he 'was dilettante in his attitude towards archaeology'. See Wilson, *Lawrence*, pp. 128–30, who assesses L. Woolley's essay in *T.E. Lawrence by his Friends*, edited by A.W. Lawrence (London, 1937). In this review, Wilson puts forward several reasons for Woolley's somewhat untruthful sketch of Lawrence.
148. Cooper, *Early Urbanism*, p. 211; Sconzo, 'Bronze Age pottery'; Paola Sconzo, 'The grave of the court pit: A rediscovered Bronze Age tomb from Carchemish', *Palestine Exploration Quarterly* 146 (2014), pp. 3–16.
149. James, *Golden Warrior*, p. 51.
150. Ibid., pp. 52–3, 60; Anderson, *Lawrence in Arabia*, pp. 33–4.
151. James, *Golden Warrior*, p. 60; Wilson, *Lawrence*, pp. 543–5. Some make the case that Lawrence's romantic vision of Arab freedom was fashioned out of the idealized image represented by his Jerablus friend Dahoum. The dedication in Lawrence's account of his part in the Arab Revolt, in *Seven Pillars of Wisdom*, is written for Selim Ahmed, this being the full name for Dahoum.
152. GB letter to her parents, 20 May 1911, Gertrude Bell Archive.
153. GB letter to her parents, 21 May 1911, Gertrude Bell Archive.
154. Lawrence letter to his mother, 23 May 1911, in M. Brown (ed.), *T.E. Lawrence: The Selected Letters* (New York, 1988), pp. 36–7.
155. Jonathan N. Tubb, 'Leonard Woolley und Thomas E. Lawrence in Karkemisch', in Trümpler, *Das Grosse Spiel*, p. 257.
156. Tubb, 'Leonard Woolley', pp. 255, 257.
157. GB letter to her parents, 21 May 1911, Gertrude Bell Archive.
158. Lawrence letter to his mother, 23 May 1911, in Brown, *T.E. Lawrence*, p. 37.
159. Bell, *Amurath*, p. 36.

160. Ibid., p. 36, fn. 1; GB diary 21 February 1909, Gertrude Bell Archive; Max von Oppenheim, 'Griechische und lateinische Inschriften aus Syrien, Mesopotamien und Kleinasien', *Byzantinische Zeitschrift* 14 (1905), pp. 1–72.

161. GB letter to her parents, 21 February 1909, Gertrude Bell Archive. She did not seem to know of H. Pognon's visit and his publication of the north tomb inscription until she returned to England, but she did mention his work in *Amurath* (p. 36, fn. 1; p. 37, fn. 1).

162. Rüdiger Gogräfe, 'Die Grabtürme von Sirrin (Osroëne)', *Damaszener Mitteilungen* 8 (1995), pp. 165–201.

163. Ibid., Abb. 2–5.

164. Ibid., p. 186.

165. The protomes are likely bulls, although their heads are now missing, so it is difficult to know their identity for certain. Bell, following Oppenheim, conjectured that these were the front parts of lions; Bell, *Amurath*, p. 36; Gogräfe, 'Grabtürme', p. 180.

166. Bell, *Amurath*, p. 36; J.B. Segal, *Edessa, 'The Blessed City'* (Oxford, 1970), p. 23; a translation of the Ma'nu inscription is provided on p. 23, fn. 4.

167. Gogräfe, 'Grabtürme', p. 180.

168. Ibid., p. 180.

169. Bell, *Amurath*, p. 37; Gogräfe, 'Grabtürme', pp. 180, 183.

170. Bell, *Amurath*, p. 37.

171. Gogräfe, 'Grabtürme', p. 183 and pl. 25b.

172. Bell, *Amurath*, p. 38; Gogräfe, 'Grabtürme', p. 186.

173. Bell, *Amurath*, p. 38.

174. Gogräfe, 'Grabtürme', pp. 184, 186.

175. GB photographs, Album J_149 and J_150, Gertrude Bell Archive.

176. Gogräfe, 'Grabtürme', p. 183 and pl. 26c.

177. Warwick Ball, *Rome in the East: The Transformation of an Empire* (London, 2000), pp. 364, 366–7; Pascale Clauss, 'Les tours funéraires du djebel Baghoûz dans l'histoire de la tour funéraire syrienne', *Syria* 49 (2002), pp. 170–1.

178. Gogräfe, 'Grabtürme', p. 199; Segal, *Edessa*, p. 29; Clauss, 'Les tours', p. 173.

179. Segal, *Edessa*, pp. 23–4.

180. Bell, *Amurath*, p. 37.

181. Ibid., p. 40.

182. Ibid., pp. 30–42.

183. Ibid., p. 47.

184. On the basis of Bell's report of basalt mills having been incorporated into tombs between Tell Munbayah and Tell Murraibet, and the fact that the local Bedouin did not know what they were, T. Wilkinson suggests that they were parts of rotary water mills for grinding grain (as opposed to saddle querns) that once existed along this stretch of the river. See Tony J. Wilkinson, *On the Margin of the Euphrates: Settlement and Land Use at Tell es-Sweyhat and in the Upper Lake Assad Area, Syria* (Chicago, 2004), p. 5. See also Bell's photograph of a basalt millstone at Abu Said, further downriver, GB photo J_204, Gertrude Bell Archive.

185. Ibid., p. 5.

186. Tony J. Wilkinson, G. Philip, J. Bradbury, R. Dunford, D. Donoghue, N. Galiatsatos, D. Lawrence, A. Ricci and S.L. Smith, 'Contextualizing early urbanism: Settlement cores, early states and agro-pastoral strategies in the Fertile Crescent during the fourth and third millennium BC', *Journal of World Prehistory*, published online, 16 April 2014, DOI 10.1007/s10963-014-9072-2.

187. Bell, *Amurath*, p. 30.
188. Ibid., p. 47.
189. É. Coqueugniot, 'Dja'de el Mughara (moyen-Euphrate), un village néolithique dans son environnement naturel à la veille de la domestication', in M. Fortin and O. Aurenche (eds), *Espace naturel, espace habité en Syrie du Nord* (Toronto, 1998), pp. 109–14.
190. Akkermans and Schwartz, *Archaeology of Syria*, pp. 50–2.
191. Bell, *Amurath*, p. 44.
192. Akkermans and Schwartz, *Archaeology of Syria*, pp. 194–6.
193. Bell, *Amurath*, pp. 30, 41, 43. At the latter site, she reports seeing, among a heap of cut stones, fragments of an entablature carved with dentils and palmettes, possibly the remnants of a tower tomb. Wilkinson conjectured that this may have been at, or near to, Tell Jouweif, occupied during the third millennium but also in the later Hellenistic period. It is also known as Shams ed-Din East; Wilkinson, *On the Margin*, pp. 5, 202.
194. Bell, *Amurath*, p. 43. This is also known as Shams ed-Din Central. Here Bell notes having seen heaps of unsquared building stones. Wilkinson, *On the Margin*, pp. 249–50.
195. Bell, *Amurath*, p. 43. Several shaft tombs belonging to an Early Bronze Age cemetery have been explored here, and it is evident that a settlement existed here as well, although the mounded site whose date is uncertain is now located within a modern village. Before the current war in Syria, it had been the place of a thriving Suq al-Ahad, or Sunday market. See Jan-Waalke Meyer, *Gräber des 3. Jahrtausands. V. Chr. im syrischen Euphrattal. 3 Ausgrabungen in Šamseddin und Djerniye* (Saarbrücken, 1991), p. 149; Wilkinson, *On the Margin*, p. 5.
196. Bell, *Amurath*, p. 47.
197. Cooper, *Early Urbanism*.
198. Ibid.
199. Bell, *Amurath*, p. 44.
200. Bell photographs, Album J_158–163, Gertrude Bell Archive; Bell, *Amurath*, Fig. 25.
201. Ibid., p. 44.
202. D. Machule, '1969–1994: Ekalte (Tall Munbāqa). Eine bronzezeitliche Stadt in Syrien', in G. Wilhelm (ed.), *Zwischen Tigris und Nil* (Mainz am Rhein, 1998), pp. 115–25.
203. Peter Werner, *Tell Munbaqa: Bronzezeit in Syrien* (Neumünster, 1998).
204. R.M. Czichon and P. Werner, *Tell Munbāqa – Ekalte – I: Die Bronzezeitlichen Kleinfunde* (Saarbrücken, 1998), Plate 1.
205. Machule, 'Ekalte (Tall Munbāqa)', p. 117.
206. Bell, *Amurath*, p. 44.
207. Christina Tonghini, *Qal'at Ja'bar Pottery: A Study of a Syrian Fortified Site of the Late 11th–14th Centuries* (Oxford, 1998).
208. Burns, *Monuments*, p. 175.
209. Tonghini, *Qal'at Ja'bar Pottery*, p. 23.
210. Bell, *Amurath*, p. 51.
211. Tonghini, *Qal'at Ja'bar Pottery*, p. 26.
212. Ibid., p. 26.
213. Bell, *Amurath*, p. 53 and Figs 33–4.
214. In 1855, Sachau was the first European to take note of this ruin; Eduard Sachau, *Reise durch Syrien und Mesopotamien* (Leipzig, 1883), p. 245; Bell, *Amurath*, p. 54, fn. 1.

215. Kassem Toueir, 'Heraqlah: A unique victory monument of Harun al-Rashid', *World Archaeology* 14 (1983), p. 296.
216. Ibid., p. 296; Marcus Milwright, *An Introduction to Islamic Archaeology* (Edinburgh, 2010), p. 80. See also the following chapters in Verena Daiber and Andrea Becker (eds), *Raqqa III: Baudenkmäler und Paläste I* (Mainz am Rhein, 2004), which provide further information about this site: Kassem Toueir, 'Das Hiraqla des Hārūn ar-Rašīd', pp. 137–42; S. Chmelnizkij, 'Überlegungen zum Planungskonzept und zur Rekonstruktion von Hiraqla', pp. 143–8; and U. Becker, 'Überlegungen zur Anlage von Hiraqla bei Raqqa', pp. 149–56, as well as pls. 88–9.
217. Toueir, 'Heraqlah', p. 298.
218. GB diary entries, 27–8 February and 1 March 1909, Gertrude Bell Archive.
219. Bell, *Amurath*, p. 54.
220. Ibid., pp. 55–6.
221. Milwright, *Introduction to Islamic Archaeology*, p. 80.
222. Stefan Heidemann, 'Die Geschichte von ar-Raqqa/ar-Rāfiqa', in S. Heidemann and A. Becker (eds), *Raqqa II. Die Islamische Stadt* (Mainz am Rhein, 2003), p. 17. See also Lorenz Korn's chapter on the Raqqa mosque and minaret, 'Die Grosse Moschee von ar-Raqqa', in Daiber and Becker, *Raqqa III*, pp. 19–23. Korn used Bell's photograph of the minaret (see pl. 4b; it is acknowledged on p. 164).
223. Bell, *Amurath*, pp. 54, 56–7; Milwright, *Introduction to Islamic Archaeology*, p. 80.
224. Bell, *Amurath*, p. 55.
225. Milwright, *Introduction to Islamic Archaeology*, p. 80.
226. K.A.C. Creswell, *Short Account of Early Muslim Architecture* (Harmondsworth, 1958), pp. 184–6.
227. Ibid., p. 187.
228. Robert Hillenbrand, 'Eastern Islamic influences in Syria: Raqqa and Qal'at Ja'bar in the later 12th century', in Julian Raby (ed.), *The Art of Syria and the Jazīra* (Oxford, 1985), pp. 27–36.
229. Lorenz Korn, 'Das Baghdad-Tor (Südosttor der Halbrundstadt)', in Daiber and Becker, *Raqqa III*, pp. 11–18.
230. Bell, *Amurath*, p. 59, fn. 1.
231. Ibid., p. 135; this point is also noted by Hillenbrand, 'Eastern Islamic influences', p. 28.
232. Ibid., p. 28.
233. For a brief yet succinct synopsis of all of the proposed dates for the Baghdad Gate and their explanations, see Stefan Heidemann, 'The citadel of al-Raqqa and fortifications in the Middle Euphrates area', in H. Kennedy (ed.), *Muslim Military Architecture in Greater Syria* (Leiden, 2006), p. 140, fn. 54.
234. Bell, *Amurath*, p. 58; GB photographs, Album J_180, J_183 and J_184, Gertrude Bell Archive. A full report on the excavations of the Qasr al-Banat has not yet appeared, although it is believed to have been reconstructed with a central courtyard that has four *iwan*s arranged around it. The back *iwan* led to the principal room of the building, while lesser rooms and corridors filled the area between and behind the *iwan*s, many of these with walls and vaults coated with plaster. Hillenbrand, 'Eastern Islamic influences', p. 37; see also Stefan Heidemann, 'Die Geschichte von ar-Raqqa/ar-Rafiqa – ein Überblick', in Heidemann and Becker, *Raqqa II*, p. 48.
235. Hillenbrand, 'Eastern Islamic influences', p. 38.

236. Bell photos J_180 and J_183, Gertrude Bell Archive. The online image of J_183 (www.gerty.ncl.ac.uk/photo_details.php?photo_id=2772) is upside down.
237. Bell photo J_184, Gertrude Bell Archive; Bell refers to this as a dome set upon squinch-arches: *Amurath*, p. 58; Hillenbrand, 'Eastern Islamic influences', p. 38.
238. See Creswell's photograph of the Qasr al-Banat, now housed in the Creswell Archive of the Ashmolean Museum of Art and Archaeology: http://creswell.as hmolean.museum/archive/EA.CA.6692-0.html.
239. Bell, *Amurath*, p. 58; Hillenbrand, 'Eastern Islamic influences', p. 36.
240. Bell, *Amurath*, p. 58; Bell acknowledges that her Swiss scholarly acquaintance, M. van Berchem, had published this inscription in F. Sarre and E. Herzfeld's *Archäologische Reise*, which was to appear shortly after *Amurath to Amurath*, so it is likely that her dating of this arcade came from him.
241. K.A.C. Creswell, *Early Muslim Architecture*, vol. 2 (New York, 1979), p. 47.
242. Compare Bell's plan, *Amurath*, fig. 36, with the plan of the mosque, Abb. 1, in N. Hagen, M. al-Hassoun and M. Meinecke, 'Die Grosse Moschee von ar-Rāfiqa', in Daiber and Becker, *Raqqa III*. Bell rightly reconstructed three entrances on the mosque's north side, *contra* Herzfeld's own estimation of five entrances. This was noted by Creswell and confirmed by the most recent German investigations; Creswell, *Early Muslim Architecture*, vol. 2, p. 48 and fns. 2–3.
243. Bell, *Amurath*, Fig. 39= GB photo J_190, Gertrude Bell Archive.
244. Bell's photograph J_185 (note that the photo's caption 'Mosque – base of minaret' is incorrect, as this belongs to the mosque arcade), Gertrude Bell Archive; see also Hillenbrand, 'Eastern Islamic influences', p. 36.
245. Bell, *Amurath*, p. 59.
246. Milwright, *Introduction to Islamic Archaeology*, p. 146.
247. Ibid., p. 148.
248. GB letter to her parents, 21 April 1909, Gertrude Bell Archive.
249. GB diary, 3 March 1909, Gertrude Bell Archive; Bell, *Amurath*, p. 67.
250. Ball, *Rome in the East*, p. 165.
251. Ibid., p. 165.
252. GB diary, 3 March 1909, Gertrude Bell Archive; Bell, *Amurath*, pp. 67–8.
253. GB photos, J_200–3, Gertrude Bell Archive; the image of the Euphrates's course is J_199.
254. Burns, *Monuments*, p. 123.
255. http://en.wikipedia.org/wiki/Halabiye_Dam.
256. Bell, *Amurath*, p. 74.
257. GB diary entries, 6–7 March 1909, Gertrude Bell Archive; Bell, *Amurath*, pp. 74–5.
258. Ibid., pp. 83–4 and fig. 48; GB photographs, Album J_213–5 are of this tomb, while Album J_216, which Bell calls Erzi East tomb, is known elsewhere as the tower of Erzî. See Clauss, 'Les tours', p. 156 and pls. 3 and 5a. It is evident that this latter tower tomb suffered considerable deterioration in the twentieth century. The doorway over the staircase of the first storey has completely vanished.
259. Ibid., p. 171.
260. Bell, *Amurath*, pp. 85–9.
261. Ibid., pp. 88–9.
262. Ibid., p. 89.
263. Alastair Northedge, 'The Islamic period in the Haditha dam area', in C. Kepinski, P. Lecomte and A. Tenu (eds), *Studia Euphratica. Le moyen Euphrate iraquien révélé par les fouilles preventives de Haditha* (Paris, 2006), p. 402.

264. Bell, *Amurath*, p. 97; Northedge, 'Islamic period', p. 402.
265. Bell, *Amurath*, p. 96, Figs 51 (J_223 and J_224) and 56 (J_232). See also Bell's photograph, J_230, looking south from the top of the minaret.
266. Christine Kepinski, Olivier Lecomte and Aline Tenu, 'Studia Euphratica, introduction', in Kepinski, Lecomte and Tenu (eds), *Studia Euphratica*, p. 15 and Fig. 2.
267. Northedge, 'Islamic period', p. 402.
268. Some of the archaeological sites are simply mentioned by Bell in her diary entries and field notebooks, but in the case of at least 60 tells, she took the time to inspect them on foot, reporting their above-ground architectural remains and artefacts (e.g. pottery) strewn on their surfaces.

Chapter 3   Ukhaidir – Desert Splendour

1. William M. Ramsay and Gertrude L. Bell, *Thousand and One Churches* (London, 1909). Reprint, with a new foreword by Robert G. Outsterhout and Mark P.C. Jackson (Philadelphia, 2008), pp. 309–11, 437, 440–1.
2. Bruno Schulz and Josef Strzygowski, 'Mschatta', *Jahrbuch der Königlichen Preuszischen Kunstsammlungen* 25 (1904), pp. 205–373.
3. Gertrude L. Bell, Review of B. Schulz and J. Strzygowski, 'Mschatta', in *Revue archéologique* 5 (1905), pp. 431–2.
4. The Mshatta façade was brought to Berlin in 1903 as a gift from the Ottoman sultan Abdul Hamid II to the German emperor Wilhelm II. Today, the Mshatta façade is part of the collection of the Museum für Islamische Kunst and is housed in the Pergamonmuseum, in Berlin. For modern scholarly discussions of the Mshatta façade and the palace, see R. Hillenbrand, 'Islamic art at the crossroads: East versus West at Mshatta', in A. Daneshvari (ed.), *Essays on Islamic Art and Architecture: In Honor of Katharina Otto-Dorn* (Malibu, 1981), pp. 63–86; Oleg Grabar, 'The date and meaning of Mshatta', *Dumbarton Oaks Papers* 41 (1987), pp. 243–7.
5. Schulz and Stryzgowski, 'Mschatta', pp. 367–70; Bell, Review of 'Mschatta', p. 432; I. Shahid, *Byzantium and the Arabs in the Sixth Century. Vol. 1, Part 1: Political and Military History.* (Washington, 1995), pp. 32–6.
6. C. Edmund Bosworth, 'Lakhmids', *Encyclopaedia Iranica* (online edition, 2012), available at www.iranicaonline.org/articles/lakhmids (accessed 29 July 2015).
7. Ernst Herzfeld, 'Die Genesis der islamischen Kunst und das Mschatta-Problem', *Der Islam* 1 (1910), pp. 106–8.
8. Moritz subsequently returned to Berlin, where he was appointed Director of the Library of the Seminar for Oriental Languages, a post he held until 1924. See G.J. Bosch, J. Carswell and G. Petherbridge (eds), *Islamic Bindings and Bookmaking: A Catalogue of an Exhibition in the Oriental Institute Museum, University of Chicago, May 18–August 18, 1981* (Chicago, 1981), p. ix.
9. Ibid.
10. While in Cairo, Bell mentions having been told that Moritz had written all of Oppenheim's book. GB diary, 17 January 1905, Gertrude Bell Archive.
11. GB letter to her mother, 8 January 1907, Gertrude Bell Archive.
12. GB diary, 27 January 1909, Gertrude Bell Archive.
13. GB diary, 28 January 1909, Gertrude Bell Archive.
14. GB letter to her mother, 29 January 1909, Gertrude Bell Archive.

15. Gertrude L. Bell, *Amurath to Amurath* (London, 1911), p. 86.
16. Ibid., pp. 119–37.
17. Ibid., p. 139.
18. GB letter to her family, 24 March 1909, Gertrude Bell Archive. Watts was in the employ of Sir William Willcocks, who at this time was in the midst of preparing for the construction of the Hindiya Barrage on the Euphrates River, a hydraulic system that would bring water to the region around the city of Hilla and restore its irrigation regimes. See R.I. Money, 'The Hindiya Barrage, Mesopotamia', *The Geographical Journal* 50/3 (1917), pp. 217–22.
19. Bell, *Amurath*, p. 140.
20. K.A.C. Creswell, *Early Muslim Architecture. Vol. 2: Early 'Abbāsids, Umayyads of Cordova, Aghlabids, Ṭūlūnids, and Samānids, A.D. 751–905* (Oxford, 1940), reprint (New York, 1979), p. 52.
21. Bell, *Amurath*, p. 140.
22. Ibid., p. 144.
23. GB letter to her family, 26 March 1909, Gertrude Bell Archive; Bell, *Amurath*, p. 144.
24. Bell, *Amurath*, p. 145.
25. Ibid.
26. Ibid.
27. GB diary, 25 March 1909; GB letter to her family, 26 March 1909, Gertrude Bell Archive. In addition, a sketch plan with these measurements, and B.T. Watts's name, are recorded on a page of Bell's field notebooks; GLB 11 (1909), London, Royal Geographic Society.
28. GB letter to her family, 26 March 1909, Gertrude Bell Archive.
29. Ibid.
30. GB diary, 27–8 March 1909; GB letter to her family, 29 March 1909, Gertrude Bell Archive.
31. Ibid.
32. Gertrude L. Bell, 'The vaulting system of Ukhaidir', *Journal of Hellenic Studies* 30 (1910), pl. X; Bell, *Amurath*, fig. 79.
33. GB letter to her family, 3 March 1911, Gertrude Bell Archive.
34. GB diary, 2 March 1911; GB letter to her family, 3 March 1911, Gertrude Bell Archive.
35. Ibid.
36. GB diary, 1–3 March 1911, Gertrude Bell Archive.
37. Gertrude L. Bell, *Palace and Mosque at Ukhaidir: A Study in Early Mohammadan Architecture* (Oxford, 1914).
38. Ibid., pls 1–3; Oskar Reuther, *Ocheïdir. Nach Aufnahmen von Mitgliedern der Babylon Expedition der Deutschen Orient-Gesellschaft* (Leipzig, 1912), pls. III–IV.
39. Creswell, *Early Muslim Architecture,* vol. 2, fig. 64.
40. A well is located nearby but still at a distance from the castle; no good water was found within the palace or in the area immediately around it. See Bell, *Palace and Mosque,* p. 1.
41. Ibid., p. 3.
42. According to Bell's calculations, the outer enclosure measured 175.80 m x 163.30 m; ibid., p. 4. Creswell's measurements were 175 m x 169 m; Creswell, *Early Muslim Architecture,* vol. 2, p. 52. The height of the outer enclosure wall was about 17 m; Bell, *Palace and Mosque,* p. 6; Creswell, *Early Muslim Architecture,* vol. 2, p. 54.

43. Bell, *Palace and Mosque*, pp. 6–7.
44. Ibid., p. 7; Creswell, *Early Muslim Architecture*, vol. 2, p. 55.
45. According to Bell's calculations, the palace structure measured about 111.40 m from north to south and 68.50 m from east to west; Bell, *Palace and Mosque*, p. 5. Creswell's measurements differ from Bell's rather considerably, particularly the east–west dimensions: 112.85 m from north to south and 81.83 m from east to west; Creswell, *Early Muslim Architecture*, vol. 2, p. 52.
46. H. Kennedy, *The Court of the Caliphs: The Rise and Fall of Islam's Greatest Dynasty* (London, 2004), p. 138.
47. Between the northern gate and the 'Great Hall' was a square room with a fluted dome (no. 4). To the right and left were long vaulted corridors (nos. 5 and 6); Bell, *Palace and Mosque*, pp. 9–10; pl. 13.
48. The Great Hall measures 7 m in width and is over 15 m in length; ibid., pp. 12–13; pl. 14.
49. Ibid., p. 24; pl. 26. See also Creswell, *Early Muslim Architecture*, vol. 2, p. 63.
50. Bell, *Palace and Mosque*, pp. 19–23. See also Creswell, *Early Muslim Architecture*, vol. 2, pp. 77–80.
51. Bell, *Palace and Mosque*, p. 26, following Reuther's reconstruction. See Reuther, *Ocheïdir*, Taf. 24: lower image. Creswell borrowed Reuther's image for his own publication. See Creswell, *Early Muslim Architecture*, vol. 2, fig. 45.
52. Bell, *Palace and Mosque*, p. 26; Creswell, *Early Muslim Architecture*, vol. 2, p. 67.
53. Bell, *Palace and Mosque*, p. 22; Reuther, *Ocheïdir*, p. 29; Creswell, *Early Muslim Architecture*, vol. 2, p. 69.
54. Bell, *Palace and Mosque*, pp. 26–7; pl. 30, Figs 1–2; Creswell, *Early Muslim Architecture*, vol. 2, p. 67 and fig. 48 (originally from Reuther, *Ocheïdir*, Taf. X, bottom image).
55. Bell, *Palace and Mosque*, p. 27; Creswell, *Early Muslim Architecture*, vol. 2, p. 68.
56. Bell, *Palace and Mosque*, pp. 27–8; Creswell, *Early Muslim Architecture*, vol. 2, p. 69.
57. Bell, *Palace and Mosque*, p. 29; Creswell, *Early Muslim Architecture*, vol. 2, p. 70.
58. Bell, *Palace and Mosque*, pp. 30–3.
59. Creswell, *Early Muslim Architecture*, vol. 2, p. 71.
60. Bell, *Palace and Mosque*, p. 32.
61. The best reconstruction of this southern arcade is illustrated by Reuther, *Ocheïdir*, Taf. XXVI.
62. Bell, *Palace and Mosque*, p. 17; Creswell, *Early Muslim Architecture*, vol. 2, p. 74.
63. Bell, *Palace and Mosque*, p. 18; Creswell, *Early Muslim Architecture*, vol. 2, pp. 75–6.
64. Bell, *Palace and Mosque*, p. 18; Creswell, *Early Muslim Architecture*, vol. 2, p. 76.
65. Bell, *Palace and Mosque*, p. 15–6; Creswell, *Early Muslim Architecture*, vol. 2, pp. 76–7.
66. Bell, *Palace and Mosque*, p. 33; Creswell, *Early Muslim Architecture*, vol. 2, p. 73.
67. Bell, *Palace and Mosque*, p. 33; Creswell, *Early Muslim Architecture*, vol. 2, p. 74.
68. Bell, *Palace and Mosque*, p. 34.
69. Ibid., pp. 36–7; pl. 43, Figs 1–2 show the Northern Annex from north and south.
70. Ibid., p. 37; Creswell, *Early Muslim Architecture*, p. 85, and fig. 69 for plan.
71. Ibid., fig. 68 and pl. 5a.
72. Bell, *Palace and Mosque*, p. 4, Map 2.
73. Creswell, *Early Muslim Architecture*, vol. 2, p. 85.

74. Ibid., p. 84.
75. GB letter to her father, 10 July 1909, Gertrude Bell Archive. The article was by Louis Massignon, 'Les chateaux des princes de Hirah', *Gazette des beaux-arts* (April 1909), pp. 297–306. See also 'Note sur le château d'Al Okhaïder', *Comptes-rendus des séances de l'Académie des Inscriptions et Belles-Lettres* 53 (1909), pp. 202–12. Massignon followed up these articles with the first volume of *Mission en Mesopotamie* (Cairo, 1910), which was chiefly concerned with Ukhaidir.
76. Creswell, *Early Muslim Architecture*, vol. 2, pp. 51–2.
77. Bell arrived at Babylon on 9 March and stayed until 11 March.
78. GB letter to her family, 11 March 1911, Gertrude Bell Archive.
79. Bell, *Palace and Mosque*, p. xi.
80. GB letter to her family, 2 April 1909, Gertrude Bell Archive.
81. Ibid.
82. Ibid.
83. Lady Elsa Richmond, 'Memories of Gertrude', Miscellaneous Item #4, Gertrude Bell Archive, University Library, Newcastle University. Lady Richmond's lectures were given at the Aeolian Hall, London, and at Rounton, Halifax and Huddersfield. They added £66 10s 6d to the Fund for the British School of Archaeology in Iraq (Gertrude Bell Memorial), as indicated on p. 4 of the Report and Accounts of the BSAI, 11 November 1931.
84. Reuther, *Ocheïdir*, Taf. XXVI.
85. Bell, 'Vaulting system', p. 81.
86. Ibid., pp. 69–81.
87. Ibid., p. 71. Brick was also used in the vault over Rooms 29 and 30, and in the columned Rooms 40 and 33. See Bell, *Amurath*, p. 153. Bell compared this feature to the earlier Sasanian tradition of brick vault-building, observed, for example, at Sarvistan, a site regarded in Bell's time as having a Sasanian date. See Bell, 'Vaulting system,' p. 72. She also noted that in cases where Sasanian builders used stone rather than brick, they cut the stones into narrow slabs to resemble brick tiles, just like in the smaller vaults at Ukhaidir; ibid., p. 73 and fig. 6, which shows a vaulted passageway constructed in stone, not brick.
88. Trudy Kawami, 'Parthian brick vaults in Mesopotamia, their antecedents and descendants', *Journal of the Ancient Near Eastern Society* 14 (1982), p. 61.
89. Bell, 'Vaulting system', p. 72, citing F.A. Choisy, *L'Art de bâtir chez les Byzantins* (Paris, 1883), p. 31. For a recent discussion of this type of vault construction, used also by the Romans, see Lynne Lancaster, 'Roman engineering and construction', in John Oleson (ed.), *The Oxford Handbook of Engineering and Technology in the Classical World* (Oxford, 2008), p. 274.
90. Bell, *Amurath*, p. 153 and fig. 109. Bell also pointed out here (p. 153, n. 1) that Dr Herzfeld, in an earlier work (Herzfeld, 'Genesis', p. 111), had stated erroneously that such a feature did not exist in Sasanian buildings.
91. Bell, 'Vaulting system', p. 72.
92. Ibid.
93. Bell, *Palace and Mosque*, p. 68, citing V. Place, *Ninive et l'Assyrie*, vol. 1 (Paris, 1867), pp. 176, 255.
94. Kawami, 'Parthian brick', p. 63, citing David Oates, 'The excavations at Tell al-Rimah, 1964', *Iraq* 27 (1965), p. 77 and pl. XXB; and David Oates, 'The excavations at Tell al-Rimah, 1968', *Iraq* 32 (1970), pp. 20–3 and pls. V–VIII.
95. Kawami, 'Parthian brick', p. 63, citing E. McCowan and R.C. Haines, *Nippur I: Temple of Enlil, Scribal Quarter, and Soundings* (Chicago, 1967), pp. 61, 77, and pls.

48A–B. See also G. Michell (ed.), *Architecture of the Islamic World: Its History and Social Meaning* (London, 1978), fig. 140 c, which illustrates a pitched brick vault over a pit from the site of Khafajeh.

96. Bell, 'Vaulting system', p. 74; *Amurath*, p. 153; *Palace and Mosque*, p. 29.
97. Bell, 'Vaulting system', p. 74; *Palace and Mosque*, p. 35.
98. Bell, *Palace and Mosque*, pp. 29–30.
99. Bell, 'Vaulting system', pp. 75–6; *Palace and Mosque*, pp. 29–30.
100. Bell, 'Vaulting system', p. 76; *Palace and Mosque*, p. 30.
101. Bell, 'Vaulting system', p. 75.
102. Ibid.
103. Ibid., pp. 75–6; *Amurath*, p. 156; *Palace and Mosque*, pp. 73, 166.
104. Letter to Gertrude Bell from M. Dieulafoy, 21 May 1910, Paris. Robinson Library Special Collections, Newcastle University, Gertrude Bell Archive, Miscellaneous, Item 13 (one of two unpublished letters from Dieulafoy to Gertrude Bell). See also Dieulafoy's opinion of the Sasanian date of Ukhaidir, after having learned of Massignon's discovery of the castle: Marcel Dieulafoy, 'Découverte par M. Massignon d'un palais fortifié près de Kerbela en Mésopotamie', *Comptes-rendus des séances de l'Academie des Inscriptions et Belles-Lettres* 52 (1908), pp. 451–2. Massignon shared Dieulafoy's opinion about Ukhaidir's Sasanian date.
105. Bell, 'Vaulting system', p. 76.
106. Ibid., p. 76; *Palace and Mosque*, pp. 111–12.
107. Oskar Reuther, who also carefully documented the presence of the groined vault at Ukhaidir, did not wholly accept Bell's arguments for a post-Sasanian date for Ukhaidir on the basis of this distinctive feature. See Reuther, *Ocheïdir*, p. 7. His own opinion appears to have been greatly influenced by his belief in the presence of groined vaulting in the building on the citadel at Amman, which was at that time believed to be a Sasanian period construction. See Schulz and Strzygowski, 'Mschatta', pp. 351–2; Reuther, *Ocheïdir*, p. 7. Creswell later weighed in on this controversial evidence himself, observing only the presence of tunnel vaults in the Amman building and thus rejecting Reuther's earlier assumption. See Creswell, *Early Muslim Architecture*, vol. 2, p. 95, n. 4. Scholars today overwhelmingly place the Amman structure, known variously as the Amman Ceremonial Building or the Domed Entrance Hall, in the Umayyad period. See Alistair Northedge and C-M. Bennett, *Studies on Roman and Islamic 'Amman: History, Site and Architecture* (Oxford, 1992); Robert Hillenbrand, *Islamic Architecture* (New York, 1994), pp. 379–81.
108. Bell, 'Vaulting system', p. 77; *Palace and Mosque*, pp. 9–10.
109. Reuther, *Ocheïdir*, pp. 29–30; Bell, *Palace and Mosque*, p. 13.
110. Reuther, *Ocheïdir*, Taf. VI illustrates a reconstructed domed corner tower. See also Bell, *Palace and Mosque*, p. 73; Creswell, *Early Muslim Architecture*, vol. 2, p. 55.
111. Bell, *Palace and Mosque*, p. 73.
112. Ibid.
113. Ibid., p. 75; see also K.A.C. Creswell, *Early Muslim Architecture. Vol. 1: Umayyads, A.D. 622–750* (Oxford, 1969), reprint (New York, 1979), p. 451, fig. 490.
114. Bell, *Palace and Mosque*, p. 75.
115. Gwendolyn Leick, 'Dome', *A Dictionary of Ancient Near Eastern Architecture* (London, 1988), p. 64.

116. Ramsay and Bell, *Thousand and One Churches*, pp. 438–46; Creswell, *Early Muslim Architecture*, vol. 1, p. 470, calls Bell's summary on pendentives from this work 'short but brilliant'.

117. Bell, 'Vaulting system', p. 79; *Palace and Mosque*, p. 73; Ramsay and Bell, *Thousand and One Churches*, pp. 438, 441, 443; Creswell, *Early Muslim Architecture*, vol. 1, pp. 467–70. In the course of her detailed discussion, Bell makes a distinction between what she refers to as a dome that is continuous with pendentives, i.e., a continuous sphere, and a dome that is not continuous with pendentives but rises, in a smaller radius, above them. The Santa Sophia dome is an example of the latter. See Ramsay and Bell, *Thousand and One Churches*, pp. 439, 443. See Creswell's objection to the use of these terms, however, and his further, fuller examination of pendentives and domes, in *Early Muslim Architecture*, vol. 1, pp. 450–71.

118. Bell, 'Vaulting system', p. 79; Creswell's own discussion of this example from Jerash, within the baths, concludes on the current evidence presented to him that these buildings are actually no later than the first half of the third century CE and are among the earliest examples of pendentives set on a square base in the entire Near East. See Creswell, *Early Muslim Architecture*, vol. 1, p. 46 and fig. 520.

119. Bell, 'Vaulting system', p. 79.

120. Ibid.

121. Ramsay and Bell, *Thousand and One Churches*, pp. 438, 442; Bell, 'Vaulting system', p. 79. Bell's photographs of Anatolian churches from Binbirkilise (Church no. 9) and Mahaletch highlight particularly well the setting of the dome in this manner. See Ramsay and Bell, *Thousand and One Churches*, Figs 42 and 205.

122. Bell, 'Vaulting system', p. 79. See Michell, *Architecture*, p. 141 for a useful illustration of the squinches used in Sasanian architecture.

123. Bell, *Palace and Mosque*, p. 73. Bell was following the widespread belief in the early twentieth century that the palace at Sarvistan dated to the fifth century CE. L. Bier challenged this assertion in the 1980s, proposing instead an eighth- or ninth-century Early Islamic date for the palace. See L. Bier, *Sarvistan: A Study in Early Iranian Architecture* (London, 1986), pp. 1–2 (for history of the research of the site) and pp. 23–52 (for his proposed date of the site).

124. Bell, *Palace and Mosque*, pp. 50–3, 73.

125. Bell, 'Vaulting system', p. 79.

126. Bell, *Amurath*, fig. 99; Bell, *Palace and Mosque*, pl. 25, fig. 2; Reuther, *Ocheïdir*, Abb. 27 shows the same feature.

127. These are Creswell's circular coffers, *Early Muslim Architecture*, vol. 2, p. 76; Bell, *Palace and Mosque*, p. 18; Reuther, *Ocheïdir*, Taf. XV, left side.

128. Bell, *Palace and Mosque*, p. 73.

129. Bell, 'Vaulting system', pp. 77, 79; *Palace and Mosque*, p. 73.

130. The discovery of a true dome with pendentives at the Umayyad hunting lodge of Qasr 'Amra in present-day Jordan, a structure universally regarded today as pre dating Ukhaidir, makes the second factor – Ukhaidir's distance from the architectural development of the pendentive – a likely reason for its more primitive dome settings.

131. Herzfeld, 'Genesis', pp. 32, 34, 51, 59, 63, 121–2, 130–1; Hillenbrand, 'Islamic art', p. 64.

132. Bell, 'Vaulting system', p. 73 and fig. 7.

133. Bell, *Palace and Mosque*, pp. 22–3; 30–1; but Creswell, *Early Muslim Architecture*, vol. 2, p. 62, in referring to the two sets of tube-like galleries on either side of the Great Hall (no. 7), notes that these were intended to be closed and inaccessible.
134. Bell, 'Vaulting system', pp. 73–4.
135. W. Andrae, *Hatra. Teil 2: nach aufnahmen von mitgliedern der Assur-expedition der Deutschen Orient-Gesellschaft* (Leipzig, 1912), fig. 37, sections e–f and fig. 152. Creswell makes reference to the same Hatra tombs in his discussion of Ukhaidir's masonry tubes. See Creswell, *Early Muslim Architecture*, vol. 2, fn. 5 on p. 89, and fig. 77 on p. 90, the latter a copy of Andrae's drawing fig. 152, first cited by Bell. Creswell also repeats Bell's reference to an apparent masonry tube found at the Sasanian site of Firuzabad, between the barrel vaults of the side chambers of the entrance *iwan* and the domed chamber (Bell, *Palace and Mosque*, p. 143, who is herself citing Marcel Dieulafoy, *L'Art antique de la Perse. Partie 4: Les monuments voûtés de l'époque achéménide* [Paris, 1885], pl. 9), although he is doubtful of this example since the visible tube appears above the crown of the vault and may be part of a vaulted ramp. See Creswell, *Early Muslim Architecture*, vol. 2, pp. 89–90.
136. Bell, 'Vaulting system', p. 74; *Amurath*, fig. 133; *Palace and Mosque*, p. 143 and n. 7.
137. Bell, *Palace and Mosque*, pp. 143–4; pl. 89, Figs 1–2.
138. Bell, 'Vaulting system', p. 77.
139. Herzfeld, 'Genesis', p. 126.
140. Ibid., p. 126, n. 81.
141. Bell, *Amurath*, p. 152.
142. Ibid., pp. 156–8.
143. Bell, *Palace and Mosque*, p. 16, n. 2. Viollet was on his way to Mesopotamia to continue investigations at the site of Samarra, which he had initiated in 1908. Much of Viollet's excavations in the summer of 1910, which were carried out together with the archaeologist André Godard, were concentrated in the area of the Dar al-Khilafa at Samarra. Herzfeld, who would work at Samarra the following year, was very critical of Viollet's findings at Samarra and the fact that he had conducted his work without the official sanction of the Ottoman government in Constantinople. See Thomas Leisten, *Excavation of Samarra. Volume I: Architecture. Final Report of the First Campaign 1910–1912* (Mainz am Rhein, 2003), pp. 4, 10–11, 24. Bell does not appear to have been particularly impressed with Viollet's archaeological abilities either, as we learn from one of her diary entries: 'He [Viollet] said that he had planned all those interesting monasteries in the Tur Abdin, but he had never heard of Khakh!' (GB diary, 4 January 1911, Gertrude Bell Archive).
144. GB letter to her mother, 5 January 1911, Gertrude Bell Archive. Bell would not have learned about Viollet's finding until January 1911. By this time, her manuscript *Amurath to Amurath* – which expressed her continuing ambivalence about Ukhaidir's date – had already been submitted for publication. This explains why the *mihrab* discovery was not reported in that book.
145. Ramsay and Bell, *Thousand and One Churches*, p. 540, n. 1.
146. Creswell, *Early Muslim Architecture*, vol. 2, pp. 94–8.
147. Bell, *Palace and Mosque*, p. 168; Michell, *Architecture*, p. 33.
148. Bell, *Palace and Mosque*, p. 161 and fig. 35.
149. Ibid., p. 161. Bell had known Enno Littmann, a leading German scholar in Near Eastern languages and Semitic philology, for a long time, having first met him in Jerusalem in 1900 (see GB diary, 1 February 1900, Gertrude Bell Archive) and

then seeing him again in her travels through Syria when he was working with the Princeton Expedition to Syria (GB letter to her mother, 3 March 1905, Gertrude Bell Archive). A professor of Arabic at Strasbourg, he had been living and lecturing (at the Cairo University) in Cairo in the winter of 1911, when Bell passed through en route to her second Mesopotamian journey, and he was a friend and colleague of Bernhard Moritz (see GB letter to her father, 13 January 1911, Gertrude Bell Archive).

150. Bell, *Palace and Mosque*, p. 165; E. Herzfeld, *Erster vorläufiger Bericht über die Ausgrabungen von Samarra* (Berlin, 1912), fig. 6.
151. Ibid., pp. 162, 168.
152. Ibid., p. 168.
153. Creswell, *Early Muslim Architecture*, vol. 2, p. 97.
154. Ibid., p. 98.
155. Ibid.
156. Ibid.
157. Hillenbrand, *Islamic Architecture*, p. 144; Kennedy, *Court*, p. 137.
158. B. Finster and J. Schmidt, 'Sasanidische und frühislamische Ruinen im Iraq, Tulul al Uhaidir, Erster vorläufiger Grabungsbericht', *Baghdader Mitteilungen* 8 (1976), pp. 7–168.
159. W. Caskel, 'Al-Uhaidir', *Der Islam* 39 (1964), pp. 28–37.
160. B. Finster and J. Schmidt, 'The origin of "desert castles": Qasr Bani Muqatil, near Karbala, Iraq', *Antiquity* 79 (2005), p. 347.
161. Caskel, 'Al-Uhaidir,' p. 37; Finster and Schmidt, 'Sasanidische', pp. 149–50; Finster and Schmidt, 'Origin', p. 347.
162. In his forward, Reuther (*Ocheïdir*, pp. 1–2) acknowledges Bell's study of Ukhaidir and thanks her for her photographs of the mosque's *mihrab*, which appear in Abbs. 22–3 of his publication. He also acknowledges her identification of the north-western sector of the palace as a mosque.
163. Herzfeld, 'Genesis', pp. 125–6.
164. The work was first published in 1940 (Oxford), revised for a second edition in 1969, and then reprinted in 1979. Creswell's discussion of Ukhaidir appears on pp. 50–100 of the reprinted 1979 edition.
165. Creswell's treatment of Ukhaidir is provided in Chapter 10 of the book (Harmondsworth, 1958). The work was revised and supplemented by James W. Allan in 1989 (Aldershot).
166. In particular, see Creswell's inclusion of Reuther's sections, *Early Muslim Architecture*, vol. 2, Figs 36 and 60, and Reuther's beautiful reconstructions of Ukhaidir's main entrance, fig. 39, the Court of Honour, fig. 44, the central *iwan* on the south side of the Court of Honour, fig. 45, and the mosque's southern arcade, fig. 58. Reuther's detailed discussions of arch construction are also slavishly repeated, pp. 61–3.
167. Ibid., pp. 59, 96.
168. Ibid., pp. 62, 73, 89.
169. Ibid., pp. 74–6, 94–5.
170. Ibid., pp. 88–9, 96.
171. See, for example, Creswell's discussions of pendentives, ibid., vol. 1, chapter 14.
172. For recent studies of architectural space, several of which use computational analyses to understand issues related to experience and human interactions within a furnished space, and the effects of access, visibility and lighting, see David L.C. Clark, 'Viewing the liturgy: a space syntax study of changing

visibility and accessibility in the development of the Byzantine church in Jordan', *World Archaeology* 39 (2007), pp. 84–104; Kevin Fisher, 'Placing social interaction: An integrative approach to analyzing past built environments', *Journal of Anthropological Archaeology* 28 (2009), pp. 439–57; C. Papadopoulos and G.P. Earle, 'Formal three-dimensional computational analysis of archaeological spaces', in E. Paliou, U. Lieberwirth and S. Polla (eds), *Spatial Analysis and Social Spaces: Interdisciplinary Approaches to the Interpretation of Historic and Prehistoric Built Environments* (Berlin, 2014), pp. 135–65.

173. GB letter to her father, 15 April 1925, Gertrude Bell Archive.
174. GB letter to her father, 3 January 1921, Gertrude Bell Archive.
175. Bell, *Palace and Mosque*, p. xii.

Chapter 4   Encounters in the Heart of Mesopotamia

1. Gertrude L. Bell, *Amurath to Amurath* (London, 1911), p. 172.
2. GB letter to her family, 2 April 1909, Gertrude Bell Archive.
3. Bell visited Babylon 9–11 March 1911 and 30 March to 2 April 1914, Gertrude Bell Archive.
4. GB letter to her family, 2 April 1909, Gertrude Bell Archive; Bell, *Amurath*, p. 172.
5. GB letter to her father, 5 May 1917, Gertrude Bell Archive.
6. GB letter to her family, 11 March 1911.
7. Irving L. Finkel and Michael J. Seymour (eds), *Babylon: Myth and Reality* (London, 2008), p. 39.
8. Joachim Marzahn, 'Robert Koldewey – Ein Lebensbild', in Ralf-B. Wartke (ed.), *Auf dem Weg nach Babylon. Robert Koldewey – Ein Archäologenleben* (Mainz, 2008), pp. 13–16.
9. Brian Fagan, *Return to Babylon: Travelers, Archaeologists, and Monuments in Mesopotamia*, revised edition (Boulder, 2007), p. 245; Finkel and Seymour, *Babylon*, p. 42.
10. Fagan, *Return to Babylon*, p. 247.
11. Joachim Marzahn, *The Ishtar Gate* (Berlin, 1995), p. 7.
12. For dating architecture according to brick inscriptions, see, for example, Robert Koldewey, *The Excavations at Babylon* (London, 1914), pp. 75–82.
13. Fagan, *Return to Babylon*, pp. 247–9; Finkel and Seymour, *Babylon*, p. 42; Gernot Wilhelm, '1898–1917: Babylon – Stadt des Marduk und Zentrum des Kosmos', in Wilhem (ed.), *Zwischen Tigris und Nil. 100 Jahre Ausgrabungen der Deutschen Orient-Gesellschaft in Vorderasien und Ägypten* (Mainz, 1998), p. 23.
14. Seton Lloyd, *Foundations in the Dust: The Story of Mesopotamian Exploration*, revised and enlarged edition (London, 1980), pp. 175–6.
15. Bell, *Amurath*, p. 171.
16. Koldewey, *Excavations*, pp. 25–30.
17. Bell, *Amurath*, p. 171.
18. Bell makes no note of the presence of glazed brick fragments on the Ishtar Gate in 1909 (she only observes this decoration in the Processional Way; see Bell, *Amurath*, p. 171 and GB diary 2 April 1909, Gertrude Bell Archive). Many pieces had already been collected and shipped back to Europe by this time. See Beate Salje, 'Robert Koldewey und das Vorderasiatische Museum Berlin', in Wartke, *Auf dem Weg nach Babylon*, pp. 129–30. The process of reconstructing the bricks of the Processional Way and Ishtar Gate started soon after they were excavated,

but World War I delayed the arrival in Berlin of much of the structures' fragmentary brick material, and not until 1930 were these magnificently reconstructed edifices revealed to the public. See Finkel and Seymour, *Babylon*, p. 57. For a full description of the desalinization process and reconstruction of the brickwork, see Marzahn, *Ishtar Gate*, pp. 14–16.

19. Bell, *Amurath*, p. 168.
20. GB diary, 2 April 1909, Gertrude Bell Archive; Koldewey, *Excavations*, p. 68.
21. GB diary, 2 April 1909, Gertrude Bell Archive; Koldewey, *Excavations*, pp. 137–8.
22. GB diary, 31 March 1914, Gertrude Bell Archive.
23. Koldewey, *Excavations*, pp. 95–100; Finkel and Seymour, *Babylon*, pp. 108–9.
24. Koldewey, *Excavations*, p. 91.
25. Wilhelm, 'Stadt des Marduk,' p. 26; Finkel and Seymour, *Babylon*, p. 112.
26. Finkel and Seymour, *Babylon*, p. 109; Stephanie Dalley, 'Nineveh, Babylon and the Hanging Gardens: Cuneiform and Classical sources reconciled', *Iraq* 56 (1994), pp. 45–58.
27. Finkel and Seymour, *Babylon*, p. 54.
28. Ibid., p. 55.
29. GB diary, 31 March 1914, Gertrude Bell Archive.
30. Finkel and Seymour, *Babylon*, p. 129.
31. Ibid., p. 55.
32. Ibid., p. 128. Wetzel's investigations in 1913 ascertained that the tower at its base originally measured some 91 m on each side and had a great staircase that led up to the tower from the south, along with two side staircases. See Koldewey, *Excavations*, pp. 183–4; Wilhelm, 'Stadt des Marduk,' p. 27; Finkel and Seymour, *Babylon*, p. 129. The number of storeys possessed by the ziggurat has been the subject of considerable debate, but based on the examination of ancient textual descriptions, it is believed to have possessed seven stages (the seventh being the temple) and stood over 70 m high. See Finkel and Seymour, *Babylon*, p. 126.
33. Article 19 i, *Antiquities Law, 1924* (Baghdad, 1924).
34. Finkel and Seymour, *Babylon*, p. 43; Magnus T. Bernhardsson, *Reclaiming a Plundered Past: Archaeology and Nation Building in Modern Iraq* (Austin, 2005), p. 138; E. Walter Andrae and R.M. Boehmer, *Bilder eines Ausgräbers. Die Orientbilder von Walter Andrae 1898–1919/Sketches by an Excavator*, second enlarged edition, English translation by Jane Moon (Berlin, 1992), pp. 141–3 and notes 65–8. Bell rightly realized that the Babylon finds could only be properly treated and preserved if they went to Berlin. See also Julia M. Asher-Greve, 'Gertrude L. Bell (1868–1926)', in Getzel M. Cohen and Martha Sharp Joukowsky (eds), *Breaking Ground: Pioneering Women Archaeologists* (Ann Arbor, 2004), p. 176.
35. GB letter to her father, 18 January 1918, Gertrude Bell Archive.
36. E.J. Keall, 'Parthians', in E.M. Meyers (ed.), *The Oxford Encyclopedia of Archaeology in the Near East* (New York, 1997), p. 249; Edward Dąbrowa, 'The Arsacid Empire', in Touraj Daryaee (ed.), *The Oxford Handbook of Iranian History* (Oxford, 2012), p. 164.
37. Jens Kröger, 'Ctesiphon', *Encyclopaedia Iranica* VI/4 (1993), pp. 446–8; an updated version is available online at http://www.iranicaonline.org/arti cles/ctesiphon (accessed 29 July 2015).
38. E.J. Keall, 'Ayvān-e Kesrā', *Encyclopaedia Iranica* III/2 (1987), pp. 155–9; an updated version is available online at www.iranicaonline.org/articles/ayvan-e-kesra-palace-of-kosrow-at-ctesiphon (accessed 29 July 2015).

39. Kröger, 'Ctesiphon.'
40. Robert Hillenbrand, *Islamic Architecture* (New York, 1994), p. 391.
41. Keall, 'Ayvān.'
42. Ibid.
43. Oscar Reuther, 'The German excavations at Ctesiphon', *Antiquity* 3 (1929), p. 441; 'Activities of the Institute of Archaeological Sciences and of the Centre for the Restoration of Monuments in Baghdad: Ctesiphon', *Centro Ricerche Archeologiche e Scavi di Torino Projects* (Torino, 2006), available at www.centros cavitorino.it/en/progetti/iraq/istituti-ctesifonte.html (accessed 29 July 2015).
44. Ibid.; see also T. Madhloom, 'Mada'in (Ctesiphon), 1970–71', *Sumer* 27 (1971), pp. 129–46, in Arabic; T. Madhloom, 'Al-Mada'in', *Sumer* 31 (1975), pp. 165–70, in Arabic; T. Madhloom, 'Restorations in al-Mada'in, 1975–1977', *Sumer* 34 (1978), pp. 119–29, in Arabic.
45. Agence France-Presse, 'Iraq to restore ancient Arch of Ctesiphon to woo back tourists', *The Raw Story* (30 May 2013), available at www.rawstory.com/rs/2013/05/30/iraq-to-restore-ancient-arch-of-ctesiphon-to-woo-back-tourists (accessed 29 July 2015).
46. Bell, *Amurath*, p. 180.
47. Ibid., p. 153 and Fig. 109, which shows the vault at Ctesiphon. This small architectural detail, insignificant to most, became the source of antagonism between Bell and the German scholar Ernst Herzfeld, who had argued previously that such inwardly projecting vaulting systems did not exist before the Islamic period. Bell's own observation at Ctesiphon, confirmed by one of her photographs, clearly showed that this architectural feature could have existed in the earlier Sasanian period. For a full discussion, see Lisa Cooper, 'Archaeology and acrimony: Gertrude Bell, Ernst Herzfeld and the study of pre-modern Mesopotamia', *Iraq* 75 (2013), pp. 157–62.
48. See Bell, *Palace and Mosque*, pp. 130–6. Bell assumes that such features were simply an Oriental interpretation of the Hellenistic style already well known in the Near East long before the Byzantine Era, and observable in Parthian architecture of the second century CE at Mesopotamian sites such as Hatra; ibid., pp. 130, 136–7. This is an argument Herzfeld would himself later make in a critical review of Reuther, and it still finds some acceptance among scholars today. See E. Herzfeld, 'Damascus: Studies in architecture: II', *Ars Islamica* 10 (1943), pp. 60–1. See also Keall, 'Ayvān'. Keall uses this argument to advocate for a third-century CE date for the construction of the Taq-i Kisra instead of the later sixth-century date accepted by Reuther and others. Whatever the case, this example demonstrates how Bell's own observations were often in line with other scholars', both past and present.
49. GB letter to her father, 22 May 1921, Gertrude Bell Archive.
50. GB letter to her father, 6 August 1921, Gertrude Bell Archive.
51. Bell stayed in Baghdad 6–12 April 1909, as evinced from her diary entries and letters.
52. Bell, *Amurath*, p. 187.
53. R. Ettinghausen and O. Grabar, *Islamic Art and Architecture, 650–1250* (New Haven, 2001), p. 51.
54. G. Michell, *Architecture of the Islamic World* (London, 1978), p. 247.
55. GB diary, 8 and 9 April 1909, Gertrude Bell Archive. See also Ettinghausen and Grabar, *Islamic Art*, pp. 216–17.
56. Bell, *Amurath*, p. 191.

57. GB letter to her mother, 14 April 1909, and GB diary, 15 March 1911, Gertrude Bell Archive. Today, this 'Abbasid Palace' is believed to have been a *madrasa*, built in the thirteenth century. See Hillenbrand, *Islamic Architecture*, pp. 223–4.
58. GB letter to her mother, 14 April 1909, and GB diary, 14 April 1909, Gertrude Bell Archive; Bell, *Amurath*, pp. 200, 204.
59. GB diary, 14 April 1909, Gertrude Bell Archive.
60. Bell, *Amurath*, p. 208.
61. Alistair Northedge, *The Historical Topography of Samarra* (London, 2007), p. 473.
62. Bell, *Amurath*, p. 208.
63. Ibid. Bell is recalling a passage from the *Gulistan* (*The Rose Garden*), composed by the medieval Persian poet Saadi Shirazi. Saadi witnessed the sack of Baghdad by the Mongols in 1258, the same year that he wrote the *Gulistan*.
64. Chase Robinson (ed.), *A Medieval Islamic City Reconsidered: An Interdisciplinary Approach to Samarra* (Oxford, 2001), p. 9; Hugh Kennedy, *The Court of the Caliphs: The Rise and Fall of Islam's Greatest Dynasty* (London, 2004), p. 149.
65. Lucien de Beylié, *Prome et Samarra* (Paris, 1907), and 'L'architecture des Abbassides au IXe siècle. Voyage archéologique à Samarra dans le basin du Tigre', *Revue archéologique* 10 (1907), pp. 1–18. Bell mentions having taken notes from de Beylié's publications while staying with the German excavators at Babylon, so it is conceivable that she became aware of his work through them. See GB diary, 3 April 1909, Gertrude Bell Archive.
66. Ernst Herzfeld, *Samarra. Aufhahmen und Untersuchungen zur islamischen Archaeologie* (Berlin, 1907).
67. Ernst Herzfeld, 'Die Genesis der islamischen Kunst und das Mschatta-Problem', *Der Islam* 1 (1910), pp. 27–63, 104–44.
68. Suzanne Marchand, 'The rhetoric of artifacts and the decline of classical humanism: The case of Josef Strzygowski', *History and Theory* 33 (1994), pp. 124–5.
69. Robert Hillenbrand, 'Creswell and contemporary Central European scholarship', *Muqarnas* 8 (1991), p. 26.
70. The 'short paper' referred to here is probably de Beylié's article in *Revue archéologique*, cited above.
71. Bell is referring here to Herzfeld's Samarra monograph, cited above.
72. GB letter to her family, 15 April 1909, Gertrude Bell Archive.
73. GB letter to her mother, 18 April 1909, Gertrude Bell Archive.
74. Kennedy, *Court*, p. 145; Northedge, *Historical Topography*, pp. 135, 140.
75. Bell crossed over to the western bank on a *kelek* twice. See GB diary, 16 and 18 April 1909, Gertrude Bell Archive. Concerning Qasr al-'Ashiq, scholars have accepted the identification of this castle with the Qasr al-Ma'shuq, mentioned by the Islamic historian al-Yaq'ubi, as the palace built by the caliph al-Mu'tamid sometime c. 877–82 CE. See Northedge, *Historical Topography*, p. 235.
76. Bell, *Amurath*, p. 209; GB diary, 15 April 1909, Gertrude Bell Archive.
77. Leisten, *Excavation*, p. 35.
78. K.A.C. Creswell, *Early Muslim Architecture. Vol. 2: Early 'Abbāsids, Umayyads of Cordova, Aghlabids, Ṭūlūnids, and Samānids, A.D. 751–905* (Oxford, 1940), reprint (New York, 1979), p. 254.
79. Ibid., pp. 259–61 and pl. 63.
80. Northedge, *Historical Topography*, p. 211.
81. Kennedy, *Court*, p. 149; Leisten, *Excavation*, p. 58.
82. GB letter to her family, 21 April 1909, Gertrude Bell Archive.

83. Leisten, *Excavation*, p. 60.
84. Bell, *Amurath*, pp. 243–6, Figs 123–4, 164–6.
85. The holy man was Muhammad al-Duri, the eleventh son of Musa al-Kazim, and the builder was Sharaf al-daulah Muslim ibn Quraish, 1061–86 CE.
86. Michell, *Architecture*, p. 251; Hillenbrand, *Islamic Architecture*, p. 325, Figs 238 and 239.
87. As noted by Herzfeld in his correspondence with Bell, and by Bell, who references van Berchem's conclusions in *Amurath*, pp. 214–5, n. 1. See also below, with further mention of van Berchem's contribution to Sarre and Herzfeld's *Archäologische Reise im Euphrat- und Tigris-Gebiet*, 4 vols (Berlin, 1911–20).
88. For a report on the destruction of the Imam al-Dur mausoleum, see Michael D. Danti, Jesse Casana, T. Paulette, K. Franklin and C. Ali, 'ASOR Cultural Heritage Initiatives (CHI): Planning for safeguarding heritage sites in Syria and Iraq, weekly report 25 – January 26, 2015', available at www.asor-syrianheritage. org/wp-content/uploads/2015/03/ASOR_CHI_ Weekly_Report_25r.pdf (accessed on 30 July 2015).
89. GB letter to her family, 21 April 1909, Gertrude Bell Archive.
90. H. Viollet, 'Le palais de'al-Moutasim fils d'Haroun al-Rachid à Samara et quelques monuments arabes peu connus de la Mésopotamie', *Comptes rendus de l'Académie des Inscriptions et des Belles-Lettres* (1909), pp. 370–5; and 'Description du palais d'al-Moutasim fils d'Haroun-al-Rachid à Samara et quelques monuments arabes peu connus de la Mésopotamie', *Mémoires presentés à l'Académie des Inscriptions et des Belles-Lettres* 12 (1909), pp. 567–94. That Bell consulted Viollet's reports is indicated by her reference to his reports in her account of Samarra in *Amurath*, pp. 209, n. 1; 210, n. 1; 235, n. 1; 237, n. 1; 238, n. 1; 240–1; 243, n. 1; 245, n. 1.
91. To be exact, Viollet published the 'Small Serdab' of the Dar al-Khilafa; see H. Viollet, 'Fouilles à Samara en Mésopotamie: Ruines du palais d' Al Moutasim', *Comptes rendus de l'Académie des Inscriptions et des Belles-Lettres* (1911), pp. 275–86; and 'Fouilles à Samara en Mésopotamie: Un palais musulman du IXe siècle', *Mémoires presentés à l'Académie des Inscriptions et des Belles-Lettres* 12 (1911), pp. 685–717.
92. Seven letters addressed by Herzfeld to Bell are housed in the Gertrude Bell Archive in the Newcastle University Library, Miscellaneous, Item 13. The letters are dated 1 and 22 November 1909; 27 August and 1 September 1910; 17 September and 29 November 1911; and 12 September 1912. For a greater discussion of the Herzfeld–Bell correspondence, see Cooper, 'Archaeology and acrimony'.
93. Hillenbrand, 'Creswell,' p. 26.
94. In letters to Bell (27 August 1910 and 29 November 1911), Herzfeld makes reference to his participation in the *Corpus Inscriptionum Arabicarum*, along with his collection of inscriptions for van Berchem. In a letter sent by van Berchem to Bell (28 October 1911), he mentions Herzfeld's prodigious information gathering. All of these letters are in the Gertrude Bell Archive, Newcastle University Library, Miscellaneous, Item 13.
95. It was in *Archäologische Reise* that the subject of the date of the Imam al-Dur mausoleum came up, along with the questionable character of the inscription that Bell claims to have seen there; van Berchem offers his own opinion about this monument and its inscriptions, respectfully including Bell's observed date within a footnote (on p. 34, n. 3), despite his doubts about its presence. For her

part, when Bell wrote up her description of the Imam al-Dur in *Amurath* (pp. 214–15, n.1), she deferred to van Berchem, who had decided that the shape of the letters indicated a ninth-century CE date. The date she had seen may point to the time of a repair of the shrine. Although she does not mention it, this was Herzfeld's suggestion, offered to her in several of his letters (see Herzfeld letters dated 1 and 22 November 1909; 27 August and 1 September 1910, Gertrude Bell Archive in the Newcastle University Library, Miscellaneous, Item 13), prior to her publication of *Amurath*.

96. For information about the Bell–van Berchem correspondence, see Asher-Greve, 'Gertrude L. Bell,' pp, 168–9 and notes 195–7.
97. M. van Berchem and J. Strzygowski, *Amida. Matériaux pour l'épigraphie et l'histoire musulmanes du Diyar-bekr, par Max van Berchem. Beiträge zur Kunstgeschichte des Mittelalters von Nordmesopotamien, Hellas und dem Abendlande, von Josef Strzygowski* (Heidelberg, 1910). Bell's contribution was a chapter on the churches and monasteries of the Tur-Abdin, pp. 224–62.
98. Remarkably, the Fondation Max van Berchem, in Geneva, houses no fewer than 177 photographs by Bell, and in van Berchem's *Opera Minora*, vol. 1 (Geneva, 1978), acknowledgement is given to Bell's collection of photos of Arab inscriptions from 1910–11. Cited from Asher-Greve, 'Gertrude L. Bell,' p. 194, n. 206.
99. Van Berchem letter to GB, 18 October 1911, in the Gertrude Bell Archive, Newcastle University Library, Miscellaneous, Item 13; translation from French to English by Emmanuelle and Henry Ritson.
100. Asher-Greve, 'Gertrude L. Bell,' p. 170 and n. 206. Letter from feuillets 145–8 in the Max van Berchem Archive, Geneva.
101. Van Berchem letter to GB, 28 October 1911, in the Gertrude Bell Archive, Newcastle University Library, Miscellaneous, Item 13; translation from French to English by Emmanuelle and Henry Ritson.
102. Hillenbrand, 'Creswell,' p. 32, n. 40.
103. Van Berchem letter to GB, 18 October 1911, in the Gertrude Bell Archive, Newcastle University Library, Miscellaneous, Item 13; translation from French to English by Emmanuelle and Henry Ritson.
104. GB letter to her mother, 28 September 1912, Gertrude Bell Archive.
105. Unpublished letter from Gertrude Bell to Professor Herzfeld, in the Gertrude Bell Archive, Newcastle University Library, Miscellaneous, Item 41; sent to the University of Newcastle from Mr E.F. Bradford of Whitby, into whose possession it came via Professor Herzfeld's late sister.
106. Bernhardsson, *Reclaiming*, p. 75.
107. Ibid. pp. 75–8.
108. Ibid., p. 78, citing from Bell's memorandum entitled 'The safeguarding of antiquities in the 'Iraq',' BLIO, L/P&S/10/689, Memorandum #85, 22 October 1918.
109. Ibid., p. 82.
110. Ibid., pp. 82–3.
111. Ibid., p. 83, citing from PRO, Kew FO 371/2883/E2883, letter from CO to FO, 14 March 1922.
112. Ibid., p. 84.
113. David Stronach, 'Ernst Herzfeld and Pasargadae', in A.C. Gunter and S.R. Hauser (eds), *Ernst Herzfeld and the Development of Near Eastern Studies, 1900–1950*

(Leiden, 2005), pp. 103–36, and Elspeth R.M. Dusinberre, 'Herzfeld in Persepolis', in Gunter and Hauser, *Ernst Herzfeld*, pp. 137–80.

114. A.C. Gunter and S.R. Hauser, 'Ernst Herzfeld and Near Eastern studies, 1900–1950', in Gunter and Hauser, *Ernst Herzfeld*, p. 20.

115. GB letters to her family, 28 March, 10 and 24 April 1923, Gertrude Bell Archive.

116. P.O. Harper, E. Klengel-Brandt, Joan Aruz and K. Benzel (eds), *Assyrian Origins: Discoveries at Ashur on the Tigris: Antiquities in the Vorderasiatisches Museum, Berlin* (New York, 1995), p. 15.

117. Gertrude L. Bell, 'The first capital of Assyria', *The Times*, 23 August 1910.

118. GB diary, 23 April 1909; GB letter to her family, 26 April 1909, Gertrude Bell Archive; Bell, *Amurath*, p. 221.

119. GB letter to her family, 26 April 1909, Gertrude Bell Archive.

120. See especially Ernst Heinrich's heartfelt appreciation for Andrae, in Andrae and Boehmer, *Bilder eines Ausgräbers*, pp. 149–54.

121. Ibid., pp. 111–22.

122. Ibid., p. 118; Finkel and Seymour, *Babylon*, p. 42.

123. Andrae and Boehmer, *Bilder eubes Ausgräbers*, p. 108.

124. See especially Andrae's reconstructions in W. Andrae, *Das wiedererstandene Assur*, revised edition with additional notes by B. Hrouda (Munich, 1977).

125. S.M. Maul, '1903–1914: Assur – Das Herz eines Weltreiches', in Wilhelm, *Zwischen Tigris*, p. 49.

126. J. Bär, 'Walter Andrae – Ein Wegbereiter der modernen Archäologie', in J. Marzahn and B. Salje (eds), *Wiedererstehendes Assur. 100 Jahre deutsche Ausgrabungen in Assyrien* (Mainz am Rhein, 2003), p. 47. Andrae returned home only twice, to complete his military service and to marry.

127. S.R. Hauser, 'The Arsacid (Parthian) Empire', in D.T. Potts (ed.), *A Companion to the Archaeology of the Ancient Near East* (Chichester, 2012), p. 1011.

128. R.W. Lamprichs, 'Aššur', in Meyers, *Oxford Encyclopaedia*, p. 228.

129. GB letter to her family, 26 April 1909, Gertrude Bell Archive.

130. J. Bär, 'Sumerians, Gutians and Hurrians at Ashur? A re-examination of Ishtar temples G and F', *Iraq* 65 (2003), p. 146; Bär, 'Walter Andrae', p. 144.

131. For the reports on excavations in the area of the Ishtar Temple, see especially W. Andrae, *Die archaischen Ischtar-Tempel in Assur* (Leipzig, 1922); W. Andrae, *Die jüngeren Ischtar-Tempel in Assur* (Leipzig, 1935); and recent updates, which provide further refinement of the earlier phases, J. Bär, *Die älteren Ištar-Tempel in Assur. Stratigraphie, Architektur und Funde eines altorientalischen Heiligtums von der zweiten Hälfte des 3. Jahrtausends bis zur Mittes des 2. Jahrtausends v. Chr.* (Saarbrücken, 2003), and Bär, 'Sumerians', pp. 143–60.

132. Andrae and Boehmer, *Bilder eines Ausgräbers*, p. 139.

133. GB letter to her family, 26 April 1909, Gertrude Bell Archive.

134. Maul, '1903–1914: Assur', p. 47.

135. GB diary, 25 April 1909, Gertrude Bell Archive: 'The long trenches are most fascinating especially one dug very deep, where the Old Assyrian houses and streets are clearly visible. These Old Assyrian houses stand very complete.' For a full discussion of Assur's houses, see C. Preusser, *Die Wohnhäuser in Assur* (Berlin, 1954), and more recent discussions, namely P. Miglus, *Das Wohngebiet von Assur. Stratigraphie und Architektur* (Berlin, 1996).

136. Bell, *Amurath*, p. 225. Bell could be talking here of the Old Assyrian house described by Andrae in *Das wiedererstandene*, pp. 180–1, and by Preusser, *Die*

Wohnhäuser, pp. 7–8, in the area south-east of the ziggurat (and near the Parthian colonnade).

137. For a full report of Assur's Parthian remains, see W. Andrae and H. Lenzen, *Die Partherstadt Assur* (Leipzig, 1933).

138. GB diary, 23–25 April 1909; 5 April 1911 (the presence of the *iwan*); GB letter to her parents, 26 April 1909; GB photographs, Album L_166, L_174, L_178, L_179, L_186 and Album Q_222, Gertrude Bell Archive.

139. Bell, *Palace and Mosque*, pp. 65–8.

140. GB photographs, Album L_167, L_168, L_169, L_170 and L171, Gertrude Bell Archive.

141. GB photographs, Album L_184 and L_185, Gertrude Bell Archive.

142. GB photograph, Album L_180, Gertrude Bell Archive.

143. GB photograph, Album L_172, Gertrude Bell Archive.

144. GB photograph, Album L_173, Gertrude Bell Archive.

145. GB photographs, Album Q_220 and Q_221, Gertrude Bell Archive.

146. GB photographs, Album Q_223 and Q_224, Gertrude Bell Archive.

147. For recent studies of how excavation records, especially archaeological photographs, highlight the subtext of power relations between foreign archaeologists and subaltern workers within seemingly benign scientific investigations of sites in the Near East and Asia, see M. Rowlands, 'The archaeology of colonialism', in K. Kristiansen and M. Rowlands (eds), *Social Transformations in Archaeology: Global and Local Perspectives* (London, 1998), pp. 327–33; Ashish Chadha, 'Visions of discipline: Sir Mortimer Wheeler and the archaeological method in India', *Journal of Social Archaeology* 2 (2003), pp. 378–401; Jennifer A. Baird, 'Photographing Dura-Europos, 1928–1937: An archaeology of the archive', *American Journal of Archaeology* 115 (2011), pp. 427–46; E. Cobb, T. Van Loan and V. Fleck, 'Representing vestiges of the past: Evaluating John Henry Haynes' contribution to nascent archaeological photography in the nineteenth century Ottoman Empire', paper presented at the Annual Meeting of the American Schools of Oriental Research, Atlanta, 2010.

148. GB letter to her mother, 14 April 1911, Gertrude Bell Archive.

149. GB photographs, Album L_174, L_187, L_188, L_189 and L_190, Gertrude Bell Archive.

150. GB photograph, Album Q_225, Gertrude Bell Archive.

151. Bell, *Amurath* p. 226.

152. Bell, *Palace and Mosque*, p. vi.

153. Bernhardsson, *Reclaiming*, pp. 85–6.

154. Andrae and Boehmer, *Bilder eines Ausgräbers*, pp. 140–1. Andrae mentions in his memoirs: 'The Babylonian Galleries of the Berlin Museum are partly due to Miss Bell.'

155. Ibid., pp. 139–40.

156. Ibid., p. 140.

157. GB letter to her family, 26 April 1909, Gertrude Bell Archive.

158. GB letter to her mother, 14 April 1911, Gertrude Bell Archive.

159. For the best descriptions of Nimrud, see M.E.L. Mallowan, *Nimrud and Its Remains* (London, 1966) and Joan Oates and David Oates, *Nimrud: An Assyrian Imperial City Revealed* (London, 2001).

160. Layard's accounts of his discoveries in Mesopotamia were best-sellers in their time. See Austen Henry Layard, *Nineveh and Its Remains*, 2 vols (London, 1849) and *Discoveries in the Ruins of Nineveh and Babylon* (London, 1953).

161. Fagan, *Return to Babylon*, p. 127.
162. For a fine overview of the British Museum's Assyrian collection, see J.E. Curtis and J.E. Reade (eds), *Art and Empire: Treasures from Assyria in the British Museum* (New York, 1995).
163. GB diary, 27 April 1909; GB letter to her family, 27 April 1909, Gertrude Bell Archive.
164. GB letter to her family, 27 April 1909, Gertrude Bell Archive. This is the same statue that was seen by A.T. Olmstead during his visit to the site around 1907–8 and published in his *History of Assyria* (New York, 1923), Fig. 81, opposite p. 164. It is one of a pair of colossal statues that had been excavated by H. Rassam back in 1854 and sketched by W. Boucher when fully intact. See C.J. Gadd, *The Stones of Assyria* (London, 1936), pl. 7, opposite p. 30, and p. 229. For additional notes on the identity and provenance of the statue, see Mallowan, *Nimrud*, pp. 231–2.
165. Also reported and photographed by Olmstead. See his *History of Assyria*, Fig. 60, opposite p. 106. Several visitors in the early twentieth century saw these items prominently exposed. See Julian Reade, 'The early exploration of Assyria', in Ada Cohen and Steven E. Kangas (eds), *Assyrian Reliefs from the Palace of Ashurnasirpal II: A Cultural Biography* (Hanover, 2010), pp. 104–5. The colossi were originally excavated by Layard and are pictured in a watercolour from his time, leaning towards one another. See Austen Henry Layard, *Discoveries in the Ruins of Nineveh and Babylon* (London, 1853), p. 337.
166. Bell, *Amurath*, p. 228; Bell, 'First capital'.
167. Gadd, *Stones*, p. 229.
168. Faraj Basmachi, *Treasures of the Iraq Museum* (Baghdad, 1975–6), p. 239, Item 17, and pl. 142.
169. Reade, 'Early exploration', pp. 103–5. Reports on the performative deliberate destruction of the Northwest Palace at Nimrud by IS include Michael D. Danti, C. Ali, T. Paulette, A. Cuneo, K. Franklin, L-A Barnes Gordon and D. Elitzer, 'ASOR Cultural Heritage Initiatives (CHI): Planning for safeguarding heritage sites in Syria and Iraq, weekly report 36 – April 13, 2015', available at www.asor-syrianheritage.org/wp-content/uploads/2015/04/ASOR_CHI_Weekly_Report_36r.pdf (accessed on 30 July 2015), and Michael Danti, Scott Branting, T. Paulette and A. Cuneo, 'ASOR Cultural Heritage Initiatives: Report on the destruction of the Northwest Palace at Nimrud', available at www.asor-syrianheritage.org/wp-content/uploads/2015/05/ASOR_CHI_Nimrud_Report.pdf (accessed on 30 July 2015).
170. Asher-Greve, 'Gertrude L. Bell', p. 168 and n. 192.
171. Gertrude L. Bell, 'The churches and monasteries of the Tur Abdin', in van Berchem and Strzygowski, *Amida*, pp. 224–62.
172. Gertrude L. Bell, 'Churches and monasteries of the Tur 'Abdin and neighbouring districts,' *Zeitschrift für Geschichte der Architektur* 9 (1913), pp. 61–112.
173. Most valuable is a monograph that includes both of Bell's academic publications on the Tur-Abdin, with an introduction, notes and report on the current state of the sites in the region by the Byzantinist M. Mundell Mango. See Gertrude L. Bell and M. Mundell Mango, *The Churches and Monasteries of the Tur 'Abdin* (London, 1982).
174. See Mango's report of, for example, the Church of Mar Cosmas, the Monastery of Mar Tahmazgerd and the Basilica at Mayafarqin, which are now completely gone: Bell and Mango, *Churches and Monasteries*, pp. 106–7 and 121–4.

Chapter 5   Further Travels and Archaeological Research, 1910–14

1. The full title of the work is *Palace and Mosque at Ukhaidir: A Study in Early Mohammadan Architecture* (Oxford, 1914).

2. The meaning of the title of Bell's book, *Amurath to Amurath*, may be evinced from the book's preface, which quotes a passage from Shakespeare's *Henry IV, Part 2* (Act V, Scene 2): 'Amurath an Amurath succeeds'; Gertrude L. Bell, *Amurath to Amurath* (London, 1911), p. viii. In Shakespeare, Amurath is a name for Murad I, a fourteenth-century sultan of the Ottoman Empire. With the use of the quote, Bell is emphasizing the unchangeable quality of the East from ancient times to the present day, in which 'conqueror falls upon the heels of conqueror, nations are overthrown and cities topple down into dust, but the conditions of existence are unaltered'; ibid., pp. vii–viii.

3. Bell was in correspondence with several scholars to whom reference is made in *Amurath to Amurath*. The Gertrude Bell Archive at Newcastle University, Miscellaneous, Item 13 includes many of those letters, including those from Ernst Herzfeld, Max van Berchem, Walter Andrae, David Hogarth, Enno Littmann, Marcel Dieulafoy, L.W. King and Flinders Petrie.

4. Evelyn Baring, first Earl of Cromer, was the British Consul-General in Egypt until 1907. Lord Cromer first met Bell in December 1906, when she made a trip to Egypt with her father and brother Hugo. Dining at Lord Cromer's Nile-side British residence in Cairo on New Year's Eve, she found him 'the nicest person in the world, without doubt' (GB letter to her mother, 1 January 1907, Gertrude Bell Archive). After that, and upon Cromer's return to England, Bell continued to see him on many occasions, finding that she shared similar views to his on a variety of subjects; this included their ardent opposition to the women's suffrage movement. See Roger Owen, 'Lord Cromer and Gertrude Bell', *History Today* 54 (2004), p. 37; Liora Lukitz, *A Quest in the Middle East: Gertrude Bell and the Making of Modern Iraq* (London, 2008), pp. 46–7, 51. Interestingly, while Bell unreservedly admired Cromer, Cromer himself did not always think so highly of Bell. On more than one occasion, writing to colleagues such as Lord Curzon and Arthur Balfour, he remarked that although he believed Bell to be clever, her judgement (especially on the broader issues of Near Eastern politics) was not always to be trusted, and that she had 'a tongue'; see Penelope Tuson, *Playing the Game: The Story of Western Women in Arabia* (London, 2003), pp. 137–8; Asher-Greve, 'Gertrude L. Bell', pp. 161–2.

5. Anderson, *Lawrence in Arabia*, p. 35.

6. Bell, *Amurath*, p. viii.

7. Bell, *Amurath*, p. ix.

8. Ellsworth Huntington, Review of Gertrude L. Bell, 'Amurath to Amurath', *Bulletin of the American Geographical Society* 44 (1912), p. 135.

9. David G. Hogarth, 'Gertrude Lowthian Bell', p. 366; Julia M. Asher-Greve, 'Gertrude L. Bell (1868–1926)', in Getzel M. Cohen and Martha Sharp Joukowsky (eds), *Breaking Ground: Pioneering Women Archaeologists* (Ann Arbor, 2004), p. 157.

10. Gertrude L. Bell, 'The east bank of the Euphrates from Tel Ahmar to Hit', *The Geographical Journal* 36 (1910), pp. 513–37.

11. Gertrude L. Bell, 'The churches and monasteries of the Tur Abdin', in Max van Berchem and Josef Stryzgowski, *Amida. Matériaux pour l'épigraphie et l'histoire*

musulmanes du DiyarBekr par Max van Berchem. Beiträge zur Kunstgeschichte des Mittelalters von Nordmesopotamien, Hellas und dem Abendlande von Josef Strzygowski (Heidelberg, 1910), pp. 224–62.

12. Gertrude L. Bell, 'The vaulting system of Ukhaidir', *Journal of Hellenic Studies* 30 (1910), pp. 69–81.

13. GB letter to her mother, 27 February 1910, Gertrude Bell Archive.

14. See above, n. 12. Bell's letters from August 1909 mention her drawing out the castle (GB letter to her mother, 17 August 1909, Gertrude Bell Archive); she then gave a lecture for the Hellenistic Society in November 1909, probably on the same topic as the journal article.

15. Bell related that her father was 'in his element' with the archaeologists they met, asking them intelligent questions. Bell humorously observed that when he was around, they all seemed far more interesting. See GB letter to her mother, undated February 1910, Gertrude Bell Archive.

16. GB letter to her mother, undated February 1910, Gertrude Bell Archive.

17. Robert B. Todd (ed.), 'Strong, Eugénie (née Sellers: 1860–1943)', *The Dictionary of British Classicists* (Bristol, 2004), p. 930.

18. Stephen L. Dyson, *Eugénie Sellers Strong: Portrait of an Archaeologist* (London, 2004), p. 76; Todd, 'Strong', p. 930.

19. Dyson, *Sellers Strong*, pp. 65–7; Todd, 'Strong', p. 930.

20. Dyson, *Sellers Strong*, pp. 111–94; Todd, 'Strong', pp. 930–1.

21. Not only was Eugénie friends with Gertrude, but she also became well acquainted with Gertrude's father, Hugh, and her step-mother, Florence; Dyson, *Sellers Strong*, p. 88. Correspondence between Eugénie and Florence Bell can be traced back to January 1900 and continued at least until late 1926, shortly after Gertrude's death; ibid., pp. 44–5, and note 70 on p. 222; p. 136 and note 29 on p. 230. In the 1926 letter, Strong wondered whether the cooling of her friendship with Gertrude was possibly due to Strong's conversion to Catholicism, which Florence denied.

22. Ibid., p. 84; GB letter to her mother, 22 February 1892, Gertrude Bell Archive.

23. Several letters of Bell's refer to 'Mr Strong' whom she also called 'my Pundit'. Strong was apparently quite impressed with Bell's proficiency in Arabic. See GB letters to her family, 13–14 February, 22–23 February, 1896, Gertrude Bell Archive.

24. Bell mentions the Strongs in a letter to her mother from London on 17 March 1899, and in another letter to her mother on 13 August 1902, Gertrude Bell Archive. The latter reports the following: 'I lunched yesterday with the Strongs. You know I do rather love that little rat – if it were only for a very genuine regard that I believe he has for me. He wants me to write a book for him, in a series on art he is bringing out for George Duckworth.'

25. Robert B. Todd (ed.), 'Ashby, Thomas (1874–1931)', *The Dictionary of British Classicists* (Bristol, 2004), pp. 29–30.

26. Ibid.

27. Ibid.

28. Dyson, *Sellers Strong*, pp. 111–27.

29. GB letter to her mother, undated February 1910, Gertrude Bell Archive.

30. GB letter to her mother, 9 (?) March 1910, Gertrude Bell Archive.

31. GB letter to her mother, undated February 1910, Gertrude Bell Archive.

32. Ibid; Katherine A. Geffcken, 'Esther van Deman and Gertrude Bell (1910)', in K. Einaudi (ed.), *Esther B. Van Deman: Images from the Archive of an American Archaeologist in Italy at the Turn of the Century* (Rome, 1991), p. 25.

33. GB letters to her parents, undated February 1910; 8, 9, 10 and 18 March 1910, Gertrude Bell Archive.
34. Katherine Welch, 'Esther B. Van Deman (1862–1937)', in Cohen and Joukowsky (eds), *Breaking Ground*, pp. 75–6.
35. Esther B. Van Deman, *The Atrium Vestae* (Washington, 1909).
36. Welch, 'Van Deman', p. 80; Esther Van Deman, 'Methods for determining the date of Roman concrete monuments', *American Journal of Archaeology* 16 (1912), pp. 230–51, 387–432.
37. Welch, 'Van Deman', pp. 82–3.
38. Ibid., p. 84. This field-intensive project required the pair to venture out into the countryside of Rome to trace the ruined aqueducts along hillsides and cliffs and through fields and valleys, and to distinguish the different aqueduct courses by their construction materials, quality of workmanship and mineral deposits. Two separate monographs on aqueducts appeared at the end of their collaboration: Esther Van Deman, *The Building of the Roman Aqueducts* (Washington, 1934); Thomas Ashby, *The Aqueducts of Ancient Rome* (Oxford, 1935). Both works were exceptional for their detailed plans, technical drawings and photographs. They are still considered valuable today, especially since much of the physical evidence for the aqueducts has since disappeared under the ever-expanding city of Rome; Welch 'Van Deman', p. 84.
39. See Welch's note from one of Van Deman's letters: 'I like Mrs. S. very much [...] She is simple and sensible'; ibid., p. 98, and note 120 on p. 108, in a letter to Randolph, 2 April 1908 (Mt. Holyoke College Archives).
40. Letter to Gertrude Bell from Van Deman, 15 July 1910, Gertrude Bell Archive; Gertrude Bell Archive at Newcastle University, Miscellaneous, Item 13.
41. GB letter to her mother, undated February 1910, Gertrude Bell Archive.
42. GB letter to her mother, 10 March 1910, Gertrude Bell Archive.
43. Ibid.
44. Geffcken, 'Esther Van Deman', p. 26.
45. Letter from Esther Van Deman to Gertrude Bell, 1 May 1910. Gertrude Bell Archive at Newcastle University, Miscellaneous, Item 13.
46. See especially Bell's careful description of the vaulting systems at Hatra: *Palace and Mosque* pp. 70–2; also her brick dimensions for Mudjdah and 'Atshan, ibid., pp. 39, 41.
47. Ibid., pp. 12–13, 15.
48. Bell's 1911 photographs, which reveal details of brick and stone architectural features, are invaluable for demonstrating techniques of construction at Ukhaidir. Gertrude Bell Archive, Newcastle University, Album P_143, P_150, P_167, P_169, P_195, P_201.
49. Letter from Esther Van Deman to Gertrude Bell, 15 July 1910. Gertrude Bell Archive at Newcastle University, Miscellaneous, Item 13.
50. Letter from Esther Van Deman to Gertrude Bell, 1 May 1910, Gertrude Bell Archive at Newcastle University, Miscellaneous, Item 13.
51. Ibid.
52. Letter from Esther Van Deman to Gertrude Bell, 15 July 1910, Gertrude Bell Archive at Newcastle University, Miscellaneous, Item 13.
53. For a good biographical coverage of this scholar, see Heinrich Drerup, 'Richard Delbrueck', in *Archäologenbildnisse: Porträts und Kurzbiographien von Klassischen Archäologen deutscher Sprache* (Mainz, 1988), pp. 188–9. Delbrück's later volumes on ivory consular diptychs (1929) and on ancient works carved in porphyry

(1932) are still widely used and consulted. His work *Hellenistiche Bauten in Latium* (Strasbourg, 1907) is still quoted from time to time, but it has been overtaken by fresh discoveries that have not affected the other two topics in anything like the same degree; Roger Wilson, pers. comm. Even before her trip to Rome, Bell had been aware of the German archaeologist's expertise, having referenced *Hellenistiche Bauten in Latium* on the earliest use of the groined vault during the Republican period in Rome (in the Tabularium) in her article on Ukhaidir's vaults (which she submitted to *The Journal of Hellenic Studies* shortly before her trip to Rome, in either late 1909 or early 1910); Bell, 'Vaulting system', p. 75 footnote 7.

54. GB letters to her family, undated February 1910; 27–8 February 1910; 9–10 and 27 March 1910, Gertrude Bell Archive.
55. GB letters to her mother, 29 March and 1 April 1910, Gertrude Bell Archive.
56. GB letter to her mother, 9 March 1910, Gertrude Bell Archive.
57. Dyson, *Sellers Strong*, p. 89, who writes: 'In 1910 Gertrude spent a prolonged period of time with Eugénie in Rome, where she developed a serious romantic attachment to Richard Delbrück, the director of the German Archaeological Institute. Indeed her father thought that she might settle there. However, personal and professional interests drew Gertrude to the Near East.'
58. See, for example, *Palace and Mosque*, p. 68 and notes 6 and 7; p. 69 and note 1; p. 70 and note 5; p. 73 and note 3; p. 123; p. 124 and notes 1, 5 and 7; p. 125 and notes 2–5; p. 136 and note 1; and p.166 and note 2.
59. Hedwig Kenner, 'Emil Reisch', in *Archäologenbildnisse*, pp. 150–1. Bell first met Dvořák on 31 March on a trip to Šibenik with other German professors: 'one was Professor Dvorjak, Strzygowski's colleague in Vienna and chief foe. I feel in hate with him at once – not on that account. He is young, fat and oily. I think him detestable'; GB letter to her family, 1 April 1910, Gertrude Bell Archive. She also lunched with Dvořák on 3 April in Split, as we know from another letter written on that day. Bell met Reisch on 2 April and went on a trip to Solin with him on 3 April; GB letter to her family, 3 April 1910, Gertrude Bell Archive.
60. Jürgen Borchhardt, 'Georg(e) Niemann', in *Archäologenbildnisse*, pp. 80–1. Bell met Niemann on 1 April 1910 and saw a ninth-century chapel at Diocletian's Gate in Split with him on 2 April; GB letters to her family, 1–2 April 1910, Gertrude Bell Archive. A letter from Bell to Esther Van Deman, written on the boat from Zara to Pola (5 April 1910), mentions meeting Niemann and knowing about his book on Diocletian's Palace, and the fact that she got from him whatever she could; Geffcken, 'Esther Van Deman', pp. 26–7. Bell also lunched with Niemann in Split on 3 April and journeyed with him and his daughter on 4 April to Zadar by boat up the coast, stopping to see Šibenik and Trogir; GB letters to her family, 4–5 April 1910, Gertrude Bell Archive. Bell was rather disparaging of Niemann in her letters, describing him as 'a sort of little gnome but very polite. He has with him a yet more gnome-like daughter, unspeakably clad' (GB letter to her family, 1 April, Gertrude Bell Archive), or in another letter 'insect-like' (GB letter to her mother, 2 April, Gertrude Bell Archive). She calls Niemann's son and daughter 'curious little gnomes, looking as if they had never come out into any light except that of the midnight oil' (GB letter to her family, 3 April 1910, Gertrude Bell Archive). Bell seemed to warm to Niemann on their trip up the coast, remarking that he became quite human when speaking about his diggings in Anatolia, and that

she enjoyed his company; GB letter to her family, 5 April 1910, Gertrude Bell Archive.

61. Gertrude Bell Archive, Newcastle University, Album E_153– 88 are all photos from the Dalmatian Coast.
62. GB letter to her family, 1 April 1910, Gertrude Bell Archive.
63. GB letter to her family, 5 April 1910, Gertrude Bell Archive.
64. Ibid.
65. GB letter to Van Deman, 5 April 1910; Geffcken, 'Esther Van Deman', p. 27.
66. GB letter to her mother, 29 March 1910, Gertrude Bell Archive.
67. GB letter to her father, 13 January 1911, Gertrude Bell Archive.
68. Ibid.
69. E. Walter Andrae and R.M. Boehmer, *Bilder eines Ausgräbers. Die Orientbilder von Walter Andrae 1898–1919/Sketches by an* Excavator, second enlarged edition, English translation by Jane Moon (Berlin, 1992), p. 140.
70. GB diary entries and letters to her family, 17 January–9 Feburary 1911, Gertrude Bell Archive.
71. GB diary, 3 March 1911; GB letter to her family, 3 March 1911, Gertrude Bell Archive. The site had also been visited by Louis Massignon in 1907; Massignon, *Mission en Mesopotamie* (Cairo, 1910), vol. 1, p. 21.
72. Bell, *Palace and Mosque*, pp. 38–9.
73. 'Kirche A' and 'Kirche B'; see also Barbara Finster and Jürgen Schmidt, 'Sasanidische und frühislamische Ruinen im Iraq', *Baghdader Mitteilungen* 8 (1976), pp. 27–39.
74. One can note especially her detail of a squinch in the back apse of 'Kirche A' – referred to in Bell's description as the 'little castle' – in which the archivolt had been decorated with a distinctive zigzag ornament in plaster, this repeating the same decoration at the base of the apse above. Overall, the ruined state of 'Kirche A' seems not to have altered significantly between Bell's visit in 1911 and Finster and Schmidt's later survey in 1973, although in the latter, one can note the complete absence of that plastered decoration of the squinch's archivolt due to the further crumbling of the very thin back wall of which it was a component. Compare Bell, *Palace and Mosque*, pl. 45 Fig. 2 (Gertrude Bell Archive, Album P_207) with Finster and Schmidt, 'Sasanidische', Taf. 18b. Finster and Schmidt's Taf. 15a is a general view of the back of the church, whose slightly more crumbled condition can be compared to Bell, *Palace and Mosque*, pl. 45, Fig. 1 (Gertrude Bell Archive, Album P_206). Bell notes that this crenellated plaster motif was observable on the archivolts above the doors at the ends of Corridors 5 and 6 at Ukhaidir; ibid., p. 38 n. 2.
75. Especially on the western side of the tower. See Bell, *Palace and Mosque*, p. 40, and P_212.
76. Compare Bell's photograph of the western side of the tower, Gertrude Bell Archive, Album P_212, with Finster and Schmidt's photo of the same side, 'Sasanidische', Taf. 9.
77. Google Earth photograph (© 2015 Google), coordinates 32°20'10.78"N, 43°49'59.69"E.
78. Bell, *Palace and Mosque*, p. 40.
79. Bell deemed the tower to be most similar to a minaret at Tauq south of Kerkuk, which is contemporary with similar thirteenth-century constructions at Baghdad; ibid., pp. 40–1; pl. 48 Fig. 1.

80. K.A.C. Creswell, *Early Muslim Architecture. Vol. 2: Early 'Abbāsids, Umayyads of Cordova, Aghlabids, Ṭūlūnids, and Samānids, A.D. 751–905* (Oxford, 1940), reprint (New York, 1979), p. 98; Robert Hillenbrand, *Islamic Architecture* (New York, 1994), p. 144; Marcus Milwright, *An Introduction to Islamic Archaeology* (Edinburgh, 2010), p. 163.
81. Finster and Schmidt, 'Sasanidische', p. 26; Hillenbrand, *Islamic Architecture*, p. 144.
82. Creswell, *Early Muslim Architecture*, vol. 2, pp. 94, 98; Finster and Schmidt, 'Sasanidische', p. 26.
83. Bell, *Palace and Mosque*, p. 41; her plan is on pl. 46, Fig. 2.
84. Ibid., p. 42; pl. 50, Figs 1–2.
85. Ibid., p. 43; pl. 49, Fig. 2; 50, Fig. 2.
86. Ibid., p. 43.
87. Creswell, *Early Muslim Architecture,* vol. 2, p. 93.
88. Ibid., p. 98.
89. Finster and Schmidt, 'Sasanidische', pp. 21–4.
90. See especially Bell's photographs, Album P_215 and P_216.
91. Creswell, *Early Muslim Architecture*, vol. 2, p. 92 and Pl. 22c can be compared to Bell, *Palace and Mosque*, pl. 49, Fig. 2 and Album P_219.
92. Ibid., pl. 51, Fig. 2 compared to Finster and Schmidt, 'Sasanidische', Taf. 5.
93. Bell, *Palace and Mosque*, pp. 38–43, and pls. 45–51.
94. Vol. IV (Paris, 1896), pls. 40, 42 and 42.
95. Bell, *Palace and Mosque*, p. 44.
96. GB letter to her mother, 21 March 1911; GB diary, 22 March 1911, Gertrude Bell Archive.
97. GB diary entries, 23–4 March 1911, Gertrude Bell Archive.
98. Ibid.
99. GB letter to her family, 28 March 1911, Gertrude Bell Archive.
100. See especially Bell's letter to her family, 28 March 1911, Gertrude Bell Archive.
101. GB diary, 25 March 1911, Gertrude Bell Archive.
102. Bell, *Palace and Mosque*, pp. 44–54, and pls. 51, fig.1, 52, Fig. 2, 53–73, Fig. 1.
103. Ibid., pp. 44–5.
104. Ibid., p. 45.
105. Ibid., p. 80. The platform stretched for approximately 372 m along its east–west axis, while from north to south it covered about 190 m, producing an enormous space upon which to lay out a monumental structure.
106. Ibid., pp. 45, 50, 80.
107. Ibid., pp. 45, 70, pl. 52, Fig. 2. While it is true that such constructions occur in early Islamic buildings such as at Qasr Kharana and Ukhaidir, offset arches and vaults were apparently never a common feature of Sasanian architecture, and Bell's statement that the feature 'is generally the case in Sasanian vault building, whether in brick or in stone' is groundless, according to Bier, *Sarvistan*, p. 30 and fn. 36. Bell was almost certainly thinking of the brick vaults in the side chambers at Sasanian Ctesiphon, which appear as offset constructions, but this brickwork supports pitched brick vaults and not mortared stone rubble, as at Qasr-i-Shirin, and therefore it represents a very different construction technology.
108. Bell, *Palace and Mosque*, pp. 83–4.
109. Bell reconstructed this porch, marked only by two grass-covered mounds, as consisting simply of two thick walls, these supporting a barrel-vaulted roof. She reports, however, having seen circular patches of brick, which may have been

the remains of columns, making possible de Morgan's reconstruction of a room flanked on either side by columns; Jacques de Morgan, *Mission scientifique en Perse*, vol. IV (Paris, 1896), p. 42; Bell, *Palace and Mosque* p. 45. Recent investigations of this particular section of the palace by an Iranian team have now confirmed the existence of two parallel lines of thick rectangular stone piers, marking the place of Bell's postulated solid walls. The Iranian work also detected additional columns both in front of and alongside the stone piers, suggesting that the hall was accommodated with porches on either side. See Yusef Moradi, 'Imarat-e Khosrow in view of the first season of archaeological excavations', in Hamid Fahimi and Karim Alizadeh (eds), *Nāmvarnāmeh: Papers in honour of Massoud Azarnoush* (Tehran, 2012), pp. 350–75.

110. The walls of this vast square space were much ruined, and nothing of the roof was preserved, but in Bell's estimation this room would have supported a vast dome, possibly covering an area of some 16 m and supported by corner piers characterized on their two inner sides by engaged columns, the remnants of which were still visible; Bell, *Palace and Mosque*, pp. 46, 74.

111. Narrow covered corridors, nos. 11 and 12, led from the hall of audience (no. 3), extended along both sides of the central area marks by Courts A and B, and gave access to the lower level of the platform at the western end of the palace, with its courts and rooms; ibid., p. 46.

112. The open courts (C–J) had groups of vaulted chambers on at least one of their ends, these distinguished by two rooms on either side of a central *iwan* opening to its full width onto the court, precisely in the manner of the earlier *iwans* of Parthian Hatra; ibid., p. 47. Latitudinally oriented rooms located behind each of the *iwan* groups were interpreted as kitchens; ibid.

113. Ibid., p. 80; Oscar Reuther, 'Sasanian art', in Arthur E. Pope, *A Survey of Persian Art* (Oxford, 1938), p. 543.

114. Bier, *Sarvistan*, p. 71, note 7; Lionel Bier, 'The Sasanian palaces and their influence in early Islam', *Ars Orientalis* 23 (1993) p. 59, and n. 18, citing Bell, *Palace and Mosque*, pp. 44–51.

115. Bier, 'Sasanian palaces', p. 59.

116. Bell, *Palace and Mosque*, p. 81.

117. Reuther, 'Sasanian art', p. 541, Fig. 153.

118. Ibid., p. 542, Fig. 154.

119. Bier, 'Sasanian palaces', p. 58.

120. Reuther, 'Sasanian art', p. 540; Bier, 'Sasanian palaces', pp. 58–9.

121. Reuther, 'Sasanian art', p. 540.

122. Ibid., p. 540.

123. Ibid., pp. 540–2.

124. Moradi, 'Imarat-e Khosrow'.

125. The structure measures 134 m by 83 m; Bell, *Palace and Mosque*, p. 51.

126. The main entrance gateway is represented by nos. 1 and 2. Courts A–C were arranged along the eastern side of the structure, flanked by small covered chambers, nos. 3–14. Many of these chambers were found covered with conical domes set over the angles on squinch arches and furnished with small niches on one of the walls, a typical Persian feature; ibid., p. 51; pl. 65, Figs 2–3.

127. These included Courts E–H and I–K and the surrounding rooms, nos. 18–34 and 35–50; ibid., pp. 52–3. At least one of the chambers (no. 39) in these wings was domed with squinches; ibid., p. 53, and pl. 68, Fig. 2.

128. Ibid., p. 90; pls. 71–2.

129. Ibid., p. 53; pl. 69, Figs 1–2.
130. Ibid., pp. 53–4; pl. 70, Figs 1–2.
131. Nos. 58–62 were observed by Bell in the south-west, while Nos. 55–7 were noted in the north-western corner of the building. Ibid., p. 54.
132. Ibid., p. 53.
133. Ibid., pl. 64.
134. Ibid, p. 90.
135. Ibid., p. 90, Fig. 10.
136. Ibid., pp. 92–4.
137. Ibid., p. 94.
138. Jürgen Schmidt, 'Qaṣr-i Šīrīn, Feuertempel oder Palast?' *Baghdad Mitteilungen* 9 (1978), p. 41.
139. Reuther, 'Sasanian art', p. 553; Figs 158–9.
140. Observed in Bell's photographs, see especially Bell, *Palace and Mosque*, pls. 67, 71–2.
141. Reuther, 'Sasanian art', p. 553.
142. Ibid., pp. 552–4.
143. Schmidt, 'Feuertempel', pp. 43–4.
144. Ibid., pp. 45–7.
145. Bier, *Sarvistan*, p. 71.
146. Ibid.
147. At Chehar Qapu, this is Court E and surrounding Rooms 18–21. At Ukhaidir, this is the mosque in the north-western corner of the palace.
148. Bier, *Sarvistan*, p. 71.
149. Bell, *Palace and Mosque*, pp. 92–4.
150. Schmidt, 'Feuertempel', p. 43.
151. Moradi, personal communication.
152. Moradi, personal communication.
153. Rüdiger Schmitt, 'Hatra', *Encyclopedia Iranica* XII/1 (2003), pp. 58–61; an updated version is available online at http://www.iranicaonline.org/arti cles/hatra (accessed 29 July 2015).
154. L. Michael White, 'Hatra', in E.M. Meyers (ed.), *The Oxford Encyclopedia of Archaeology in the Near East* (New York, 1997), p. 484.
155. Ibid., pp. 484–5.
156. Joachim Marzahn, '1907–1911: Hatra. Feldarchäologie im Schnelldurchlauf', in G. Wilhelm (ed.), *Zwischen Tigris und Nil* (Mainz am Rhein, 1998), pp. 68–73.
157. Fu'ad Safar and M.A. Mustafa, *Hatra: The City of the Sun God* [Arabic title *Al-Ḥaḍr, Madi⁻nat al-shams*] (Baghdad, 1974). Hatra's listing as a World Heritage Site is available at http://whc.unesco.org/en/list/277 (accessed 22 June 2015).
158. GB diary, 27 January 1909, Gertrude Bell Archive.
159. Andrae's investigations at Hatra would result in a two-volume report on its architecture: Walter Andrae, *Hatra nach Aufnahmen von Mitgliedern der Assur Expedition der Deutschen Orient-Gesellschaft*, 2 vols (Leipzig, 1908 and 1912).
160. GB diary, 24 April 1909, Gertrude Bell Archive.
161. Ibid.; GB letter to her family, 26 April 1909, Gertrude Bell Archive.
162. The whereabouts of the letter is not known, but that it existed is indicated by Andrae's reply to her in a letter dated 20 June 1910. Gertrude Bell Archive, Newcastle University, Miscellaneous, Item 13.
163. Ibid.
164. Ibid.
165. GB letter to her mother, 14 April 1911, Gertrude Bell Archive.

166. Ibid.
167. Ibid.
168. Ibid.
169. Michael Sommer, *Hatra. Geschichte und Kultur einer Karawanenstadt im römisch-parthischen Mesopotamien* (Mainz am Rhein, 2003), p. 8.
170. For a detailed assessment of each of the Hatra pieces destroyed in the Mosul Museum, see Christopher Jones, 'Assessing the damage at the Mosul Museum, Part 1: The Assyrian artifacts' (27 February 2015). Available at https://gatesofni neveh.wordpress.com/2015/02/27/assessing-the-damage-at-the-mosul-mus eum-part-1-the-assyrian-artifacts/ (accessed 30 July 2015).
171. For information on the recent destruction of Hatra inflicted by IS, see Michael D. Danti, C. Ali, T. Paulette, A. Cuneo, K. Franklin, L-A Barnes Gordon and D. Elitzer, 'ASOR Cultural Heritage Initiatives (CHI): Planning for safeguarding heritage sites in Syria and Iraq, weekly report 35 – April 6, 2015', available at www.asor-syrianheritage.org/wp-content/uploads/2015/04/ASOR_CHI_Weekly_ Report_35r.pdf (accessed 30 July 2015), and Christopher Jones, 'Assessing the damage at Hatra' (7 April 2015), available at http://gatesofnineveh.wordpress. com/2015/04/07/assessing-the-damage-at-hatra/ (accessed 30 July 2015).
172. Bell, *Palace and Mosque*, pp. 70–3.
173. Ibid., pp. 66–8.
174. GB letter to her father, 10 November 1922, Gertrude Bell Archive.
175. Ibid.
176. Bell, *Palace and Mosque*, Chapter V, 'The Façade', pp. 122–44, and Chapter VI, 'The Mosque', pp. 145–60.
177. Ibid., Chapter IV, pp. 55–121.
178. See also the discussion of Strzygowski's scholarship and methodology in Chapter 2, above.
179. Ernst Herzfeld, 'Die Genesis der islamischen Kunst und das Mschatta-Problem', *Der Islam* 1 (1910), pp. 27–63, 104–44; for Herzfeld's date of Mshatta, see p. 143 in this work. See also Thomas Leisten, 'Concerning the development of the Hira-style revisited', in Ann C. Gunther and Stefan R. Hauser (eds), *Ernst Herzfeld and the Development of Near Eastern Studies, 1900–1950* (Leiden, 2004), p. 375.
180. Jonathan Bloom, 'Introduction', in Jonathan Bloom (ed.) *Early Islamic Art and Architecture* (Aldershot, 2002), p. xvi.
181. Leisten, 'Development of the Hira-style', p. 375.
182. Suzanne Marchand, 'The rhetoric of artifacts and the decline of classical humanism: The case of Josef Strzygowski', *History and Theory* 33 (1994), p. 125.
183. Lisa Cooper, 'Archaeology and acrimony: Gertrude Bell, Ernst Herzfeld and the study of pre-modern Mesopotamia', *Iraq* 75 (2013), pp. 143–69.
184. Bell, *Palace and Mosque*, pp. 60–2.
185. Ibid., and Fig. 5 Building G. This may also be seen in F. von Luschan, D. Humann and R. Koldewey, *Ausgrabungen in Sendschirli*, vol. 2 (Berlin, 1898), p. 184, Fig. 83.
186. Bell, *Palace and Mosque*, pp. 62–3, Figs 6–8.
187. Ibid., p. 63.
188. GB diary, 5 April 1911, Gertrude Bell Archive: 'At lunch we discussed for long the origin of the liwan [*iwan*]. They have got a liwan here, probably later, on top of temple wall, looking east. The liwan is the gate, originally where the king transacted all business. It is the khilani Look up Singirli. Achaemenid palaces not found in old Assyria, the room is always closed. Introduced avowedly on Hittite

models, but so far not found at Boghaz Keui except of course in gate. Reappears in Sasanian times, either singly or with a closed room behind, and so passes to Arab.'

189. Bell, *Palace and Mosque*, p. 62, footnote 4. This was published in F. Sarre and E. Herzfeld, *Iranische Felsreliefs* (Berlin, 1910), p. 186.

190. Bell, *Palace and Mosque*, pp. 65–6, and Fig. 9. The peristyle is observed, for example, in the small Parthian palace at Nippur. For a more recent discussion of this and other Parthian structures, see especially Malcolm Colledge, *Parthian Art* (Ithica, NY, 1977); E.J. Keall, 'The Arts of the Parthians', in R.W. Ferrier (ed.), *The Arts of Persia* (New Haven, 1989), pp. 48–59.

191. Bell, *Palace and Mosque*, p. 66.

192. Colledge, *Parthian Art*, p. 63; Keall, 'Parthians', p. 249.

193. Bell, *Palace and Mosque*, p. 68.

194. Ibid.

195. Ibid., pp. 68–9. From her footnotes, it is evident that Bell was using R. Delbrück's *Hellenistiche Bauten in Latium* as the authoritative guide for the uses and development of the cut stone vault in the Mediterranean coastal regions and especially Italy; ibid., pp. 68–9, notes 6 and 7 on p. 68 and notes 1 and 2 on p. 69; see also White, 'Hatra', p. 484.

196. Bell, *Palace and Mosque*, pp. 68–9; E.J. Keall, 'Some thoughts on the early *Eyvan*', in Dickran K. Kouymijian (ed.), *Near Eastern Numismatics, Iconography, Epigraphy and History: Studies in Honor of George C. Miles* (Beirut, 1974), p. 124; Edward J. Keall, 'Architecture ii. Parthian Period', *Encyclopedia Iranica* II/3 (1986), pp. 327–9; an updated version is available online at http://www.iranicaonline.org/articles/architecture-ii (accessed 29 July 2015).

197. Bell, *Palace and Mosque*, p. 66 and Fig. 10.

198. Ibid., pp. 75–6, pl. 73, Fig. 2; Dietrich Huff, 'Fīrūzābād', *Encyclopedia Iranica* IX/6 (1999) pp. 633–6; an updated version is available online at www.iranicaonline.org/articles/firuzabad (accessed 29 July 2015). Lionel Bier, 'Sasanian Palaces in Perspective', *Archaeology* 35 (1982), p. 33.

199. Bell, *Palace and Mosque*, p. 75.

200. Ibid., p. 74, note 1 for the presumed date of Sarvistan, and p. 78.

201. Ibid., p. 74, note 1 for date of Qasr-i-Shirin, and p. 80.

202. Ibid., pp. 82–4.

203. Ibid., p. 56; C. Edmund Bosworth, 'Lakhmids', *Encyclopaedia Iranica* (online edition, 2012), available at www.iranicaonline.org/articles/lakhmids (accessed 29 July 2015).

204. Bell, *Palace and Mosque*, pp. 55–6.

205. Bell, citing the Islamic historian Mas'udi, who was describing the magnificent *hira* at the Lakhmid capital itself, 'al-Hirah; ibid., pp. 58–9, 86.

206. Ernst Herzfeld, *Erster vorläufiger Bericht über die Ausgrabungen von Samarra* (Berlin, 1912), p. 40. Herzfeld's discussion of Balkuwara and its link to a *hira* is also mentioned in a letter he wrote to Bell, 17 September 1911 (from Ctesiphon), Gertrude Bell Archive, Newcastle University, Miscellaneous, 13. Bell, *Palace and Mosque*, pp. 58–9, 86–7; Hillenbrand, *Islamic Architecture*, p. 405; Leisten, 'Development of the Hira-style', pp. 377–8.

207. Keall, 'Some thoughts', pp. 124–9.

208. Ibid., and Figs 2, 4–5.

209. Ibid., p. 124, Fig. 1; Malcolm Colledge, *Parthian Art* (Ithaca, NY, 1977), p. 63 and Fig. 26.

210. Oleg Grabar, 'Ayvān', *Encyclopedia Iranica* III/2 (1987), pp. 153–5; an updated version is available online at www.iranicaonline.org/articles/ayvan-palace (accessed 29 July 2015).

211. Oskar Reuther, 'Parthian architecture: A history', in Arthur E. Pope (ed.), *A Survey of Persian Art. Vol. 1: Pre-Achaemenid, Achaemenid, Parthian and Sasanian Periods* (London, 1938), p. 429; Keall, 'Architecture ii. Parthian Period'.

212. F. Oelmann, 'Hilani und Liwanhaus', *Bonner Jahrbücher* 127 (1922), pp. 189–236.

213. Reuther, 'Parthian architecture', p. 429.

214. Hillenbrand, *Islamic Architecture*, p. 395. Elsewhere in his book, Hillenbrand compares a formal chamber, often on an upper storey, equipped with a window at which royal persons could make official appearances, to the earlier *bit hilani*; ibid., pp. 385, 402. This interpretation of the Hittite *bit hilani* has its adherents, particularly among those who see in it an equation with the word *ḥln*, known from Biblical and Canaanite texts as a type of multi-storeyed palatial building equipped with a royal 'window of appearances'. See Irene Winter, 'Art as evidence for interaction: Relations between the Neo-Assyrian Empire and North Syria as seen from the monuments', in H-J. Nissen and J. Renger (eds), *Mesopotamia und seine Nachbarn* (Berlin, 1982), p. 363. In the context of much-later Ukhaidir, such a form could indeed have provided the inspiration for the three-storeyed gatehouse section of the northern section of palace and the high windows that look down upon the interior 'Court of Honour'. If this is the interpretation of the *bit hilani* to which Hillenbrand is alluding, it refers to a somewhat different definition of the complex from that originally noted by Koldewey and must be treated as a separate example of a possible cultural borrowing from architectural traditions of the earlier ancient Near East.

215. Winter, 'Art as evidence', p. 363.

216. Irene Winter, '"Seat of kingship" / "A wonder to behold": The palace as construct in the ancient Near East', *Ars Orientalis* 23 (1993), pp. 33–4.

217. Ibid., pp. 38–9.

218. Bell, *Palace and Mosque*, p. 97. Bell was particularly influenced by the investigations of Rudoph-Ernest Brünnow and Alfred von Domaszewski, who had carried out an extensive survey of Roman remains in 1897–8, publishing their findings in their monumental *Die Provincia Arabia*, 3 vols (Strassburg, 1904–9). Bell appears also to have been in personal correspondence with Brünnow, as she acknowledges him for having provided her with a plan of Dumeir, which she included in her book. Bell had visited Dumeir, a Roman fort on the road between Damascus and Palmyra in present-day Syria, in February 1911, on her way across the Syrian desert to Ukhaidir.

219. Bell, *Palace and Mosque*, pp. 114–17. Part of her interest in this castle stemmed from the fact that it had been recently visited by her friend Bernhard Moritz, who had, in the few hours that he spent there, discovered an inscription that argued for its Umayyad date; ibid., p. 111; B. Moritz, 'Ausflüge in der Arabia Petraea', in *Mélanges de la Faculté Orientale de Beyrouth* 3 (1908), p. 429, see also Stephen Urice, *Qasr Kharana in the Transjordan* (Durham, NC, 1987) pp. 10–11. Bell was also familiar with the earlier reports published by Alois Musil, who had visited Qasr Kharana three times and was responsible for the first detailed ground-plans of the building, one of which Bell reproduced; see A. Musil, *Kusejr 'Amra* (Wien, 1907); Bell, *Palace and Mosque*, p. 114, Fig. 29. From her own diaries and letters, we know that Bell visited Qasr Kharana on 3–6 January 1914. She carefully examined the

castle, taking photographs, drawing plans, copying Kufic inscriptions and overall doing 'much more at it than anyone else'; GB letter to her family, 5 January 1914, Gertrude Bell Archive. Regrettably, Bell never published any of her data on Qasr Kharana, although her extensive photographs, plans and notes make it clear that her original intent had been to do so. Bell's 1914 photographs of Qasr Kharana are available through the Newcastle photographic archives: Gertrude Bell Archive, Newcastle University, Album X_009–010, Album Y_077–132. Her field book containing her notes, measurements and plans of Qasr Kharana from 1914 are housed at the Royal Geographic Society in London (GLB 15).

220. Bell, *Palace and Mosque*, pp. 117–18. While in Bell's time Mshatta was thought to be attributable to the Umayyad caliph Yazid II, who died in 724 CE, its construction is now generally equated with al-Walid II, around 744 CE. Ibid., p. 117; Hillenbrand, 'Islamic art', p. 64. Oleg Grabar, 'The date and meaning of Mshatta', *Dumbarton Oaks Papers* 41 (1987), pp. 243–7.

221. Cooper, 'Archaeology and acrimony', p. 166.

222. Philip J. Dear, 'Ukhaidir and its lessons', *The British Architect* (11 June 1915), p. 292.

223. Ibid.

224. Anonymous, Review of Gertrude L. Bell, 'Palace and Mosque at Ukhaidir. A Study in Early Mohammadan Architecture', *The Athenaeum* (30 May 1914), p. 767.

225. K.A.C. Creswell, Review of Gertrude L. Bell, 'Palace and Mosque at Ukhadir. A Study in Early Mohammadan Architecture', *The Burlington Magazine for Connoisseurs* 26 (October 1914), p. 35; Dear, 'Ukhaidir', p. 292.

226. 'Review', *The Athenaeum*, p. 768; see also A., Review of Gertrude L. Bell, 'Palace and Mosque at Ukhaidir. A Study in Early Mohammadan Architecture', *Journal of Roman Studies* 4 (1914), pp. 113–14, which expresses similar praise.

227. Marcel Dieulafoy, Review of Gertrude L. Bell, 'Palace and Mosque at Ukhaidir. A Study in Early Mohammadan Architecture', *Journal des savants* 12 (September– November 1914), pp. 393–5, and 397.

228. Ibid., p. 398.

229. Hillenbrand, 'Creswell', p. 26.

230. A., 'Review', pp. 113–14.

231. Creswell, 'Review', pp. 35–6. The same review is repeated by Creswell in the *Journal of the Royal Asiatic Society of Great Britain and Ireland* (1914), pp. 784–8.

232. Hillenbrand, 'Creswell', p. 26.

233. GB letter to her mother, 18 November 1913, Gertrude Bell Archive.

234. Bell was awarded the medal in 1918 'for her important explorations and travels in Asia Minor, Syria, Arabia and on the Euphrates'. See http://www.rgs.org/NR/rdonlyres/C5962519-882A-4C67-803D-0037308C756D/0/GoldMedalrecipents.pdf (accessed 18 June 2015).

235. Janet Wallach, *Desert Queen* (New York, 1996), p. 136.

236. Ibid., pp. 142–3.

Chapter 6   Mesopotamia and Iraq – Past and Present Entwined

1. Bell's political activities are described at length in several biographies of her. See especially H.V.F. Winstone, *Gertrude Bell* (London, 1978); Janet Wallach, *Desert Queen* (New York, 1996); Georgina Howell, *Gertrude Bell: Queen of the Desert, Shaper*

of Nations (New York, 2006); Liora Lukitz, *A Quest in the Middle East: Gertrude Bell and the Making of Modern Iraq* (London, 2008). For Bell's participation in the 1919 Paris peace talks, see Margaret Macmillan, *Paris 1919* (New York, 2003), pp. 398–400. For Bell's part in war-time and post-war activities in Mesopotamia and the wider Middle East, see also Penelope Tuson, *Playing the Game: The Story of Western Women in Arabia* (London, 2003), chapters 4 and 5; Peter Sluglett, *Britain in Iraq: Contriving King and Country* (London, 2007); Priya Satia, *Spies in Arabia: The Great War and the Cultural Foundations of Britain's Covert Empire in the Middle East* (Oxford, 2008).

2. Julia M. Asher-Greve, 'Gertrude L. Bell (1868–1926)', in Getzel M. Cohen and Martha Sharp Joukowsky (eds), *Breaking Ground: Pioneering Women Archaeologists* (Ann Arbor, 2004), p. 177.

3. Ibid.

4. Quoted in Howell, *Queen of the Desert*, p. 139.

5. Howell, *Queen of the Desert*, p. 139, reports that when reading Milton in her schooldays, Bell wanted 'to stand on her head for joy'. Bell's most serious engagement with poetry came with her English translations of poems by the mystical Persian poet Hafiz, which she completed in 1897, not long after her travels to Persia. See Gertrude L. Bell, *Poems from the Divan of Hafiz* (London, 1897); Lukitz, *A Quest*, p. 26; Howell, *Queen of the Desert*, pp. 56–9.

6. Wallach, *Desert Queen*, p. 48; Howell, *Queen of the Desert*, p. 121.

7. Billie Melman, *Women's Orients: English Women and the Middle East, 1718–1918* (London, 1992), pp. 206–7; B. Hodgson, *Dreaming of the East: Western Women and the Exotic Allure of the Orient* (Vancouver, 2005), p. 172.

8. Gertrude L. Bell, *The Desert and the Sown* (London, 1907), reprint, with a new introduction by Rosemary O'Brien (New York, 2001), p. 1.

9. Chapter Six, entitled 'Romance', of an unfinished manuscript by Bell. Robinson Library Special Collections, Newcastle University, Gertrude Bell Archive, Miscellaneous, Item 20. The excerpt also appears transcribed in Lukitz, *A Quest*, p. 242, and partially in Magnus T. Bernhardsson, *Reclaiming a Plundered Past: Archaeology and Nation Building in Modern Iraq* (Austin, 2005), p. 64.

10. GB letter to her mother, 11 April 1899, Gertrude Bell Archive.

11. Bell, *Desert and the Sown*, p. 249.

12. Gertrude L. Bell, *Amurath to Amurath* (New York, 1911), p. 180.

13. 'Romantic orientalism: Overview', *The Norton Anthology of English Literature*. *Norton Topics Online* (2010–15), available at www.wwnorton.com/college/english/nael/romantic/topic_4 (accessed 29 July 2015).

14. F.N. Bohrer, *Orientalism and Visual Culture: Imagining Mesopotamia in Nineteenth-Century Europe* (Cambridge, 2003), pp. 49–55.

15. Ibid., p. 49.

16. Quoted by E. Frahm, 'Images of Assyria in nineteenth- and twentieth-century western scholarship,' in S. Holloway (ed.), *Orientalism, Assyriology and the Bible* (Sheffield, 2006), p. 74.

17. Ibid., p. 77.

18. Bohrer, *Orientalism and Visual Culture*, p, 147.

19. A.H. Layard, *Nineveh and Its Remains* (London, 1849), vol. 1, p. 6; quoted by Bohrer, *Orientalism and Visual Culture*, p. 147.

20. Layard, *Nineveh and Its Remains*, pp. 6–7.

21. Bohrer, *Orientalism and Visual Culture*, p. 149.

22. Eckart Frahm, 'Images of Assyria', p. 81.

23. Howell, *Queen of the Desert*, pp. 63–4.
24. Such historical figures are referred to, for example, in Bell's chapter 'Romance'.
25. David G. Hogarth, *Accidents of an Antiquary's Life* (London, 1910), p. 1; quoted in Bernhardsson, *Reclaiming*, p. 95.
26. Bell, *Amurath*, p. 108.
27. As discussed in Chapter 5 above, in Shakespeare's *Hamlet*, Amurath is a name for Murad I, a fourteenth-century sultan of the Ottoman Empire. Many other sultans named Murad ruled after him.
28. Bell, *Amurath*, pp. vii–viii.
29. Bell, *Amurath*, pp. 144–5.
30. GB letter to her father, 18 April 1918, Gertrude Bell Archive.
31. Bell, 'Romance'.
32. Bell, *Amurath*, p. 226.
33. Bell, 'Romance'.
34. Besides in her 'Romance' chapter, cited above, it also appears in her diary entry for 31 March 1914, Gertrude Bell Archive.
35. Bell, *Amurath*, p. 226.
36. Adam Hill, *Stepping Stones in the Stream of Ignorance: D.G. Hogarth as Orientalist and Agent of Empire* (MA thesis, Southern Illinois University Edwardsville, 2008), pp. 10, 25, 44.
37. Bernhardsson, *Reclaiming*, p. 94; Hill, *Stepping Stones*, pp. 44–5.
38. Richard Hingley, *Roman Officers and English Gentlemen: The Imperial Origins of Roman Archaeology* (London, 2000), pp. 49–50; F. Haverfield, J.L. Strachan Davidson, E.R. Bevan, E.M. Walker, D.G. Hogarth and Lord Cromer, 'Ancient imperialism', *The Classical Review* 24 (1910), pp. 113–14.
39. Edward Said, *Orientalism* (New York, 1979). Said makes particular reference to Hogarth as an agent of imperialism on pp. 197 and 223–4.
40. See Chapter 4 above; E. Walter Andrae and R.M. Boehmer, *Bilder eines Ausgräbers. Die Orientbilder von Walter Andrae 1898–1919/Sketches by an Excavator*, second enlarged edition, English translation by Jane Moon (Berlin, 1992), p. 139.
41. Margaret MacMillan, *Paris 1919* (New York, 2001), pp. 11–14.
42. Ibid., pp. 399–400.
43. Winstone, *Gertrude Bell*, pp. 214–5; Wallach, *Desert Queen*, pp. 230, 243–5; MacMillan, *Paris 1919*, p. 400; Sluglett, *Britain in Iraq*, p. 27.
44. A.K. Bennison, *The Great Caliphs: The Golden Age of the 'Abbasid Empire* (London, 2009), p. 5.
45. Ibid.
46. Ibid.
47. Ibid.
48. Howell, *Queen of the Desert*, p. 335.
49. Lukitz, *A Quest*, p. 152.
50. Ibid., quoting from G.L. Bell, 'The fealty of the tribes, a chapter in the history of Iraq', Robinson Library Special Collections, Newcastle University, Gertrude Bell Archive, Miscellaneous, Item 20. See also GB letter to her father, 31 July 1921, Gertrude Bell Archive.
51. Lukitz, *A Quest*, p. 152.
52. Bell, *Amurath*, pp. 181–3.
53. GB letter to her father, 6 August 1921, Gertrude Bell Archive.
54. GB letter to her father, 24 October 1922, Gertrude Bell Archive; Bernhardsson, *Reclaiming*, p. 117.

55. Ibid., p. 123.
56. *Antiquities Law* (Iraq) (Baghdad, 1924), Article 22, p. 9.
57. Bernhardsson, *Reclaiming*, pp. 123–4.
58. Ibid., pp. 121, 125.
59. *Antiquities Law*, Article 19(i), p. 6.
60. See, for example, Bell's misgivings about awarding the excavation permit to the Oxford expedition for the site of Kish, which consisted of only one individual; GB letter to her father, 30 January 1923, Gertrude Bell Archive. In another letter, Bell expresses her hopes that Yale University will ask for a permit to dig at Warka (Uruk), since it is a big mound and its excavations should be sponsored by a big, rich institution; GB letter to her mother, 31 March 1926, Gertrude Bell Archive.
61. GB letter to her father, 1 March 1923; GB letter to her father, 4 March 1925; GB letter to her father, 6 March 1924, describes how one gold scarab was won by a toss of a rupee; GB letter to her father, 16 March 1926, Gertrude Bell Archive.
62. GB letter to a parent, 24 March 1924; GB letter to her mother, 25 March 1925; GB letter to her mother, 31 March 1926, Gertrude Bell Archive.
63. GB letter to her father, 13 October 1923; GB letter to her mother, 3 March, 1926; GB letter to her father, 16 June 1926, Gertrude Bell Archive; Bernhardsson, *Reclaiming*, pp. 152–3.
64. Ibid., p. 152.
65. Ibid., pp. 150–1.
66. Ibid., p. 151.
67. Ibid., pp. 142–5.
68. Bernhardsson, *Reclaiming*, pp. 118–19, 152; J.F. Goode, *Negotiating for the Past: Archaeology, Nationalism, and Diplomacy in the Middle East, 1919–1941* (Austin, 2007), pp. 198–9; W.L. Cleveland, *The Making of an Arab Nationalist: Ottomanism and Arabism in the Life and Thought of Sati' al-Husri* (Princeton, 1971), pp. 61–5.
69. Goode, *Negotiating*, p. 216; Bernhardsson, *Reclaiming*, p. 202.
70. Goode, *Negotiating*, p. 216; Bernhardsson, *Reclaiming*, p. 202.
71. Ibid., pp. 120–1.
72. GB letter to her father, 12 December 1921, Gertrude Bell Archive.
73. Bell seems to have found the division of the finds at Ur particularly challenging, as related in her letters to her parents. See GB letter to her father, 1 March 1923; GB letter to her father, 6 March 1924; GB letter to her father, 4 March 1925, Gertrude Bell Archive.
74. Bernhardsson, *Reclaiming*, p. 153. See especially Bell's letters to her parents in 1926, in which she admits to her lack of knowledge in arranging a museum – GB letter to her father, 24 February 1926; GB letter to her mother, 23 March 1926; GB letter to her mother, 7 July 1926 – and that her museum work would include many mistakes: GB letter to her mother, 6 April 1926, Gertrude Bell Archive.
75. Rory Stewart, 'The queen of the quagmire', *The New York Review of Books* (25 October 2007).
76. Ibid.
77. GB letter to her mother, 5 September 1920, Gertrude Bell Archive.
78. GB letter to her family, 23 August 1920, Gertrude Bell Archive.
79. GB letter to her family, 27 April 1909, Gertrude Bell Archive.

BIBLIOGRAPHY

Primary Sources/Documents

Gertrude Bell Archive, Robinson Library, Special Collections, Newcastle University (Newcastle upon Tyne, United Kingdom):

Letters from Gertrude Bell to members of her family.
Diary entries.
Photographs (administered by the School of History, Classics and Archaeology, Newcastle University).
Miscellaneous Items from the Gertrude Bell Archive:
> Miscellaneous Item 4: Lecture by Lady Elsa Richmond entitled 'Memories of Gertrude'.
> Miscellaneous Item 13: Letters to Gertrude Bell from Walter Andrae, Marcel Dieulafoy, Ernst Herzfeld, Max Van Berchem and Esther Van Deman.
> Miscellaneous Item 20: Chapter by Bell entitled 'Romance', from an unfinished manuscript; Essay by Bell, 'The fealty of the tribes, a chapter in the history of Iraq'.
> Miscellaneous, Item 41: Letter from Gertrude Bell to Ernst Herzfeld.

Papers of Gertrude Margaret Lowthian Bell, Royal Geographical Society (London): Field notebooks, GLB 9, 11, 14 and 15.

Publications

'Activities of the Institute of Archaeological Sciences and of the Centre for the Restoration of Monuments in Baghdad: Ctesiphon', *Centro Ricerche Archeologiche e Scavi di Torino Projects* (Torino, 2006). Available at www.centroscavitorino.it/en/progetti/iraq/istituti-ctesifonte.html (accessed 29 July 2015).
Agence France-Presse, 'Iraq to restore ancient Arch of Ctesiphon to woo back tourists', *The Raw Story*, 30 May 2013. Available at www.rawstory.com/rs/2013/05/30/iraq-to-restore-ancient-arch-of-ctesiphon-to-woo-back-tourists (accessed 29 July 2015).
Ainsworth, W.F., *A Personal Narrative of the Euphrates Expedition*, 2 vols (London, 1888).

Akkermans, Peter and Glenn Schwartz, *The Archaeology of Syria* (Cambridge, 2003).

Anderson, Scott, *Lawrence in Arabia* (Toronto, 2013).

Andrae, E. Walter, *Hatra nach Aufnahmen von Mitgliedern der Assur Expedition der Deutschen Orient-Gesellschaft*, 2 vols (Leipzig, 1908 and 1912).

—— *Die archaischen Ischtar-Tempel in Assur* (Leipzig, 1922).

—— *Die jüngeren Ischtar-Tempel in Assur* (Leipzig, 1935).

—— *Das wiedererstandene Assur* (Leipzig, 1938). Revised edition with additional notes by B. Hrouda (Munich, 1977).

Andrae, E. Walter and R.M. Boehmer, *Bilder eines Ausgräbers. Die Orientbilder von Walter Andrae 1898–1919/Sketches by an Excavator*. Second enlarged edition, English translation by Jane Moon (Berlin, 1992).

Andrae, E. Walter and H. Lenzen, *Die Partherstadt Assur* (Leipzig, 1933).

Anonymous, Review of Gertrude L. Bell, 'The Desert and the Sown', *The Spectator* (16 February 1907), p. 17.

—— Review of Gertrude L. Bell, 'Palace and Mosque at Ukhaidir. A Study in Early Mohammadan Architecture', *Journal of Roman Studies* 4 (1914), pp. 113–14.

—— Review of Gertrude L. Bell, 'The Desert and the Sown', *The Academy* (2 March 1907), pp. 210–11.

—— Review of Gertrude L. Bell, 'Palace and Mosque at Ukhaidir. A Study in Early Mohammadan Architecture', *The Athenaeum* (30 May 1914), pp. 767–8.

Antiquities Law (Iraq) (Baghdad, 1924).

Ashby, Thomas, *The Aqueducts of Ancient Rome* (Oxford, 1935).

Asher-Greve, Julia M., 'Gertrude L. Bell (1868–1926)', in Getzel M. Cohen and Martha Sharp Joukowsky (eds), *Breaking Ground: Pioneering Women Archaeologists* (Ann Arbor, 2004), pp. 142–97.

Baird, Jennifer A., 'Photographing Dura-Europos, 1928–1937: An archaeology of the archive', *American Journal of Archaeology* 115 (2011), pp. 427–46.

Ball, Warwick, *Rome in the East: The Transformation of an Empire* (London, 2000).

Bär, Jürgen, *Die älteren Ištar-Tempel in Assur. Stratigraphie, Architektur und Funde eines altorientalischen Heiligtums von der zweiten Hälfte des 3. Jahrtausends bis zur Mittes des 2. Jahrtausends v. Chr.* (Saarbrücken, 2003).

—— 'Sumerians, Gutians and Hurrians at Ashur? A re-examination of Ishtar temples G and F', *Iraq* 65 (2003), pp. 143–60.

—— 'Walter Andrae – Ein Wegbereiter der modernen Archäologie', in J. Marzahn and B. Salje (eds), *Wiedererstehendes Assur. 100 Jahre deutsche Ausgrabungen in Assyrien* (Mainz am Rhein, 2003), pp. 45–52.

Barker, Andrew D. 'Ptolemy (Claudius Ptolemaeus)', in Simon Hornblower and Antony Spawforth (eds), *The Oxford Classical Dictionary*, 3rd revised edition, online version (Oxford, 2005). Available at www.oxfordreference.com.ezproxy.library.ubc. ca/view/10.1093/acref/9780198606413.001.0001/acref-9780198606413-e-5426? rskey=0VLpTP&result=5438 (accessed 29 July 2015).

Basmachi, Faraj, *Treasures of the Iraq Museum* (Baghdad, 1975–6).

Becker, Udo, 'Überlegungen zur Anlage von Hiraqla bei Raqqa', in Verena Daiber and Andrea Becker (eds), *Raqqa 3: Baudenkmäler und Paläste I* (Mainz am Rhein, 2004), pp. 149–56.

Bell, Gertrude L., *Safar Nameh: Persian Pictures* (London, 1894).

—— *Poems from the Divan of Hafiz* (London, 1897).

—— Review of B. Schulz and J. Strzygowski, 'Mschatta', in *Revue archéologique* 5 (1905), pp. 431–2.

────── Review of Karl Holzmann, 'Binbirklisse: Archäologische Skizzen aus Anatolien. Ein Beitrag zur Kunstgeschichte des Christlichen Kirchenbaues', *Revue archéologique* 7 (1906), pp. 219–20.

────── 'Notes on a journey through Cilicia and Lycaonia', *Revue archéologique* 7 (1906), pp. 1–29, 219–20; 385–414; 8 (1906), pp. 7–36, 225–52, 390–401; 9 (1907), pp. 18–30.

────── *The Desert and the Sown* (London, 1907). Reprint, with a new introduction by Rosemary O'Brien (New York, 2001).

────── 'The churches and monasteries of the Tur Abdin', in Max van Berchem and Josef Stryzgowski, *Amida. Matériaux pour l'épigraphie et l'histoire musulmanes du DiyarBekr par Max van Berchem. Beiträge zur Kunstgeschichte des Mittelalters von Nordmesopotamien, Hellas und dem Abendlande von Josef Strzygowski* (Heidelberg, 1910), pp. 224–62.

────── 'The east bank of the Euphrates from Tel Ahmar to Hit', *The Geographical Journal* 36 (1910), pp. 513–37.

────── 'The first capital of Assyria', *The Times*, 23 August 1910.

────── 'The vaulting system of Ukhaidir', *Journal of Hellenic Studies* 30 (1910), pp. 69–81.

────── *Amurath to Amurath* (London, 1911).

────── 'Churches and monasteries of the Tur 'Abdin and neighbouring districts', *Zeitschrift für Geschichte der Architektur* 9 (1913), pp. 61–112.

────── *Palace and Mosque at Ukhaidir: A Study in Early Mohammadan Architecture* (Oxford, 1914).

────── 'The safeguarding of antiquities in the Iraq', BLIO, L/P&S/10/689, Memorandum #85, 22 October 1918.

Bell, Gertrude L. and M. Mundell Mango, *The churches and monasteries of the Tur 'Abdin* (London, 1982).

Bell, Lady (Florence) (ed.), *The Letters of Gertrude Bell*, 2 vols (London, 1927).

Bennison, Amira K., *The Great Caliphs: The Golden Age of the 'Abbasid Empire* (London, 2009).

Berchem, Max van and Josef Strzygowski, *Amida. Matériaux pour l'épigraphie et l'histoire musulmanes du Diyar-bekr, par Max van Berchem. Beiträge zur Kunstgeschichte des Mittelalters von Nordmesopotamien, Hellas und dem Abendlande, von Josef Strzygowski* (Heidelberg, 1910).

Bernhardsson, Magnus T., *Reclaiming a Plundered Past: Archaeology and Nation Building in Modern Iraq* (Austin, 2005).

Bier, Lionel, 'Sasanian Palaces in Perspective', *Archaeology* 35 (1982), pp. 29–36.

────── *Sarvistan. A Study in Early Iranian Architecture* (University Park and London, 1986).

────── 'The Sasanian palaces and their influence in early Islam', *Ars Orientalis* 23 (1993), pp. 57–66.

Bloom, Jonathan, 'Introduction', in Jonathan M. Bloom (ed.), *Early Islamic Art and Architecture* (Aldershot, 2002).

Bohrer, Frederick N., *Orientalism and Visual Culture: Imagining Mesopotamia in Nineteenth-Century Europe* (Cambridge, 2003).

Borchhardt, Jürgen, 'Georg(e) Niemann', in *Archäologenbildnisse: Porträts und Kurzbiographien von Klassischen Archäologen deutscher Sprache* (Mainz, 1988), p. 80.

Bosch, G.J., J. Carswell and G. Petherbridge (eds), *Islamic Bindings and Bookmaking: A Catalogue of an Exhibition in the Oriental Institute Museum, University of Chicago, May 18–August 18, 1981* (Chicago, 1981).

Bosworth, C. Edmund, 'Lakhmids', *Encyclopaedia Iranica* (online edition, 2012). Available at www.iranicaonline.org/articles/lakhmids (accessed 29 July 2015).

Brown, Malcolm (ed.), *T.E. Lawrence: The Selected Letters* (New York, 1988).

Brünnow, Rudoph-Ernest and Alfred von Domaszewski, *Die Provincia Arabia*, 3 vols (Strassburg, 1904–9).

Bryce, Trevor, *The World of the Neo-Hittite Kingdoms* (Oxford, 2012).

Bunnens, Guy, *Tell Ahmar: 1988 Season* (Leuven, 1990).

—— *A New Luwian Stele and the Cult of the Storm-God at Til Barsib-Masuwari* (Louvain, 2006).

—— 'Assyrian empire building and Aramization of culture as seen from Tell Ahmar/Til Barsib', *Syria* 86 (2009), pp. 67–82.

—— 'Looking for Luwians, Aramaeans and Assyrians in the Tell Ahmar stratigraphy', in S. Mazzoni and S. Soldi (eds), *Syrian Archaeology in Perspective: Celebrating 20 Years of Excavations at Tell Afis* (Pisa, 2013), pp. 177–97.

—— 'A third-millennium temple at Tell Ahmar (Syria)', paper delivered at the 9th International Congress on the Archaeology of the Ancient Near East, Basel, 12 June 2014.

Burgoyne, Elizabeth, *Gertrude Bell: From Her Personal Papers, 1889–1914* (London, 1958).

—— *Gertrude Bell: From Her Personal Papers, 1914–1926* (London, 1961).

Burns, Ross, *Monuments of Syria: An Historical Guide* (London, 1992).

Butler, Howard Crosby, *Architecture and Other Arts* (New York, 1903).

'Butler: Catalogue of Photographs', *Research Photographs of Princeton University* (Princeton, 2015). Available at www.princeton.edu/researchphotographs/archaeological-archives/butler/ (accessed 29 July 2015).

Caskel, Werner, 'Al-Uhaidir', *Der Islam* 39 (1964), pp. 28–37.

Chadha, Ashish, 'Visions of discipline: Sir Mortimer Wheeler and the archaeological method in India', *Journal of Social Archaeology* 2 (2003), pp. 378–401.

Chesney, F.R., *The Expedition for the Survey of the Rivers Euphrates and Tigris, carried on by order of the British government, in the years 1835, 1836, and 1837; preceded by geographical and historical notices of the regions situated between the rivers Nile and Indus*, 4 vols (London, 1850).

Chmelnizkij, S., 'Überlegungen zum Planungskonzept und zur Rekonstruktion von Hiraqla', in Verena Daiber and Andrea Becker (eds), *Raqqa 3: Baudenkmäler und Paläste I* (Mainz am Rhein, 2004), pp. 143–8.

Choisy, F.A., *L'Art de bâtir chez les Byzantins* (Paris, 1883).

Clark, David L.C., 'Viewing the liturgy: A space syntax study of changing visibility and accessibility in the development of the Byzantine church in Jordan', *World Archaeology* 39 (2007), pp. 84–104.

Clauss, Pascale, 'Les tours funéraires du djebel Baghoûz dans l'histoire de la tour funéraire syrienne', *Syria* 49 (2002), pp. 155–94.

Cleveland, W.L., *The Making of an Arab Nationalist: Ottomanism and Arabism in the Life and Thought of Sati' al-Husri* (Princeton, 1971).

Cobb, E., T. Van Loan and V. Fleck, 'Representing vestiges of the past: Evaluating John Henry Haynes' contribution to nascent archaeological photography in the nineteenth-century Ottoman Empire', paper delivered at the Annual Meeting of the American Schools of Oriental Research, Atlanta, 2010.

Colledge, Malcolm, *Parthian Art* (Ithaca, NY, 1977).

Cooper, Lisa, *Early Urbanism on the Syrian Euphrates* (London, 2006).

——— 'Archaeology and acrimony: Gertrude Bell, Ernst Herzfeld and the study of premodern Mesopotamia', *Iraq* 75 (2013), pp. 143–69.

Coqueugniot, É., 'Dja'de el Mughara (moyen-euphrate), un village néolithique dans son environnement naturel à la veille de la domestication', in M. Fortin and O. Aurenche (eds), *Espace naturel, espace habité en Syrie du Nord* (Toronto, 1998), pp. 109–14.

Creswell, K.A.C., Review of Gertrude L. Bell, 'Palace and Mosque at Ukhaidir. A Study in Early Mohammadan Architecture', *Journal of the Royal Asiatic Society of Great Britain and Ireland* (July 1914), pp. 784–8.

——— Review of Gertrude L. Bell, 'Palace and Mosque at Ukhaidir. A Study in Early Mohammadan Architecture', *The Burlington Magazine for Connoisseurs* 26 (October 1914), pp. 35–6.

——— *Short Account of Early Muslim Architecture* (Harmondsworth, 1958). Revised edition, supplemented by James W. Allan (Aldershot, 1989).

——— *Early Muslim Architecture. Vol. 1: Umayyads, A.D. 622–750* (Oxford, 1969). Reprint (New York, 1979).

——— *Early Muslim Architecture. Vol. 2: Early 'Abbāsids, Umayyads of Cordova, Aghlabids, Tūlūnids, and Samānids, A.D. 751–905* (Oxford, 1940). Reprint (New York, 1979).

Crow, Jim, 'Gertrude Bell – Fotografin und Archäologin', in Charlotte Trümpler (ed.), *Das Grosse Spiel. Archäologie und Politik zur Zeit des Kolonialismus (1860–1940)* (Essen, 2008), pp. 597–607.

Crowfoot, John Winter, 'I. Binbirkilise (Madenschehr)', in J. Strzygowski, *Kleinasien. Ein Neuland der Kunstgeschichte* (Leipzig, 1903), pp. 1–41.

Curtis, John E. and J.E. Reade (eds), *Art and Empire: Treasures from Assyria in the British Museum* (New York, 1995).

Czichon, R.M. and P. Werner, *Tell Munbāqa – Ekalte – I: Die Bronzezeitlichen Kleinfunde* (Saarbrücken, 1998).

Dalley, Stephanie, 'Nineveh, Babylon and the Hanging Gardens: Cuneiform and Classical sources reconciled', *Iraq* 56 (1994), pp. 45–58.

Danti, Michael, S. Branting, T. Paulette and A. Cuneo, 'ASOR Cultural Heritage Initiatives: Report on the destruction of the Northwest Palace at Nimrud', Available at http://www.asor-syrianheritage.org/wp-content/uploads/2015/05/ASOR_CHI_Nimrud_Report.pdf (accessed 30 July 2015).

Danti, Michael D., C. Ali, T. Paulette, A. Cuneo, K. Franklin, L-A. Barnes Gordon and D. Elitzer, 'ASOR Cultural Heritage Initiatives (CHI): Planning for safeguarding heritage sites in Syria and Iraq, weekly report 35 – April 6, 2015'. Available at www.asor-syrianheritage.org/wp-content/uploads/2015/04/ASOR_CHI_Weekly_Report_35r.pdf (accessed 30 July 2015).

——— 'ASOR Cultural Heritage Initiatives (CHI): Planning for safeguarding heritage sites in Syria and Iraq, weekly report 36 – April 13, 2015'. Available at www.asor-syrianheritage.org/wp-content/uploads/2015/04/ASOR_CHI_Weekly_Report_36r.pdf (accessed 30 July 2015).

Danti, Michael D., Jesse Casana, T. Paulette, K. Franklin and C. Ali, 'ASOR Cultural Heritage Initiatives (CHI): Planning for safeguarding heritage sites in Syria and Iraq, weekly report 25–January 26, 2015'. Available at www.asor-syrianheritage.org/wp-content/uploads/2015/03/ASOR_CHI_Weekly_Report_25r.pdf (accessed 30 July 2015).

de Bellefonds, Pascale Linant, 'Vogüé, (Charles-Jean-) Melchior de', *Grove Art Online*. *Oxford Art Online* (Oxford, 2007–15). Available at www.oxfordartonline.com. ezproxy.library.ubc.ca/subscriber/article/grove/art/T090069 (accessed 29 July 2015).

de Beylié, L., 'L'architecture des Abbassides au IXe siècle. Voyage archéologique à Samarra dans le basin du Tigre', *Revue archéologique* 10 (1907), pp. 1–18.

—— *Prome et Samarra* (Paris, 1907).

de Morgan, Jacques, *Mission scientifique en Perse*, vol. IV (Paris, 1896).

Dear, Philip J., 'Ukhaidir and its lessons', *The British Architect* (11 June 1915), pp. 292–9.

Dębrowa, Edward, 'The Arsacid Empire', in Touraj Daryaee (ed.), *The Oxford Handbook of Iranian History* (Oxford, 2012), pp. 164–86.

Delbrück, Richard, *Hellenistiche Bauten in Latium* (Strassburg, 1907).

Dhorme, Édouard, 'René Dussaud (1868–1958)', *Revue de l'histoire des religions* 153 (1985), pp. 149–53.

Dieulafoy, Marcel, *L'Art antique de la Perse. Partie 4: Les monuments voûté de l'époque achéménide* (Paris, 1885).

—— 'Découverte par M. Massignon d'un palais fortifié près de Kerbela en Mésopotamie', *Comptes-rendus des séances de l'Academie des Inscriptions et Belles-Lettres* 52 (1908), pp. 451–2.

—— Review of Gertrude L. Bell, 'Palace and Mosque at Ukhaidir. A Study in Early Mohammadan Architecture', *Journal des savants* 12 (September–November 1914), pp. 385–98.

Dirven, Linda, 'Author of "De Dea Syria" and his cultural heritage', *Numen* 44 (1997), pp. 153–79.

Drerup, Heinrich, 'Richard Delbrueck', in *Archäologenbildnisse: Porträts und Kurzbiographien von Klassischen Archäologen deutscher Sprache* (Mainz, 1988), pp. 188–9.

Dusinberre, Elspeth R.M., 'Herzfeld in Persepolis', in A.C. Gunther and S.R. Hauser (eds), *Ernst Herzfeld and the Development of Near Eastern Studies, 1900–1950* (Leiden, 2004), pp. 137–80.

Dyson, Stephen L., *Eugénie Sellers Strong* (London, 2004).

Elsner, Jás, 'The birth of Late Antiquity: Riegl and Stzygowski in 1901', *Art History* 25 (2002), pp. 375–6.

Ettinghausen, Richard and Oleg Grabar, *Islamic Art and Architecture, 650–1250* (New Haven, 2001).

Fagan, Brian, *Return to Babylon: Travelers, Archaeologists, and Monuments in Mesopotamia*, revised edition (Boulder, 2007).

Finkel, Irving L. and Michael J. Seymour (eds), *Babylon: Myth and Reality* (London, 2008).

Finster, Barbara and Jürgen Schmidt, 'Sasanidische und frühislamische Ruinen im Iraq', *Baghdader Mitteilungen* 8 (1976), pp. 3–169, pls. 1–79.

—— 'The origin of "desert castles": Qasr Bani Muqatil, near Karbala, Iraq', *Antiquity* 79 (2005), pp. 339–49.

Fisher, Kevin, 'Placing social interaction: An integrative approach to analyzing past built environments', *Journal of Anthropological Archaeology* 28 (2009), pp. 439–57.

Fletcher, C.R.L., 'David George Hogarth, President R.G.S. 1926–27', *The Geographical Journal* 71 (1928), pp. 321–44.

Frahm, Eckart, 'Images of Assyria in nineteenth- and twentieth-century western scholarship', in S. Holloway (ed.), *Orientalism, Assyriology and the Bible* (Sheffield, 2006), pp. 74–94.

Gadd, C.J., *The Stones of Assyria* (London, 1936).

Gawlikowski, Michal, 'Thapsacus and Zeugma: The crossing of the Euphrates in antiquity', *Iraq* 58 (1996), pp. 123–33.

Geffcken, Katherine A., 'Esther van Deman and Gertrude Bell (1910)', in K. Einaudi (ed.), *Esther B. Van Deman: Images from the Archive of an American Archaeologist in Italy at the Turn of the Century* (Rome, 1991), pp. 24–7.

Gill, David, 'Hogarth, David George (1862–1927)', *Oxford Dictionary of National Biography* (Oxford, 2004). Available at www.oxforddnb.com.ezproxy.library.ubc. ca/view/article/33924 (accessed 29 July 2015).

Gilliot, Claude, 'Yaqut', in J.W. Meri (ed.), *Medieval Islamic Civilisation: An Encyclopedia* (London, 2006), pp. 869–70.

Gogräfe, Rüdiger, 'Die Grabtürme von Sirrin (Osroëne)', *Damaszener Mitteilungen* 8 (1995), pp. 165–201.

Goode, James F., *Negotiating for the Past: Archaeology, Nationalism, and Diplomacy in the Middle East, 1919–1941* (Austin, 2007).

Gossman, Lionel, *The Passion of Max von Oppenheim: Archaeology and Intrigue in the Middle East from Wilhelm II to Hitler* (Cambridge, 2013).

Grabar, Oleg, 'The date and meaning of Mshatta', *Dumbarton Oaks Papers* 41 (1987), pp. 243–7.

――― 'Ayvān', *Encyclopedia Iranica* III/2 (1987), pp. 153–5; an updated version is available online at www.iranicaonline.org/articles/ayvan-palace (accessed 29 July 2015).

Greene, Kevin and Tom Moore, *Archaeology: An Introduction*, 5th edition (London, 2010).

Grigor, Talinn, 'Orient oder Rom? Qajar "Aryan" architecture and Strzygowski's art history', *Art Bulletin* 89 (2007), pp. 562–90.

Gunther, Ann C. and Stefan R. Hauser, 'Ernst Herzfeld and Near Eastern studies, 1900–1950', in A.C. Gunther and S.R. Hauser (eds), *Ernst Herzfeld and the Development of Near Eastern Studies, 1900–1950* (Leiden, 2004), pp. 3–44.

Hagen, Norbert, Mustafa al-Hassoun and Michael Meinecke, 'Die Grosse Moschee von ar-Rāfiqa', in Verena Daiber and Andrea Becker (eds), *Raqqa 3: Baudenkmäler und Paläste I* (Mainz am Rhein, 2004), pp. 25–40.

Harper, Prudence O., E. Klengel-Brandt, J. Aruz and K. Benzel (eds), *Assyrian Origins: Discoveries at Ashur on the Tigris: Antiquities in the Vorderasiatisches Museum, Berlin* (New York, 1995).

Hauser, Stefan R., 'The Arsacid (Parthian) Empire', in D.T. Potts (ed.), *A Companion to the Archaeology of the Ancient Near East* (Chichester, 2012), pp. 1001–20.

Haverfield, F., J.L. Strachan Davidson, E.R. Bevan, E.M. Walker, D.G. Hogarth and Lord Cromer, 'Ancient imperialism', *The Classical Review* 24 (1910), pp. 105–16.

Hawkins, David, 'Karkamiš', *Reallexikon der Assyriologie und Vorderasiastischen Archäologie* (Berlin, 1976–80), pp. 426–46.

――― 'Carchemish', in E.M. Meyers (ed.), *The Oxford Encyclopedia of Archaeology in the Near East* (New York, 1997), pp. 423–4.

――― *Corpus of Luwian Inscriptions. Volume 1: Inscriptions of the Iron Age* (Berlin, 2000).

Heidemann, Stefan, 'Die Geschichte von ar-Raqqa/ar-Rāfiqa', in Stefan Heidemann and Andrea Becker (eds), *Raqqa II. Die Islamische Stadt* (Mainz am Rhein, 2003), pp. 9–56.

――― 'The citadel of al-Raqqa and fortifications in the Middle Euphrates area', in H. Kennedy (ed.), *Muslim Military Architecture in Greater Syria* (Leiden, 2006), pp. 122–50.

Herzfeld, Ernst, *Samarra. Aufhahmen und Untersuchungen zur islamischen Archaeologie* (Berlin, 1907).
—— 'Die Genesis der islamischen Kunst und das Mschatta-Problem', *Der Islam* 1 (1910), pp. 27–63, 104–44.
—— *Erster vorläufiger Bericht über die Ausgrabungen von Samarra* (Berlin, 1912).
—— 'Damascus: Studies in architecture: II', *Ars Islamica* 10 (1943), pp. 13–70.
Hill, Adam, *Stepping Stones in the Stream of Ignorance: D.G. Hogarth as Orientalist and Agent of Empire* (MA thesis, Southern Illinois University Edwardsville, 2008).
Hillenbrand, Robert, 'Islamic art at the crossroads: East versus West at Mshatta', in A. Daneshvari (ed.), *Essays on Islamic Art and Architecture: In Honor of Katharina Otto-Dorn* (Malibu, 1981), pp. 63–86.
—— 'Eastern Islamic influences in Syria: Raqqa and Qal'at Ja'bar in the later 12th century', in Julian Raby (ed.), *The Art of Syria and the Jazīra* (Oxford, 1985), pp. 27–36.
—— 'Creswell and contemporary Central European scholarship', *Muqarnas* 8 (1991), pp. 23–35.
—— *Islamic Architecture* (New York, 1994).
Hingley, Richard, *Roman Officers and English Gentlemen: The Imperial Origins of Roman Archaeology* (London, 2000).
Hodgson, Barbara, *Dreaming of the East: Western Women and the Exotic Allure of the Orient* (Vancouver, 2005).
Hogarth, David G., *Devia Cypria: Notes of an Archaeological Journey in Cyprus in 1888* (London, 1889).
—— *A Wandering Scholar in the Levant* (New York, 1896).
—— *The Nearer East* (New York, 1902).
—— 'Geographical conditions affecting populations in the east Mediterranean lands', *The Geographical Journal* 27 (1906), pp. 465–77.
—— 'Problems in exploration: I. Western Asia', *The Geographical Journal* 32 (1908), p. 549–63.
—— 'Carchemish and its neighbourhood', *University of Liverpool Annals of Archaeology and Anthropology* 2 (1909), pp. 165–84.
—— *Accidents of an Antiquary's Life* (London, 1910).
—— *Carchemish. Report on the Excavations at Jerablus on Behalf of the British Museum I: Introductory* (London, 1914).
—— 'Obituary: Gertrude Lowthian Bell', *The Geographical Journal* 68 (1926), p. 363–8.
—— *The Life of Charles M. Doughty* (London, 1928).
Howell, Georgina, *Gertrude Bell: Queen of the Desert, Shaper of Nations* (New York, 2006).
Huff, Dietrich, 'Fīrūzābād', *Encyclopedia Iranica* IX/6 (1999), pp. 633–6; an updated version is available online at www.iranicaonline.org/articles/firuzabad (accessed 29 July 2015).
Huntington, Ellsworth, Review of Gertrude L. Bell, 'Amurath to Amurath', *Bulletin of the American Geographical Society* 44 (1912), pp. 134–5.
Jackson, Mark P.C., 'A critical examination of Gertrude Bell's contribution to archaeological research in central Asia Minor', in Charles Tripp and Paul Collins (eds), *Gertrude Bell and Iraq – A Life and Legacy Conference Publication* (London, in press).
James, Lawrence, *The Golden Warrior: The Life and Legend of Lawrence of Arabia* (London, 1990).

Jones, Christopher, 'Assessing the damage at the Mosul Museum, Part 1: The Assyrian artifacts' (27 February 2015). Available at https://gatesofnineveh.wordpress. com/2015/02/27/assessing-the-damage-at-the-mosul-museum-part-1-the-assyr-ian-artifacts/ (accessed 30 July 2015).

—— 'Assessing the damage at Hatra' (7 April 2015). Available at https:// gatesofnineveh.wordpress.com/2015/04/07/assessing-the-damage-at-hatra/ (accessed 30 July 2015).

Kawami, Trudy S., 'Parthian brick vaults in Mesopotamia, their antecedents and descendants', *Journal of the Ancient Near Eastern Society* 14 (1982), pp. 61–7.

Keall, Edward J., 'Some thoughts on the early *Eyvan*', in Dickran K. Kouymijian (ed.), *Near Eastern Numismatics, Iconography, Epigraphy and History: Studies in Honor of George C. Miles* (Beirut, 1974), p. 123–30.

—— 'Architecture ii. Parthian Period', *Encyclopedia Iranica* II/3 (1986), pp. 327–9; an updated version is available online at http://www.iranicaonline.org/articles/ architecture-ii (accessed 29 July 2015).

—— 'Ayvān-e Kesrā', *Encyclopaedia Iranica* III/2 (1987), pp. 155–9; an updated version is available online at www.iranicaonline.org/articles/ayvan-e-kesra-palace-of-kosrow-at-ctesiphon (accessed 29 July 2015).

—— 'The arts of the Parthians', in R.W. Ferrier (ed.), *The Arts of Persia* (New Haven, 1989), pp. 48–59.

—— 'Parthians', in Eric Meyers (ed.), *The Oxford Encyclopedia of Archaeology in the Ancient Near East* (Oxford, 1995), pp. 249–50.

Kennedy, Hugh, *The Court of the Caliphs: The Rise and Fall of Islam's Greatest Dynasty* (London, 2004).

Kenner, Hedwig, 'Emil Reisch', in *Archäologenbildnisse: Porträts und Kurzbiographien von Klassischen Archäologen deutscher Sprache* (Mainz, 1988), pp. 150–1.

Kepinski, Christine, Olivier Lecomte and Aline Tenu, 'Studia Euphratica, introduction', in C. Kepinski, O. Lecomte and A. Tenu (eds), *Studia Euphratica: Le moyen Euphrate iraquien révélé par les fouilles preventives de Haditha* (Paris, 2006), pp. 9–19.

Kiepert, Richard, 'Syrien und Mesopotamien zur Darstellung der Reise des D. Max Freiherrn von Oppenheim von Mittelmeere zu Persischen Golf, 1893, Westliches Blatt und Östliches Blatt', in M. von Oppenheim, *Von Mittelmeer zum Persischen Golf* (Berlin, 1899–1900).

Koldewey, Robert, *Die wiedererstehende Babylon: die bisherigen Ergebnisse der deutschen Ausgrabungen* (Leipzig, 1913).

—— *The Excavations at Babylon* (London, 1914).

Korn, Lorenz, 'Das Baghdad-Tor (Südosttor der Halbrundstadt)', in Verena Daiber and Andrea Becker (eds), *Raqqa 3: Baudenkmäler und Paläste I* (Mainz am Rhein, 2004), pp. 11–18.

—— 'Die Grosse Moschee von ar-Raqqa', in Verena Daiber and Andrea Becker (eds), *Raqqa 3: Baudenkmäler und Paläste I* (Mainz am Rhein, 2004), pp. 19–23.

Kröger, Jens, 'Ctesiphon', *Encyclopaedia Iranica* VI/4 (1993), pp. 446–8; an updated version is available online at http://www.iranicaonline.org/articles/ctesiphon (accessed 29 July 2015).

Kwarteng, Kwasi, *Ghosts of Empire: Britain's Legacies in the Modern World* (London, 2011).

Lamprichs, R.W., 'Aššur,' in Eric Meyers (ed.), *The Oxford Encyclopedia of Archaeology in the Ancient Near East* (Oxford, 1995), pp. 225–8.

Lancaster, Lynne, 'Roman engineering and construction', in John P. Oleson (ed.), *The Oxford Handbook of Engineering and Technology in the Classical World* (Oxford, 2008), pp. 256–84.

Lawrence, A.W. (ed.), *T.E. Lawrence by His Friends* (London, 1937).

Lawrence, T.E., *Seven Pillars of Wisdom* (New York, 1991).

Layard, Austen Henry, *Nineveh and Its Remains*, 2 vols (London, 1849).

―――― *Discoveries in the Ruins of Nineveh and Babylon* (London, 1853).

Leick, Gwendolyn, *A Dictionary of Ancient Near Eastern Architecture* (London, 1988).

Leisten, Thomas, *Excavation of Samarra. Volume I: Architecture. Final Report of the First Campaign 1910–1912* (Mainz am Rhein, 2003).

―――― 'Concerning the development of the Hira-style revisited', in Ann C. Gunther and Stefan R. Hauser (eds), *Ernst Herzfeld and the Development of Near Eastern Studies, 1900–1950* (Leiden, 2004), pp. 371–84.

Lloyd, Seton, *Foundations in the Dust: The Story of Mesopotamian Exploration*, revised and enlarged edition (London, 1980).

Lukitz, Liora, *A Quest in the Middle East: Gertrude Bell and the Making of Modern Iraq* (London, 2008).

Machule, D., '1969–1994: Ekalte (Tall Munbāqa). Eine bronzezeitliche Stadt in Syrien', in G. Wilhelm (ed.), *Zwischen Tigris und Nil* (Mainz am Rhein, 1998), pp. 115–25.

MacMillan, Margaret, *Paris 1919* (New York, 2001).

Madhloom, T., 'Mada'in (Ctesiphon), 1970–71', *Sumer* 27 (1971), in Arabic, pp. 129–46.

―――― 'Al-Mada'in', *Sumer* 31 (1975), in Arabic, pp. 165–70.

―――― 'Restorations in al-Mada'in, 1975–77', *Sumer* 34 (1978), in Arabic, pp. 119–29.

Mallowan, M.E.L., *Nimrud and Its Remains*, 2 vols (London, 1966).

Marchand, Suzanne, 'The rhetoric of artifacts and the decline of classical humanism: The case of Josef Strzygowski', *History and Theory* 33 (1994), pp. 106–30.

Marchetti, Nicolò, 'Karkemish on the Euphrates: Excavating a city's history', *Near Eastern Archaeology* 75 (2012), pp. 132–47.

Marquand, Allan, 'Strzygowski and his theory of early Christian art', *Harvard Theological Review* 3 (1910), pp. 361–2.

Marzahn, Joachim, *The Ishtar Gate* (Berlin, 1995).

―――― '1907–1911: Hatra. Feldarchäologie im Schnelldurchlauf', in G. Wilhelm (ed.), *Zwischen Tigris und Nil. 100 Jahre Ausgrabungen der Deutchen Orient-Gesellschaft in Vorderasien und Ägypten* (Mainz am Rhein, 1998), pp. 68–73.

―――― 'Robert Koldewey – Ein Lebensbild', in Ralf-B. Wartke (ed.), *Auf dem Weg nach Babylon. Robert Koldewey – Ein Archäologenleben* (Mainz, 2008), pp. 8–27.

Massignon, Louis, 'Les chateaux des princes de Hirah', *Gazette des beaux-arts* (April 1909), pp. 297–306.

―――― 'Note sur le château d'Al Okhaïder', *Comptes-rendus des séances de l'Académie des Inscriptions et Belles-Lettres* 53 (1909), pp. 202–12.

―――― *Mission en Mesopotamie* (Cairo, 1910).

Matthews, John F., 'Ammianus Marcellinus', In Simon Hornblower and Antony Spawforth (eds), *The Oxford Classical Dictionary*, 3rd revised edition, online version (Oxford, 2005). Available at www.oxfordreference.com.ezproxy.library. ubc.ca/view/10.1093/acref/9780198606413.001.0001/acref-9780198606413-e-361?rskey=Oqh5jT&result=363 (accessed 29 July 2015).

Maul, S.M., '1903–1914: Assur – Das Herz eines Weltreiches', in Gernot Wilhelm (ed.), *Zwischen Tigris und Nil: 100 Jahre Ausgrabungen der Deutschen Orient-Gesellschaft in Vorderasien und Ägypten* (Mainz am Rhein, 1998), pp. 47–65.

McCowan, E. and R.C. Haines, *Nippur I: Temple of Enlil, Scribal Quarter, and Soundings* (Chicago, 1967).

Melman, Billie, *Women's Orients: English Women and the Middle East, 1718–1918* (London, 1992).

Meyer, Jan-Waalke, *Gräber des 3. Jahrtausands. V. Chr. im syrischen Euphrattal. 3 Ausgrabungen in Šamseddin und Djerniye* (Saarbrücken, 1991).

Michell, G., *Architecture of the Islamic World* (London, 1978).

Miglus, Peter, *Das Wohngebiet von Assur. Stratigraphie und Architektur* (Berlin, 1996).

Milwright, Marcus, *An Introduction to Islamic Archaeology* (Edinburgh, 2010).

Money, R.I., 'The Hindiya Barrage, Mesopotamia', *The Geographical Journal* 50/3 (1917), pp. 217–22.

Moradi, Yusef, 'Imarat-e Khosrow in view of the first season of the archaeological excavations', in Hamid Fahimi and Karim Alizadeh (eds), *Nāmvarnāmeh: Papers in honour of Masoud Azarnoush* (Tehran, 2012), pp. 350–75.

Moritz, Bernhard, 'Ausflüge in der Arabia Petraea', in *Mélanges de la Faculté Orientale de Beyrouth* 3 (1908), pp. 387–436.

Morray, David, 'Ibn Jubayr, Abu'l-Husayn Muhammad B. Ahmad', in J.W. Meri (ed.), *Medieval Islamic Civilisation: An Encyclopedia* (London, 2006), pp. 358–9.

Musil, A., *Kusejr 'Amra* (Wien, 1907).

Northedge, Alistair and C-M. Bennett, *Studies on Roman and Islamic 'Amman: History, Site and Architecture* (Oxford, 1992).

—— 'The Islamic period in the Haditha dam area', in C. Kepinski, P. Lecomte and A. Tenu (eds), *Studia Euphratica. Le moyen Euphrate iraquien révélé par les fouilles preventives de Haditha* (Paris, 2006), pp. 397–415.

—— *The Historical Topography of Samarra* (London, 2007).

Oates, David, 'The excavations at Tell al-Rimah, 1964', *Iraq* 27 (1965), pp. 62–80.

—— 'The excavations at Tell al-Rimah, 1968', *Iraq* 32 (1970), pp. 1–26.

Oates, David and Joan Oates, *Nimrud – An Assyrian Imperial City Revealed* (London, 2001).

Oelmann, F., 'Hilani und Liwanhaus', *Bonner Jahrbücher* 127 (1922), pp. 189–236.

Olin, Margaret, 'Art history and ideology: Alois Riegl and Josef Strzygowski', in Penny S. Gold and Benjamin C. Sax (eds), *Cultural Visions: Essays in the History of Culture* (Amsterdam, 2000), pp. 151–70.

Olmstead, A.T., *History of Assyria* (New York, 1923).

Oppenheim, Max von, 'Griechische und lateinische Inschriften aus Syrien, Mesopotamien und Kleinasien', *Byzantinische Zeitschrift* 14 (1905), pp. 1–72.

—— *Der Tell Halaf und die verschleierte Göttin* (Berlin, 1908).

Ousterhout, Robert G., *John Henry Haynes: A Photographer and Archaeologist in the Ottoman Empire 1881–1900* (Hawick, 2011).

Owen, Roger, 'Lord Cromer and Gertrude Bell,' *History Today* 54 (2004), p. 37.

Papadopoulos, C. and G.P. Earle, 'Formal three-dimensional computational analysis of archaeological spaces', in E. Paliou, U. Lieberwirth and S. Polla (eds), *Spatial Analysis and Social Spaces: Interdisciplinary Approaches to the Interpretation of Historic and Prehistoric Built Environments* (Berlin, 2014), pp. 135–65.

Place, Victor, *Ninive et l'Assyrie*, vol. 1 (Paris, 1867).

Popham, Arthur E., *Bibliographie de Salomon Reinach* (Paris, 1936).

Preusser, Conrad, *Die Wohnhäuser in Assur* (Berlin, 1954).

Purcell, Nicholas, 'Itineraries', in Simon Hornblower and Antony Spawforth (eds), *The Oxford Classical Dictionary*, 3rd revised edition, online version (Oxford, 2005). Available at www.oxfordreference.com.ezproxy.library.ubc.ca/view/10.1093/acref/9780198606413.001.0001/acref-9780198606413-e-3362?rskey=OsMVw6&result=3375 (accessed 29 July 2015).

———— 'Peutinger Table', in Simon Hornblower and Antony Spawforth (eds), *The Oxford Classical Dictionary*, 3rd revised edition, online version (Oxford, 2005). Available at www.oxfordreference.com.ezproxy.library.ubc.ca/view/10.1093/acref/9780198606413.001.0001/acref-9780198606413-e-4911?rskey=AG7I6H&-result=4 (accessed 29 July 2015).

———— 'Strabo', in Simon Hornblower and Antony Spawforth (eds), *The Oxford Classical Dictionary*, 3rd revised edition, online version (Oxford, 2005). Available at www.oxfordreference.com.ezproxy.library.ubc.ca/view/10.1093/acref/9780198606413.001.0001/acref-9780198606413-e-6094?rskey=PcXfj8&result=6108 (accessed 29 July 2015).

Ramsay, William M., *The Historical Geography of Asia Minor* (London, 1890).

Ramsay, William M. and Gertrude L. Bell, *The Thousand and One Churches* (London, 1909). Reprint, with a new foreword by Robert G. Outsterhout and Mark P.C. Jackson (Philadelphia, 2008).

Reade, Julian, 'The early exploration of Assyria', in Ada Cohen and Steven E. Kangas (eds), *Assyrian Reliefs from the Palace of Ashurnasirpal II: A Cultural Biography* (Hanover, NH, 2010), pp. 86–106.

Reinach, Salomon, 'Gertrude Bell', *Revue archéologique* 24 (1926), pp. 265–7.

Renfrew, Colin and Paul Bahn, *Archaeology: Theories, Methods and Practice* (London, 1991).

Reuther, Oskar, *Ocheïdir. Nach Aufnahmen von Mitgliedern der Babylon Expedition der Deutschen Orient-Gesellschaft* (Leipzig, 1912).

———— 'The German excavations at Ctesiphon,' *Antiquity* 3 (1929), pp. 434–51.

———— 'Parthian architecture: A history', in Arthur E. Pope (ed.), *A Survey of Persian Art. Vol. 1: Pre-Achaemenid, Achaemenid, Parthian and Sasanian Periods* (London, 1938), pp. 411–44.

———— 'Sasanian art', in Arthur E. Pope (ed.), *A Survey of Persian Art. Vol. 1: Pre-Achaemenid, Achaemenid, Parthian and Sasanian Periods* (London, 1938), pp. 493–578.

Robinson, Chase (ed.), *A Medieval Islamic City Reconsidered: An Interdisciplinary Approach to Samarra* (Oxford, 2001).

Rodrigue, Aron, 'Totems, taboos, and Jews: Salomon Reinach and the politics of scholarship in fin-de-siècle France', *Jewish Social Studies* 10 (2004), pp. 1–19.

'Romantic orientalism: Overview', *The Norton Anthology of English Literature. Norton Topics Online* (2010–2015). Available at www.wwnorton.com/college/english/nael/romantic/topic_4 (accessed 29 July 2015).

Roobaert, A. and G. Bunnens, 'Excavations at Tell Ahmar-Til Barsib', in G. del Olmo Lete and J.-L. Montero Fenollós (eds), *Archaeology of the Upper Syrian Euphrates: The Tishrin Dam Area* (Barcelona, 1999), pp. 163–78.

Rowlands, M. 'The archaeology of colonialism', in K. Kristiansen and M. Rowlands (eds), *Social Transformations in Archaeology: Global and Local Perspectives* (London, 1998), pp. 327–33.

Sachau, Eduard, *Reise durch Syrien und Mesopotamien* (Leipzig, 1883).

Safar, Fu'ad and M.A. Mustafa, *Hatra: The City of the Sun God* [Arabic title *Al-Ḥaḍr, Madīnat al-shams*] (Baghdad, 1974).

Said, Edward, *Orientalism* (New York, 1978).

Salje, Beate, 'Robert Koldewey und das Vorderasiatische Museum Berlin', in Ralf-B. Wartke (ed.), *Auf dem Weg nach Babylon. Robert Koldewey – Ein Archäologenleben* (Mainz, 2008), pp. 125–43.

Sarre, Frederick and Ernst Herzfeld, *Iranische Felsreliefs* (Berlin, 1910).

———— *Archäologische Reise im Euphrat- und Tigris-Gebiet*, 4 vols (Berlin, 1911–20).

Satia, Priya, *Spies in Arabia: The Great War and the Cultural Foundations of Britain's Covert Empire in the Middle East* (Oxford, 2008).

Schaeffer, Claude, 'Salomon Reinach: Born 29 August 1859: Died 4 November, 1932', *Man* 33 (1933), pp. 51–2.

Schmidt, Jürgen, 'Qaṣr-i Šīrīn, Feuertempel oder Palast?', *Baghdad Mitteilungen 9* (1978), pp. 39–47.

Schmitt, Rüdiger, 'Hatra', *Encyclopedia Iranica* XII/1 (2003), pp. 58–61; an updated version is available online at http://www.iranicaonline.org/articles/hatra (accessed 29 July 2015).

———— 'Isidorus of Charax', in *Encyclopedia Iranica* XIV/2 (2007), pp. 125–7; an updated version is available online at http://www.iranicaonline.org/articles/ isidorus-of-charax (accessed 29 July 2015).

Schneider, Ute, 'Die Kartierung der Ruinenlandschaften. Späte Würdigung', in Charlotte Trümpler (ed.), *Das Grosse Spiel. Archäologie und Politik zur Zeit des Kolonialismus (1860–1940)* (Essen, 2008), pp. 40–7.

Schnell, Andréa Elizabeth, *Gertrude Bell: An Orientalist in Context* (MA thesis, McGill University, 2008).

Schulz, Bruno and Josef Strzygowski, 'Mschatta', *Jahrbuch der Königlichen Preuszischen Kunstsammlungen* 25 (1904), pp. 205–373.

Sconzo, Paola, 'Bronze Age pottery from the Carchemish region at the British Museum', *Palestine Exploration Quarterly* 145 (2013), pp. 334–8.

———— 'The grave of the court pit: A rediscovered Bronze Age tomb from Carchemish', *Palestine Exploration Quarterly* 146 (2014), pp. 3–16.

Segal, J.B., *Edessa, 'The Blessed City'* (Oxford, 1970).

Shahid, Irfan, *Byzantium and the Arabs in the Sixth Century. Vol. 1, Part 1: Political and Military History* (Washington, 1995).

Silverstein, Adam, 'Ibn Khurradadhbih', in J.W. Meri (ed.), *Medieval Islamic Civilisation: An Encyclopedia* (London, 2006), pp. 359–61.

Sluglett, Peter, *Britain in Iraq: Contriving King and Country* (London, 2007).

Snipes, Kenneth, 'Lucian', in Alexander P. Kazhdan (ed.), *The Oxford Dictionary of Byzantium* (Oxford, 1991); an updated version is available online at www. oxfordreference.com.ezproxy.library.ubc.ca/view/10.1093/acref/9780195046526. 001.0001/acref-9780195046526-e-3209?rskey=eMTOu3&result=3209 (accessed 29 July 2015).

Sommer, Michael, *Hatra. Geschichte und Kultur einer Karawanenstadt im römisch-parthischen Mesopotamien* (Mainz am Rhein, 2003).

Stewart, Rory, 'The queen of the quagmire', *The New York Review of Books* (25 October 2007).

Stronach, David, 'Ernst Herzfeld and Pasargadae,' in Ann C. Gunter and Stefan R. Hauser (eds), *Ernst Herzfeld and the Development of Near Eastern Studies, 1900–1950* (Leiden, 2004), pp. 103–35.

Strzygowski, Josef, *Orient oder Rom* (Leipzig, 1901).
—— *Kleinasien, ein Neuland der Kunstgeschichte* (Leipzig, 1903).
—— Review of Gertrude L. Bell, 'Notes on a journey through Cilicia and Lykaonia' (in *Revue archéologique* 1906 and 1907), *Byzantinische Zeitschrift* 16 (1907), pp. 378–81.
Szymaszek, Maciej, 'The lost screens of the churches of Mar Cyriacus in Arnas and Mar 'Azaziel in Kefr Zeh (Tur 'Abdin, Turkey)', *Eastern Christian Art* 9 (2012–13), pp. 107–18.
—— 'Josef Strzygowski in the letters and diaries of Gertrude Lowthian Bell', in P.O. Scholz and M.A. Dlugosz (eds), *Von Biala nach Wien: Josef Strzygowski und die Kunstwissenschaften zum 150. Geburtstag von Josef Strzygowski* (Vienna, 2015), pp. 99–112.
Talmon-Heller, Daniella, 'Abū l-Fidā', al-Malik al-Mu'ayyad 'Imād al-Dīn', in G. Krämer, D. Matringe, J. Nawas and E. Rowson, *The Encyclopaedia of Islamic Three* (Leiden, 2008), 2008/1: pp. 39–40.
Teichmann, Gabriele, 'Max Freiherr von Oppenheim – Archäologe, Diplomat, Freund des Orients', in Charlotte Trümpler (ed.), *Das Grosse Spiel. Archäologie un Politik zur Zeit des Kolonialismus (1860–1940)* (Essen, 2008), pp. 238–49.
Thureau-Dangin, François, 'Tell Ahmar', *Syria* 10 (1929), pp. 185–205.
Thureau-Dangin, François and Maurice Dunand, *Til-Barsib* (Paris, 1936).
Todd, Robert B. (ed.), 'Ashby, Thomas (1874–1931)', *The Dictionary of British Classicists* (Bristol, 2004), pp. 28–31.
—— 'Strong, Eugénie (née Sellers: 1860–1943)', *The Dictionary of British Classicists* (Bristol, 2004), pp. 930–2.
Tolmacheva, Marina A. 'Geography', in J.W. Meri (ed.), *Medieval Islamic Civilisation: An Encyclopedia* (London, 2006), pp. 284–8.
Tonghini, Christina, *Qal'at Ja'bar Pottery: A Study of a Syrian Fortified Site of the Late 11th–14th Centuries* (Oxford, 1998).
Toueir, Kassem, 'Heraqlah: A unique victory monument of Harun al-Rashid', *World Archaeology* 14 (1983), pp. 296–304.
—— 'Das Hiraqla des Hārūn ar-Rašīd', in Verena Daiber and Andrea Becker (eds), *Raqqa 3: Baudenkmäler und Paläste I* (Mainz am Rhein, 2004), pp. 137–42.
Trigger, Bruce G., *A History of Archaeological Thought* (Cambridge, 1989).
Tubb, Jonathan N., 'Leonard Woolley und Thomas E. Lawrence in Karkemisch', in Charlotte Trümpler (ed.), *Das Grosse Spiel. Archäologie un Politik zur Zeit des Kolonialismus (1860–1940)* (Essen, 2008), pp. 250–61.
Tuplin, Christopher J., 'Xenophon', in Simon Hornblower and Antony Spawforth (eds), *The Oxford Classical Dictionary*, 3rd revised edition, online version (Oxford, 2005). Available at www.oxfordreference.com.ezproxy.library.ubc.ca/view/10.1093/acref/9780198606413.001.0001/acref-9780198606413-e-6914?rskey=uw-S84T&result=6928 (accessed 29 July 2015).
Tuson, Penelope, *Playing the Game: The Story of Western Women in Arabia* (London, 2003).
Tweedale, Geoffrey, 'Bell, Sir (Isaac) Lowthian, first baronet (1816–1904)', *Oxford Dictionary of National Biography* (Oxford, 2004). Available at http://www.oxforddnb.com.ezproxy.library.ubc.ca/view/article/30690 (accessed 29 July 2015).
Urice, Stephen, *Opera Minora*, vol. 1 (Geneva, 1978).
—— *Qasr Kharana in the Transjordan* (Durham, NC, 1987).

Van Deman, Esther B., *The Atrium Vestae* (Washington, 1909).

—— 'Methods for determining the date of Roman concrete monuments', *American Journal of Archaeology* 16 (1912), pp. 230–51, 387–432.

—— *The Building of the Roman Aqueducts* (Washington, 1934).

Viollet, Henri, 'Description du palais d'al-Moutasim fils d'Haroun-al-Rachid à Samara et quelques monuments arabes peu connus de la Mésopotamie', *Mémoires presentés à l'Académie des Inscriptions et des Belles-Lettres* 12 (1909), pp. 567–94.

—— 'Le palais de'al-Moutasim fils d'Haroun al-Rachid à Samara et quelques monuments arabes peu connus de la Mésopotamie', *Comptes rendus de l'Académie des Inscriptions et des Belles-Lettres* (1909), pp. 370–5.

—— 'Fouilles à Samara en Mésopotamie: Ruines du palais d'al Moutasim', *Comptes rendus de l'Académie des Inscriptions et des Belles-Lettres* (1911), pp. 275–86.

—— 'Fouilles à Samara en Mésopotamie: Un palais musulman du IXe siècle', *Mémoires presentés à l'Académie des Inscriptions et des Belles-Lettres* 12 (1911), pp. 685–717.

von Luschan, F., D. Humann and R. Koldewey, *Ausgrabungen in Sendschirli*, vol. II (Berlin, 1898).

Wallach, Janet, *Desert Queen* (New York, 1996).

Watenpaugh, H.Z., *The Image of an Ottoman City: Imperial Architecture and Urban Experience in Aleppo in the 16th and 17th Centuries* (Leiden, 2004).

Welch, Katherine, 'Esther B. Van Deman (1862–1937)', in G.M. Cohen and M.S. Joukowsky (eds), *Breaking Ground: Pioneering Women Archaeologists* (Ann Arbor, 2006), pp. 68–108.

Werner, Peter, *Tell Munbaqa: Bronzezeit in Syrien* (Neumünster, 1998).

White, L. Michael, 'Hatra', in Eric Meyers (ed.), *Oxford Encyclopedia of the Archaeology of the Ancient Near East* (New York, 1997), pp. 484–5.

Wilhelm, Gernot, '1898–1917: Babylon – Stadt des Marduk und Zentrum des Kosmos', in Gernot Wilhem (ed.), *Zwischen Tigris und Nil. 100 Jahre Ausgrabungen der Deutschen Orient-Gesellschaft in Vorderasien und Ägypten* (Mainz, 1998), pp. 15–28.

Wilkinson, Tony J., *On the Margin of the Euphrates: Settlement and Land Use at Tell es-Sweyhat and in the Upper Lake Assad Area, Syria* (Chicago, 2004).

Wilkinson, Tony J., G. Philip, J. Bradbury, R. Dunford, D. Donoghue, N. Galiatsatos, D. Lawrence, A. Ricci and S.L. Smith, 'Contextualizing early urbanism: Settlement cores, early states and agro-pastoral strategies in the Fertile Crescent during the fourth and third millennia BC', *Journal of World Prehistory*, published online, 16 April 2014, DOI 10.1007/s10963-014-9072-2.

Wilson, Jeremy, *Lawrence of Arabia* (New York, 1990).

Winstone, H.V.F., *Gertrude Bell* (London, 1978).

Winter, Irene, 'Art as evidence for interaction: Relations between the Neo-Assyrian Empire and North Syria as seen from the monuments', in H-J. Nissen and J. Renger (eds), *Mesopotamia und seine Nachbarn* (Berlin, 1982), pp. 355–82.

—— '"Seat of kingship"/"A wonder to behold": The palace as construct in the ancient Near East', *Ars Orientalis* 23 (1993), pp. 27–55.

Woolley, C.L., *Carchemish. Report on the Excavations at Jerablus on Behalf of the British Museum II: The Town Defences* (London, 1921).

Woolley, C.L. and R.D. Barnett, *Carchemish. Report on the Excavations at Jerablus on Behalf of the British Museum III: The Excavations in the Inner Town, and the Hittite Inscriptions* (London, 1952).

INDEX